ACCIDENTAL ABORTION RISK

ACTIVE NANODEVICES WARNING

ADDICTION INDICATOR

ADDICTION RISK

AUTOMOTIVE POLLUTION HAZARD

AUTONOMOUS DEVICE WARNING

BACK INJURY HAZARD

BEDBUG INFESTATION HAZARD

CHOKING HAZARD FOR SMALL CHILDREN

CLIMATIC CHANGE HAZARD

CORROSIVE MATERIAL HAZARD

COSMIC THREAT

ELECTROCUTION HAZARD

ENVIRONMENTAL HAZARD

ESCALATOR INJURY HAZARD

EXISTENTIAL THREAT

FIRE HAZARD

FLOOD HAZARD

FOOT INJURY HAZARD

FOSSIL FUEL POLLUTION/DEPLETION HAZARD

HEALTH HAZARD

HEARING LOSS HAZARD

HIGH "YUCK FACTOR"

HIP INJURY HAZARD

ALLERGY RISK

ANIMAL CRUELTY
ALERT

ASPHYXIATION
HAZARD

AUTOMOTIVE
ACCIDENT
HAZARD

BICYCLE SAFETY
HAZARD

BIFLATION
HAZARD

BIOHAZARD

CANCER HAZARD

CREEPING
SOCIALISM
WARNING

DANGER OF
DEATH

DEFLATION
HAZARD

DENTAL HAZARD

EXPLOSIVE
HAZARD

FALLING
OBJECTS
HAZARD

FALSE ALARM
RISK

FATAL DISEASE
INDICATOR

GENDERCIDE
ALERT

GENERAL
WARNING
SYMBOL

GENOCIDAL
DEATH RAY
HAZARD

GEOMAGNETIC
DISTURBANCE
HAZARD

IDENTITY
HAZARD

INFECTIOUS
DISEASE HAZARD
(ANIMAL-TO-HUMAN)

INFECTIOUS
DISEASE HAZARD
(HUMAN-TO-HUMAN)

INHALATION
HAZARD

ENCYCLOPEDIA PARANOIACA

The Definitive Compendium of Things You Absolutely, Positively Must Not Eat, Drink, Wear, Take, Grow, Make, Buy, Use, Do, Permit, Believe, or Let Yourself Be Exposed to, Including an Awful Lot of Toxic, Lethal, Horrible Stuff That You Thought Was Safe, Good, or Healthy; All Sorts of Really Bad People Who Are Out to Get, Cheat, Steal from, or Otherwise Take Advantage of You; and a Whole Host of Existential Threats and Looming Dooms That Make Global Warming, Giant Meteors, and Planetary Pandemics Look Like a Walk in the Park (with Its High Risk of Skin Cancer, Broken Bones, Bee Stings, Allergic Seizures, Animal Attacks, Criminal Assaults, and Lightning Strikes)

COMPILED BY

HENRY BEARD *and* **CHRISTOPHER CERF**

and the Staff of the Cassandra Institute

SIMON & SCHUSTER PAPERBACKS
IN ASSOCIATION WITH THE CASSANDRA INSTITUTE AND
THE INSTITUTE OF EXPERTOLOGY

New York   London   Toronto   Sydney   New Delhi

Simon & Schuster Paperbacks
A Division of Simon & Schuster, Inc.
1230 Avenue of the Americas
New York, NY 10020

First Simon & Schuster trade paperback edition November 2013

SIMON & SCHUSTER PAPERBACKS and colophon are registered
trademarks of Simon & Schuster, Inc.

For information about special discounts for bulk purchases,
please contact Simon & Schuster Special Sales at
1-866-506-1949 or business@simonandschuster.com.

The Simon & Schuster Speakers Bureau can bring authors
to your live event. For more information or to book an event,
contact the Simon & Schuster Speakers Bureau at
1-866-248-3049 or visit our website at www.simonspeakers.com.

Designed by Kyoko Watanabe

Manufactured in the United States of America

10   9   8   7   6   5   4   3   2   1

The Library of Congress has cataloged the hardcover edition as follows:
Beard, Henry.
    Encyclopedia paranoiaca / Henry Beard and Christopher Cerf.
        p.   cm.
    1. Death—Humor.   I. Cerf, Christopher.   II. Title.
    PN6231.D35B43 2012
    818'.602—dc23   2012010796

ISBN 978-1-4391-9955-8
ISBN 978-1-4391-9956-5 (pbk)
ISBN 978-1-4391-9957-2 (ebook)

For Gwyneth and Katherine

PREFACE

THE BOOK YOU HOLD IN YOUR HANDS IS THE FRUIT (POSSIBLY toxic) of years of labor by the Cassandra Institute's worldwide cadre of researchers. It could literally save your life—perhaps more than once. We apologize in advance if it fails to do so.

Our original aim was purely academic: to produce a comprehensive and authoritative inventory of the perils, menaces, threats, blights, banes, and other assorted pieces of Damoclean cutlery that—according to those most qualified to offer guidance on such matters—currently hover over humanity. But almost immediately after beginning our review of the data our dedicated staffers had amassed, we reached the inescapable conclusion that—for our planet and all of us who inhabit it—the End was far nigher than anyone had previously anticipated. It was our urgent duty, we quickly realized, to publicize our apocalyptic findings as widely and persuasively as possible.

Furthermore, we recognized the need to present the alarming information our research had uncovered in a volume whose heft and gravitas would ensure that the admonitions it contained would not go unheeded, and whose handy, search-friendly layout would make it as easy (but not nearly as hazardous) as rolling off a log for our readers to identify the hundreds of grave and immediate risks facing them every day, and, in those rare cases where corrective strategies are actually available, to take appropriate steps to avoid or mitigate the danger.

With that goal in mind, a hastily convened meeting of the Institute's Board of Advisers concluded that, because of the ease of perusal that an alphabetized, cross-referenced, and thoroughly footnoted text provides and, frankly, the sense of authority that such a format automatically commands, the ideal vehicle for conveying the often literally earthshaking results of our inquiries would be the encyclopedia.

In reaching its decision, the Board was mindful that the term *encyclopedia* is derived from *enkiklios* ("general") and *paidea* ("knowledge"), a pair of words in Greek, the traditional language of calamity, which also contributed the word *paranoia*—not to mention *apocalypse, catastrophe, cataclysm, hecatomb,* and all of the countless *phobias*—to the English vocabulary.

Nor did our advisers fail to remind us that the first true encyclopedia was *Naturalis Historia,* or *Natural History,* the extraordinary compendium of ancient knowledge assembled by the great Roman writer Pliny the Elder. The earliest version of his thirty-seven-volume masterwork was published between 77 and 79 AD, and his zeal for cataloging the earth's wonders was a constant inspiration to us. But, sadly, Pliny also serves as a haunting harbinger of the fate that awaits those who choose to ignore the hazards—hidden or not so hidden—lurking everywhere in the natural world he studied so obsessively.

In August of 79 AD, while Pliny was correcting, revising, and adding new material to his manuscript in the seaside town of Misenum, where he was stationed as a commander of the Roman fleet, the great volcano Vesuvius that dominated the coastline a short distance to the south began to erupt. Ever the curious scholar, Pliny resolved to get a firsthand look at the spectacular geological phenomenon and set off toward Herculaneum in a small boat. As his flimsy craft approached the shore, it was repeatedly pummeled by hunks of pumice, cascades of red-hot cinders, and lumps of molten rock falling from the sky. Warned by his helmsman to head back to the safety of their home port, he refused, uttering the timeless phrase **FORTES FORTUNA ADIUVAT** ("Fortune favors the brave"). He died the next morning, probably of suffocation, on the beach at Stabiae, a little less than five kilometers from the doomed city of Pompeii. We at the Cassandra Institute salute his memory, but feel compelled to echo the caution voiced long ago by that savvy unheeded helmsman with a Latin phrase of our own: **PULLUS PARVUS RECTE DIXIT** ("Chicken Little was right").

—Henry Beard and Christopher Cerf

ENCYCLOPEDIA
PARANOIACA

A

abdominal cramping. See: **sushi, sashimi, and ceviche.**

abortion, accidental. See: **parsley.**

abstinence. Abstinence is the one method of birth control or protec-

tion against sexually transmitted infections that is considered morally acceptable by a significant number of
the world's religions. And, on a more practical level, as
Planned Parenthood points out on its website, it is the
only way "to be absolutely sure that you won't have an
unintended pregnancy or get a sexually transmitted disease (STD)."[1]
It's hardly a surprise, therefore, to hear doctors such as Joanna K.
Mohn of the New Jersey Physicians Resource Council assert that "abstinence is the best and healthiest" safe-sex choice.[2]

But, in your quest for a long and robust life, should you follow
her advice? Well, according to noted British epidemiologist George
Davey Smith, M.D., D.Sc., and his colleagues at Bristol University
and Queen's University of Bristol, the answer is a resounding no. In
a decadelong study published in the *British Medical Journal,* Davey
Smith and his associates tracked the mortality and sexual behavior
of 918 middle-aged males and found that the men who reported the
lowest "orgasmic frequency" rate died off twice as fast as those who
experienced the most orgasms.[3] Follow-up research, codirected by the
University of Bristol's Shah Ebrahim, Ph.D., not only validated Davey
Smith's results, but also demonstrated specifically that men who have
three or more orgasms a week are 50 percent less likely than those who
don't to die from a heart attack or a stroke.[4] And a fourteen-year study
conducted at the College of Public Health at the National Taiwan University produced convincing evidence that sexual activity was inversely
proportional to mortality rates not only for men, but for women, too.[5]

The bad news about abstinence doesn't stop there. A landmark
study led by Monique G. Lê of the French National Institute of
Health and Medical Research found that women who never engage
in intercourse, or do so only rarely (less than once per month), have

a significantly increased chance of contracting breast cancer.[6] And, in a much-quoted article entitled "Is Sex Necessary?," *Forbes* magazine's Alan Farnham cites research, "some rigorous, some less so," suggesting that failing to have sex at least once or twice a week is also associated with, among other things, a less robust immune system, an increased risk of prostate cancer, higher incidences of depression, and, in postmenopausal women, vaginal atrophy. Clearly the time-honored cliché "The safest sex is no sex" needs further examination. See: **birth-control pills; condoms; "safe sex"; sexual activity;** and **sexually transmitted diseases (STDs)**.

accelerated puberty in females. See: **bisphenol A.**

acoustically toxic homes. See: **wind turbine syndrome.**

acrylamide. Acrylamide, an industrial chemical widely used in the

manufacture of cement and for treating raw sewage, is a known carcinogen and neurotoxin. So you can imagine the dismay that greeted the surprise discovery, by a team of Swedish scientists in 2002, that substantial concentrations of this altogether unappetizing substance are present in many of the things we really like to eat. Acrylamide, it turns out, is formed whenever carbohydrate-rich, starchy foods are fried, toasted, roasted, or baked. The Swedish researchers found that potato chips, baked potatoes, and french fries contain particularly worrisome amounts of the toxic compound, and to a lesser degree so do cookies, breads, and breakfast cereals.[7] According to the U.S. Food and Drug Administration, acrylamide is also lurking in coffee, cigarette smoke, and black olives, and (perhaps offering some consolation to anyone with a taste for junk food, a hot cup of java, and a smoke) it shows up in whopping amounts in prune juice.[8]

"This is not just another food scare. This is an issue where we find a substance that could give cancer, in foods, and in significant amounts," Jørgen Schlundt, the director of the World Health Organization's Food Safety Program, told ABC News shortly after the Swedish results were announced.[9] Schlundt's worst fears were confirmed in 2007 when a study by the University of Maastricht in the Netherlands established "a direct link" between acrylamide and uterine and ovarian cancer, and demonstrated that women who consumed 40 micrograms of acrylamide a day (roughly the amount in a medium-size bag of potato chips) had twice the cancer risk of their naughty-nosh-averse peers.[10]

And if that's not enough to concern you, consider this: The consumption of acrylamide has also recently been linked, by researchers at the Albert Einstein College of Medicine and Iona College in New York State, to neurodegenerative diseases in the brain, including Alzheimer's;[11] and, in a Polish study published in the *American Journal of Clinical Nutrition,* to an increased risk of atherosclerosis and heart attacks.[12]

To be fair, not *all* the news about acrylamide is depressing: Scientists are reporting steady progress in finding ways to reduce the amount of the toxin produced when foodstuffs are manufactured or prepared.[13] But what can you do to protect yourself in the meantime? Well, the website RawFoodLife advises that you avoid cooked foods altogether. "Cooking anything at all that contains proteins combined with sugar or carbs creates acrylamide," they warn. Such foods include "almost all fruits and veggies," they add ominously, so even "being a vegan or vegetarian doesn't protect you!"[14]

If that's too radical a proposition for your taste, you might prefer the following recommendations from well-known Los Angeles nutritionist Alyse Levine, M.S., R.D.: "Completely eliminate French fries and potato chips from your diet," or at the very least, cut down on them; "avoid overcooking or using extremely high temperatures when cooking foods"; and "scrape the darker crumbs off toast and other baked items before consuming them."[15]

Shape magazine contributing editor Cynthia Sass, M.P.H., R.D., agrees with Levine, and also has a few constructive tips of her own to add. "Wrap burgers in crisp lettuce leaves in place of buns," she suggests; "opt for steamed brown rice instead of roasted corn or potatoes"; snack on fresh fruits instead of cookies; and forgo that second cup of morning coffee in favor of "a tall glass of H_2O."[16]

And, of course, as Mary Ann Johnson, Ph.D., of the American Society for Nutrition points out, if you're a smoker, avoiding acrylamide poisoning offers you one more good reason to quit.[17]

See: **food, undercooked; lettuce; brown rice; fruits, whole; bottled water; tap water; quitting smoking.**

activists, finger-wagging. See: **Nanny Statism.**

acute lymphocytic leukemia. See: **candlelight dinners.**

ADD/ADHD. See: **bisphenol A; food containers, plastic; soy.**

adware. See: **malware.**

aerosol/chemtrails plasma weapons. See: **tectonic nuclear warfare.**

agflation. *Agflation* is a term coined in 2007 by financial analysts at

Merrill Lynch to describe the alarming escalation in food prices that was occurring at the time—a trend that was briefly interrupted by the 2008 global banking crisis, but that resumed with equally worrisome intensity in 2010 and 2011. In an article called "The Agonies of Agflation," *The Economist* attributes the soaring prices of international agricultural commodities to climate-change-influenced crop failures, increased consumption of feed-dependent protein-intensive diets in the developing world, wider use of expensive fertilizers, and last but hardly least, government-subsidized fuel-substitution programs, such as the production of corn-based ethanol, that are forcing up the price of crops used to feed people and livestock.

Agflation, the magazine points out, not only contributes to overall inflation; it also has a pernicious tendency to crowd out purchases of nonessential products, particularly in countries where the cost of food represents a significant percentage of disposable income, like China (33 percent) and India (46 percent).[18] Long term, falling demand throughout non-agricultural sectors of the economy increases the risk of factory closings, layoffs, and widespread unemployment.

In the meantime, the more immediate and visible impacts of rising food prices, as the *New York Times* noted in a June 2011 article, are "worsened hunger for tens of millions of poor people, and destabilizing politics in scores of countries, from Mexico to Uzbekistan to Yemen. The Haitian government was ousted in 2008 amid food riots, and anger over high prices has played a role in the recent Arab uprisings." Gawain M. Kripke, policy director of Oxfam America, calls attention to the heartbreaking fact that almost one billion people around the world do not have enough to eat. "That's almost certain to increase as prices rise, especially if they rise in an aggressive manner, which they are." Kripke also cautions that the recent price spikes were symptoms of environmental and market pressures on world food supplies and a "polite warning" of worse such disruptions to come. "We may get much more rude warnings soon,"[19] he adds ominously.

Clearly agflation is no picnic, but in terms of its purely economic consequences, it's only one factor in a more pernicious form of price and market disruption known as "biflation." See: **biflation.** See also: **biofuels.**

air fresheners. "Air fresheners have become a staple in many Ameri-can homes and offices," notes the Natural Resources Defense Council, "marketed with the promise of creating a clean, healthy, and sweet-smelling indoor atmosphere." However, the Council warns, "many of these products contain phthalates (pronounced *thal-ates*)— hazardous chemicals known to cause hormonal abnormalities, birth defects, and reproductive problems." NRDC reports that it independently tested fourteen different commercially available air fresheners, none of which listed phthalates as an ingredient, and "uncovered these chemicals in 86 percent (12 of 14) of the products tested, including those advertised as 'all-natural.'"[20]

As if that weren't bad enough, a recent study conducted by scientists at the University of California, Berkeley, and the Lawrence Berkeley National Laboratory found that, in addition to phthalates, many widely marketed air fresheners also contain ethelyne-based glycol ethers, which are classified as hazardous pollutants by the U.S. Environmental Protection Agency, and terpenes, a class of chemicals that are not in themselves toxic, but that research indicates may react with ozone in the air to produce a number of toxic compounds.[21] (Note: According to the UC Berkeley–Lawrence Berkeley researchers, ozone is the primary constituent of smog, and can enter your home from "infiltration of outdoor air." It is also produced indoors by copying machines and laser printers, and, ironically, by room air-purifying machines that *purposely* emit ozone to cleanse the very air

whose quality you were aiming to improve with your air freshener.[22])
See: **laser printers; room air purifiers.**

air purifiers. See: **room air purifiers.**

airplane cabins. Surfaces inside airplanes could make you sick, spe-

cifically your airline seat and the restrooms, warns
world-famous University of Arizona microbe hunter
Charles P. Gerba, Ph.D., in an article published on the
popular women's health website Lifescript.com. "There
are no rules and regulations about disinfecting restrooms or [seat-back] trays between flights," Gerba says. "We're talking
about 50 people per toilet—which can make airplane restrooms just
about the germiest place ever."

So, if you have to fly, what can you do to protect yourself? Gerba
advises you to pack a carry-on bottle of hand sanitizer (make sure it's
no larger than 3.4 ounces so you'll be able to get it through airport
security!) and a package of disinfectant wipes. When you sit down,
clean the armrests and your tray table with one of the wipes, Gerba
says. Use the hand sanitizer after using the restroom. In addition,
Lifescript offers travelers the following tidbit of Gerba advice: "Say
'no, thanks' to reusable airline pillows or blankets, which could still be
contaminated with the germs of previous passengers. Instead, pack a
wrap and your own inflatable pillow or neck rest."[23] See also: **airplane
seat pockets; crossing your legs; hand sanitizers, alcohol-based.**

airplane seat pockets. Airplane seat pockets are such a biological

hazard that they require special attention, even from
folks already knowledgeable about protecting themselves from the microbial threats presented by the restrooms, armrests, tray tables, pillows, and blankets one
regularly encounters while flying (See: **airplane cab-
ins**). According to Douglas Wright of *Budget Travel* magazine, "reaching into that pocket is akin to putting your hand in someone else's
purse and rummaging among their used tissues and gum wrappers.
Toenail clippings and mushy old French fries are even nastier sur-
prises that have been found in seat pockets." If you want to avoid

contracting a cold, the flu, or something far worse, Wright advises, "avoid stashing things in the seat pocket," or, if you absolutely insist on doing so, bring along a plastic bag in which you can place magazines and other personal items to shield them from contamination.[24] (Take care not to touch the outside of the plastic bag once it's been in the seat pocket!) One question Wright doesn't address, by the way, is what to do if an aircraft emergency requires you to consult the airline safety card that's customarily stored in your seat-back pocket. Here's hoping you never find yourself in a position where you have to confront this difficult conundrum.

airport screening procedures. See: **Nanny Statism.**

algorithmic trading. See: **flash crash.**

alluvial litter. See: **beach, a day at the.**

aluminum. "Aluminum poses a very serious danger to the human body," warns the Internet-based organic health information service, the Global Healing Center. "It can make you very ill." For example, the Center points out, "Some people are allergic to aluminum and will develop a skin rash (contact dermatitis)." But, frankly, that's the least of your worries. Far more serious health problems with "possible" links to aluminum toxicity, according to the Center, include malfunction of the blood-brain barrier, autism and learning disorders in children, mental retardation in infants, stomach and intestinal ulcers, gastrointestinal disease, Parkinson's disease, speech problems, hyperactivity, liver disease, headaches, heartburn, nausea, constipation, colicky pain, premature osteoporosis, lack of energy, anemia, and flatulence.[25] In addition, although the results remain inconclusive, the aluminum present in antiperspirant deodorants—which, it's been theorized, enters women's bodies through the nicks they incur while shaving under their arms—has been linked in some studies to increased rates of Alzheimer's disease[26] and breast cancer.[27] (For more about aluminum-based antiperspirants and their possible connection to Alzheimer's and breast cancer, see: **deodorant sprays, antiperspirant.**)

And if that's not enough to depress you, perhaps this will: In addition to antiperspirants, aluminum is present in a dizzying variety of other products we use every day, including astringents, baby powder, baking powder, buffered aspirin, cake mix, cookware, dentures, diarrhea remedies, foil, food containers, hemorrhoid medications, lipsticks, nasal sprays, processed cheese, self-rising flour, table salt, talcum powder, vaccines, and vaginal douches. Furthermore, the Global Healing Center warns, "acid rain breaks down aluminum in the earth which then runs off into our water supplies" and contaminates the seafood we eat. Indeed, aluminum is so ubiquitous, there's almost no way we can avoid it completely.[28]

But, says NaturalNews.com, there are many things we can do to *limit* unnecessary exposure. Among their suggestions: "Avoid aluminum-can beverages altogether." "Avoid aluminum cookware and opt for cast iron, glass, or copper cookware instead." "Use wax paper instead of aluminum foil." And "buy baking powder that is aluminum free." In addition, NaturalNews.com points out, "discerning consumers" can find good deodorant products that don't contain aluminum.[29]

Nonetheless, recommends the Global Healing Center, "since there is really no way to be 100% aluminum free, it's best to measure and remove [it] from your body." Luckily, the Center's founder and research director, Dr. Edward F. Group III, has created two products to help you do just that—"The Aluminum Heavy Metal Test" ($22.95), a simple at-home checkup you can perform on yourself to see if your levels are within safe parameters, and "Dr. Group's Heavy Metal Cleanser" (the starter kit costs only $199.95), which can help you remove aluminum and other metallic poisons from your tissue. You can learn more about these products by visiting Global Health Center's website, at www.globalhealingcenter.com. The goal, the Center reminds us, is to flush aluminum residues "before they have time to do serious damage to your body."[30]

America, decline and fall of. See: **Nanny Statism; superpower collapse soup.**

America, fructosification of. See: **sugar.**

ammonia-treated meat products. See: **"slimeburgers."**

anaphylactic shock. See: **condoms, allergic reactions to.**

animal feces, liquefied. See: **tap water.**

anisakis worms, parasitic. See: **sushi, sashimi, and ceviche.**

anthrax, pulmonary. See: **runny nose.**

antibacterial and antiviral products. Antibacterial and antiviral sprays, soaps, deodorants, and kitchen and bathroom cleaners; toothpaste and mouthwash with "germ-fighting" additives; microbe-resistant toys, blankets, pillows, clothing, and shower curtains; and even anti-bacterial chopsticks—all of these products are prolifer-ating like wildfire these days. It's easy to understand why: The public (quite appropriately!) has become far better educated about how eas-ily and rapidly not only colds and the flu, but also more serious infec-tious diseases like SARS, hepatitis A, meningitis, and tuberculosis, can spread throughout the population. But, unfortunately, this is a case where the cure is literally far worse than the disease. Why? Well, for one thing, a growing body of research has revealed that the overuse of antibacterial agents is creating a whole new generation of **superbugs** (q.v.), resistant not only to the agents themselves, but also to antibiot-ics. The problem has become so pressing that the Canadian Medical Association has actually called for a ban on all antibacterial household products.[31]

And that's hardly the only issue: Most antibacterial products contain triclosan or triclocarban, chemicals that, according to Gina Solomon, M.D., M.P.H., a senior scientist at the Natural Resources Defense Council, "pollute our rivers and streams, are toxic to wildlife, can enter and accumulate in people's bodies, and disrupt hormone systems." [32] "In a study of male rats, Dr. Solomon informs us, triclosan caused "decreased sperm count" and "damage to the reproductive sys-tem," and "disrupted the production of androgens"—the hormones responsible for promoting the development of male sexual characteristics. "The reason I care about male rats," she adds, "is that male humans have identical hormones and hormone-responses." So what can we do to protect ourselves? "Read the ingredients on your products," Dr. Solomon advises, "and get rid of anything containing triclosan or triclocarban."[33] (Precisely how she proposes you should "get rid" of these items without further "polluting our streams and rivers," and "poisoning our wildlife," is a question she leaves for another day.) See also: **toothpaste, antimicrobial.**

antiperspirants. See: **deodorant sprays, antiperspirant.**

anxiety, relaxation-induced. See: **meditation.**

Apophis. See: **Asteroid 99942 Apophis.**

apple juice. According to Mehmet Oz, M.D., host of television's

highly popular *Dr. Oz Show,* "Some of the best known brands in America have arsenic in their apple juice."[34] How did it get there? "American apple juice is made from apple concentrate, 60% of which is imported from China,"[35] the *Dr. Oz Show* website explains. Indeed, in just one package of juice, "there can be apple concentrate from up to seven countries. Although arsenic has been banned in the U.S. for decades, it's not always regulated in other countries where it may be in the water supply or used in pesticides contaminating the juice you're giving to your children." Dr. Oz points out that the U.S. Environmental Protection Agency has established a limit on how much arsenic is permissible in drinking water—10 parts per billion. What so greatly alarms Dr. Oz is that, when his show had three dozen samples from five different brands of apple juice tested, ten of the samples—that is, almost a full third of them—were found to contain amounts of arsenic higher than the EPA's limit for water.[36]

The Food and Drug Administration has taken issue with Dr. Oz's apple juice warning, noting, among other things, that Dr. Oz's tests didn't distinguish between inorganic arsenic and organic arsenic, which passes through the body more easily and is therefore less dangerous.[37]

But Dr. Oz has no use for such distinctions. "The FDA should not allow more arsenic in our apple juice than we allow in our drinking water," he maintains.[38] Patty Lovera, assistant director of Food & Water Watch, agrees. "There's no doubt that *The Dr. Oz Show* investigation into arsenic levels in apple juice shocked a lot of people, especially parents who consider apple juice to be a nutritious staple in their kids' diets," she says. "It is unacceptable that a toxic chemical like arsenic is allowed to contaminate our food and drink, and we all need to demand higher standards of protection for our families."[39] (Note: Arsenic is far from the only health hazard presented by apple juice, or, for that matter, by fruit juices in general. For details, see: **fruit juice.**)

apple seeds. With all the fuss about the dangers presented by the

high sugar content of apples, and the risks posed by the pesticide residues frequently found on apple peels (See: **apples**), perhaps the greatest health danger presented by the fruit—that its seeds contain deadly cyanide poison—is often overlooked. And, as Cecil Adams points out in his nationally syndicated *Straight Dope* column (which, as Adams himself notes, has been "fighting ignorance since 1973"), inattention to this little detail can "most certainly do you in." Specifically, Adams writes, the fruits of all members of the rose family (which include not only apples, but also cherries, apricots, peaches, plums, and almonds) contain substances known as cyanogenetic glycosides, which, on ingestion, release hydrogen cyanide gas through an enzymatic reaction. "Symptoms of cyanide poisoning are excitement, convulsions, respiratory distress, and spasms," Adams informs us. "Another warning sign is death, which can occur without any of the other symptoms." The good news, according to Adams, is that "sub-lethal doses of cyanide gas are detoxified and passed out of the body rapidly, so it's impossible to slowly poison yourself over a period of time." The bad news, however, is "that one gluttonous binge will put you away forever."[40] (Note: For more detailed information about avoiding and/or treating cyanide poisoning from fruit seeds and pits, see: **bowl of cherries.**) See also: **apples; apples, peeling; apple juice.**

apples. "An apple a day keeps the doctor away," the old saying tells us,

but, unfortunately, this advice is horribly misguided. One problem is that apples have a far higher sugar content than many other fruits—more that twice as much as strawberries and cranberries, for example, and significantly more than plums, melons, papayas, and kiwis (to name just a few). Even more ominous, however, is the fact that, as Roanoke, Virginia, physician Dr. Kristie Leong reports, "Surveys have shown that pesticide residues were found on more than ninety percent of apples tested. Some apples contained the residues of as many as eight different pesticides. In fact, peaches and apples top the list of the most pesticide contaminated fruits on the market." [41] Does this mean it's time to give up apples altogether? Not necessarily, writes Dr. Leong; you might consider peeling them before eating. "Although peeling an apple may not eliminate all of the pesticides since some can penetrate into the body of the apple," she notes, "it should lower their levels." See: **apples, peeling.** See also: **apple juice; apple seeds; fruits, whole;** and **sugar.**

apples, peeling. Since apples have been identified as one of the most

pesticide-laden foods on the market, many physicians and nutritionists have recommended peeling them before serving or eating them (See: **apples**). But, before doing so, readers would be wise to consider a 2007 Cornell University study indicating that the most widely touted health benefits of eating apples come not from the apples themselves, but from their peels. "We found that several compounds [present only in the apple peels] have potent anti-proliferative activities against human liver, colon and breast cancer cells," explains Cornell associate professor Rui Hai Liu, who led the study. Indeed, as *Science Daily* suggested in their article covering Dr Liu's research, it's probably time to retire the phrase "An apple a day keeps the doctor away" and replace it with "An apple peel a day might keep cancer at bay." [42] See also: **apples; apple seeds.**

apricots. Experts the world over have hailed the apricot, both for its taste and for its health benefits. But before indulging, it's important to note that this delicious and mineral-rich fruit can present a serious, or even fatal, health hazard. The problem, as the North Carolina State University Department of Horticultural Science points out on its helpful web resource "Poisonous Plants of North Carolina," is that apricot seeds—located inside the stone at the center of the fruit—contain a highly toxic substance called amygdalin that, when ingested, can cause gasping, weakness, excitement, pupil dilation, spasms, convulsions, coma, and even respiratory failure.[43] Indeed, as nationally syndicated columnist Cecil Adams points out, Turkey, "a big apricot country," has reported at least nine cases of lethal poisoning from apricot seeds in recent years. "Unfortunately," writes Adams, "victims of such poisonings have a habit of kicking the bucket before doctors have a chance to ask them how many seeds they've eaten," so what constitutes a lethal dose is "hard to pin down."[44]

With Adams's advice in mind, we urge you to consider the following testimonial from author Rebecca Wood, winner of a James Beard Award and the Julia Child Cookbook Award: "My mother always puts a few apricot pits into her preserves for, she said, 'The flavor.' As a child, her logic was beyond my ken as apricot kernels are nastily bitter. Today, I take my hat off to mom and the perennial kitchen wisdom she still serves up. According to both Oriental Medicine and alternative medicine, these kernels are anti-carcinogenic."[45] And, as you now know, they're also deadly poisonous. Furthermore, the U.S. Federal Drug Administration has officially determined that the use of apricot kernels in treating cancer is not only a "major health fraud" but also a "potentially lethal" practice.[46] We take *our* hat off to Rebecca for living to savor the bitterness of her mom's preserves.

arctic melting. See: **global warming; sea levels, rising.**

ARkStorm. See: **California superstorm.**

armadillos. These strange and ancient creatures, which are native to

the American Southwest, are not only a fairly common victim of roadkill on highways in Texas and Louisiana, they are also uniquely capable of exacting an unexpectedly nasty form of revenge on anyone foolish enough to retrieve one of their carcasses for a tasty dish of *azotochitli chili* (or "turtle-rabbit" stew, from its Aztec name). Thanks to their unusually low body temperature, armadillos are the only wild animals that are known carriers of *Mycobacterium leprae*, the surprisingly fragile bacteria that cause the often severe and disfiguring inflammatory affliction known as Hansen's disease, or, more commonly, leprosy. Ironically, although armadillos are an indigenous New World species, and leprosy was unknown in the Americas before its introduction at the time of Christopher Columbus, the "little armored one" (*armadillo* in Spanish), which has a current infection rate of nearly 20 percent in some areas of the South, is uniquely positioned to return the favor to descendants of the European settlers. And since most U.S. citizens who display early symptoms of the malady turn out to have recently visited countries in South America, Africa, and Asia where leprosy is endemic, and hence are correctly diagnosed and promptly given powerful multiple-dose antibiotics, the fifty to eighty individuals each year who complain of numbness in their skin or other signs of peripheral nerve damage but do not report any overseas travel or contact with anyone infected with leprosy are often left untreated until the disease has progressed past the point of effective therapy. "These patients have always been a puzzle," admitted Dr. Anthony Fauci, director of the National Institute of Allergy and Infectious Diseases. The best—and seemingly least necessary advice imaginable—comes from Dr. Richard W. Truman, a researcher at the National Hansen's Disease Program in Baton Rouge, Louisiana: "The important thing is that people should be discouraged from consuming armadillo flesh or handling it."[47] See also: **leprosy.**

arsenic. See: **apple juice; brown rice; coal; cosmetics; solar energy.**

arteriosclerosis. See: **neckties.**

artificial nails, nurses with. See: **nurses with artificial nails.**

arugula. See: **leafy green vegetables.**

aspartame is an artificial sweetener discovered by accident in 1965 by a scientist working for G. D. Searle and Company who was trying to perfect an antiulcer drug. Now marketed as a sugar substitute under such brand names as NutraSweet, Equal, and Canderel, aspartame is much sweeter than sugar, has almost no genuine food value, and is, in small doses, relatively noncaloric. The chemical was approved, under a cloud of controversy, by the U.S. Food and Drug Administration (FDA) for use as a dry food additive and tabletop sweetener in 1981. Aspartame's "clean bill of health" came shortly after recently elected president Ronald Reagan's new FDA commissioner, Dr. Arthur Hull Hayes Jr., took office, and Hayes's decision continues to raise eyebrows—not only because an FDA-appointed panel had voted against approval on the basis of concerns that the sweetener might be a carcinogen, but also because then G. D. Searle president, Donald Rumsfeld (yes, *that* Donald Rumsfeld), had been a member of Reagan's election transition team when Hayes was picked for his job. Two years later, in June 1983, the FDA approved aspartame for use in carbonated beverages, setting the stage for an international explosion in the use of the synthetic, nonnutritive sweetener.[48] (Three months after the aspartame-carbonated-beverages decision, under attack for accepting corporate gifts, Arthur Hull Hayes Jr. resigned, and, shortly thereafter, in November 1983, he became a "Senior Scientific Consultant" to Burson-Marsteller, G. D. Searle's PR agency. But that's another story.[49])

Today, aspartame is used in over six thousand consumer products worldwide including breath mints, cereals, chewing gum, cocoa mixes, flavored waters, fruit and vegetable drinks, ice cream, "nutritional bars," and yogurt, and enjoys widespread popularity as a tabletop sweetener.[50] But, through the years its use has continually been dogged by safety controversies—most notably by a pair of studies conducted by the European Ramazzini Foundation in Bologna, and published in the journal *Environmental Health Perspectives*, that found statistically significant increases in lymphomas and leukemias in rats to whom aspartame had been fed.[51] But the FDA, after considering the Italians' evidence, affirmed that the agency had no reason to alter its previous conclusion that aspartame is safe as a general-purpose sweetener in food.[52]

So what should we believe? Well, Andrew Weil, M.D., the best-selling author and award-winning founder of the Arizona Center of

Integrative Medicine, agrees that many claims about the acute risks involved in using aspartame are overblown. "I've seen no scientific support for assertions on the Internet that there is an 'aspartame disease' or that it worsens symptoms of multiple sclerosis, lupus, and fibromyalgia," Weil writes.[53] However, he adds, "because I have seen a number of patients, mostly women, who report headaches from this substance, I don't regard it as free from toxicity. Women also find that aspartame aggravates PMS (premenstrual syndrome)."[54] Furthermore, Weil notes, aspartame is suspected of being an "excitotoxin," a type of compound that, if consumed in sufficient quantities, "can damage nerve cells by overstimulating them." As a result of these concerns, Dr. Weil's advice is to "follow the precautionary principle. In other words, don't use it."[55] See: **sugar; sucralose.**

asphyxiations, childhood. See: **hot dogs.**

Asteroid 99942 Apophis. An asteroid 350 meters in diameter (about 1,100 feet) named after the malignant Egyptian deity Apep, the Uncreator, and a villain in the TV science-fiction series *Stargate SG-1,* is scheduled to approach within a few thousand miles of the earth on the ominous date of Friday, the thirteenth of April 2029. Although recent astronomical observations indicate that it is likely to miss our home planet during this close encounter, it may come near enough to pass through a "gravitational keyhole" as it speeds by, resulting in orbit-modifying effects that would set up a direct hit on April 13, 2036. If that later collision were to occur, the potential impact could in theory produce an explosion equivalent to an 880-megaton nuclear blast, and, depending on the precise point of impact along a projected path of entry—officially known as the "Path of Risk"—across southern Russia, the Pacific (uncomfortably close to the coastlines of California and Mexico), and Central and South America, would cause up to 10 million casualties.[56] See: **Asteroid 99942 Apophis, attempting to deflect.**

Asteroid 99942 Apophis, attempting to deflect. Anatoly Perminov, chief of Russia's Federal Space Agency, Roscosmos, recently announced plans to intercept and deflect the asteroid Apophis, which he declared would "surely collide with Earth." But American astronomer Paul Chodas of NASA's Near-Earth Object (NEO) Program Office insists that, as scientists get a more exact fix on the asteroid's orbit, "the possibility of an impact is going down," declining from an estimated 1 in 45,000 chance of a direct hit to about 1 in 250,000. And he warns that deploying a spacecraft to alter Apophis's orbit could pose its own risks, since a slight but ultimately lethal miscalculation could lead to a botched interception that ends up nudging the piece of interplanetary debris into a collision course with Earth instead of bumping it out of one. "You have the potential of increasing the impact probability with failures in the mission," Chodas cautioned. "You could make matters worse." With that perspicacious caveat in mind, it is worth noting that Apophis is one of two close-approaching bits of celestial detritus that the European Space Agency is considering as possible targets of its long-planned, though obliviously designated, Don Quijote mission to study the effects of impacting an asteroid with a spacecraft.[57]

atherosclerotic plaques. See: **dairy products.**

ATM card cloning. See: **identity theft.**

ATM receipts. See: **bisphenol A.**

attention deficit hyperactive disorder. See: **bisphenol A; food containers, plastic; soy.**

automobile crashes, fatal, alcohol-related. See: **smoking bans.**

autumn leaves. Fall foliage is known for its beauty; so much so that

thousands of tourists drive into the countryside each autumn in search of the spectacularly colorful vistas it provides. But most that do are probably unaware that the very leaves that lured them into taking to the road represent one of most lethal—and multipronged—

driving hazards that any motorist can face. "Wet leaves on the road surface can make stopping difficult, and piles of leaves can obscure potholes, curbs and street markings,"[58] cautions Rich White, executive director of the Car Care Council. And that's only the beginning. Inadvertently stop your car atop a pile of dry leaves, and before you know it, the heat from your car's catalytic converter can set them ablaze. "If that happens, your car can be engulfed in mere minutes and destroyed by the conflagration,"[59] warns automotive expert Matthew C. Keegan. "Protect your car from this deadly menace and avoid the leaves!"[60]

avian flu. See: **flu pandemic.**

B

babesiosis. See: **tick-borne diseases.**

baby boys, urogenital abnormalities in. See: **food containers, plastic.**

baby oil. See: **polyvinyl chloride (PVC).**

baby powder. See: **aluminum; talcum powder.**

back, sleeping on your. See: **sleeping on your back.**

backdoors. See: **malware.**

bacon. See: **high-fat, high-calorie food addiction.**

Baconator triple. Wendy's "Baconator triple" sandwich—which fea-

tures three quarter-pound burger patties "piled high with Applewood smoked bacon, mayo, ketchup, and sliced American cheese" all served up on a "premium bun"—delivers 1,130 calories, 38 grams of saturated fat, 345 milligrams of cholesterol, 3,150 milligrams of sodium, and 11 grams of sugar. This impressive bundle of dubious nutritional achievements has earned the Baconator triple the note-worthy number one spot on the *Daily Beast*'s heralded "40 Deadliest Fast Food Meals" list.[1]

bagels. "Holey smokes!" exclaims the *Daily Beast*. "While doughnuts' nutritional value and fat content don't do a body good, when it comes to calories, many are better than your average New York bagel," the popular website advises. "For one plain, dry bagel (yum!), one can eat two glazed Dunkin' Donuts. Not that we recommend this."[2]
See also: **doughnuts.**

bagworms. See: **blueberries.**

baked goods, commercial. See: **trans fats.**

baked potatoes. See: **acrylamide.**

ballet pumps. See: **low-heel shoes.**

banana equivalent dose. Usually referred to as the "BED" of any natural or artificial object or any human activity, this comparative calculation of the amount of potentially damaging radiation likely to be received by any given individual is based on the fact that all bananas emit about 0.0001 millisieverts of radioactivity using the current standard unit of measurement of radiation intensity, which is equivalent to roughly .01 millirem on the older Roentgen Equivalent Man scale. The unexpected ionizing properties of the banana are a result of the very high potassium content of this curved, sweet-fleshed, yellow fruit harvested from an intensively cultivated tropical herbaceous plant of the genus *Musa*. Since all primordial potassium consists of a small percentage (around 0.0117 percent) of the unstable isotope potassium-40, which has an impressive 1.25 billion-year half-life, some radioactivity will invariably be absorbed by anyone who ingests anything with a lot of potassium in it, like, say, a banana.[3] Interestingly, it will also be "hot" enough to be detected by sensors employed by national security personnel to screen cargo for radiological terror weapons at border crossings, and in fact, as the National Threat Initiative reports, "current radiation portal monitors are subject to false alarms caused by legitimate radioactive materials (i.e., kitty litter, bananas, and ceramics)."[4]

So, should we jump to the conclusion that, yes, we should eat no bananas? Well, just to put things in perspective, one dental X-ray subjects a patient to a dose equivalent to fifty bananas, the average daily dose everyone typically receives from all sources is on the order of one hundred bananas, and a one-way jet flight from New York to Los Angeles adds up to pretty much a whole supermarket aisle's worth of nuclear fruit—four hundred bananas. On the other hand, consuming even a single one of these tasty snacks exposes the eater to a .01 millirem of radiation, a radiological shellacking thirty times greater than the .003 millirem dose someone living right at the very doorstep of a nuclear plant would receive over an entire year.[5]

So at the risk of going "bananas" over this subject, perhaps out of simple prudence we should cut down on our consumption of this popular but arguably perilous food item. As a consolation, it is worth noting that a kilogram (one liter) of beer has barely one-tenth the BED of a kilogram (about two pounds) of bananas,[6] and unless that beverage was consumed from an aluminum container, the discarded receptacle poses less risk of causing physical harm than a carelessly disposed-of banana peel. See **aluminum.**

banks, "too big to fail." See: **"doom loop"; zombie banks.**

banning everything that can be used to kill people. Patrick Moore, Ph.D., who helped found Greenpeace, has become increasingly concerned about what he sees as an ill-advised and counterproductive trend toward banning everything that can be used to kill people. "Over the past 20 years, one of the simplest tools—the machete— has been used to kill more than a million people in Africa, far more than were killed in the Hiroshima and Nagasaki nuclear bombings combined,"[7] writes Moore, who, in his role as chairman of Greenspirit

Strategies, Ltd., is now an outspoken defender of (among other things) nuclear energy,[8] synthetic pesticides,[9] and the use of polyvinyl chloride in consumer products,[10] all of which, he says, have been unfairly and inaccurately demonized by "activist misinformation and scare tactics."[11] "What are car bombs made of?" Moore asks. "Diesel oil, fertilizer and cars. If we banned everything that can be used to kill people, we would never have harnessed fire."[12] See: **nuclear energy; polyvinyl chloride.**

bar soap. Allison Janse, who wrote *The Germ Freak's Guide to Outwitting Colds and Flu* with the help of University of Arizona microbiologist Charles P. Gerba, Ph.D., strongly advises you to use dispenser soaps instead of bar soaps. Why? "Because bar soaps can be laden with germs passed from person to person," she explains.[13]

baseball caps. When you go out in the sun, do you wear a baseball cap to shield your skin from potentially damaging ultraviolet radiation? Well, your concern is well placed, but, the Skin Cancer Foundation cautions, you're kidding yourself if you think a mere baseball cap offers the kind of protection you truly need. "Baseball caps and visors shade the face but leave neck, lower face, and ears exposed," the Foundation warns. What's required instead is "a broad-brimmed hat," which will go "a long way toward preventing skin cancer in often-exposed areas like the neck, ears, scalp, and face," they advise. "Opt for a 3-to-4 inch brim that extends all around the hat."[14] See: **sun exposure, insufficient.**

bath salts. Methylenedioxypyrovalerone (MDPV), a powerful "designer drug" with stimulative, hallucogenic, psychosis-inducing, and addictive properties rivaling those of methamphetamine and cocaine, and with equally severe withdrawal symptoms, has recently been packaged and widely marketed in the United States as "bath salts" under brand names such as Ivory Wave, Tranquility, Cloud Nine, White Lightning, Red Dove, White Dove, Bliss, Hurricane

Charlie, and Lovey Dovey. The products—which are typically inhaled, smoked, or ingested—have been banned throughout most of Europe and Australia, but, because they are not "marketed for human consumption," they have yet to be classified as a scheduled drug or controlled substance in the United States, except in Florida and Louisiana, where troubling episodes resulting from misuse of the powders have become widespread.[15] (Three reported examples: A Panama City, Florida, woman became convinced her mother was a "monster" and attacked her with a machete[16]; also in Panama City, seven officers were needed to subdue a man who literally tore a radar unit out of a squad car with his teeth[17]; and, worst of all, a twenty-one-year-old Covington, Louisiana, boy slit his own throat and then shot himself in the head after snorting some "Cloud Nine."[18]) "You can buy this drug legally—that's right, legally!—at gas stations and convenience stores across this country," noted an outraged Dr. Mehmet Oz on a March 2011 edition of his syndicated *Dr. Oz Show*. "Your own kids might be doing it."[19] One small consolation: While ingesting these "tub drugs" has been compared to smoking meth and taking acid at the same time ("users completely lose their mind while having superhuman energy" reports Joe Weber of *Death + Taxes* magazine[20]), there is no evidence that accidentally utilizing these chemical compounds for their advertised, though fraudulent, purpose as bath enhancers would produce any "trouble bubbles" or other harmful effects. Nevertheless, a Code Orange Rubber Duckie Alert seems drastically overdue.

bathroom floor, walking barefoot on. According to Safety.com

 (which bills itself as "the ultimate safety site"), you should never walk barefoot into the bathroom. Always wear foot protection, such as shoes, slippers, or flip-flops, the site advises, "to prevent contact with germs on the floor, which can cause conditions such as athlete's foot."[21] See: **flip-flops.**

baths. Did you ever stop to think that every time you take a bath you're immersing yourself in a "bacterial soup?" That's the term Dr. Philip M. Tierno Jr., director of clinical microbiology and immunology at the New York University Medical Center, used, during a 2010 *Today* show appearance, to describe our bathwater and all the fecal contaminants (such as *E. coli, streptococcus,* and *NS staph aureus*) that regularly get washed off our own bodies, and those of other bathers, and then thrive and multiply in the moist and warm environment the bathtub provides.[22] Indeed, writes Melissa Breyer, senior editor of the Care2 News Network's "Healthy & Green Living" section, "many garbage cans are cleaner than bathtubs, which can ring in at about 100,000 bacteria per square inch."[23]

So what can we do to protect ourselves from this microbial nightmare? Well, for starters, Professor Mary K. Harrison of the University of Florida's Institute of Food and Agricultural Sciences recommends that every family member "wash out the bathtub after each use."[24] *Woman's Day* magazine goes a step further and suggests that your tub should be sprayed with a disinfectant every time someone bathes in it.[25] But, unfortunately, these precautions—helpful though they may be—utterly fail to address the *new* stew of pathogens you bring to the bathtub each time you use it, because they're on your body when you plop into it. There's just no getting around it, writes Yvonne Rodenhiser, a frequent contributor of health and hygiene articles to Yahoo.com; if your goal is to "get really clean," you're just going to have to forswear the bathtub altogether and take a shower instead.

But, you may argue, luxuriating in the bathtub is oh-so-much more relaxing than showering. Well, Rodenhiser feels the same way, and she's come up with an ingenious compromise. "Avoid hopping into the bath right away," she suggests. "Instead, take a quick shower first and lather up and rinse off to wash away all those germs that you don't want to have in your bath water. Then take your bath. You will be clean and your bath water will stay clean so you can relax and be germ free when you get out."[26] See: **showers.**

bathtub toys. See: **rubber duckies.**

battery cages. See: **eggs.**

beach, a day at the. This popular diversion is generally thought of as

a pleasant and relaxing way to pass a few idle hours, and, as a phrase, it is often employed metaphorically—and inappropriately—as a synonym for any inherently effortless, risk-free activity, but a protracted period of time spent at the seaside is in fact fraught with hidden, and not so hidden, perils. Quite apart from shark attacks, excess cancer-inducing sun exposure, tsunamis, and drowning risks, a trip to the shore is likely to bring the unsuspecting beachgoer into contact with an awesome array of littoral debris. A partial list of the articles collected during the 2008 spring and fall beach sweeps conducted at 115 sites on the New Jersey shore by volunteers of Clean Ocean Action provides a sobering snapshot of the alluvial litter likely to be encountered on any given stretch of recreational coastline in the developed world: 36,041 pounds of refuse were recovered, comprising some 289,976 separate items, ranging from plastic bags, bottles, wrappers, lids, straws, stirrers, knives, forks, spoons, cigar tips, disposable diapers, tampon applicators, syringes, and condoms to fishhooks, nails, Christmas tree lights, shotgun shells, a bowling ball, a bottle of holy water, a truck-bed liner, a refrigerator door, a large noose, thirty feet of construction fencing, and a ballerina tutu.[27] See also: **summertime sex.**

beauty products. See: **cosmetics.**

BED. See: **banana equivalent dose.**

bedbugs. Technically known as *Cimex lectularius,* these tiny nest-

dwelling insect parasites feed exclusively on the blood of warm-blooded animals, and their all-time favorite host is Yours, and Ours, Truly, Homo sapiens. Ranging in size from about as big as a poppy seed to as much as a quarter inch in length, with flat, oval bodies, these tenacious household pests tend to infest bedding, furniture, carpets, and other warm, dark places from which they emerge during the night to bite their victims.[28] Although the Centers for Disease Control (CDC) have stated unequivocally that "bed bugs have never been shown to transmit disease," the CDC's *Emerging Infectious Diseases* information site goes on to report meticulously, and revoltingly, "bed bug bites can result in clinical manifestations; the most common are small clusters of extremely pruritic, erythematous papules or wheals that represent repeated feedings by a single bed bug. Less common but more severe manifestations include grouped vesicles, giant urticaria, and hemorrhagic bulbous eruptions." [29]

The CDC site lists several chemicals that pest control specialists have employed during recent attempts to combat the nocturnal parasites, but the tiny bloodsuckers have evolved in recent decades to the point where they can survive even the most potent and toxic pesticides (including the now-outlawed DDT, malathion, and diazinon), so these less powerful poisons are, for all practical purposes, useless in eradicating bedbug populations. "What we'd like is something you can spray on the floor and two months later a bug will pick up a lethal dose from walking across it," says Dr. Dini M. Miller, Ph.D., a Virginia Tech entomologist who is one of the nation's few academic experts on bedbugs. But alas, she laments, "it doesn't exist. Most of the things we have now, you almost have to spray directly on the bug to do anything to him." "Or," she adds helpfully, "hit him with the can." Indeed, as a recent *Newsweek* article on the bedbug scourge reports, "people sometimes do extreme things to get rid of them—such as setting off dozens of insect bombs in a room." This can be "quite effective," the magazine observes ruefully, "if the house blows up as a result." [30]

(Note: *Newsweek*'s musings are not as outlandish as they sound. According to the California Department of Pesticide Regulation, a number of such explosions occur every year, typically when homeowners use too many foggers and don't shut off pilot lights in ovens, stoves, and water heaters.[31]) So just to update that venerable bedtime benediction: "Good night, sleep tight, don't let the bedbugs bite, but if you're munched on by mattress mites, and you want to gas those parasites, be sure to shut off your pilot lights!"

———

Now that you know how impossible it is to get rid of bedbugs, you'll probably be relieved to hear that experts have come up with dozens of effective strategies you can use to prevent them from infesting your home in the first place. Here's a summary of some of the easiest and most practical:

- When you're traveling, Dr. Dini Miller, the Virginia Tech expert quoted above, points out, there might be bedbugs in your hotel room. So, when you get there, before opening your suitcase, you should "pull back all of the bedding at the head of the bed to look for evidence"; "check the underside of the mattress tag and the seams of the mattress and the boxsprings"; and "remove the head board from the wall and inspect the back of it."[32] (Bedbug .com says you should always bring a flashlight with you when you travel to help with such inspections.[33]) If you find anything, call the front desk and change rooms.[34]

- To protect your luggage in your hotel room, Dr. Miller continues, never place your suitcase on the bed; "inspect the luggage stand" and make sure that, when you put your bag on it, it's not touching the wall; "keep your clothing in your bag, don't use the drawers"; and don't put your shoes under the bed or in the closet.[35] (To be *extra* safe, advises American Museum of Natural History entomologist Louis N. Sorkin, M.S., keep your luggage in the bathtub instead of the bedroom—bedbugs don't like it there.[36])

- Upon returning home, says Dr. Miller, unpack right away (but not in your bedroom!) and send all your packed clothes—clean or dirty—to the laundry. (Bedbug.com recommends that you unpack your luggage *outdoors*, if at all possible, and vacuum the inside and outside of it before you bring it into the house.[37]) And, if your bag is the kind that won't be damaged by the process, adds Miller, sanitize it in your clothes dryer before putting it away.[38]

- When taking a taxi, recommends Bedbug.com, keep your bags on your lap "if at all possible" and "avoid using the trunk or storage compartments." And, if you take your jacket or coat off, don't put it on the seat next to you; hang it from the garment hook.[39]

- "You don't know what comes in and out of people's houses, even if you are related to them," warns Bedbug.com. So, the next time you visit friends or family, it is strongly advised that you pack your antibedbug encasements—yes, all of them, pillow, mattress, and box-spring protectors.[40] What, you don't have antibug pillow, mattress, and box-spring protectors? Bedbug.com will be happy to sell you a set complete with "patent pending zipper technology" for a modest $89.95.[41]

bedspreads, hotel. When you arrive in a hotel room after checking in, "the first thing you need to do is remove that disgusting quilted comforter," writes Allison Janse, who, in collaboration with famed University of Arizona microbe hunter Charles P. Gerba, Ph.D., authored *The Germ Freak's Guide to Outwitting Colds and Flu.* "There's a reason why they're so hideous looking. It's to hide the dirt and stains!" Janse explains. "Just think of how many naked people have sat on that comforter and done who knows what on it. Remember Mike Tyson's rape trial when they found body fluids from previous guests on his hotel bedspread?"[42]

bee-colony collapse disorder. See: **colony collapse disorder.**

beef trimmings, ammonia-treated. See: **"slimeburgers."**

belching. See: **omega-3 fish oil supplements.**

benzene poisoning. See: **candlelight dinners; carpeting, new.**

beta-carotene. See: **carrots.**

beverage garnishes. See: **lemon wedges.**

bicycle saddles. Riding a bicycle for recreation, for local errands, or for a daily commute would seem to be a healthy way for a guy to get some much-needed exercise, but before you "saddle up" for a trip on that Trek or get set for a stationary workout in a spinning class, consider this: Men who ride bikes with the traditional crotch-numbing knob-nosed saddle seat are putting themselves at risk for erectile dysfunction. As Dr. Steven Schrader of the Division of Applied Research Technology (DART) at the National Institute of Occupational Safety and Health (NIOSH) outlined the problem based on a recent examination of bike-patrol police officers in several U.S. cities, "The traditional bicycle saddle has a narrow nose or horn that protrudes under the groin as the cyclist straddles the bicycle . . . 25% or more of the body weight [of the cyclist] is supported where the groin contacts the saddle nose. Bearing weight on this region of the saddle compresses the nerves and arteries in the groin . . . and may lead to a loss of sensation and a decrease in blood supply to the genitals. This can contribute to the sexual and reproductive health effects that have been reported with bicycling."[43]

The study confirmed the results of a previous piece of research by Dr. Schrader on saddle-seat erectile dysfunction provocatively titled "Cutting Off the Nose to Save the Penis," which found that noseless bike seats improved blood flow to the penis, erectile function, and penile sensation. Dr. Schrader emphasized that the male groin "was never meant to bear pressure. Within a few minutes the blood oxygen levels go down by 80 percent." He also provided this succinct statement of the advantages of the new no-nose bicycle seat over the traditional design: "There's as much penis inside the body as outside. When you sit on a regular bike saddle, you're sitting on your penis."[44]

Sergeant Joe Andruzzi, commander of the 450-man bike-patrol unit of the Chicago Police Department and a senior member of the International Police Mountain Bike Association, agreed heartily with Dr. Schrader's recommendations about saddle seat replacements: "I encourage any officers who are concerned about their reproductive health to try a no-nose saddle. If you do, be patient. Your body needs time to adjust. Just know that if you make the switch, your penis will thank you for it."[45] See also: **erectile dysfunction.**

biflation. *Biflation* is a term used to describe a complex and poten-

tially devastating economic phenomenon in which deflation and inflation both occur simultaneously. Biflation can be set in motion by a sudden increase in the money supply by a central bank (such as, say, the

2009–2011 quantitative easing program undertaken by the U.S. Federal Reserve), which can spark a sharp spike in the price of commodity-based assets, such as food, energy, and clothing—especially in an environment in which other factors, such as the rapid development of economies in Asia, have already created a rising demand for such assets. The increase in the cost of these essential goods leads to a decrease in purchasing power available for the acquisition of longer-term, debt-based, nonessential assets like homes, household furnishings, automobiles, boats, electronic goods, and even stocks, and the prices of these items fall due to the decreased volume of money chasing them.[46] The resulting "mixflation," as it is sometimes termed, is a disruptive blend of growth-sapping deflationary expectations and destabilizing inflationary pressures, and, according to *Wall Street Journal* columnist Al Lewis, we've been experiencing it for several years now. "Everything you already own—a house, a car, a stock portfolio—has rapidly declined in value," he points out. "Everything you actually need to buy—food, gasoline, medicine, education—is going up."[47] All in all, not a pretty picture, but not quite as dire an outlook as the one offered in a pure deflationary spiral. See: **deflation.**

biocide. See: **Medea hypothesis, the.**

biodebridement. See: **maggot therapy.**

biofuels. Biofuels, such as ethanol made from corn, have been widely heralded as an environmentally friendly replacement for fossil fuels, principally because they are "renewable" (the crops they are made from can be regrown and re-harvested), whereas fossil fuels, by definition, are not, and will therefore be in ever-shorter supply. In addition, biofuels appear to have a better "carbon footprint" than fossil fuels because, in theory, when you burn biofuels, you're burning the same carbon that plants removed from the air while they were growing, whereas, when you burn coal, oil, or natural gas, you're spewing fossilized carbon into the air. However, as social-change strategist Joe Brewer explains in his informative article "The Coming Biofuels Disaster," the harmful impacts from large-scale biofuel production may be even greater than the problem it is designed to solve. For one thing, it is shifting crop yields and land implementation away from food production. "Basic economics tells us that the cost of goods go up when supply decreases," Brewer notes, and, indeed, the growing demand for grains to produce fuel has already led to dramatic increases in the cost of food—a phenomenon known as **agflation** (q.v.)—and a concurrent increase in the number of hungry people in less developed countries. "We are starving poor people to feed our cars!" Brewer says.[48]

Furthermore, the process of growing the crops used for making biofuels consumes tremendous quantities of fossil fuels. "Corn receives more synthetic fertilizer than any other crop, and that fertilizer is made from fossil fuels—mostly natural gas," explains UC Berkeley professor Michael Pollan, prizewinning author of *The Omnivore's Dilemma*. "Corn also receives more pesticide than any other crop, and most of that pesticide is made from petroleum. To plow or disc the cornfields, plant the seed, spray the corn and harvest it takes large amounts of diesel fuel, and to dry the corn after harvest requires natural gas. So by the time your 'green' raw material arrives at the ethanol plant, it is already drenched in fossil fuel." And all that is before you even start to distill the corn into ethanol, which itself is an energy-intensive process that necessitates the burning of still more fossil fuels.[49]

When all is said and done, according to Professor David Pimentel, Ph.D., and his colleagues at Cornell University's Department of Ecology and Evolutionary Biology, "the total energy input to produce a liter of ethanol is 7,474 kcal. However, a liter of ethanol has an energy value of only 5,130 kcal. Based on a net energy loss of 2,344 kcal of ethanol produced, 46% more fossil energy is expended than is produced as ethanol."[50] In short, concludes Michael Pollan, "making ethanol from corn is an environmentally and economically absurd proposition." So why the big rush to do it? Because we have such a powerful lobby promoting the growth and consumption of corn, Pollan says. Each year, the United States grows more than 10 billion bushels, "far more than we can possibly eat—though God knows we're doing our best, bingeing on corn-based fast food and high fructose corn syrup till we're fat and diabetic." "We can't eat much more of the stuff without exploding," Pollan concludes, "so the corn lobby is targeting the next unsuspecting beast that might help chomp through the surplus: your car."[51]

bird flu. See: **flu pandemic.**

birth-control pills. According to Sara Newmann, M.D., M.P.H., of  the Bixby Center for Global Reproductive Health at the University of California, San Francisco, birth-control pills have an 8 percent failure rate, largely because it's so hard to remember to take them at exactly the same time every day. If you're at all forgetful, therefore, you might want to consider an alternative birth-control method. Furthermore, Newmann points out, birth-control pills can cause breast tenderness, nausea, spotting, and low sex drive.[52] And, of course, as the Mayo Clinic pointedly reminds us, "birth control pills won't protect you from sexually transmitted infections."[53] Finally, ABC News has recently reported that a number of experts, including pharmacoepidemiologist Dr. Susan S. Jick of the Boston University School of Public Health, are increasingly worried about a substance called drospirenone contained in several brands of a relatively new, heavily marketed, and extremely popular type of oral contraceptive known as "combination birth control pills." Research suggests that these products may trigger significantly more blood clots than other birth-control pills—clots with the potential to cause serious breathing problems, a stroke, or even death.[54] The Mayo Clinic shares Dr. Jick's concern. "Consult your health care provider as soon as possible," the Clinic advises, "if you're taking combination birth control pills and have: abdominal pain; breast lump; chest pain; depression; difficulty speaking; eye problems, such as blurred or double vision or loss of vision; fainting; jaundice (yellowish discoloration of the skin); new or worsening headaches; seizure; severe allergic skin rash; severe leg pain or swelling; or severe mood swings."[55] See: **abstinence; condoms; "safe sex"; sexual activity.**

birth defects. See: **air fresheners; commuting by train; parsley; tap water.**

bisphenol A. This organic compound, which is commonly referred to by the abbreviation BPA, is widely employed by the food and beverage industry in the epoxy linings of the ubiquitous metal cans in which many food products, including soups, sauces, fruits, vegetables, and fish and meat entrées are packaged and the transparent, shatterproof, polycarbonate plastic bottles that are used as containers for sodas, sparkling and flavored waters, and juices. BPA is also present in a dizzying array of consumer goods, including compact discs, dental sealants, baby bottles, teething rings, sippy cups, and the thermal paper used in credit-card and ATM receipts. BPA is cheap to produce, durable, antiseptic, flavorless, stable, and corrosion-resistant, but this commercially valuable chemical is also a potentially powerful synthetic estrogen that can disrupt normal endocrine function,[56] and more than one hundred studies conducted around the world since 1997 have linked even low doses of BPA, and its close chemical cousins, bisphenol AF, bisphenol B, bisphenol F, and bisphenol S to prostate and breast cancer, reproductive abnormalities, accelerated puberty in females, low sperm counts in males, neurological effects similar to attention-deficit/ hyperactivity disorder, diabetes, obesity, and a possible doubling of the risk of coronary heart disease.[57] And in a 2004 survey of 2,157 people between the ages of six and eighty-five in the United States conducted by the Centers for Disease Control, 93 percent were found to have detectable levels of BPA in their urine samples. "Children had higher levels than adolescents, and adolescents had higher levels than adults," according to endocrinologist Retha Newbold of the U.S. National Institute of Environmental Health Sciences, noting that "it is the unborn baby and children that investigators are most worried about."

The BPA apparently leached out of the linings of cans when they were heated during food preparation or the interiors of bottles when they were washed in hot water, an insidious process identified in a study by Scott Belcher, an endocrine biologist at the University of Cincinnati, who found that BPA becomes soluble more than fifty times faster when exposed to hot liquids than it would under normal conditions. And although BPA breaks down quickly into an easily excreted waste product—glucuronide—the CDC also found trace amounts of that particular by-product in most of the urine samples, suggesting some degree of continuous contamination.[58] "There is low-level exposure, but regular low-level exposure," explained chemist Steven Hentges, executive director of the polycarbonate/SPA global group of the American Chemistry Council. "It is presumably in our diet." This disturbing supposition was recently confirmed by Randy Hartnell, whose Washington state–based health food company, Vital Choice, began marketing products in BPA-free packaging after making an expensive changeover to an alternative can-lining material. Hartnell was understandably flabbergasted when a Consumer Union test of a container of his tuna fish came up positive for BPA. "What we're hearing is the stuff is just omnipresent," Hartnell lamented. "Is it in the cutting board? The gloves that people wear who are working on the fish? Is it in the tuna itself? We don't know. We're trying to find out."[59]

While there may be some uncertainty about the severity and extent of the effects of the routine ingestion of small doses of BPA, Scott Belcher warns that containers made of or lined with the compound should never be microwaved, utilized to store heated liquids or foods, or washed in hot water, either by hand or in a dishwasher. Belcher summed up his concerns by saying that "based on my knowledge of the scientific data there is reason for caution," noting matter-of-factly, "I have made a decision for myself not to use them."[60] His viewpoint was seconded by Frederick vom Saal, a BPA researcher at the University of Missouri, Columbia. "This is a bad chemical," vom Saal stated flatly, "and it should not be used the way it is used."[61]

black holes, tiny. See: **Large Hadron Collider.**

black olives. See: **acrylamide.**

black swans. A descriptive metaphor employed by the economist, philosopher, and phenomenally successful investor Nassim Nicholas Taleb to characterize extremely rare, highly improbable, and inherently unforeseeable events that have enormous and frequently (although not always) disastrous consequences—consequences that our society, Taleb feels, is massively unprepared to cope with. In classical times, the term *black swan* was used by philosophers to illustrate the utility of relying on past observation as the basis for arriving at conclusions about the future. Since no one had ever seen a black swan, it made sense to assume that all swans were white, a pretty safe bet that went unchallenged until a Dutch explorer discovered a black swan in western Australia in 1697 and promptly named the nearby Swan River after the celebrated dusky-feathered outlier. Black swan events typically come as a complete surprise, have a huge impact, and then are explained away in hindsight by the same experts who contemptuously dismissed the possibility of their ever occurring in the first place. Such consequential incidents in recent history include World War I, the terrorist attacks of 9/11, and the stock-market crashes of 1929 and 2008.

Compounding the difficulty of dealing with the aftermath of these disruptive episodes is the near impossibility of preparing for the worst, particularly in the field of financial planning, since the worst we generally anticipate is often the wrong worst, and when a truly unforeseen worst takes place, our prospects are worsened by a lack of preparation or a misallocation of resources to the preparation for the wrong worst that makes the actual worst that comes along that much worse. On the bright side, black swan events include a number of out-of-the-blue fortuitous happenstances, like the invention of the printing press, the discovery of the New World, and the development and widespread adoption of the personal computer and the Internet, all of which coincidentally made the writing and publication of this book possible. On a somewhat less sunny note, the occurrence of yet another far less beneficial black swan event may mean that instead of idly perusing these pages, you are instead crumpling them up and using them to stoke the meager fire that is warming you in the ruins of a devastated civilization.[62]

bladder distention, urinary. See: "**holding it in.**"

blankets, airplane. See: **airplane cabins.**

Blarney Stone. Several hundred thousand people make their way

 each year to the top of Blarney Castle, near Cork, Ireland, to kiss the legendary "Stone of Eloquence," better known as the Blarney Stone. Indeed, doing so—which involves climbing the long, winding staircase to the top of the castle and leaning backward over the parapet while someone "firmly holds your feet"—is supposedly guaranteed to turn you into a brilliant and persuasive speaker.[63] "But given that up to 400,000 mouths from all over the world touch the stone each year," warns the popular travel website TripAdvisor.com, "putting your own to the grimy attraction (no easy task in itself) may be too high a price for the promised 'gift of gab.'" In fact, TripAdvisor is so concerned about the possibility of tourists' contracting something more sinister than oratory skills from planting a wet one on the Blarney Stone that its editors have officially anointed the historic slab "the World's Germiest Attraction."[64]

blindness. See: **mascara; neckties.**

bloating. See: **fruit juice; omega-3 fish oil supplements.**

blood clots. See: **crossing your legs; socks and stockings with elastic tops.**

Bloody Mary mixes. See: **high-fructose corn syrup (HFCS).**

blueberries. Do you love blueberries? Well, sadly, so do blueberry

 maggots and bagworms. That's why blueberry producers douse their product with so much pesticide that the fruit has earned a place on the Environmental Working Group's "Dirty Dozen" list of fruits and veggies you should make a point of buying only if they're organically grown.[65] See also: **organic food.**

bodice rippers. See: **romance novels.**

bone-marrow failure disorders. See: **candlelight dinners.**

botnets. One of the most insidious ways that hackers and computer criminals use **malware** (q.v.) is to open a "back door" to a computer—yours, for example—so that it can be taken over by outsiders. Once they've transformed it into a "zombie" machine, writes *The Economist,* they can link it up to thousands, if not millions, of others around the world to create a "botnet" that, in turn, can be employed by the cybercrooks to steal identities (again, including yours); to send spam, viruses, worms, and Trojans; to cripple major corporate or government computer networks by overloading them with bogus requests; and, of course, to infect still more computers. According to *The Economist,* as many as 100 million computers worldwide have already been infected, and the number is growing every day.[66] So how can you tell if your computer has been compromised and, as the *Consumerist* blog's Meg Marco elegantly puts it, "is being controlled and used for evil?"[67] The answer, sadly, is that you probably can't. But, according to the Federal Trade Commission, there may be a few telltale signs: "You may receive emails accusing you of sending spam; you may find email messages in your 'outbox' that you didn't send; or your computer suddenly may operate more slowly or sluggishly." If any of these things are happening to you, suggests the FTC, "disconnect from the Internet right away."[68] (The FTC has a lot of other excellent advice for dealing with malware and botnets, too; you can access it at http://www.ftc.gov/bcp/edu/pubs/consumer/alerts/alt132.shtm. Of course, if you've already "disconnected from the Internet" because you suspect your machine is part of a "zombie army," you'll probably find it difficult to take advantage of the agency's good counsel.) See also: **cyberwarfare; malware; Trojan horse.**

bottled water. Over 50 percent of all Americans are now drinking  bottled water, paying, to quote the Natural Resources Defense Council (NRDC), "from 240 to 10,000 times more" than they typically would for an equivalent amount of tap water.[69] Their willingness to ante up this extraordinary premium is based, of course, on the assumption that bottled water comes from pristine, unspoiled places, and, therefore, that it is purer, healthier, and better tasting than the water they could get directly from their faucets. But is this assumption merited? Emphatically not, says the NRDC, which points out in their report "Bottled Water: Pure Drink or Pure Hype" that the Federal Drug Administration allows water bottlers to identify their product as "spring water," even though it may be brought to the surface using a pumped well, and even though it may be treated with chemicals. Among the "more interesting" approved brands of bottled water NRDC tested, according to the report, were several labeled "spring water" (at least one with mountains and a lake pictured on the bottle) that actually came "from an industrial parking lot next to a state-designated industrial waste site in Millis, Massachusetts," and that were contaminated with "dangerous levels of industrial solvents"; and another, branded "Pure Glacier Water from the Last Unpolluted Frontier," whose actual source was the Juneau, Alaska, municipal water supply.[70]

And, to make matters worse, the rise in bottled water consumption presents a legitimate environmental hazard. For example, the U.S. Council of Mayors reports that because they're made from petroleum, the plastic water bottles produced for U.S. consumption use up 1.5 million barrels of oil per annum. That much energy, according to the Council, could power 250,000 homes or fuel 100,000 cars for a year.[71] Furthermore, the number of unrecycled plastic water bottles going into landfills almost quadrupled during the decade ending in 2008.[72] Knowing all this, is it still wise to spend up to ten thousand times more for a sip of bottled water than for an equivalent amount of tap water? You decide. See: **tap water.** See also: **bisphenol A.**

bottles, plastic. See: **bisphenol A; bottled water.**

bovine growth hormone, recombinant. See: **milk.**

bowl of cherries. Someone's life may be a bowl of cherries, but if the

individual in question is a toddler, it might be a very short life indeed. On its helpful website, the Childcare Network has posted a list of twelve foods "that pose a significant choking risk to small children." Number one on their rundown of the Deadly Dozen—"cherries with pits."[73] The pediatric staff at Health Castle echoes that verdict with its own stern warning: "Beware of cherries with pits. Both the cherry and the pit are choking hazards."[74] And the AgriLife Extension Service at Texas A&M University provides the metaphorical—though potentially lethal—"cherry on top" with the reminder that "all cherry pits contain small amounts of cyanide and cause poisoning if eaten in large quantities."[75] Indeed, warns chemist and biomedical scientist Anne Marie Helmenstine, Ph.D., "if you eat enough cherry pits, you could die." Luckily, adult humans can detoxify small amounts of cyanide compounds, Dr. Helmenstine writes, so if you happen to swallow a pit while eating a cherry pie "you'll be fine." However, she cautions, chewing the pits "makes them much more hazardous to your health." Keep that in mind before you allow yourself to absentmindedly bite down on a cherry! And furthermore, Helmenstine advises, "children and pets are much more likely to suffer poisoning from eating the [pits] than adults." Therefore, she says, "it's important to seek immediate medical attention" if a child or pet is known to have eaten several pits. "Usually," she concludes, "the plan of action is to pump the stomach or induce vomiting."[76] See: **ipecac.** See also: **apple seeds; beach, a day at the; piece of cake.**

BPA. See: **bisphenol A.**

brain damage. See: **compact fluorescent lightbulbs (CFLs); hot tubs; yoga.**

brain glucose metabolism, increased. See: **cell phones, radiation hazards.**

brain injury, traumatic. See: **hiccups; runny nose.**

brain tumors. See: **headaches; hot dogs.**

Brazilian Blowout, the. The hair-straightening treatment known as the Brazilian Blowout has been hailed as "life-changing" by women who have struggled their entire lives with hard-to-manage hair. The treatment—the results of which can last for several months—has become so popular, Fox News reports, "that even pre-teens are pressuring their moms for the pricey trip to the salon ($200–$500 per visit) . . . and are often getting it."[77] Unfortunately, however, studies in Canada and Oregon have shown that Brazilian Blowout solution has the potential to be "life-changing" in a way that its adherents may not have bargained for: It contains significant amounts of a substance whose presence in the widely promoted beauty product should make salon goers' hair stand on end instead of relaxing into soft, silky tresses. Following reports of breathing problems, swollen eyes, coughing, and spontaneous nosebleeds among stylists at an Oregon salon, researchers at Oregon Health and Science University's Center for Research on Occupational and Environmental Toxicology (CROET) and the Oregon Occupational Health and Safety Division tested 105 samples of the shampoolike formulation and found high levels of formaldehyde, a toxic irritant and sensitizing agent that, in addition to the extremely unpleasant short-term symptoms exposure to its fumes can produce, has been identified as a known human carcinogen by both the International Agency for Research on Cancer and the U.S. Environmental Protection Agency. More that one-third of the samples came from bottles labeled "formaldehyde-free," yet the formaldehyde content of even these samples ranged from 6.3 percent to 10.6 percent.[78] After its own investigation, Health Canada issued a strong recommendation that "stylists who use Brazilian Blowout treatments should immediately stop using the affected products."[79]

But perhaps the most hair-raising warning comes from Deirdre Imus, founder and president of the Imus Environmental Health Center at Hackensack University: "Listen ladies: The gas-like masks offered to customers and worn by your stylists should be a big tip-off that something about this product is probably not good for you and certainly not good for children."[80]

breakfast cereals. See: **acrylamide; aspartame; granola bars; high fructose corn syrup (HFCS);** and **vitamin A supplements.**

breast milk, decreased ability to produce. See: **french fries.**

broken toes. See: **flip-flops.**

brominated flame retardants. See: **salmon, farmed.**

brown rice. Health food adherents suffered a rude shock in 2007
 when Andrew Meharg, Ph.D., the chair of biogeo-
chemistry at the University of Aberdeen in Scotland,
announced that he had discovered potentially dangerous levels of arsenic in brown rice, which has long been
the iconic staple of the macrobiotic diet.[81] Arsenic, of
course, is famously poisonous, and it's also a known carcinogen. According to Dr. Meharg, rice absorbs considerably more of the deadly
toxin than most other crops do because the water used to flood rice
paddies is able to "mobilize" arsenic that occurs naturally in the soil,
or that has collected there because of pesticide contamination, or as a
result of runoff from industrial and mining sites.

Why is brown rice more dangerous than, say, the white rice or "pol-
ished rice" that is consumed in so much of the world? Because, Dr.
Meharg explains, the outer grain, where much of the arsenic he found
in the tainted rice was "localized," is removed in the manufacture of
white rice, but in brown rice, it remains in place. (Ironically, it's the
fiber and nutrients concentrated in the outer grain that established
"brown rice" as a macrobiotic favorite in the first place.) Perhaps most
disturbing of all, says Dr. Meharg, is the fact that arsenic is a "non-
threshold carcinogen," which means that exposure to any amount of
the poisonous element, no matter how small, poses a health risk.[82] In
a recent interview, Professor Meharg assured the *Daily Mail* that he
"does not let his children eat the suspect rice," and he suggested "other
consumers might take the same decision."[83]

brownstones. Brownstones are thought by many to be among the
 sturdiest, and therefore the safest, structures in which
one can live. Before choosing to inhabit such buildings,
however, readers would be wise to heed the advice of
geophysicist Mary Lou Zoback, who serves as vice
president of earthquake risk applications for Risk Management Solutions, Inc., in Newark, California. The brownstones in

many urban areas were built without earthquakes in mind, Zoback cautions. "They crumble well," she points out.[84]

brushing your teeth after meals. Did your parents, or, perhaps, your
 dentist, teach you that you should always brush your teeth after meals? If you've followed this advice throughout your life, Dr. Phil Stemmer, B.D.S., the founder and clinical director of London's Fresh Breath Centre, has some bad news for you: You may have done irreparable damage to the enamel of your teeth. In fact, he warns, it's absolutely essential that you *not* brush until at least an hour after eating "because the food acids and sugars temporarily weaken the protective enamel on the teeth. If you clean your teeth too soon, you are actually brushing away at the enamel before it hardens again." The best routine? "Brush your teeth *before* meals," Dr. Stemmer advises, "and then freshen up after eating using an alcohol-free mouthwash."[85]

bubble nucleation. See: **vacuum metastability event.**

bunions. See: **high-heel shoes.**

butter. See: **dairy products.**

C

cabbage. See: **leafy green vegetables.**

cabs, taxi. See: **bedbugs.**

caffeine. The caffeine found in coffee and tea, and also in cola and
 energy drinks, may help wake you up in the morning or give you an occasional shot of needed energy, but, according to Livestrong.com, the health and fitness website operated by the Lance Armstrong Foundation, "it can also pose dangerous risks." For example,

people who drink coffee regularly generally register higher blood pressure readings than those who do not; indeed, Sheldon G. Sheps, M.D., a hypertension specialist at the Mayo Clinic, says the amount of caffeine found in just two to three cups of coffee can raise a person's systolic pressure (the top number in a blood pressure reading) as much as 14 millimeters of mercury (mm Hg) and diastolic pressure (the bottom number) as much as 13 mm Hg. Such increases, Sheps cautions, can prove particularly dangerous for folks who already have high blood pressure or heart-related diseases. In addition, Livestrong informs us, research reports indicate that caffeine, when ingested in sufficient quantities, "may cause the body to rid itself of calcium—a nutrient vital in supporting bone strength." For example, a study of elderly women with calcium deficiencies, published in the *Journal of Bones and Mineral Research* in 2009, found that those who consumed caffeine frequently exhibited significantly greater instances of osteoporosis and bone fractures than women who did not.

Furthermore, warns Roland R. Griffiths, Ph.D., a behavioral pharmacology expert at the Johns Hopkins University School of Medicine, the basic mechanisms that cause people to become dependent upon caffeine are similar to classic drug addiction. As a result, he says, people who routinely ingest caffeine may experience withdrawal symptoms if, say, their morning coffee is delayed or missed. "Symptoms of caffeine withdrawal," Livestrong notes, "include headache, lethargy, foggy thinking, depressed or irritable mood, and even nausea or vomiting."[1] In sum, if you use caffeine habitually, it's probably past time for you to "wake up and smell the coffee." See also: **coffee; tea, a nice hot cup of.**

cake, piece of. Using the descriptive term *a piece of cake* to character-

ize the degree of difficulty of any given task is definitely a half-baked proposition. Virtually all cakes are made of wheat flour, a fairly benign-seeming farinaceous product that harbors two unrelated, but equally grave, latent dangers. The first of these lurking menaces is the potential for enormous dust explosions precipitated by random sparks in airborne clouds of the finely ground cereal grains, like the spontaneous combustion event in the historic Great Mill Disaster of May 2, 1878, that leveled the Washburn "A" Mill in Minneapolis, causing the immediate deaths of fourteen millworkers and igniting a conflagration that killed four more people and destroyed five other nearby mills.[2] The second hidden peril is celiac disease, an inherited form of wheat-gluten intolerance affecting many individuals with Northern European ancestry that transforms that scrumptious dessert item into a slow-acting but potentially deadly poison. As noted by the Mayo Clinic, "celiac disease can cause abdominal pain and diarrhea. Eventually the decreased absorption of nutrients (malabsorption) that occurs with celiac disease can cause vitamin deficiencies that deprive your brain, peripheral nervous system, bones, liver, and other organs of vital nutrients." In extreme cases, celiac disease can also lead to "loss of bone density (osteoporosis) . . . several forms of cancer, including intestinal lymphoma and bowel cancer . . . as well as seizures and a form of nerve damage known as peripheral neuropathy."[3]

California superstorm. As if earthquakes weren't enough of a threat to the nation's largest, richest, and, meteorologically speaking, most temperate state, recent improvements in weather satellite imagery have made it possible for scientists to spot telltale high-altitude wind currents that indicate the presence of "atmospheric rivers"— giant streams of moisture-laden air that flow in from the tropical Pacific Ocean and onto the California coast. These immense weather systems can exceed two hundred miles in width and two thousand miles in length and have the potential to deliver torrential downpours of up to ten feet of rain over much of central California in a period of just a few weeks. A deluge of this magnitude actually occurred in the winter of 1861–1862, and it dumped enough rain on the Central Valley in forty-five days to flood vast tracts of the state from Sacramento to Bakersfield, a stretch of land some three hundred miles long and twenty miles wide. Marcia K. McNutt of the U.S. Geological Survey (USGS) notes that the inundation basically turned "the Sacramento Valley into an inland sea, forcing the state capital to be moved from Sacramento to San Francisco for a time, and requiring Governor Leland Stanford to take a rowboat to his inauguration."

According to a study conducted by a team of scientists from the USGS, FEMA (the Federal Emergency Management Agency), and CalEMA (its state counterpart), if a "superstorm" of the same magnitude were to hit modern-day California, it would bring a volume of water equivalent to fifty Mississippi Rivers in a period of about four weeks. The entire coastal region from north of San Francisco all the way to San Diego would suffer property losses in excess of $400 billion, one in four houses in the state could experience some flood damage, widespread landslides and mudslides would severely damage the highway network, and the state would have to absorb at least another $325 billion in lost agricultural and tourist business revenue.[4] "We think this event happens once every 100 to 200 years or so," says Lucy Jones, chief scientist of the U.S. Geological Survey's Survey of Multi-Hazards Demonstration Project, "which puts it in the same category as our big San Andreas earthquakes." But a tempest of the biblical proportions and duration envisioned in the study (which its authors aptly dubbed an "ARkStorm," short for "Atmospheric River k = 1000") would have a total cost "nearly three times the loss deemed to be realistic for a severe southern California earthquake, an event with roughly the same annual occurrence probability."[5] As Jones noted, "Floods are as much a part of our lives in California as earthquakes are," adding grimly, "We are probably not going to be able to handle the biggest ones."[6]

Canary Islands mega-tsunami. See: **Cumbre Vieja mega-tsunami.**

Canderel. See: **aspartame.**

candlelight dinners. To many of us, candlelight dinners represent
 the epitome of romance—occasions to be longed for, treasured, and remembered. But, as a 2009 study conducted by scientists at the University of South Carolina has demonstrated, we pay a high price for those intimate moments: Candlelight dinners—especially in enclosed spaces—can be unhealthy, hazardous, and even life-threatening. The reason, explains Amid Hamidi, coauthor of the study, is that paraffin candles—those most frequently used in homes and

restaurants—are petroleum-based, and when they are burned, they emit dangerous chemicals such as benzene, which has been linked to bone-marrow failure disorders (aplastic anemia and acute lympho-cytic leukemia, for example) and toluene, which, even in low to moderate amounts, can cause confusion, tiredness, weakness, nausea, loss of memory, loss of appetite, color-blindness, and hearing disorders, and, when inhaled in larger quantities, frequently leads to unconsciousness and death.[7]

canned foods. See: **bisphenol A.**

carbofuran poisoning. See: **oranges.**

carpeting, new. As the always informative website SilentMenace.com

 points out, new carpeting can be found in many homes and in most businesses and schools, and it contains "more bad things than you want to imagine . . . Infants crawl and children play for hours on it, all the while inhaling its fumes, and businesses subject workers to newly-installed carpeting, poisoning them with a stew of chemicals, allergens and toxic dust." The biggest menace posed by new carpeting, according to SilentMenace.com, is the fact that it releases "volatile organic compounds (VOC's), such as toluene, benzene, formaldehyde, ethyl benzene, styrene, and acetone."[8] Inhaled in sufficient quantities, the U.S. Environmental Protection Agency advises, VOCs can cause "conjunctival irritation, nose and throat discomfort, headache, allergic skin reaction, dyspnea, declines in serum cholinesterase levels, nausea, emesis, epistaxis, fatigue, and dizziness. Some organics can cause cancer in animals; some are suspected or known to cause cancer in humans."[9]

"If you've ever felt queasy or lightheaded in a room recently floored with new carpeting," notes SilentMenace.com, "this is most likely why." And, the website adds, VOCs are hardly the only problem: "Other compounds in new carpeting that affect our health are adhesives, stain protectors, moth proofing and flame retardants. Moth proofing chemicals contain naphthalene, which is known to produce toxic reactions, especially in newborns. Fire retardants often contain polybrominated diphenyl ether (PBDE). Recent reports have indicated that exposure to even low concentrations of these chemicals may result in irreparable damage to the nervous and reproductive systems." SilentMenace.com points out that the most dangerous exposure to new carpeting is in places of business. Since most of today's corporate suites are "closed environments," the website explains, "not only each of the offices, but the entire building is a sealed, controlled environment, where the air is constantly re-circulated." The result, of course, is that virtually none of the polluted air from the new carpeting ever has a chance to escape. "Add the many photocopiers, chemical cleaners and air 'fresheners' that are most likely in place," adds SilentMenace.com, "and what you have in practically any indoor American office is a virtual toxic wasteland."

So what can you do to try to stay healthy? The sad reality, says SilentMenace.com, is that "management most likely isn't going to rip up thousands of dollars of new carpeting simply because of you." But that doesn't mean you're helpless to act. "If new carpeting in your place of business is making you sick, you may be able to get a doctor's excuse to remain away from work until the carpeting is aired out," SilentMenace.com advises. Furthermore, says the website, if you can get a doctor to certify you as a "person with multi-chemical sensitivities," you can invoke the Americans with Disabilities Act of 1990 to obtain a medical order forbidding your employer from exposing you to new carpet fumes and other indoor pollution hazards. Before attempting this stratagem, however, SilentMenace.com urges you to "check with your attorney on your rights." "Management," they point out, "can be justified to fire anyone who creates a chaotic scene and disrupts the company's conduct of business." [10] See: **carpeting, old.** See also: **air fresheners; copying machines; ink-jet printers; laser printers.**

carpeting, old. "Older carpets can be more of a hazard than new

ones," warns SilentMenace.com. "Not only may they contain the chemicals banned from more recent production, they also have had years to accumulate pounds of dust mites, dirt, pesticides and other toxins brought in on shoes, feet and pet's paws. At home, the chemicals from sprays and insect foggers settle in the rug and remain there for years. If your place of business is serviced by an exterminator or has had its walls recently painted, the VOC's can remain in the carpet indefinitely and seep out long after the exterminator leaves and the walls no longer smell of paint." What can you do to reduce your exposure to carpet toxins? Well, recommends SilentMenace.com, if you're a homeowner, the answer is simple: "Get rid of the carpeting." When it comes to getting the company where you work to do the same, however, the website acknowledges, "you're pretty much at their mercy." [11] That doesn't mean, however, that you shouldn't "demand that safety measures be established to minimize . . . the dangers that over-exposure to hazardous chemicals can have on your health," SilentMenace. com insists. "Just because you don't feel bad today that doesn't mean that you won't develop problems later on as chemicals that have been accumulating in your body slowly decimate your organs, glands, nervous system and even your bone marrow." [12]

carrots. According to Australia's Macular Degeneration Foundation, the notion that eating carrots is good for your eyes is nothing but a myth, and a dangerous one at that. Indeed, Foundation director Dr. Paul Beaumont warns that eating too many carrots actually increases your chances of going blind, because foods rich in beta-carotene—like carrots—can damage the eye's protective shield, doubling a person's risk of contracting macular degeneration. Does that mean that those who want to protect their eyes have no recourse? Hardly. According to Dr. Beaumont, there are *other* foods that, like carrots, are rich in the eye-friendly antioxidant lutein, but that, *unlike* carrots, contain no harmful beta-carotene. Beaumont specifically recommends spinach and egg yolks.[13] See **spinach; eggs.**

Cascade Range volcanoes. If you're one of the hundreds of thousands sands of Americans and Canadians who reside in or near the Cascade Mountain Range—including those dwelling in such major metropolitan areas as Portland, Seattle, Tacoma, and Vancouver—you are living in constant danger of suffering the direct or indirect effects of a volcanic eruption. Adding to "the great risk posed by volcanic activity in the region," the National Disaster Education Coalition (NDEC) points out, is the fact that "individual Cascades volcanoes can lie dormant for many centuries between eruptions," which means that the hazards are "not always apparent." However, when these volcanoes *do* erupt, the Coalition warns, "high-speed avalanches of hot ash and rock (pyroclastic flows), lava flows, and landslides can devastate areas 10 or more miles away, and huge mudflows of volcanic ash and debris (lahars) can inundate valleys more than 50 miles downstream."[14]

The United States Geological Survey has specifically labeled ten active Cascades volcanoes in Washington, Oregon, and California—Mount Baker, Crater Lake, Glacier Peak, Mount Hood, Lassen Peak, Mount Newberry, Mount Rainier, Mount Shasta, South Sister, and Mount St. Helens (whose eruption in 1980 unleashed a catastrophic lahar that buried twenty-three square miles in up to six hundred feet of mud and rock[15])—as "very high threat volcanoes."[16] If you live near one, the NDEC advises, it behooves you to develop a "volcano-specific family disaster plan." For advice on how to do it, the Coalition suggests, "contact your local emergency management agency, American Red Cross chapter, or state geological survey or department of natural resources."[17] See also: **Mount Rainier** and **lahars.** (Note: The volcanism in the Cascades Range is a by-product of a tectonic process called subduction. For more details, and for a discussion of other potentially dire consequences of tectonic activity in the Cascades region, see: **Cascadia Subduction Zone.**)

Cascadia Subduction Zone. About 50 miles west of the Pacific coast

of North America, stretching for 680 miles from Vancouver Island in British Columbia to Cape Mendocino in Northern California, lies the Cascadia Subduction Zone, an area in which the oceanic Juan de Fuca Plate (accompanied by two associated smaller plates, the Explorer Plate and the Gorda Plate) is colliding with, and plunging under, the edge of the continental North American Plate. Geologists call this process subduction, and for hundreds of years at a time, an

ocean plate and continental plate that are colliding in such a manner can remain locked together, a process that creates almost unimaginably great, and ever-increasing, pressure. Finally, the rocks along the plate boundary reach the point where they can no longer withstand the stress, and they rupture abruptly, permitting the massive plates to snap past each other with cataclysmic speed. The result is what scientists call a megathrust earthquake, the most violent seismic event our planet can produce, and to make matters worse, because such quakes are almost always undersea events, they more often than not trigger devastating tsunamis. For example, the four most intense temblors ever recorded—the 1960 Valdivia (Chile) earthquake and tsunami; the 1964 Prince William Sound (Alaska) earthquake and tsunami; the 2004 Sumatra-Andaman earthquake and tsunami; and the 2011 Great East Japan earthquake and tsunami—were all megathrust events.[18]

The bad news for the Pacific Northwest is that the Cascadia Subduction Zone has a long geological record of producing megathrust earthquakes, and many scientists say there's a strong possibility one could occur there at any time within the next few decades. "It's not if, but when," warns Yumei Wang, the leader of the Oregon Department of Geology and Mineral Industries' Geohazards Team. "The average time between magnitude 8 and larger Cascadia earthquakes is about 240 years. The last megaquake, estimated as a magnitude 9, occurred in 1700—that's 311 years ago. In geologic terms, Cascadia is '9 months pregnant' and overdue."[19] And when the event occurs—since the "Cascadia" region includes three large cities, Portland, Seattle, and Vancouver—it promises to be one of the greatest natural disasters ever to strike North America. "The amount of devastation is going to be unbelievable," says Rob Witter, a coastal geologist in Wang's Oregon Department of Geology and Mineral Industries. "People aren't going to be ready for this."[20]

Echoing Witter's concern is Brigadier General Mike Caldwell, interim director of Oregon's Emergency Management Agency. "The reaction time [after] the predicted 8 to 9 magnitude earthquake could be as few as 6 to 7 minutes, up to 15 to 20 minutes before a potential 60 foot (or higher) tsunami strikes our coastal communities," he warned in congressional testimony delivered in April 2011, shortly after the

Great East Japan quake. "We also predict that most, if not all tsunami warning sirens will most likely not be operational due to the significant earthquake. Bridges and roadways will be impassable to vehicles. Communication systems will probably be damaged and probably not functional. Structures will be demolished and injuries and death are a given." In sum, Caldwell concluded, the Cascadia quake and tsunami is "a known major disaster waiting to happen . . . These are our choices: Prepare, or cross our fingers and hope this event happens on someone else's watch."[21] See also: **Oregon–Washington–British Columbia mega-tsunami; mega-tsunamis; Cascade Range volcanoes.**

cedar chests, self-locking. See: **yard sales.**

celery. As a result of peak consumer demand during the holiday sea-

son, *Prevention* magazine tells us, 75 percent of America's celery crop is grown during the autumn and winter, "when rain and wind promote the growth of bacteria and fungal diseases. And because we eat the entire stalk, it must be sprayed repeatedly to ward off pests." ("Nobody likes to find a caterpillar-damaged stalk in their celery bunch," explains Stuart Reitz, Ph.D., a research entomologist with the U.S. Department of Agriculture.) The consequence of all those pesticide applications is that celery ranks near the top of the Environmental Working Group's "Dirty Dozen" list of foods so laden with toxins that, if conventionally grown, you'd be best to avoid them altogether. *Prevention* agrees. If you're going to buy celery, they advise, make sure it was raised organically.[22] See: **organic food.**

celiac disease. See: **cake, piece of.**

cell phones, biohazards of. See: **phones, biohazards of.**

cell phones, radiation hazards of. Although a large number of previ-

ous studies had found no evidence of any measurable physical effects from the long-term use of cell phones, a recently published research paper in the *Journal of the American Medical Association* reports troubling indications that the electromagnetic emanations from mobile communications units can accelerate certain cerebral functions in the area of the brain nearest to the antenna. A little less than an hour of continuous exposure to the comparatively feeble output of nonionizing radiation produced by the devices when held close to the head caused a measurable increase in glucose production in portions of the brain immediately adjacent to the activated phone, the researchers concluded, raising new questions about the safety of cell-phone usage.[23]

According to the study's lead author, Dr. Nora D. Volkow, "our results give evidence that the human brain is sensitive to the effects of radiofrequency-electromagnetic fields from acute cell phone exposure."[24] And the study concluded that "in healthy participants and compared with no exposure, 50-minute cell phone exposure was associated with increased brain glucose metabolism in the region closest to the antenna."[25] Although Dr. Volkow stressed that the new research was preliminary, it is worth noting that if the long-term impact on the human brain of very heavy cell-phone use does in fact turn out to be truly damaging, a small, but by no means inconsequential, compensation for the ultimate loss of this ubiquitous and invaluable tool for global interconnectivity would be a fairly immediate and substantial reduction in the earth's current population of boorish, banshee-voiced, blabber-happy buttwipes. See also: **colony collapse disorder.**

ceramics. Many common ceramic products produce higher-than-normal readings in routine radiation inspections, either because of the presence of radionuclides like potassium-40 in the clay they are made of, or due to trace amounts of uranium oxide or sodium urate found in the glazes they are sealed with, and sometimes colored with as well, as in the classic case of the vivid, orange- and red-hued—and, in more ways than one, "hot"—Fiesta Ware from the 1930s and 1940s that is much sought after by collectors. Dr. Paul W. Frame of the Oak Ridge Associated Universities recalls being at a truck weighing station when a vehicle transporting ceramic toilets set off radiation monitors, and, citing another memorable alarm, reports an incident when "health physicists at Oak Ridge reported excessively high readings while surveying newly purchased urinals for the men's restroom.

Perhaps," Dr. Frame suggests drily, "they should have been spelled 'uranyls.'"[26] (Although Frame's brave, if flippant, response to being ceramically irradiated might be considered commendable, readers would be wise to remember the twin warnings from author and well-known antinuclear activist Helen Caldicott, M.D., that "there is no such thing as a safe dose of radiation," and that "radiation is cumulative."[27]) See also: **banana equivalent dose.**

cereal. See: **acrylamide; aspartame; granola bars; high-fructose corn syrup (HFCS); vitamin A supplements.**

ceviche. See: **sushi, sashimi, and ceviche.**

chancroid. See: **sexually transmitted diseases; condoms.**

Chandrasekhar limit. See: **IK Pegasi.**

chard. See: **leafy green vegetables.**

checks, counterfeit. See: **identity theft.**

cheese. See: **dairy products.**

cheesecake. See: **high-fat, high-calorie food addiction.**

cherries. Did you know that cherry pits contain cyanide? So do the seeds and pits of several other related fruits, such as apples, plums, almonds, pears, and apricots.[28] For more information about this—not to mention other hazards presented by what Mark Rieger, author of *Introduction to Fruit Crops*, calls "the most dangerous species in the Rose family"[29]—see: **bowl of cherries.**

cherry tomatoes. See: **grapes.**

chewing gum. "Many women are troubled by lines around their mouth," writes Kristie Leong, M.D. "These vertical lines, visible at the border of the lips, are referred to by dermatologists as marionette lines," she says, and a good way to prevent—or, at least, delay—their appearance is to eliminate bad habits that can lead to their premature development. One such habit, Leong points out, is chewing gum. It may sound harmless, she warns, but "repeatedly contorting the mouth muscles and overusing the jaw contributes to breakdown of collagen and elastin and causes mouth lines to appear sooner."[30]

chicken. "Never mind cigarettes; the Surgeon General should slap a warning label on chicken," writes Jim Gorman in *Men's Health* magazine. "Recent nationwide testing by Consumers Union, the advocacy group behind *Consumer Reports,* notes that of the 484 raw broilers examined, 42 percent were infected by *Campylobacter jejuni,* and 12 percent by *Salmonella enteritidis,*" Gorman says, adding that recent U.S. Department of Agriculture research shows similar *Salmonella* levels. "Now add in the fact that we each consume about 70 pounds of chicken a year—more than our intake of beef, pork, or turkey—and it's a wonder broilers don't come with barf bags," Gorman concludes.[31]

Why have chickens have become so bacteria ridden? Perhaps this description of how most "broilers" in America are raised, written by Michael Specter of *The New Yorker* after he ventured into an untended chicken shed on the Delmarva Peninsula, will offer a clue: "Every window was covered with thick blackout curtains, and it seemed as if nothing at all were inside . . . I unfastened the latch, swung it open, and walked inside. I was almost knocked to the ground by the overpowering smell of feces and ammonia. My eyes burned and so did my lungs, and I could neither see nor breathe. I put my arm across my mouth and immediately moved back toward the door, where I saw a dimmer switch. I turned it up. There must have been thirty thousand chickens sitting silently on the floor in front of me. They didn't move, didn't cluck. They were almost like statues of chickens, living in nearly total darkness, and they would spend every minute of their six-week lives that way. Despite the ventilation system, there wasn't much air in the room, and I fled quickly."[32] As a consequence of such methods, says Gerald Kuester, a former U.S. Department of Agriculture microbiologist, the "final product is no different than if you stuck it in the toilet and ate it."[33]

"Bad chicken kills at least 1,000 people each year and costs several billion dollars annually in medical costs and lost productivity," *Time* magazine reports. "An uncooked chicken has become one of the most dangerous items in the American home."[34]

chicken feathers, hydrolyzed. See: **salmon, farmed.**

Chicken McNuggets. Anthony Bourdain, the noted chef, best-selling author, and globe-trotting host of the "food and cultural adventure" TV series *No Reservations,* is famous, among many other things, for claiming that the most disgusting thing he'd ever eaten was a Chicken McNugget[35]—even worse, one might infer, than an unwashed warthog rectum he tried to digest in Namibia (which, he says, was "equally full of sand and crap in every mouthful" and had "a permeating odor of burning reflux"[36]) and a fermented shark that was served to him in Iceland ("They celebrate their hardy Viking roots by eating shark that has essentially rotted and is then marinated in lactic acid for six months," Bourdain explains[37]). When Sean O'Neal interviewed Anthony Bourdain for the *A.V. Club* in 2008, he gave the intrepid culinary explorer a chance to reconsider, and found that his opinion of McNuggets had indeed softened a bit. "Given the choice between reliving the warthog experience and eating a McNugget, I'm surely eating the McNugget," Bourdain said. "But at least I knew what the warthog was. Whereas with the McNugget, I think that's still an open question. Scientists are still wondering."[38] (Note: We *do* know, however, from the invaluable X-Ray Vision-aries health blog, that a twenty-piece order of Chicken McNuggets offers up 1,030 calories and sixty-five grams of fat. That's the primary reason that the blog has chosen McNuggets as one of the "100 Most Unhealthy Foods in the American Diet."[39])

child abuse, fiscal. See: **fiscal child abuse.**

childhood asphyxiations. See: **hot dogs.**

chlamydia. See: **sexually transmitted diseases; romance novels.**

chlorine bleach. "Chlorine," warns the Wisconsin Department of
Health Services, "is a poisonous, greenish-yellow gas
described as having a choking odor. It is a very corrosive, hazardous chemical. Household bleach, used to
whiten fabrics or remove mold from surfaces, is a 5%
solution of a stabilized form of chlorine." As a result,
liquid chlorine bleach and its vapors can badly irritate your eyes. It
can cause nose and throat irritation, and merely touching it can cause
skin problems. Accidentally drinking even a tiny amount can induce
stomach irritation, nausea, and vomiting. Drinking more can kill
you. Bleach fumes from chlorine bleach can cause pulmonary embo-
lisms. Allowing chlorine bleach to come in contact with ammonia
products (and, by the way, simple human, dog, or cat urine contains
ammonia) produces gases called chloramines, the inhalation of
which can be quickly fatal. "If you are using bleach in the work place,"
notes Jennifer Lance, founder of the Eco Child's Play website,
"OSHA (Occupational Safety and Health Administration), which
regulates the safety of the work place, will require you use a mask and
gloves to handle the chemical to protect yourself. Do you use those
precautions at home? Were you even aware you needed to?"[40] We
have another question: Is this the kind of product you want anywhere near your family? You decide. (Note: Jennifer Lance suggests
that, as an alternative to using chlorine bleach in your laundry, you
make your own solution by mixing hydrogen peroxide and water in
about a 50:50 ratio.[41]) See: **handkerchiefs; laundry; hydrogen
peroxide.**

chlorine washes. According to WorldPoultry.net, which bills itself as
the "gateway to the global poultry industry," chlorine
washes are frequently used to "reduce harmful bacteria
levels on vegetables, fruits and poultry." Indeed, the
Center for Science in the Public Interest, in an important position paper published in 2009, pointed to

chlorine washes as at least a partial solution to America's growing produce contamination problem[42] (See: **leafy green vegetables**). But, WorldPoultry.net reports, research has demonstrated that "because of chlorine's sensitivity to food components and extraneous materials released in chlorinated water treatments, many bacteria survive." Furthermore, the website warns, "Chlorine is toxic at high concentrations, may produce off-flavors and undesirable appearance of certain food products, and it can only be used in conjunction with specialized equipment and trained personnel. In addition, chlorine may be harmful to the environment."[43] Clearly another solution to detoxifying our increasingly hazardous food supply is needed.

chloroform poisoning. See: **toothpaste, antimicrobial.**

chronic myrocardial ischemia. See: **hiccups.**

climate change. See: **global warming.**

clothing, spontaneous ignition of. See: **hydrogen peroxide.**

clowns. Have you ever hired a clown to liven up a birthday party for one of your children? If so, then a recent survey in Britain of adolescents' attitudes toward these presumably lovable circus performers suggests you may have unknowingly subjected your unsuspecting offspring to some severe psychological damage. In a 2006 canvass of the young patients in children's wards in British hospitals by the University of Sheffield, researchers interviewed more than 250 children aged four to sixteen, and were clearly surprised when every single one of the tots expressed a deep dislike of clowns. The study, titled "Space to Care," was undertaken as part of an effort to design a more child-friendly environment in what are typically grim and sterile medical facilities. "As adults we make assumptions about what works for children," said Penny Curtis, a senior lecturer in research at the university, who like her colleagues had assumed that visits by Bozo and his brethren would be a source of cheer for the youngsters. "We found that clowns are universally disliked by children," Ms. Curtis conceded ruefully. "Some found them frightening and unknowable."[44] Interestingly, also in 2006 and also in Britain, organizers of the annual Bestival rock festival on the Isle of Wight abruptly canceled their plans to make the classic clown costume of big floppy shoes and curly red wigs the theme for the popular fancy-dress event at that year's shindig after receiving hundreds of complaints from ticket holders who suffer from a fear of clowns, or *coulrophobia*. Said festival organizer Rob da Bank, a leading DJ on BBC's Radio 1, "We had so many people with clown phobias contact us I am worried everyone might end up hiding in the woods."[45]

coal. "Among all industrial sources of air pollution, none poses greater risks to human health and the environment than coal-fired power plants," advises the Clean Air Task Force (CATF) in its September 2010 report, *The Toll from Coal: An Updated Assessment of Death and Disease from America's Dirtiest Energy Source.* "Emissions from coal-fired power plants contribute to global warming, ozone smog, acid rain, regional haze, and—perhaps most consequential of all from a public health standpoint—fine particle pollution." Indeed, a study commissioned by the Task Force calculates that in 2010, 3,200 deaths in the U.S. alone were directly attributable to the fine particles emitted by the nation's more than five hundred coal-fired plants.[46] Furthermore, according to CATF, coal-fired power plants generate 130 million tons of solid power-plant waste (PPW) every year—"enough to fill the Grand Canyon." "Laden with heavy metals and other harmful toxics known to contaminate water supplies," CATF continues, "these wastes cause injury and death to livestock and wildlife, and threaten human health with birth defects, cancer, and organ and neurological damage. PPW is routinely dumped in unlined impoundments, landfills, and mines throughout the United States, allowing hazardous chemicals such as arsenic, chromium, and lead to leach into surface and ground waters."[47] Is it any wonder that *New Scientist*'s Fred Pearce has labeled coal "*the* killer." "Of all the fossil fuels," he writes, "coal is the one that could make this planet uninhabitable."[48] See also: **fossil fuels; global warming; exercise, outdoor.**

coffee. As you undoubtedly already know, a major ingredient of coffee—not to mention other popular beverages such as tea, and cola and energy drinks—is caffeine, a stimulant which has been shown to contribute to bone density and high-blood-pressure problems, and is also, in itself, an addictive substance. (For more details, see: **caffeine.**) In addition, the U.S. Food and Drug Administration has found that coffee contains acrylamide, a much-publicized neurotoxin and carcinogen that is also formed in many carbohydrate-rich, starchy foods when they are fried, baked, or roasted. (See: **acrylamide.**) In short, you probably already have adequate reasons to avoid coffee altogether. But if you need a few more, consider the following environmental and socioeconomic data about world coffee production, assembled by the Toronto-based establishment Merchants of Green Coffee (whose worthy—and, as you'll see, somewhat daunting—mission is "to lead the evolution of the coffee industry to a sustainable state 'from tree to cup'"[49]):

- "Every cup of coffee consumed destroys roughly three square centimeters of rainforest, making coffee a leading cause of rainforest destruction."
- "Coffee ranks as one of top three most heavily pesticide sprayed crops in the world."
- "Coffee processing is a major cause of water contamination in many producing countries."
- "Supply chain imbalances exploit millions of small subsistence farmers."[50]

Makes you yearn for a piping hot cup of joe, doesn't it? See also: **coffee mugs.**

coffee mugs. "Reusing your coffee mug is great for the environment but may not be so great for your health," writes Danielle Braff in *Men's Health* magazine. Indeed, according to research conducted by noted University of Arizona microbiologist Charles P. Gerba, Ph.D., 20 percent of office mugs carry fecal bacteria, and 90 percent are covered in other germs. A major factor in turning your morning cup of java into a "handy desktop cesspool," Braff says, is that "most people tend to clean their cups with bacteria-laden sponges or scrub brushes instead of in a dishwasher. That bacteria transfers to the mug and can live there for 3 days." So what should you do? "Bring your mug home daily to be washed in the dishwasher, and make sure it goes through the dry cycle, which uses the hottest temperatures and zaps every last germ," Braff advises.[51] See: **dishwashers.** See also: **sponges.**

cognitive decline. See: **soy.**

collagen breakdown. See: **chewing gum.**

colony collapse disorder. Whenever there is a buzz about perils linked to bees, the most widely cited risk involving these hardworking and ubiquitous pollinators and honey producers is the spread in the last few decades of the dread Africanized hybrid "killer bee" (a relatively minor menace considerably amplified by the release of several aptly categorized sensationalist B-movies), but in recent years a far more profound threat has appeared in the world of apiculture—the killed bee. Beginning in 2006, beekeepers in North America and Europe have observed a sudden and sharp decline in the number of their Western honeybee colonies, including a loss in the United States alone of 2.5 million colonies—literally billions of bees—recorded by the Apiary Inspectors of America.[52]

The abrupt and entomologically alarming disappearance of between 20 percent and 70 percent of the bees in the affected hives has been variously attributed to a number of possible factors, including infestations by *Varroa destructor* mites, the spread of insect diseases (particularly the *Nosema apis* and *Nosema ceranae* viruses, Israel acute paralysis virus, and invertebrate iridescent virus type 6), malnutrition, pesticides, the effects of the introduction of pest-controlling genetically modified crops,[53] and even radiation from cell phones.[54] Thus far no specific cause has been identified, and as a recent report from the

U.S. Department of Agriculture noted, it seems more likely that "a combination of environmental stresses may set off a cascade of events and contribute to a colony where worker bees are more susceptible to pests and pathogens." [55]

Since honeybees are almost exclusively responsible for the pollination of dozens of commercially important crops, including almonds, apples, avocados, blackberries, cantaloupes, cherries, cranberries, cucumbers, kiwis, pears, pumpkins, raspberries, soybeans, strawberries, and watermelons, the prospect of their virtual extinction is a source of profound concern to everyone in agribusiness. "It's a very serious situation," said Troy Fore, executive director of the American Beekeeping Federation. "Some of the numbers are just horrifying." [56] And California beekeeper David Bradshaw lamented, "I have never seen anything like it. Box after box are just empty. There's nobody home." [57]

According to bee expert Professor Jürgen Tautz of Würzburg University, "It is not a sudden problem. It has been happening for a few years now. Five years ago in Germany there were a million hives, now there are less than 800,000. If that continues, there will be eventually no bees. Bees are not only working for our welfare." Professor Tautz added pointedly, "they are also perfect indicators of the state of the environment. We should take note." [58]

Colorado tick fever. See: **tick-borne diseases.**

color-blindness. See: **candlelight dinners.**

combination birth-control pills. See: **birth-control pills.**

Comet Catalina. On May 26, 2005, NASA's Jet Propulsion Lab made a preliminary determination that a recently discovered comet named "Catalina 2005 JQ5" might be on a collision course with the earth. "Comet Catalina" (as the object was dubbed for short) appeared to be significantly larger and faster-moving than any of the other "near earth objects" identified by the JPL, and, therefore, it presented a far more devastating potential threat to our planet. Experts were quick to reassure the public, however, that future observations would lead to a considerably more accurate calculation of the comet's exact orbit—a calculation that would almost certainly rule out any possibility of the earth's being directly impacted. Imagine their surprise, then, when additional data showed that Comet Catalina was not *less*, but *more*, likely than previously thought to score what *New Scientist* magazine termed a "perfect bulls-eye" on terra firma. If the comet does end up striking the earth, it's estimated that it will do so with the almost unimaginable impact of 6 billion tons of TNT.[59] But Catalina's approach is not scheduled until June 11, 2085, so readers may not choose to devote undue worry to it, at least until they see if the earth survives its more imminent close encounter with the asteroid Apophis on April 13, 2036. (See: **Asteroid 99942 Apophis.**)

commercial baked goods. See: **trans fats.**

commodities. James Debevec, founder and CEO of the Absolute Value Fund, points out that of all the asset classes, the one that has historically performed the worst is commodities. Indeed, he notes, several hundred years of data analyzed by the Foundation for the Study of Cycles reveal that commodities have generated "astonishingly low returns"—significantly less that the rate of inflation. A principal reason that commodities are such poor investments, Debevec points out, is that they have no yield. "Actually," he writes, "with storage costs and security costs they have *negative* yield. This stands in marked contrast to almost all other asset classes that provide some sort of return on investment." "So," he concludes, "after reading all this why would anybody ever buy commodities at all?"[60] Great question! See: **treasury bonds, U.S.**

commuting by bicycle. The U.S. Small Business Administration argues that commuters who live relatively near their place of business can save gas, help the environment, and get some beneficial exercise by riding their bikes to work instead of driving.[61] But before accepting this apparently well-meaning advice at face value, you'd be wise to consider the fact that one of the world's largest technical services firms, the UK's Jacobs Engineering Group, recently banned cycling as a commuting option for its employees because they—and, apparently, their insurance providers—feel it is just too risky. "It's patently obvious that if you are struck by a wayward vehicle when you are on a bicycle or motorbike you are going to be more severely affected than if you were in a car," the company noted. "The reason for this policy is to protect our employees from other vehicles on the road."[62] You might expect an organization as "green" as San Francisco's Bay Area Air Quality Management District to disagree, but they issued a similar ban in 2007, and for exactly the same reason. "The potential for serious injury is much greater riding a bicycle than driving a car in the event of an accident," BAAQMD's human resources director, Mike Rich, explained to staffers.[63] A second reason people frequently reject biking as a commuting option is the fear that they'll arrive at the office too sweaty and smelly to conduct the day's business in a professional manner. (Jeff Peel of the League of American Bicyclists acknowledges that this is a legitimate concern, but points out, in a *U.S. News* interview, that many fitness clubs offer shower-only memberships for bike or running commuters, and if you can't find one near your workplace that does, "it's amazing how far you can get with a sponge bath in a regular bathroom." "Baby wipes work like a charm," he adds.[64]) And a third—and perhaps in some people's minds the most serious—issue for commuters to ponder before making a bicycle their vehicle of choice is the very real risk that cycling can lead to impotency. For more about this, see: **bicycle saddles.** See also: **commuting by car; commuting by train; exercise, outdoor.**

commuting by car. "Despite the fact that nobody likes sitting in traf-

fic," notes Discovery Communication's "sustainability blog," Treehugger.com, "we are increasingly driving to work alone in our cars, all the while contributing to global warming and making ourselves miserable."[65] The U.S. Environmental Protection Agency offers sobering statistics to back up TreeHugger's assertion. "In 2002 alone," the Agency reports, "5.7 billion gallons of fuel were wasted in traffic congestion—more than 500 times the amount of oil spilled by the *Exxon Valdez*—unnecessarily releasing 50 million tons of carbon dioxide into the atmosphere."[66] The obvious solution to all this waste and unhappiness, the U.S. Small Business Association advises, is for commuters "to avoid driving whenever possible. Many cities have improved public transportation systems and added more bike trails in an effort to reduce carbon emissions. By choosing one of these alternatives, you will save gas money while greatly reducing the size of your carbon footprint. If you don't have an alternative to driving, consider carpooling with a coworker or two. Sharing the ride will drastically reduce the impact on the environment."[67]

For those with access to convenient train service, commuting by rail does seem an attractive alternative. According to the American Public Transportation Association (APTA), public transit in the United States is already saving approximately 4.2 billion gallons of gasoline and about 37 million metric tons of carbon dioxide annually. Indeed, says APTA, "taking public transportation far exceeds the combined benefits of using energy-efficient light bulbs, adjusting thermostats, weathering one's home, and replacing a refrigerator."[68] Furthermore, as OfficeArrow.com, a website for office professionals, points out, train travel offers many other benefits to commuters. "You don't have to find a parking space," they advise. "If you come prepared, the time you spend on the train can be turned into useful time for business, like working on your laptop." Or, if you prefer, you can use those extra hours for personal projects, such as "reading a good book."[69]

Last but not least, Great Britain's Association of Train Operating Companies is quick to remind us, a major boon to rail commuters is the option of "relaxing with a glass of wine or beer after a long day of work." ("The vast majority of passengers who choose to drink alcohol do so responsibly," the Association assures us, lest we had any doubts.)[70] And if that's not enough to convince you to leave your gas-guzzler in the garage, perhaps this will: A study funded by the Robert Wood Johnson Foundation and supervised by Richard E. Wener, Ph.D., of the Polytechnic University in Brooklyn found that switching from driving to taking the train offers commuters significant health advantages. "Train commuters were four times more likely to walk 10,000 steps each workday than were car commuters," Wener and his team reported. "Some 40.4 percent of train commuters walked at least

10,000 steps per day, while 14.8 percent of car commuters walked that much. The CDC [Centers for Disease Control] recommends a daily physical activity standard of 10,000 steps." Worse still, the researchers found, "people commuting by car reported significantly more stress and a more negative mood than did those commuting by train."[71] To quote the APTA's catchy and memorable slogan, isn't it time to "dump the pump, save money, and ride transit?"[72] See: **commuting by bicycle; commuting by train.**

commuting by train. A *New York Daily News* investigation in 2003

found that riding public transit to work "may be much more than a daily chore—it could be making you sick." According to reporter Alison Gendar, who broke the news about the paper's in-depth, four-week probe, train and subway cars, buses, station stairways, and ticket machines "are a breeding ground for a shocking cocktail of germs, bugs and bacteria."

After duly warning us that what we're about to read might be a "stomach-churning" experience, Gendar goes ahead and gives us the gruesome details anyway. *Daily News* researchers, she says, found "*E. coli, enterococcus,* and *streptococcus viridians*"—which frequently cause diarrhea, dental caries, and urinary infections, not to mention the "churning" stomachs Gendar warns us about—"hitching rides on New York subway car surfaces, and on the escalator handrail of the 125th Street and Broadway subway station"; "*aspergillus* and *penicillium* molds—which cause emphysema and sick building syndrome—growing along the Number 2 and Number 5 platforms at the 149th Street and Grand Concourse subway station in the Bronx"; and, worst of all, *strep a* and *staph aureus* bugs—the microbes responsible for "flesh-eating disease," rheumatic fever, and antibiotic-resistant MRSA infections—on a commuter railroad ticket machine at Grand Central Station and a Thirty-fourth Street Metrocard vending device. New York commuter trains "get cleaned between runs each night, and an 'extraordinary cleaning' every 90 days," Gendar reports, but, she quotes "medical experts" as telling her, "the work is undermined by commuters displaying an appalling ignorance of basic hygiene."[73]

And, if the possibility of contracting a life-threatening disease isn't enough to discourage you from commuting by rail, consider the discovery, made after Navy SEALS successfully raided Osama bin Laden's headquarters in Pakistan, that the radical Islamist leader had been planning an attack on America's railroads. "Anyone, even a member of al-Quaida, could purchase a train trip ticket and board an Amtrak train without so much as a question asked from an Amtrak official," New York senator Charles Schumer declared at a May 2011 news conference. "That's a glaring loophole." [74]

Well, you may protest, my health might be in danger if I commute by rail, and I acknowledge the risk of a terrorist attack, but at least my chance of being in an *accident* will be smaller if I go to work on the train than if I commute by car. And, to bolster your argument, you might cite claims made by public transit advocacy organizations, such as this one from Light Rail Now!: "It doesn't take a rocket scientist to figure out that, with a litany of metro area motor vehicle accidents recited on every single morning radio broadcast in virtually any major American city, the automobile has got to be at the 'Darth Vader' end of the safety spectrum." [75]

But crusading Los Angeles accident attorney (and former U.S. marine) Michael P. Ehline, Esq., feels strongly that the railroad industry is getting a free pass in the cars vs. trains commuting argument, and he's made it his personal mission to set things right. "People do not realize the dangers that can be waiting for them any day of the week on the train," he writes. "Dangers can lurk anywhere from the train station to the train itself. When walking in the train station, there are often wet floors that have recently been mopped where a slip and fall injury can occur." Furthermore, notes Ehline, "the rider has no protection such as seatbelts in case the train comes to a halt quickly or if there is an accident of any type." Worse still, he points out, unlike automobile commuters, "the train rider has no control," so if an accident should occur "there is no time to be prepared for the impact." In addition, "the train is often crowded, greatly increasing the odds of an injury due to standing on the train." The hordes of passengers waiting to board trains offer yet another hazard, Ehline complains, increasing the odds you might be "pushed, shoved and otherwise maneuvered" into circumstances "where injuries are possible." And even when you leave the train, the danger persists. "Many people are injured by closing doors," Ehline cautions.

Just to be sure train riders understand exactly what they may be facing, Ehline provides a helpful list of the specific injuries that could befall them "no matter how minor the accident is": "lacerations, cuts, scrapes, broken bones, back injuries, head injuries, spinal cord and brain injuries," not to mention, of course, the "hundreds of deaths associated with train accidents." Train crashes can also cause frightful collateral damage, Ehline reminds us, such as the "spillage of deadly toxins, solid and gas. Sometimes railroad crashes will contaminate whole neighborhoods and cause birth defects."[76]

"The railway company is responsible for reasonably checking to make sure these tragic events won't happen," Ehline assures us, but, unfortunately, "many of these companies put profits over people" and their "hired gun investigators" are trained "to defeat liability." Things, however, are not as bleak as they might seem, Ehline assures us, because his company, Ehline Law Firm PC, "is the great equalizer" and it's "just a phone call away." "Make an appointment today," Ehline urges, "even if you're uncertain you have a case . . . The Ehline Law Firm PC., will make it happen for you. Do or die. Semper Fi."[77] (For more information, visit www.ehlinelaw.com.) See: **commuting by bicycle; commuting by car.**

compact fluorescent lightbulbs (CFLs). Compact fluorescent light-bulbs, "the squiggly, coiled bulbs that generate light by heating gases in a glass tube, are generally considered to use more than 50 percent less energy and to last several times longer than incandescent bulbs," reports MSNBC's Alex Johnson, and, as a result, they are "touted by environmentalists as a more efficient and longer-lasting alternative to the incandescent bulbs that have lighted homes for more than a century." However, Johnson cautions, CFLs, as the new-fangled bulbs are known for short, are "running into resistance from waste industry officials and some environmental scientists" who warn that the bulbs' innards pose a significant threat to health and to our surroundings. The reason: "All CFLs contain mercury, a neurotoxin that can cause kidney and brain damage," Johnson writes. Indeed, he says, just one average CFL bulb contains enough mercury to contaminate as many as six thousand gallons of water to a point beyond safe drinking levels. The bulbs are harmless enough unless they break, but if they do, you and your family face the immediate danger of mercury poisoning.

To prevent that, the Environmental Protection Agency provides a detailed program for how to handle the situation. You should air out the room for fifteen minutes, double-bag the broken shards (wearing gloves as you do so), and "use duct tape to lift the residue from flooring," the EPA recommends. Furthermore, the Agency says, don't vacuum up the remains of the compact fluorescent lightbulb immediately, as this will only spread the toxic mercury. And later on, when you finally *do* vacuum, throw out the vacuum cleaner bag immediately afterward.[78]

Alas, the problems don't end there. Even if you never break a single CFL, these admittedly long-lasting bulbs will eventually burn out and you'll have to dispose of them. And, once you do, says John Skinner, executive director of the Solid Waste Association of North America, they're almost certain to shatter before they get to the landfill. "They'll break in containers, or they'll break in a dumpster or they'll break in the trucks. Workers may be exposed to very high levels of mercury when that happens," he worries. Moreover, Skinner laments, when bulbs break in your neighborhood, they could end up contaminating your soil.[79] See: **incandescent lightbulbs.** See also: **lightbulb efficiency standards.**

competitiveness of the United States, weapons designed to undermine. See: **global warming, attempting to mitigate.**

computer algorithm–driven trading. See: **flash crash.**

computer sex. See: **cybersex.**

computer viruses. See: **botnets; malware; Trojan horses.**

condiment containers. See: **ketchup, relish, and mustard containers.**

condoms. For over half a century, condoms have been hailed by many

as a near panacea, purportedly offering protection against a wide variety of serious problems ranging from unwanted pregnancies to the contraction of sexually transmitted diseases. But, according to an article in *Rubber World* magazine written by Dr. C. Michael Roland of the U.S. Naval Research Laboratory in Washington D.C., if you're counting on condoms to reduce your chances of contracting HIV, well, you have another think coming. The HIV virus is only about 0.1 microns in size, Dr. Roland explains—small enough to pass through what he calls "intrinsic flaws"—in layman's terms, "naturally occurring holes"—in the latex used to make prophylactic devices. Indeed, according to Dr. Roland, in research based on U.S. government condom leakage standards, 33 percent of all condoms tested allowed HIV-size particles through.[80] And, he says, to make matters worse, evidence suggests that "spermicidal agents such as nonoxonol-9 may actually ease the passage."[81]

Unfortunately, the news is not much better when it comes to other sexually transmitted diseases. In a "male condom fact-sheet" updated in April 2011, the Centers for Disease Control and Prevention (CDC) warn that STDs such as genital herpes, human papillomavirus [HPV] infection, syphilis, and chancroid—which are transmitted primarily by skin-to-skin contact rather than by an exchange of genital fluids—can be spread even when a condom is used, because the condom "may not cover all infected areas or areas that could become infected."[82] Noted Canadian obstetrician-gynecologist and health researcher Stephen J. Genuis, M.D., puts it more bluntly. "No degree of condom education will curb the transmission of these organisms," he writes.[83]

Well, you may say, at least condoms can protect against unwanted pregnancies, right? The answer is yes, sorta—but not nearly as well as you might have hoped. According to the Mayo Clinic, the failure rate of the average male condom, when employed exactly as it should be, is about 2 percent. But add the human error that comes from normal use to the mix (slippage, misapplication, etc.) and the failure percentage, according to the American Pregnancy Association (APA), increases over sevenfold, to 14 percent to 15 percent. This means, the APA reminds us, "that 14–15 people out of every 100 will become pregnant during the first year of use."[84] Is that amount of risk acceptable? You decide.

And here's one final tip about condoms from the CDC: If you or your partner *do* decide to use one, keep oil-based lubricants such as Vaseline or Johnson's baby oil in the medicine cabinet.[85] According to a joint study (or was it a "study of joints"?) conducted by scientists from UCLA, USC, and the Mariposa Foundation, "As little as sixty seconds' exposure of commercial latex condoms to mineral oil, a common component of hand lotions and other lubricants used during sexual intercourse, caused approximately 90% decreases in the strength of the condoms, as measured by their burst volumes in the standard ISO (International Standards Organization) Air Burst Test."[86]

In short, as Cecil Adams has warned in his famous *Straight Dope* column, "You'd be foolish to make condoms your only defense." "Abstinence," he advises, and, in the case of sexually transmitted infections, "avoidance of high-risk sex partners" are "far more effective strategies."[87] See: **abstinence.** See also: **condoms, allergic reactions to; romance novels; summertime sex.**

condoms, allergic reactions to. Before you decide to use a **condom**

(q.v.), it's important for you and your partner to know that some men and women can have an allergic reaction to the latex used to make it, and that such reactions can be fatal. Symptoms, according to noted author and physician Andrew Weil, M.D., include "a hives-like rash and itching, dryness and, sometimes, shortness of breath, welts, and eczema." And, he warns, latex allergy "can also lead to life-threatening anaphylactic shock."[88] Such shocks typically occur within "minutes of exposure," the Australasian Society of Clinical Immunology and Allergy informs us, "and must be promptly treated by adrenaline injection."[89] You can avoid this risk altogether, Dr. Weil suggests, by opting for polyurethane condoms. "However," he points out, "the polyurethane products have higher breakage rates than latex condoms and therefore may not be as effective in preventing transmission of HIV and other sexually transmitted infections." Condoms made of lambskin are also available, Dr. Weil notes, "but are too porous to prevent transmission of disease." [90]

convertibles. See: **driving with the top down.**

convulsions. See: **apricots.**

cookies. See: **acrylamide; high-fructose corn syrup (HFCS); trans fats.**

copying machines. "Did you ever wonder where the riskiest place to work in your office might be?" asks AOL Jobs blogger Lisa Johnson Mandell. "By the window, perhaps, where you could be injured by shattering glass? How about by the front door of a ground floor business, where a drunk driver could jump the curb and run into you?" It may surprise you that neither of these obvious choices is the right answer. No, says Mandell, "the worst place to work" in the office is right by the copying machine. Why? Well, for one thing, copying machines emit chemicals called volatile organic compounds (VOCs) which, to quote Mandell, "have a nasty tendency to be linked to maladies such as asthma and even cancer." [91] In addition, the tiny toner particles associated with copiers have—according to nano-Control, an international foundation that studies the health effects of emissions from office machines—been linked to "toxic and allergic reactions in the lungs," and to heart diseases and even cancer. [92]

Furthermore, the Workers Health Centre, Australia's oldest workers' health and safety service, cautions all those with office jobs that a potentially hazardous form of oxygen, ozone, is formed during the operation of high-voltage machines such as photocopiers, and by ultraviolet emission from photocopier lamps. As a consequence, the Centre warns, if you work near an improperly ventilated copying machine, you could be exposed to concentrations of this "odorous gas" capable of causing irritation to your eyes, lungs, throat, and nasal passages; headaches; shortness of breath; dizziness; general fatigue; and "temporary loss of olfactory sensation." Moreover, the Centre says, "prolonged inhalation of ozone levels of a few parts per million is known to damage the lungs," and "some authorities" suggest that a concentration as small 0.1 parts per million "might have the effect of causing premature aging and shortened lifespan."[93]

In sum, as the always helpful website SilentMenace.com puts it, "This ain't the Disney Channel, boys and girls; photocopier pollution is *serious* business." The obvious solution, SilentMenace says, is to persuade your boss to have your office copier "moved to a separate room and vented to the outside by installing exhaust vents similar to those used above the oven in an average home." But, if he or she refuses to do this, the website cautions, "*the* only choice you'll have is to remove yourself from the source(s) of the poisoning, in other words, to find another position in the company (not likely, as you'll be labeled a troublemaker) or, most probably, leave your job." Well, there *is* one other "drastic" alternative, SilentMenace advises. You *could* "wear a paint respirator mask that's equipped with replaceable vapor filters while on the job. Are you willing to do that? And is your boss willing to allow you to spook others and tarnish the company's image by wearing one?" "Probably not," the website concludes.[94] (Note: Dry-toner copiers and laser printers utilize the same technology, so laser printers present many of the same health hazards. For specific details, see: **laser printers.**)

coral reef bleaching. Sponge Bob must be peeing in his square pants—his happy undersea city of Bikini Bottom appears to be doomed. In the last few decades, over one-fifth of the world's coral reefs have disappeared after widespread episodes of catastrophic bleaching triggered by sharply rising ocean-water temperatures.[95] The reefs, which are aptly described as "rainforests of the sea,"[96] occupy less than 1 percent of the total marine environment, but are home to over 25 percent of the ocean's biodiversity[97] and provide a direct global economic benefit in jobs, food, and tourism of $375 billion a year to the more than 500 million people who live within sixty kilometers of the shallow coastal seas where extensive coral colonies are found. The often vast submerged structures composed of calcium carbonate excreted over centuries by coral polyps have fallen victim from the very beginning of the twenty-first century to hundreds of increasingly severe incidents of this telltale lethal whitening phenom-enon.[98] A recent review of historical data found that "published re-cords of coral reef bleaching events from 1870 to the present suggest the frequency . . . scale . . . and severity (over 95% mortality in some areas) of recent bleaching disturbances are unprecedented in the sci-entific literature."[99]

A particularly devastating outbreak in 2005 that affected 80 per-cent of all the reefs in twenty-two countries in the tropical Atlantic and Caribbean destroyed or degraded beyond recognition over 40 percent of the total subaqueous acreage. "Heat stress during the 2005 event exceeded any observed in the Caribbean in the prior 20 years, and regionally-averaged temperatures were the warmest in at least 150 years," according to C. Mark Eakin, Ph.D., coordinator of the National Oceanic and Atmospheric Administration's Coral Reef Watch Pro-gram. "This severe, widespread bleaching and mortality will undoubt-edly have long-term consequences for reef ecosystems, and events like this are likely to become more common as the climate warms."[100] And a recent report by the Institute of Physics concluded that "increasing ocean acidification, a direct result of growing atmospheric CO_2 levels, could lead to a rapid decline of coral reefs and the marine ecosystem in the 21st century."[101] See also: **global warming.**

corn. See: **biofuels; high-fructose corn syrup (HFCS).**

corn lobby. See: **biofuels.**

coronary heart disease. See: **smoking; trans fats.**

cosmetics. "Given the choice, we think most consumers would not put arsenic or lead on their lips and faces," says biolo-gist Rick Smith, coauthor of *Slow Death by Rubber Duck: The Secret Danger of Everyday Things* and execu-tive director of the Toronto-based advocacy group Environmental Defence Canada. But, according to a 2011 research study conducted by Smith's organization, you risk doing just that whenever you apply commonly available makeup products such as "foundations, concealers, powders, blushes and bronzers, mascaras, eyeliners, eyeshadows, lipsticks and glosses." Environmental Defence's study was designed to see whether four specific heavy metals designated by Health Canada as "toxic"—arsenic, cadmium, lead, and mercury—were present in a broad array of "widely used" cosmetic products. The good news is that none of the makeup samples contained mercury. The bad news is that the other three metals were present in a truly disturbing proportion of the products. For example, 96 percent of the cosmetics contained lead, over half contained cadmium, and 20 percent contained arsenic.

According to Environmental Defence, the presence of these metals in the body has been linked to a variety of nightmarish health problems, "including cancer; reproductive and developmental disorders; neurological problems; memory loss; mood swings; nerve, joint and muscle disorders; cardiovascular, skeletal, blood, immune system, kidney and renal problems; headaches; vomiting, nausea and diarrhea; lung damage; contact dermatitis; brittle hair; and hair loss. Many are suspected hormone disrupters and respiratory toxins, and for some like lead, there is no known safe blood level." To make matters worse, the highest concentrations of arsenic, cadmium, and lead were all found in lip glosses, which, precisely because they're worn on the lips, are particularly likely to be ingested.[102]

And furthermore, heavy metals are not the only toxic substances routinely found in cosmetics. To give just three examples from a report issued by the Nova Scotia Allergy and Environmental Health Association, many lipsticks contain **aluminum** (q.v.), a known toxin in humans, to make them long-lasting; coal-tar dyes, the major coloring agent in makeup, has been linked to dermatitis and skin cancer; and the industrial foaming agents present in many bubble baths have been demonstrated to cause skin rashes, bladder, kidney, and urinary tract infections, genital disorders, eye irritations, and respiratory problems.[103]

Finally, there is growing international concern about chemicals called phthalates that are widely used in cosmetics. Phthalates are industrial plasticizers that are added to lotions and sunscreen products to moisturize and soften skin, to nail polishes and hair sprays to impart flexibility to them after they dry, and to fragrances to give them more staying power. According to the Natural Resources Defense Council,

"Phthalates are known to interfere with production of the male hormone, testosterone, and have been associated with reproductive abnormalities. Numerous animal studies have linked prenatal exposure to certain phthalates with decreases in testosterone, malformations of the genitalia, and reduced sperm production." As a consequence of such findings, the European Union instituted a ban on all beauty products containing phthalates in 2004, although the United States has yet to follow suit.[104] Indeed, reports the *Earth Island Journal,* "more than 500 cosmetics sold in the United States contain chemicals banned from beauty products in Europe, Canada, and Japan." In short, the *Journal* concludes, the state of cosmetics safety is "not a pretty picture."[105] Isn't it time your reconsidered that "natural look"?

cottage cheese. See: **high-fructose corn syrup (HFCS).**

cough drops. See: **cough syrup.**

cough syrup. Got a hacking cough, and feel like a soothing spoonful

of cough syrup might be just the ticket? Well, think again—unless you want to gain weight, and increase your risk of getting a truly serious disease. The problem, as eHow Health.com points out, is that "many liquid cough suppressants and expectorants contain high fructose corn syrup," a product that, because most of us are eating far too much fructose already, can lead us not only to obesity, but also to diabetes, heart disease, and/or cancer (see: **sugar**). "Flavored varieties designed to taste better for children tend to have higher amounts of the sweetener," eHow cautions.[106] Not convinced the cure may be worse than the affliction? Then consider this: Delta Dental Plans' SmileWay oral health information website warns that ingredients such as high-fructose corn syrup and sucrose in over-the-counter cough syrups—and in many commercially available cough drops, too—"contribute to decay when the bacteria in your mouth feed on the sugars, breaking them down and forming acids that attack the enamel of your teeth."[107] See also: **high-fructose corn syrup (HFCS).**

coulrophobia. See: **clowns.**

cramping, abdominal. See: **sushi, sashimi, and ceviche.**

cranberry sauce. See: **high-fructose corn syrup (HFCS).**

Crater Lake. See: **Cascade Range volcanoes; lahars.**

cream. See: **dairy products.**

creams and lotions. See: **lotions and creams.**

credit-card data skimming; credit-card hacking programs. See: **identity theft.**

credit-card receipts. See: **bisphenol A.**

crop failures, climate-change-influenced. See: **agflation; global warming.**

crossing your legs. Did you know that sitting with your legs crossed can kill you? According to a research study conducted by K. R. Aryal and H. al-Khaffaf of the Burnley General Hospital in Lancashire, England, and published in the *European Journal of Vascular and Endovascular Surgery* in 2006, sitting with crossed legs can injure the endothelium of the veins in the legs, which can act as a precursor to deep venous thrombosis (DVT), the formation of a blood clot in a deep vein, a condition which can, in turn, lead to a pulmonary embolism. Sitting on an *airplane* with your legs crossed, particularly on a long trip, increases your risk of a life-threatening clot still further, the researchers found.[108] The respected South African website Health24.com concurs. "People should avoid sitting with crossed legs and wearing tight garments below the waist," their medical advisers urge.[109] See also: **socks and stockings with elastic tops.**

crying while eating. See: **laughing or crying while eating.**

CT scans. See: **X-ray computed tomography.**

Cumbre Vieja mega-tsunami. Every summer, thousands of vaca-
tioners flock to the Canary Islands to romp on the rolling, sun-drenched dunes and beaches of this exotic
Atlantic archipelago, and to explore its rugged cliffs
and picturesque forests. But, unbeknown to most of
them, on La Palma, one of the Canaries, lies what Brit-
ish journalist Ian Gurney, writing in the *Daily Express,* characterizes as
"a major global catastrophe in the making, a natural disaster so big that
it could flatten the Atlantic coastlines of Britain, Europe, North Africa
and the United States of America and cause enormous damage to
London and other UK cities." [110] The source of this potential calamity
is the Cumbre Vieja Volcano, which last erupted in 1971. Geologists
fear that the entire left flank of the volcano—an area of land more than
eight times the size of Manhattan island—is unstable and could slide,
virtually intact, into the Atlantic, during a future eruption.

Were this to happen, Stephen N. Ward and Simon Day of the
Institute of Geophysics and Planetary Physics at the University of
California at Santa Cruz predict, the gravitational energy released
would equal the force of "all the world's nuclear weapons combined."
As a consequence, the east coast of North America would be slammed
by a series of waves as high as a ten-story building, and substantial,
if smaller, tsunamis would also inundate the Atlantic shorelines of
Britain, Spain, Portugal, and France. "A La Palma tsunami would not
be the end of the world but it would make for quite a day," [111] they
conclude. In short, it's hard to argue with Dr. Day's suggestion that
"Cumbre Vieja needs to be monitored closely for any signs of impending volcanic activity and for the deformation that would precede collapse." [112] See also: **mega-tsunamis.**

cuticle cuts. See: **nail salons.**

cutlery contamination. See: **dishwashers.**

cutting boards. "If you have a choice between licking a cutting board
or a toilet seat . . . pick the toilet seat," advises famed University of
Arizona microbe hunter Charles P. Gerba, Ph.D.[113] (who, it must be
said, appears to take unrestrained glee at such comparisons). There

are more than two hundred times more pathogens on a cutting board than the toilet seat, explains Gerba, and one of the principal reasons is that far too many of us merely give our cutting boards a quick rinse after using them, rather than thoroughly washing them.[114] ("Put the cutting board in the dishwasher after you use it," urges Gerba's frequent coauthor, Allison Janse[115]—advice that, at least if you're using a wood cutting board, the folks at the website What'sCookingAmerica .net fervently hope you won't take. "Wood is porous and will soak up water causing the cutting board to crack when it dries," they explain.[116])

Furthermore, as many cooks already know, it's absolutely essential to have at least two separate cutting boards—one for slicing and dicing fruits and vegetables, and the other for carving meat, so the fecal bacteria from your meat, poultry, and seafood dishes won't end up coating your produce, and the germs and pesticide residue from your veggies and fruit won't contaminate your steak, pork, chicken, or fish. Indeed, according to nationally syndicated columnist Cecil Adams's "Straight Dope Science Advisory Board," to be *truly* safe, you should add a third, separate cutting board just for fowl. Why? Because chicken is "considered a walking petri dish of germs," they say, and "non-chicken meats" are not always cooked thoroughly enough to "be certain everything is dead." (Of course, at a certain point, remembering which cutting board is which can become a nightmare; to help you keep everything straight, several manufactures now offer color-coded boards—red for meat, green for produce, and yellow for poultry.)

If you insist on using only one cutting board, the Straight Dope Science Advisory Board warns, it's critically important to keep it thoroughly disinfected throughout the food preparation process. The "current advice," they say, is to flood it after each use for several minutes with a 5 percent chlorine bleach solution (about two tablespoons of bleach to a quart of water) and then wipe it with vinegar to remove the bleach. (While this approach "may be scientifically sound," the Board concludes, it's pretty much calculated to turn your dinner into a "midnight snack.")[117] See: **chlorine bleach; dishwashers; cutting boards, plastic; cutting boards, wood.**

cutting boards, plastic. According to microbiologists Dean O. Cliver

and Nese O. Ak, experiments they conducted at the University of Wisconsin's Food Research Institute demonstrate that plastic cutting boards are less safe to use than wooden ones, because wooden cutting boards have an innate ability to kill food-poisoning bacteria that "survive very nicely" on plastic boards. When Cliver and Ak purposely contaminated wooden boards with organisms such as *Salmonella, Listeria,* and *E. coli,* the *New York Times* reports, they found that "99.9 percent of the bacteria died off within three minutes on the wooden boards, while none died on the plastic ones." Furthermore, when contaminated boards were left unwashed overnight at room temperature, "bacterial counts increased on the plastic, but none of the organisms could be recovered from the wooden boards the next morning." "The researchers tested boards made from seven different species of trees and four types of plastic and found similar results," the *Times* says. "Wood was safer than plastic, regardless of the materials used." [118] See: **cutting boards, wood.** See also: **cutting boards.**

cutting boards, wood. While acknowledging research indicating that

wood cutting boards may contain enzymes that can kill pathogens, the Food News Service's Ochef website, dedicated to "providing answers to life's vexing cooking questions," cautions that keeping your board sanitary is far more important than "what it's made of." And therefore, to protect you and your family from food-related illnesses, Ochef votes strongly in favor of plastic cutting boards, because, unlike wooden ones, you can throw them in the dishwasher "where we know they get really, really clean." [119] San Francisco gourmet chef Danny Alfaro couldn't agree more. "Nonporous surfaces like plastic are easier to clean than wood and thus better in terms of food safety," he writes. "Wood is naturally porous, and those tiny fissures and grooves in wooden cutting boards can harbor bacteria. Which is why cutting boards made of wood aren't allowed in commercial kitchens. That being the case, why use them at home?" [120] See: **cutting boards, plastic; dishwashers.** See also: **cutting boards.**

cyanide poisoning. See: **apple seeds; apricots; cherries; peaches.**

cybersex. Also widely referred to as **computer sex, Internet sex,** **netsex, MUDsex,** and **TinySex,** this popular form of electronic intimacy has the advantage of being both sanitary and anonymous, but the quality of the romantic experience clearly depends heavily on the creativity of one's cyberpartner, as this randomly selected example of an actual online encounter reported on an illuminating web page titled *Adventures in Cybersex* so graphically illustrates:

> **bloodninja:** Wanna cyber?
>
> **Katie_007:** Sure, you into vegetables?
>
> **bloodninja:** What like gardening an shit?
>
> **Katie_007:** Yeah, something like that.
>
> **bloodninja:** Nothing turns me on more, check this out: You bend over to harvest your radishes.
>
> (pause)
>
> **Katie_007:** is that it?
>
> **bloodninja:** You water your tomato patch. Are you ready for my fresh produce?
>
> **Katie_007:** I was thinking of like, sexual acts INVOLVING vegetables . . . Can you make it a little more sexy for me?
>
> (pause)
>
> **bloodninja:** I touch you on your lettuce, you massage my spinach . . . sexily. I ride your buttocks like they were amber waves of grains.
>
> **Katie_007:** Grain doesn't really turn me on . . . I was thinking more along the lines of carrots and zucchinis.
>
> **bloodninja:** my zucchinis carresses your carrots. Damn baby you're right, this shit is HOTT.
>
> **Katie_007:** (pause)
>
> **bloodninja:** My turnips listen for the soft cry of your love. My insides turn to celery as I unleash my warm and sticky cauliflower of love.
>
> **Katie_007:** What the f*ck is this madlibs? I'm outta here.
>
> **bloodninja:** Yeah, well I already unleashed my cauliflower, all

over your olives, and up in your eyes. Now you can't see.
Bitch.

Katie_007: whatever.[121]

Certified sex addiction therapist Shari Cohn, M.S.S.W., L.C.S.W., S.C., C.S.A.T., worries that cybersex addiction in the United States is reaching epidemic proportions. "Internet sex is very powerful and potentially very destructive," she writes, and over 15 million Americans are "using cybersex in ways that are risky and showing signs of compulsivity."[122] The Cassandra Institute would like to believe that, by reprinting the Internet conversation reproduced above, and encouraging potential cybersex addicts to read it as often as possible, we are taking a small but meaningful step toward reversing this alarming trend.

cyberwarfare. A good deal of attention has been paid to the clearly dire national security threats posed by weapons of mass destruction, but we may have nearly as much to fear from "weapons of mass disruption"—premeditated raids by hostile programmers on sensitive Internet sites and telecommunications nodes that could gravely threaten our critical network-dependent, computer-driven infrastructure. Steven Chabinsky, a senior FBI official responsible for cybersecurity, points to the inherent vulnerability of advanced, wired societies to electronic assaults, noting that "given enough time, motivation, and funding, a determined adversary will always—always—be able to penetrate a targeted system."

A U.S. Joint Forces Command review of the novel challenges posed by the looming cyberwar threat supplied an apt analogy for the impact of the new information technologies on warfare, concluding that "in much the same way that air power transformed the battlefield of World War II, cyberspace has fractured the physical barriers that shield a nation from attacks on its commerce and communication."[123] Sounding an even more apocalyptic alarm, Sir Robert Fry, the former deputy commanding general of coalition forces in Iraq, predicts that a full-scale sneak hack-attack could lead to "the instantaneous failure of the systems that animate and sustain modern life. At a stroke, computer systems, power grids, industrial production, and financial markets could fail, with untold consequences for civil governance and social cohesion: an electronic Pearl Harbor." [124]

Sadly, an investigation by the Center for Strategic and International Studies suggests that we are no better prepared for this potentially disastrous surprise attack than we were for the devastating Japanese air strike in 1941, thanks in large part to a "desperate shortage" in the United States of individuals with the skills necessary to "design secure systems, write safe computer code, and create the ever more sophisticated tools needed to prevent, detect, mitigate, and reconstitute from damage due to system failures and malicious acts." [125] And after a long career serving in the front lines of the emerging struggle for the effective domination of cyberspace, the former head of the National Security Agency and director of national intelligence Admiral Mike McConnell offered a similarly downbeat assessment of the American military's readiness to engage effectively in information warfare, declaring that "cyberwar has already started, and we are losing it." [126] See also: **malware.**

cystic fibrosis. See: **runny nose.**

D

dairy products. The Physicians Committee for Responsible Medi-

cine (PCRM) warns that there are numerous health risks associated with dairy products, and the organization strongly suggests that you eliminate them from your diet. Among the problems that the Committee enumerates:

- Dairy products—including cheese, ice cream, milk, butter, and yogurt—"contribute significant amounts of cholesterol and fat to the diet."
- Several cancers, including ovarian, breast, and prostate cancer, have been linked to the consumption of dairy products.
  Of particular concern in connection with increased cancer risks, the PCRM advises, is the presence in cow's milk of a

compound called insulin-like growth factor (IGF-1), which "has been shown to occur in increased levels in the blood by individuals consuming dairy products on a regular basis."

- "Epidemiological studies of various countries show a strong correlation between the use of dairy products and the incidence of insulin-dependent diabetes."
- Lactose intolerance is common among many populations, including a majority of Asian Americans, African Americans, and Native Americans. Symptoms include "gastrointestinal distress, diarrhea, and flatulence."
- Dairy products contain proteins, sugar, and saturated and unsaturated fats that "may pose health risks for children and lead to the development of chronic diseases such as obesity, diabetes, and formation of atherosclerotic plaques that can lead to heart disease."
- And finally, as *Encyclopedia Paranoiaca* details in our entry on milk, the synthetic compound recombinant bovine growth hormone (rBGH) is commonly injected into dairy cows to increase the production of milk. "Because the cows are producing quantities of milk nature never intended," the Physicians Committee points out, "the end result is mastitis, or inflammation of the mammary glands. The treatment requires the use of antibiotics, and traces of these and the hormones themselves have been found in samples of milk and other dairy products." (See: **milk.**)

Okay, you might ask, if I'm not going to consume any dairy products, where else can I get the calcium, potassium, riboflavin, and vitamin D that these foods and drinks provide? Well, the Physicians Committee for Responsible Medicine recommends fruits, vegetables (specifically leafy greens), soy milk, tofu, and calcium-fortified products such as breakfast cereals and juices. These "nutrient-rich foods" can help you meet your dietary requirements "with ease," the PCRM says, and "without the health risks" presented by dairy.[1] See: **fruits, whole; leafy green vegetables; soy; acrylamide; fruit juice.**

dam collapses and failures, catastrophic. See: **hydroelectric power.**

daylight saving time. The next time spring rolls around and you

make a mental note to set that alarm clock forward one hour, the key word you need to remember isn't *clock*— it's *alarm!* According to Dr. Till Roenneberg, a leading chronobiologist and professor at the Institute for Medicinal Psychology at Ludwig-Maximilians-University in Munich, Germany, our bodies' natural circadian time orientation, which is set by light and darkness to a basic twenty-four-hour cycle, never properly adjusts to gaining an "extra" hour of sunlight at the end of the day. Dr. Roenneberg warns that "the consequences of that [failure to adjust] is that the majority of the population has drastically decreased productivity, decreased quality of life, increased susceptibility to illness, and is just plain tired." This "social jet lag," as Dr. Roenneberg describes it, is caused by the fact that "light doesn't do the same things to the body in the morning and evening. More light in the morning would advance the body clock, and that would be good. But more light in the evening would even further delay the body clock."

An even more urgent wake-up call comes from Sweden, where Imre Janszky of the Karolinska Institute's Department of Public Health Sciences in Stockholm and Dr. Rickard Ljung of the Swedish National Board of Health and Welfare report evidence that, at least in Sweden, heart attack rates spike in the days just after the annual spring time change. The two researchers concluded that "the most likely explanation to [*sic*] our findings are disturbed sleep and disruption of biological rhythm." [2]

All of which raises the unsettling question of whether, on that next fateful Saturday night in March, when we twiddle with the reset button on our happily glowing bedside snoozebuster, we are in fact hitting the trigger of a ticking time bomb, and instead of springing forward, we're about to suddenly pitch forward, facedown.

death rattle. See: **hiccups.**

debit-card cloning. See: **identity theft.**

debris, littoral. See: **beach, a day at the.**

Decade of the Living Dead. See: **zombie banks.**

decreased sperm count. See: **antibacterial and antiviral products; bisphenol A.**

deep-fried foods. See: **trans fats.**

deep venous thrombosis (DVT). See: **crossing your legs.**

deficit hysteria. "Deficit hysteria is rising to fever pitch in Washing-

ton," writes Darrell Delamaide of the *Wall Street Journal* Digital Network's MarketWatch.com. " 'Fiscal nightmare,' 'buried under a mountain of debt,' 'awash in red ink'—these are some of the colorful phrases being bandied about by politicians, pundits and even journalists ostensibly reporting facts . . . Yet, if you look out the window, you don't see any red ink or mountains of debt. The only nightmare is unemployment continuing near 10% and ongoing waves of foreclosures—neither of which is attributable to the federal deficit and neither of which will be fixed by budget cuts." But, warns Delamaide, there *is* cause for alarm. "There is the possibility that the government, held under the sway of misguided and obsolete economic theories and driven by a not-so-hidden corporate agenda, will make genuinely harmful cuts in both discretionary spending and entitlement programs—cuts that will cause real and needless misery to millions . . . The overwrought hysteria of the deficit hawks—one economist calls them deficit terrorists—has already sabotaged government stimulus that could have rebooted the economy much more quickly and alleviated unemployment to a greater extent."[3]

deflation. An economy is considered to be experiencing deflation

when there is too little money available to buy the goods its businesses produce, and with a scarcity of money and a glut of goods, the prices of those goods start to fall. Although the prospect of declining prices would seem on its face to be a good thing—a sort of nationwide sales event—the ultimate effect is a catastrophic "cash crisis." Because businesses make less profit on the goods they produce, they cut their production. With less production, businesses need fewer workers, so they undertake a series of layoffs. The newly laid-off workers have less money, so they in turn stop buying goods, and businesses cut employment even further. As unemployment spreads, consumption takes a nosedive, inventories of unsold goods clog warehouses, factories close, debts are unpaid, housing prices plummet, foreclosures rise, banks go belly-up, the stock market tanks, and since everyone thinks that prices will go still lower and things will get worse, even people fortunate enough to have access to money stop spending it.

This vicious circle of shrinking economic activity is usually described as a "deflationary spiral" and blamed at least in part on a "liquidity trap" that is sprung when central banks can't—or won't—cut interest rates far enough or increase the money supply fast enough to restart the economy.[4] It happened in the United States during the Great Depression in the 1930s and more recently in Japan in the 1990s, and a growing number of financial experts, including James Bullard, president of the Federal Reserve Bank of St. Louis, and Mohamed El-Erian, CEO of PIMCO, the world's largest bond fund, worry that the United States is once again, to use El-Erian's phrase, "on the road to deflation."[5] Indeed, warned Heiner Flassbeck, a senior economist at the UN Conference on Trade and Development (UNCTAD), as he presented his agency's 2010 annual report, "the world economy at this moment in time" faces "a dramatic deflationary danger."[6] The good news is that most economists agree that there is a cure—aggressively expansive fiscal and monetary policy. The bad news is that many economists *also* believe that the cure, if not actually worse than the disease itself, might trigger a considerably more serious contagion.[7] See: **inflation.**

dehydration. See: **water, drinking too little.**

delirium and unconsciousness. See: **water, drinking too little.**

dental floss. Every time you visit your dentist, does he or she warn

you to floss more often? And do you go home vowing to change your ways, only to slip back into nonflossing mode within a few days at most? If so, your inaction may indeed be hurting your gums. But, far more important, it may also be adding years to your life. The reason, according to the Environmental Health Association of Nova Scotia (EHANS), is that most dental floss is coated with polytetrafluoroethylene (PTFE). PTFE, EHANS warns, is "related to the coating on non-stick cookware, a chemical which is considered to be carcinogenic." Fortunately (or unfortunately, if you *really* hate flossing), there are alternatives to dental floss coated with PTFE—some flosses are unwaxed, and others use beeswax, rather than PTFE, to reduce friction. Among the brands EHANS recommends are Tom's of Maine Naturally Waxed Anti-Plaque Floss and (for those ethically opposed to using animal products, even for nondietary purposes) EcoDenT Vegan Floss.[8] See: **vegetarianism and veganism.**

dentures. See: **aluminum.**

deodorant sprays, antiperspirant. Human body odor is caused by

bacteria that grow rapidly in accumulations of perspiration under the armpits, and then trigger biochemical reactions that break down organic compounds in that perspiration to create *volatile carboxylic acids,* pungent-smelling chemicals that give "BO" its characteristic unpleasant aroma. Antiperspirant deodorant sprays are designed to control body odor by reducing or eliminating the underarm perspiration in which the bacteria grow.[9] As effective as these sprays may be for this purpose, there is a potential hazard in their use: Some of the deodorant inevitably finds its way inside the human body, either because aerosol spray droplets are inhaled, because it's absorbed through pores in the skin, or because it enters the bloodstream directly through the nicks that occur when women shave under their arms.[10]

Why is this a problem? Well, for one thing, many antiperspirant deodorants contain preservatives called parabens that mimic the female hormone estrogen, which is listed as a known carcinogen by the National Institute of Environmental Health Sciences (NIEHS).[11] In addition, the majority of such deodorants also contain **aluminum** (q.v.), one of the very few basic molecular elements that is neither essential for, nor beneficial to, organic life; indeed, some individuals with aluminum allergies typically develop contact dermatitis when exposed to it. Aluminum, in large doses, is also a potent neurotoxin and can disrupt the blood-brain barrier and even cause genetic damage.

Furthermore, there is inconclusive but obviously quite disquieting evidence that aluminum concentrations in the human body may contribute to the development or progression of two very serious ailments: breast cancer and Alzheimer's disease. In the case of breast cancer, there is concern that estrogen-mimicking aluminum salts in the antiperspirants, like the parabens the products also contain, may hasten the growth of tumors, and although many experts argue that there is no data to support this theory, the noted British toxicologist Philip W. Harvey, Ph.D., observes sagely that "absence of evidence is not evidence of absence of a harmful effect. These chemicals are being directly applied daily, by very large numbers of people, and the long-term health effects of exposure are essentially unknown."[12]

As for Alzheimer's disease, the potential contribution from aluminum exposure to the growth of disabling amyloid plaques is equally speculative and circumstantial, but considering the potential consequences of failing to address any contributing factor that might speed the onset of the malady's devastating symptoms, the possibility is difficult to dismiss out of hand. As the Alzheimer's Society of the UK notes, "Alzheimer's is a common disease with multiple causes, while aluminum is widespread in the environment, and there are no methods that allow us to measure an individual's 'body burden' of lifetime exposure to this element."[13] Does this mixed message of ambiguous information provide enough of a basis on which to raise a stink, as it were, about antiperspirant deodorant sprays? Frankly, that's hard to say, but the best advice would seem to be—*do* sweat it!

deregulation feedback loops. See: **income inequality.**

dermatitis, contact. See: **aluminum; cosmetics; deodorant sprays, antiperspirant.**

desertification, subtropical. See: **global warming.**

diet soda. "Just as you were starting to feel virtuous for having
 switched from sugary sodas to low- or no-calorie sub-
stitutes," writes MSNBC.com's Linda Carroll, "a new
study comes along suggesting that diet sodas might be
bad for your head and your heart." The study, funded
by the National Institutes of Health and conducted by
researchers at the University of Miami and Columbia University, followed 2,500 New Yorkers who drank diet soda every day and "found
that daily diet soda drinkers had a 61 percent higher risk of so-called
vascular events, including stroke and heart attack, than those who did
not drink any diet soda,"[14] Carroll reports. "Our study says that diet
soda may be just as bad for your health as regular soda that has been
previously associated with obesity and diabetes," says Mitchell Elkind,
M.D., a neurology professor at Columbia's College of Physicians and
one of the study's principal investigators. Elkind's advice: "Stick to
water, juice, tea or coffee: things that people have been drinking for
millennia."[15] See: **bottled water; tap water; fruit juice; tea; coffee.**
See also: **aspartame; sucralose.**

differential accumulation. See: **stagflation.**

difficulty speaking. See: **birth-control pills.**

dime-store trinkets, hand-me-down. See: **yard sales.**

Ding Dongs. See: **high-fat, high-calorie food addiction.**

disembowelment, accidental. See: **hot tubs.**

dishrags. See: **sponges.**

dishwashers. According to a 2011 study conducted by scientific researchers at the University of Ljubljana in Slovenia, and published in
the British journal *Fungal Biology,* recently evolved microbes toxic

enough to kill you could well be festering in your dishwashing machine. The researchers studied 189 domestic dishwashers in 101 different cities around the world and found that a shocking 62 percent of them contained fungi on the rubber lining in the door. "More than half of these," reports the British newspaper the *Telegraph*, "included the black yeasts *Exophiala dermatitidis* and *E. phaeomuriformis* which are known to be dangerous to human health."[16]

What startles scientists most about these findings was the ability of the two species—both of which have a record of causing fatal infections in humans—to withstand the blistering heat, high salt concentrations, and aggressive detergents they are exposed to during a typical dishwasher cycle. "This is a combination of extreme properties not previously observed in fungi," reports the scientific news website Science Daily. The widespread presence in some of our most common household appliances of these extremophilic pathogens—that is, pathogens able to thrive in conditions hostile to most life on earth—"suggests that these organisms have embarked on an extraordinary evolutionary process that could pose a significant risk to human health in the future."[17] And if that's not enough to terrify you, consider the following quote from the coauthor of the University of Ljubljana study, Dr. Nina Gunde-Cimerman. "One thing that is not in the report is that we tested the dishes after they had been cleaned in these dishwashers and they were full of this black yeast, so too the cutlery that you put in your mouth,"[18] she says. "I wash my dishes now by hand."[19]

diversification, portfolio. See: **portfolio diversification.**

doctors, incompetent. A recent survey of more than a thousand doc-
tors in the United Kingdom and just under two thousand in the United States revealed that roughly the same percentage of physicians in both countries—a little under 20 percent, or nearly one in five—reported having encountered an incompetent colleague at some point during the previous three years. The study, conducted by re-

searchers at Cambridge University, Harvard University, and several major hospitals and medical schools, found that only about 70 percent of either nation's doctors who had worked with an incapable or unqualified medical practitioner reported the individual in question to superiors or to a supervisory board, and that of those who failed to blow the whistle on their underperforming compatriot, about a third of the American doctors and half of the British physicians refrained from doing so either because they feared retribution or doubted that anything would be done about the situation. As an interesting, and somewhat worrisome footnote, the survey also discovered that although the medical systems in the two countries are quite different, an almost equal number of physicians in both nations—again, about one in five—did *not* agree with the statement "Doctors should put patients' welfare above the doctors' own financial interest."[20]

doctors' offices. "Doctors' offices are virtual petri dishes," warns Allison Janse in *The Germ Freak's Guide to Outwitting Colds and Flu,* the handy medical guidebook she authored in collaboration with famed environmental microbiologist Charles P. Gerba, Ph.D. "Think about it: A group of sick people are forced to wait in a holding tank of contagion while their diseases commingle, mutate, and reproduce," she writes. "If you're just going for a well visit, chances are you'll be sick before you leave." If you absolutely *have to* visit a physician, Janse advises, you should schedule an early-morning appointment, when "the office has just been cleaned and not many people have been there to sneeze and slobber on the magazines, the door handles, and the pen you sign in with." She also suggests that you bring your own reading material, and that, the moment you get home, you "give your hands a thorough decontamination" and also change your clothes and put them in the wash.[21] See: **hand washing; laundry.**

doggie bags. "Ditch the doggie bag," advises Allison Janse in *The Germ Freak's Guide to Outwitting Colds and Flu,* the practical, if disturbing, guidebook she authored with the help of noted University of Arizona microbe hunter Charles P. Gerba, Ph.D. "After your entrée was cooked, placed on a warmer, served, half eaten, and left unrefrigerated while you made small talk and drove home, the bacterial count was climbing." If you just can't resist the temptation to bring those leftovers home, Janse cautions, "you have about ninety minutes from the time the food was served" to get it into your refrigerator. Even then, she says, you must reheat it to 160 degrees or more and eat it within twenty-four hours or you're asking for trouble.[22]

dogs. While acknowledging that "many groups support the health benefits of pets," the National Center for Infectious Diseases warns that "dogs can carry a variety of germs that can make people sick." For example, the Center reports, "puppies may pass the bacterium *Campylobacter* in their feces (stool). This germ can cause diarrhea in people. Puppies and some adult dogs often carry a variety of parasites that can cause rashes or illness in people." Furthermore, the Center continues, "dogs in urban or rural areas can carry the bacterium *Leptospira* (lep-TO-spy-ruh)," which causes the disease leptospirosis (lep-to-spi-roh-sis), also known as swineherd's disease or swamp fever, an extremely unpleasant ailment whose symptoms include (among many others) coughs, high fever, muscle pain or rigidity, severe headaches, skin rashes, abdominal pain and vomiting, enlarged lymph glands, conjunctivitis, liver damage, and kidney failure. Worse still, the Center concludes, "dogs can also carry rabies, a deadly viral disease." Armed with this knowledge, what can we do to protect ourselves? "Thoroughly wash your hands with running water and soap after contact with dogs, dog saliva, or dog feces (stool)," the Center advises.[23] And, adds veterinarian Lisa Conti, D.V.M., M.P.H., director of the Florida Health Department's Division of Environmental Health, you absolutely should not permit a dog to lick or kiss you. "Dogs have bacteria around their mouths you don't want on your face,"[24] she explains. See: **hand washing.**

dollar-denominated holdings. See: **investments, domestic.**

"doom loop." This colorful term coined by Andy Haldane, the executive director for financial stability of the Bank of England, refers to the fiscally ruinous consequences of unstated but implied government commitments to bail out major financial institutions during severe financial crises, such as the 2009 recovery package that left British taxpayers on the hook for £1.5 trillion in debts, or about $2 trillion. The continuing reliance on what, based on past experience with previous rescues, everyone correctly assumes will be an inevitable, last-minute, political intervention to save the country from an economic collapse has the unintended effect of encouraging more of the same irresponsible behavior that caused the crisis in the first place, because banks and their shareholders are spared from suffering any consequences for failing to maintain adequate capital reserves to cover unanticipated losses.[25]

As Haldane notes in a paper he coauthored with a Bank of England colleague, economist Piergiorgio Alessandri, the reluctant public assumption of unsecured private liabilities is typically accompanied by a firmly stated official pledge that this is a "one-time-and-never-again" move. But the stakes of economic failure are so high that such government assurances lack credibility. Knowing this, Haldane argues, bank owners are incentivized to adapt ever-riskier strategies "to boost shareholder return and, whether by accident or design, game the state." In short, says Haldane, the massive 2009 bailout, which in one fell swoop transformed the United Kingdom from a highly solvent nation into one of the world's largest debtors, merely ensured that the bankers will "double their bets" the next time, and that when their bacon needs saving again, the price will be even higher. "This adds to the cost of future crises," Haldane observes. "And the larger these costs, the lower the credibility of 'never again' announcements. This is a 'doom loop.'"[26]

Haldane's trenchant observation was echoed, in July 2011 testimony before the U.S. Congress, by Simon Johnson, an MIT economist and former chief economist of the International Monetary Fund, who clearly sees many of the same troubling symptoms of institutional dysfunction in Wall Street and Washington. "A financial system with dangerously low capital levels—hence prone to major collapses—creates a nontransparent contingent liability for the federal budget in the United States," Johnson stated. "This can only lead to further instability, deep recessions, and damage to our fiscal balance sheet, in a version of what the Bank of England refers to as a 'doom loop.'"[27] See also: **zombie banks.**

Doomsday Argument, the. First advanced by the Australian-born theoretical astrophysicist Brandon Carter in the early 1980s, and later supported and refined by J. Richard Gott III of the Department of Astrophysical Science at Princeton, this essentially statistical deduction makes the case that the members of the human race who are alive today are randomly situated roughly halfway along what will eventually prove to be the entire life span of Homo sapiens. Another way to look at things is to accept the premise that, given our presumed average position in the history of mankind, about half of all the human beings who will ever live have already been born.

Although the mathematical calculations that support this theory are mind-bendingly complex, the underlying predictive presumption is actually quite simple. Usually referred to as the Copernican principle, this venerable philosophical concept states that, from a strictly probabilistic point of view, the odds are that we are not special people in a special place at a special time, but rather just a bunch of ordinary folks who happened to show up on a fairly lackluster planet during the middle of a pretty ho-hum era.[28] As Professor Gott summed up our terminal dialectic predicament: "Making only the assumption that you are a random intelligent observer, limits for the total longevity of our species of 0.2 million to 8 million years can be derived at the 95% confidence level. Further consideration indicates that we are unlikely to colonize the galaxy."[29]

The reason for this rather gloomy conclusion, Jim Holt explains in *Lingua Franca* magazine, is that if humanity *did* manage to survive long enough to make it to the stars, an estimated 500 quadrillion more of us would be born in the future, and those of us living now "would be among the first 0.00001 percent of all members of the human species to exist." "Are we really so special?" Holt asks. If not, he argues, the only reasonable conclusion is "Doom soon."[30] Intriguingly, a concept that contradicts the Doomsday Argument's basic presumption of an essential mediocrity pervading physical reality and in the process raises the distinct possibility that we are the only highly developed technological civilization in our galaxy—and possibly the entire universe—provides equally compelling evidence for our inevitable demise. See **Fermi's paradox.**

doorknobs and doorplates, public restroom. Noted University of

Arizona microbiologist Charles P. Gerba, Ph.D., has pointed out the paradox that even after washing your hands properly in a public restroom, you often can't exit the place without having to use a door whose knob, handle, or plate is virtually certain to have been contaminated by other, far less conscientious bathroom visitors. Gerba and his writing colleague Allison Janse recommend the following strategies for dealing with this dilemma: (1) Time your departure so it coincides with someone else's arrival so you can slide out without touching the door. (2) Use a tissue to cover the doorknob, and then dispose of it immediately. "If there's no trashcan, throw it on the floor," suggest Gerba and Janse, "and eventually management will get a clue." (3) Use your nondominant hand (i.e., your left one if you're right-handed) to open the door, and then wash it elsewhere as soon as possible thereafter. "Chances are you're less likely to touch your nose, mouth, or eyes with your non-dominant hand," they explain. (4) If you're confronted with a handle you have to turn, use your pinkie "so you have only a one-in-ten chance of touching anything important if you forget to wash later." (5) Open the door using your sleeve as a covering. "Just remember to wash your shirt when you get home," Gerba and Janse advise.[31]

doughnuts. "Within the sweets spectrum, desserts like ice cream and

apple pie have some redeeming value—the calcium in dairy products and the antioxidants in fruit," writes Martica Heaner in the *New York Times*. "Even chocolate contains beneficial phytochemicals." But, according to Jayne Hurley, a senior nutritionist at the Center for Science in the Public Interest, doughnuts have absolutely nothing to offer but a panoply of unhealthy ingredients. They are chock-full of sugar, refined flour, and the fats known to increase heart disease risk:

saturated fat and partially hydrogenated oil that is loaded with trans fat, Hurley cautions. Indeed, says Heaner, a doughnut containing anything even vaguely nutritious is hard to find. "In a glazed blueberry Krispy Kreme, for example, there is not a blueberry in sight," she reports. "The 'fruit' is concocted from sugar, corn syrup, corn cereal, partially hydrogenated oil, natural and artificial flavors and dyes." Perhaps the following comment on doughnuts by the New York Obesity Research Center's Carla Wolper sums them up best: "When it comes to health, the only thing good about them is the hole."[32] See also: **sugar; trans fats.**

drinking from a straw. "People who drink out of a straw often have a
 characteristic pattern of lines and wrinkles around their mouth," advises Roanoke, Virginia, physician and health writer Kristie Leong, M.D., who notes that dermatologists often calls such wrinkles "marionette lines." "If you want skin that still looks youthful as you age," Leong advises, "avoid the drinking straw habit."[33]

drive-by downloads. See: **malware.**

drivers, courteous. Common courtesy is one of the keys to driving
 safety, right? Not so, advises Joseph D. Younger, automotive editor of AAA New York's *Car & Travel* magazine. On the contrary, Younger warns, courteous drivers are one of the great potential safety *hazards* on the road today. "Drivers who cede their legal right of way, thinking that they're doing you a favor, might actually put you at risk," he cautions. "The other driver may ... not notice what's behind him on his right," explains AAA driving instructor Karen Blackburn, whom Younger quotes in his landmark auto safety article, "When Courtesy Turns Dangerous." "Inviting you to a potential collision is not doing you a favor." But, you might think, if the courteous act of a friendly driver leads to a head-on collision with an oncoming truck, at least I won't be legally liable. Well, think again. "The other driver has no legal liability," says Blackburn. "It's all on you." So what are we to do? "Rather than relying on the kindness of strangers," Younger sug-

gests, "consider routes that avoid left turns entirely." Blackburn agrees. "Can you go to the next intersection and safely make a U-turn?" she asks. "Can you make a series of three right turns to get back to the original intersection?"[34] See: **U-turns.**

driving with the top down. According to a joint study undertaken by

dedicated researchers at the St. Louis University School of Medicine and the Ear Institute of Texas, occupants of convertible automobiles being driven with their tops down and side windows open at speeds in excess of 55 mph experience enough noise to cause measurable hearing loss. The diligent joyriders put five late-model ragtops through their paces at 55 mph, 65 mph, and 75 mph and found that regardless of the design of the vehicle or its operating speed, "when the convertible cars were driven with the top open, high levels of noise were consistently recorded." Using the definition of 85 decibels (dbs) identified by the National Institute for Occupational Safety and Health as the standard measure of "excessive noise exposure," the dogged experimenters recorded sound levels ranging from 82.5 dbs, which is about the racket emitted by a small lawn mower, to 104 dbs, which is close to the raucous howl of a chain saw. The "mean noise exposure" was 85.3 dbs at 55 mph, 88.4 dbs at 65 mph, and 89.9 dbs at 75 mph. In their conclusion, the hard-driving team cautioned that motorists who tool around in their jalopies with the top down "are potentially at increased risk of noise-induced hearing loss," adding that hearing-protection devices like earplugs or headphones would not be recommended owing to "safety and legal concerns" that could arise if drivers wearing noise-canceling gear became less responsive to the sirens of approaching emergency vehicles.[35]

drowsiness. Is your teenage son or daughter—or a teenage friend—

exhibiting drowsiness? If so, warns the U.S. Substance Abuse and Mental Health Services Administration (SAMHSA), it could be a sign that he or she is using heroin.[36] (For information and referrals, call the National Clearinghouse for Alcohol and Drug Information at 800-729-6686.)

Dumpster-diving. See: **identity theft.**

dust mites, dust mite feces. See: **carpeting, old; pillows and mattresses.**

DVT (deep venous thrombosis). See: **crossing your legs.**

E

eating, laughing or crying while. See: **laughing or crying while eating.**

economic superiority of the United States, weapons designed to undermine. See: **global warming, attempting to mitigate.**

eczema. See: **condoms, allergic reactions to.**

ED. See: **erectile dysfunction.**

eggs. According to the *New York Times,* "97% of all eggs produced in  the United States are from hens that live in tightly packed battery cages."[1] In the event you don't know what a "battery cage" is, you may find the following description of life in such cages, excerpted from the website of People for the Ethical Treatment of Animals, informative: "Because the hens are crammed so closely together, these normally clean animals are forced to urinate and defecate on one another. The birds have part of their sensitive beaks cut off so that they won't peck each other out of frustration created by the unnatural confinement. After their bodies are exhausted and their production drops, they are shipped to slaughter, generally to be turned into chicken soup or cat or dog food because their flesh is too bruised and battered to be used for much else."[2] One way you can help end this cruelty, and perhaps protect your own health in the bargain, is by refusing to buy industrially produced eggs. As world-renowned Princeton University philosopher and bioethicist Peter Singer has written, "As consumers, we have the power—and the moral obligation—to refuse to support farming methods that are cruel to animals and bad for us."[3] See also: **eggs, breakfast buffet.**

eggs, breakfast buffet. When you're on the road, do you enjoy going

to the free breakfast buffet offered by your hotel or motel and helping yourself to a heaping portion of scrambled eggs? Big mistake! Many hotel restaurants purposely undercook the eggs a bit so they won't dry out in the buffet display, warns eFoodAlert.com. As a result, they may not have been heated enough to guarantee killing any *Salmonella* bacteria that might be present. And, once contaminated eggs are sitting at room temperature, the salmonella can multiply rapidly, increasing the danger of a food-poisoning outbreak with every passing minute.[4] (Of course, quite apart from the danger of pathogen exposure, eating eggs, especially nonorganic ones, is hardly *ever* a healthy or ethical choice. For more details, see: **eggs.** See also: **organic food.**)

elastin breakdown. See: **chewing gum.**

electronic piracy. See: **identity theft.**

encephalitis. See: **headaches; hiccups.**

energy consumption, runaway. See: **superpower collapse soup.**

environmental tobacco smoke (ETS). See: **smoking.**

Equal. See: **aspartame.**

erectile dysfunction. Usually abbreviated to "ED," this fairly com-

mon—and now widely publicized—form of male sexual impotence affects about 18 million Americans, and is four times more likely to be experienced by sixty-year-old men than forty-year-olds. It can be treated by one of three heavily marketed phophodiesterase (PDE5) inhibitors, sildenafil (Viagra), vardenafil (Levitra), and tadalafil (Cialis), but if your idea of a good time isn't sitting with the object of your desire on a deserted beach in that pair of side-by-side claw-footed bathtubs they show in all those TV ads, you might want to arrange instead to travel to a more exotic locale, like the Amazon, where you could get bitten by *Phoneutria nigriventer,* the Brazilian wandering spider, whose toxin, PhTx3, causes prolonged, albeit often painful, erections, and, occasionally, death.[5]

Dr. Kenia Pedrosa Nunes, a researcher at the Medical College of Georgia, in Augusta, who is studying the amatory arachnid's venom to see if it can be harnessed into a more effective treatment for ED, reports that "when a human is bitten by this spider, we can observe many different symptoms, including priapism, a condition in which the penis is continually erect."[6] Tx2-6, a component of the tumescence-promoting substance secreted by the four-inch-long spider (whose favored habitat, appropriately enough, is banana plantations), has been successfully tested on flaccid rats, but for now, you'll have to take your chances with the love bug itself, which has been reliably reported to have improved the sex lives of men in Brazil.[7] Yes, its sting can be fatal, but your odds of surviving are excellent according to Rod Crawford, the curator of arachnids at the University of Washington's Burke Museum, who notes that only ten of seven thousand humans bitten by the erotogenic insect have died from the bite.[8] See also: **bicycle saddles; meat-induced impotence; smoking.**

escalator handrails. Southern Arizona's largest provider of health care services, the Carondet Health Network, has one primary message for those venturing out in public during flu season, and it's this: "Don't touch an escalator handrail with your hands."[9] Noted New York University microbiologist Philip M. Tierno Jr., Ph.D., couldn't agree more. Interviewed by Fox News's Diana Rocco after returning from a ride on his hometown Big Apple's mass transit system, Tierno had this to say: "The subway system is filthy. They've got rats on the subway. The other day I had a roach crawling on my legs. You've got germs from thousands of people touching the [escalator handrails] who sneeze and don't cover their hands and put them on the rails. So the germs are everywhere and there's nothing you can do about it."[10] The University of Arizona's germ specialist, Charles Gerba, Ph.D., is happy to join the chorus. "Escalator handrails are loaded with germs," he warns. "Don't touch them if you can manage without it."[11] See: **escalators.**

escalators. In January 2009, in New York City, more than a dozen students were injured on a field trip to a movie theater. As reported by CBS *Early Show* correspondent Susan Koeppen, "a screw sticking out of the side of an escalator caught on one boy's pants. He fell, causing those behind him to fall like dominos." According to the injured students' teacher, Frank Cammallere, "It was mayhem. Kids were yelling at me, screaming, 'Save me, Mr. Cammallere! Save me! Save me!' They felt like they were getting sucked in by the escalator."

Sadly, such incidents are all too common. "Every year," says Koeppen, "nearly 10,000 people are sent to the emergency room because of escalator accidents. Many are children." "It's unbelievable what an escalator can do to human flesh," notes nationally certified escalator inspector Kevin Doherty. "I think a lot of people climb on these escalators assuming that they're regularly checked, when, in fact, they're not," Doherty says. The problem, he points out, is that there are no federal regulations that require escalators to be inspected, so it's left to each individual state or city to determine how often escalators should be checked—if at all. "They *should* be inspected," Doherty argues. "They're deadly; they're killing people; and they have killed people; and they maim children."

The *Early Show* took Doherty on a tour of escalators in train stations, movie theaters, and shopping malls in New York City and what he found was truly dismaying: missing escalator teeth where folks step off at the top, which could allow shoelaces to get sucked in ("It would have taken the shoe lace, it would have taken the shoe, and it would have taken your foot," comments Doherty); screws, like the one responsible for injuring Frank Cammallere's schoolchildren, protruding from side walls; and dangerous gaps between the moving steps and side walls where clothing could become entangled, causing serious falls ("You're falling onto a piece of metal at an uncontrolled speed. You'll smash your head open," Doherty points out helpfully).

Indeed, Doherty reported, 60 percent to 70 percent of the escalators he examined had safety violations so serious that "if I had the authority, I would have taken them out of service immediately." "That dangerous?" asked CBS's Koeppen. "Absolutely. No question about it," Doherty replied. So what can we do, other than avoiding escalators altogether, to improve our odds against an escalator accident? CBS News offers three important tips: (1) Keep you feet and clothing away from the sides of the escalator; (2) Try to stand near the middle of the step; and (3) Most important of all, adults should *always* hold the handrail, and children should hold their hands.[12] See: **escalator handrails.**

escarole. See: **leafy green vegetables.**

ethanol. See: **biofuels; agflation.**

e-threats. See: **botnets; malware; Trojan horse.**

evacuation posture, incorrect. See: **toilet, sitting on the.**

exercise ball, using in place of a desk chair to counter the health
 risks of too much sitting. Citing hard-to-dispute statistics showing that sitting for hours a day at your desk can significantly enhance your odds of dying from a heart attack or cancer, James A. Levine, M.D., Ph.D., director of the Non-Exercise Activity Thermogenesis (NEAT) Laboratory at the Mayo Clinic, recommends trading in your traditional office chair for an exercise ball. ("Sitting on this kind of large, inflatable ball requires you to shift slightly from side to side to keep your balance," he writes, thus helping you keep to a minimum the motionless inactivity that studies have proven can take years off your life span.[13]) But, you may ask, how does spending hours a day sitting on an exercise ball—or as it's known in some circles, a "stability ball" or "Swiss ball"—stack up from a safety point of view? Not very well, advises Livestrong.com, the health, fitness, and lifestyle website

founded and chaired by champion cyclist Lance Armstrong. One risk that should not be overlooked, the website warns, is the possibility that you might fall off the ball; another is "excessive strain from continued muscular exertion"; a third is the total lack of back support; and a fourth is that your spherical desk-chair substitute might accidentally "roll into aisles and cause problems for workers looking ahead rather than at the floor." But last, and probably scariest of all, is "the potential risk of a sudden deflation." "Simply rolling your exercise ball over a fallen thumbtack might cause it to suddenly deflate," Livestrong. com cautions. "If you're sitting on it when this happens, a serious injury might result."[14] See also: **sitting down; stand-up desks.**

exercise, discomfort during. If you feel discomfort in your upper

body, including the chest, arms, or neck while you exercise, warns health and exercise professional Dawna Theo, it could be a sign that you are having a heart attack.[15] Be advised! (In this context, it may be useful to consider the Mayo Clinic's suggestion that the risk of heart attacks and other heart problems can be mitigated by the use of **omega-3 fish oil supplements,** q.v.).

exercise, indoor. As the Center for Innovation in Engineering and

Science Education (CIESE) has pointed out, research has consistently demonstrated that exposure to the fine particles that pollute the air in many areas of the world significantly increases one's risk of "premature death." As a result, many, including the Center itself, have concluded that your chances of survival will increase if you reduce strenuous outdoor activity (see: **exercise, outdoor**). Does this mean, however, that strenuous *indoor* activity is less perilous? Hardly. As Jane E. Brody reveals in her instructive *New York Times* article "Dangers of Indoor Air Pollution," the air you breathe in your own home "may be hazardous to your health—more dangerous, in fact, than the outdoor air in the most polluted of cities."[16] Luckily, however, there are ways in which the dangers of indoor exercise can be mitigated. For example, CIESE suggests, you can help reduce indoor particle levels by cutting back on your use of such notorious particle producers as candles and fireplaces, or by using a room air purifier. See: **room air purifiers; exercise, lack of.** See also: **gyms.**

exercise, lack of. You probably already know that the lack of regular exercise can be harmful to your health in any number

of ways. But, because you may not be clear on the *specific* diseases (and other undesirable medical conditions) that failure to engage in enough physical activity can lead to, *Encyclopedia Paranoiaca* has compiled the following alphabetical list, culled from a variety of sources including the Mayo Clinic, the *New York Times,* and the BBC World Service: arthritis, breast cancer, colon cancer, coronary heart disease, dementia, depression, diabetes, diminished strength, flabby body, high blood pressure, lack of endurance, lack of energy, low self-esteem, metabolic syndrome, obesity, osteoporosis, poor muscle tone, poor posture, shortness of breath, and strokes.[17] Before you plunge, at our behest, into a vigorous physical program to prevent these problems, however, it's incumbent on us to inform you that a team of medical researchers at Tufts University in Boston has recently discovered that engaging in exercise more than triples a person's chance of having a heart attack in the hours immediately afterward. Nonetheless, Issa Dahabreh, M.D., the scientist who led the study, stresses that her team's findings should not deter you from working out. Indeed, she says, "people who exercise regularly have a much smaller risk, if any." But she does recommend that sedentary folks who make the commitment to get in shape should increase their exercise level gradually so as not to place undue stress on their hearts.[18] See: **exercise, discomfort during; exercise, indoor; exercise, outdoor; gyms.** See also: **sex.**

exercise, outdoor. "Health studies have shown a significant association between exposure to fine particles and prema-

ture death," warns the Center for Innovation in Engineering and Science Education (CIESE) in its invaluable "Particulate Matter Primer." And, contrary to popular opinion, the problem is neither temporary nor local. "Particle pollution is a year round problem in many areas of the country," CIESE cautions. Indeed, they point out, fully "one out of every three people in the United States is at a higher risk of experiencing [fine-particle-pollution-related] health effects." The obvious solution: Cut back on outdoor exercise. "Your chances of being affected by particles increase the more strenuous your activity and the longer you are active outdoors," the "Particulate Matter Primer" advises. "If your activity involves prolonged or heavy exertion, reduce your activity time or substitute another that involves less exertion." [19] See: **exercise, indoor; gyms;** and **exercise, lack of.** See also: **coal.**

extinction, mass. See: **mass extinction.**

extreme weather events, more frequent. See: **global warming.**

extremophilic pathogens. See: **dishwashers; hairspray.**

F

face touching. One of the most important—and least frequently observed—rules for not catching the flu or other virus-borne diseases is "Don't touch your face!" "Your hands can be laden with influenza virus, but if you're not touching your eyes, nose, and lips, you are not transmitting that virus (to yourself)," explains Mark Nicas, an adjunct professor of environmental health sciences at the University of California, Berkeley. When you do rub your eye, or touch your nostrils or mouth, or scratch your ear, however, you're giving the pathogens a perfect route into your body.[1] The bad news, according to well-known University of Arizona infectious disease expert Charles P. Gerba, Ph.D., and his frequent writing colleague, Allison Janse, is that "the average person touches her mouth, nose, eyes, and ears one to three times every five minutes. The average child does this ten times every five minutes." Gerba and Janse find these statistics puzzling and unacceptable. "Don't touch your face or ears until you wash your hands," they admonish. "Stop doing this! You just did it again. Really, you've got to find a new nervous habit."[2]

factory farms. See: **meat, eating; chicken; eggs; farmers' markets.**

false vacuum. See: **vacuum metastability event; Large Hadron Collider.**

farmers' markets. According to *Food Safety News,* an Internet-based newspaper that reports daily on food safety issues, consumers who shop in markets selling food grown locally because they think the comestibles they buy there will be healthier or safer may be flirting with danger. Benjamin Chapman, Ph.D., a food safety specialist at North Carolina State University who is quoted on the site, warns that farmers' markets may actually be *less* safe than grocery stores and supermarkets "because there's less pressure on a vendor at a [farmers'] market to implement risk reduction. At a grocery store, growers have all these specifications they have to hit, but that's absent in the farmers' market."[3]

And as if that weren't troubling enough, Joel Grover and Matt Goldberg of NBC News in Los Angeles, who conducted a "hidden-camera investigation" of farmers' markets in 2010, discovered that many of the claims made by the vendors they encountered were "flat-out lies." "We bought produce at farmers' markets across the LA area, and then made surprise visits to farms where we were told the produce was being grown," Grover and Goldberg reported. In several cases, they said, "we found farms full of weeds, or dry dirt, instead of rows of the vegetables that were being sold at the markets." It turned out that some of this produce actually came from industrial farms, some in the States and some in Mexico. Furthermore, the NBC reporters had five batches of "pesticide-free" berries they bought in Los Angeles farmers' markets tested at a state-certified laboratory and learned that three of them did, in fact, contain pesticides.

So, how do you, the customer, know if a farmer at a farmers' market is selling locally grown produce that actually came from his or her farm? According to Grover and Goldberg, the market operators they interviewed recommended asking the vendors you buy from "a lot of questions. Ask for the exact location of the farm where the produce is grown. If they claim their produce is 'pesticide-free,' ask them what methods they use to control pests on their crops. Ask exactly when the produce was picked." "If the farmer can't give you specific answers, or seems unwilling to answer your questions," the market operators concluded, "you should walk away."[4] See: **supermarkets.**

farmers, small subsistence, exploitation of. See: **coffee.**

fast-food salads. See: **salads, fast-food.**

faucets. Since the tap on the sink is likely to be the first thing people touch after exiting the toilet stall, says famous University of Arizona microbiologist Charles P. Gerba, Ph.D., "it usually has the most bacteria of any item you are likely to touch in a public restroom."[5] Luckily, notes Lisa B. Bernstein, M.D., a professor at Emory University's School of Medicine, the widespread adoption of automatically activated devices such as hands-free faucets and hot-air hand-drying machines is making confrontations with pathogen-laden bathroom fixtures less commonplace than they used to be.[6] But, urges Philip M. Tierno Jr., Ph.D., author of *The Secret Life of Germs,* whenever you *do* have to wash your hands in a restroom with traditional plumbing, always "use a paper towel or a wad of tissue to shut off the faucet and turn the door handle." See: **faucets, hands-free; hand-drying machines, hot-air.**

faucets, hands-free. Because you don't have to touch them with bacteria-laden fingers to turn them on, hands-free faucets are widely assumed to be more hygienic than regular ones, and, as a result, an increasing number of restroom operators around the world have been having them installed in their facilities. But a startling new study at Johns Hopkins Hospital in Baltimore may change that. In research presented at the annual meeting of the Society for Health Care Epidemiology in April 2011, the Hopkins team, led by infectious disease expert Dr. Lisa L. Maragakis, discovered that electronic "no-touch" faucets were more likely to be contaminated with the bacteria that cause Legionnaires' disease than the old-fashioned manual type. Indeed, the *Los Angeles Times* reports, microbe counts were so much higher in the "new fangled plumbing" that Johns Hopkins Hospital has actually ripped out the machines already in place in patient care areas, and has "elected to purchase traditional fixtures" for new clinical buildings scheduled to open after the study was completed. According to the *Times*, Hopkins investigators believe that the bacteria counts in the electronic-eye faucets were so inflated because "they have a complicated system of valves that is difficult to clean." "Newer is not necessarily better when it comes to infection control," says Dr. Maragakis.[7] See: **faucets.** See also: **hand-drying machines, hot-air.**

Fermi's paradox. The discouraging premise contained in the so-called **Doomsday Argument** (q.v.)—that we, as a species, are nothing special and are probably never going to amount to much—is challenged by a contradictory, but equally glum, notion known as Fermi's paradox. As first postulated by its namesake, Enrico Fermi, the Nobel Prize–winning physicist who helped lay the groundwork for the atom bomb and nuclear energy, this celebrated head-scratcher poses the question: If there are hundreds of billions of galaxies, each with hundreds of billions of stars, why isn't there any evidence of intelligent life somewhere else in the universe? There are a number of logical explanations for this phenomenon, including the possibility that there are in fact aliens out there but they are too far away in space and time to contact us, or there are some other yet undiscovered communication problems; or that they are out there somewhere, maybe quite close by, but they are (perhaps wisely) avoiding us. Still, with between 200 and 400 billion stars in our galaxy, and about that same number of galaxies in the universe, and given the huge amount of time that has passed since the Big Bang—at least 10 billion years—you would think we would have heard or seen *something* by now.[8]

We are sorry to report, however, that we may in fact be utterly alone, and truly unique, and that our very solitude is not evidence of our exceptional achievement, but rather a strong predictor of our inevitable extinction. This dismal conclusion is based on the concept of the "Great Filter," a descriptive term for the plausible assumption that all life needs to go through nine critical stages on the path of existence—and overcome some major hurdles—to get to the point where it is capable of interstellar communication and travel:

1. It must appear in its simplest form on a hospitable planet.
2. It must display a reproductive capacity, like RNA.
3. It must evolve into a simple single-cell prokaryotic organism.
4. It must evolve into a more complex eukaryotic single-cell organism.
5. It must develop sexual reproduction.
6. It must evolve into multicell life-forms.
7. It must eventually evolve into tool-using animals with large brains.
8. It must create a twenty-first-century-level civilization.
9. And . . . it can then proceed to colonize the universe.

Alas, it seems to be a safe bet that although life that has made it through steps one through six may indeed be abundant throughout the universe, there is some unavoidable event or universal negative factor lurking in steps eight and nine that acts as an insurmountable barrier to further evolution, and that like just about every living thing that has ever come down the cosmic pike, we are about to hit the wall, big-time. As Oxford philosophy professor Nick Bostrom stated the case: "There must be (at least) one Great Filter—an evolutionary step that is extremely improbable—somewhere on the line between Earth-like planet and colonizing-in-detectable-ways civilization. If the Great Filter isn't in our past, we must fear it in our (near) future. Maybe almost every civilization that develops a certain level of technology causes its own demise."[9]

fiat currencies. See: **stagflation.**

Fiesta Ware. See: **ceramics.**

fine-particle-pollution-related health effects. See: **exercise, indoor; exercise, outdoor; street canyons; warm, sunnny days.**

fire retardants. See: **carpeting, new; salmon, farmed.**

fireworks permits. See: **Nanny Statism.**

fiscal child abuse. *Fiscal child abuse* is a term coined by Boston Uni-

versity economics professor Laurence J. Kotlikoff and his colleague, Richard Munroe, to describe the irresponsible, and unsustainable, levels of debt that today's adults (Kotlikoff terms them the "gerontocracy"[10]) are imposing on "young and future Americans." "We've spent six decades passing the generational buck," Kotlikoff and Munroe point out, "taking ever-larger sums from the young and giving them to the old, while promising the young their turn, when old, to expropriate their own offspring. This massive Ponzi scheme is turning the American Dream into the American Nightmare." Can anything be done about this calamity? The good news, say Kotlikoff and Munroe, is that indeed something can. All that's required, they suggest, is to scrap our health care system, to eliminate Social Security and replace it with mandatory saving in "personal security accounts" whose assets are invested in a diversified global index fund, to get rid of the current income tax system in favor of a tax on consumption, and to slash defense spending by "declaring victory in our unwinnable wars and bringing the troops home." "This all may sound radical," Kotlikoff and Munroe conclude. "It's not. Our progeny only have 100 cents out of every dollar they earn to surrender to Uncle Sam. And if their tax rates get too high, they will have a simple response: 'Hasta la vista, baby.'"[11]

fish breath. See: **omega-3 fish oil supplements.**

flame retardants. See: **carpeting, new; salmon, farmed.**

flares, solar. See: **severe space weather events.**

flash crash. A little after 2:42 P.M. on May 6, 2010, the Dow Jones In-

dustrial Average plummeted 600 points in five minutes flat, which, when combined with an earlier sharp decline of over 300 points, added up to a nerve-shattering plunge of almost 1,000 points, or about 10 percent of the entire value of the widely followed financial index.

Some twenty minutes later, the stock exchange ticker recorded an equally abrupt and inexplicable rally, and the Dow recovered virtually all of the precipitous 600-point drop in share prices, finally closing the dizzying trading day with a drop of about 350 points, or just over 3 percent of total market capitalization. According to an early report on the Big Board donnybrook issued by the Securities and Exchange Commission (SEC), "almost 200 stocks briefly lost almost all their value during the flash crash, trading in many cases for a single penny." [12]

A more comprehensive analysis, issued in September 2010 by the SEC and its sister regulatory agency, the Commodity Futures Trading Commission (CFTC), attributed the wild gyrations in the markets to the high-speed computer algorithm–driven trading of huge blocks of stocks in an effort to reap individually minuscule but cumulatively significant profits from tiny movements in the prices of millions of shares. This massive surge in trading led to what one researcher termed "order flow toxicity" as liquidity providers—potential buyers of cheap stocks—deserted the market en masse when mind-bending bid-and-asked price mismatches began to dominate the stock quotations. [13]

In an opinion piece published exactly one year after the debacle, former Delaware senator Edward Kaufman and Michigan senator Carl Levin neatly summarized the Wall Street roller-coaster ride: "One year ago, the stock market took a brief and terrifying nose-dive. Almost a trillion dollars in wealth momentarily vanished." The two market-savvy solons went on to offer what proved to be an eerily prophetic prediction of the extreme market volatility that took place just a few months later, in August of 2011, warning that "algorithmic trading has caused mini-flash crashes since, and surveys suggest that most investors and analysts believe it's only a matter of time before the Big One." Bemoaning the lack of effective oversight of the markets provided by the SEC and the CFTC, the pair of farsighted lawmakers concluded ominously—and presciently, "They're right to be afraid." [14]

flesh-eating pneumonia. See: **superbugs.**

flip-flops. "Ah, the casual, comfortable flip-flop: A symbol of summertime, an emblem of relaxation—and a *harbinger of death*?" So

 writes the *Today* show's Laura T. Coffey in the lead paragraph of an article provocatively titled "Can Your Flip-Flops Kill You?" "OK, well, that may be overstating it a little bit," Coffey confesses, "but not by too terribly much, health experts say." [15] The risks associated with flip-flops are numerous, and they are, indeed, serious.

First of all, according to a recent study conducted at Auburn University, when you wear flip-flops, you tend to scrunch your toes to keep the flip-flop on your foot while your heel is lifted in the air. This motion, the researchers report, "stretches the plantar fascia, the connective tissue that runs from heel to toe, causing inflammation, pain along the sole, heel spurs and tired feet in general." Furthermore, according to the Auburn team, the flip-flop wearers they studied noticeably "altered their gait, taking shorter strides and turning their ankles inward, likely to keep the flip-flop from falling off." Long-term ankle and hip problems, the researchers warn, will most likely be the result.[16]

Second, notes Mallika Marshall, M.D., of Massachusetts General Hospital, "Flip-flops don't offer much in the way of support: no arch support, no heel cushioning, and no shock absorption. That can cause foot pain, tendonitis, and even sprained ankles if you trip." A third reason wearing flip-flops can be dangerous, adds Dr. Marshall, is that "your toes and feet are exposed, making them susceptible to falling objects or people stepping on your toes. Doctors are seeing more nail injuries and broken or bruised toes, which wouldn't happen if you covered the front of your feet." [17]

The fourth concern is a far more disquieting one—the fact that wearing flip-flops increases your risk of contracting a deadly melanoma. "Flip-flops . . . leave the tops of the feet dangerously exposed to sun damage," cautions Dr. Rebecca Tung, director of the Division of Dermatology at Loyola University Medical Center in Maywood, Illinois. Compounding the problem, Dr. Tung advises, is that people frequently forget to apply sunscreen to their feet before they venture outside wearing flip-flops.[18] "Skin cancer on the feet can be really dangerous because the spots are easier to miss, especially if they're between the toes," notes Mass. General's Dr. Marshall.[19]

And finally we come to our fifth and last flip-flop problem: the risk that you'll contract a painful, or possibly even a fatal, infectious disease as a result of wearing them. According to *Today*'s Laura Coffey, the University of Miami recently set up a mobile lab to test people's flip-flops and found that they were covered with bacteria from fecal matter, skin, and respiratory germs, microbes that cause yeast infection and diaper rash, and, even worse, the germ *Staphylococcus aureus,* which, as Philip M. Tierno Jr., Ph.D., the director of clinical microbiology and immunology at New York University's Langone Medical Center, warns, "can make you very sick or kill you." Not only can these germs easily get on your (mostly) unprotected flip-flop-clad feet, Tierno says, but, since flip-flops frequently need to be adjusted for comfort because "they flop around," we touch them with our hands far more frequently than we do regular shoes.[20] "Shoes perform two functions," concludes Pennsylvania podiatrist Dr. Richard Maleski. "They protect your feet and support your feet." Quite obviously, flip-flops do neither.[21]

floor lamps, halogen torchiere, pre-1997. See: **yard sales.**

floss, dental. See: **dental floss.**

flu pandemic. Although the issuance of several false alarms predict-
ing influenza outbreaks—particularly the swine flu panic of 1976 and the more recent bird flu scare—and the widespread availability of generally effective annual flu shots have combined to make the threat of a global epidemic appear pretty remote,[22] it's worth noting that as of 2006, flu still retained its coveted number one position on the "The Top 10: Epidemic Hall of Infamy" list prepared by the University of California at Davis. When you consider that the next nine presumably less catastrophic global contagions on the dishonor roll are small-pox, plague, cholera, tuberculosis, malaria, AIDS, yellow fever, polio, and measles, it becomes apparent that this mostly relatively mild viral infection is in fact nothing to sneeze at.[23]

The reason for the heightened concern? Although the other

historic scourges on the horror roster of communicable disease are either currently fairly well contained, or sufficiently well understood to be treatable to some degree with modern medical interventions, influenza remains something of a medical mystery. And much of what we *do* know about the potential lethality of this ubiquitous bug comes from studies of the catastrophic Spanish Flu Epidemic of 1918, whose impact was neatly summarized by FLU.gov: "It is estimated that approximately 20 to 40 percent of the worldwide population became ill and that over 50 million people died. Between September 1918 and April 1919, approximately 675,000 deaths from the flu occurred in the U.S. alone. Many people died from this very quickly. Some people who felt well in the morning, became sick by noon, and were dead by nightfall."[24]

And a report prepared for the Centers for Disease Control by Dr. Jeffrey Tautenberger of the Armed Forces Institute of Pathology and Dr. David Morens of the National Institute of Allergies and Infectious Diseases emphasized that the factors that led to the extreme lethality of the twentieth century's notorious "killer flu"—death rates five to twenty times higher than predicted, the fact that healthy young adults were most likely to die from the disease, and the near-simultaneous onslaught of three separate severe waves of infection within one year—remain a profound epidemiological puzzle, and that "even with modern antiviral and antibacterial drugs, vaccines, and prevention knowledge, the return of a pandemic virus equivalent in pathogenicity to the virus of 1918 would likely kill more than 100 million people worldwide. A pandemic virus with the pathogenic potential of some recent H5N1 avian virus outbreaks could cause substantially more deaths." As for the likelihood of a recurrence in the near future of what they termed "the Mother of All Pandemics," Drs. Tautenberger and Morens stressed that "predictions are only educated guesses. We can only conclude that since it happened once, analogous conditions could lead to an equally devastating pandemic."[25]

"flu, voodoo." See: **zombification.**

foggy thinking. See: **caffeine.**

food choices, increased government control over. See: **Nanny Statism.**

food containers, plastic. Before using a plastic food container, warns *Real Simple* magazine, you should call the 800 number of the company that made it and ask if it contains polycarbonate plastic. If it does, you should stop in your tracks and seriously consider storing your edibles in something else.[26] Why? Because as Nena Baker describes in her book *The Body Toxic,* the chemical building block of polycarbonate plastic is **bisphenol A** (q.v.), a chemical linked to "prostate and breast cancer, urogenital abnormalities in baby boys, a decline in semen quality, early onset of puberty in girls, type 2 diabetes, obesity, and neurobehavioral problems such as attention-deficit/hyperactive disorder." But if you're not going to use plastic food containers, what should you use instead? Baker suggests you consider aluminum containers (although, before using one, she advises, you should "make sure the container is not lined with bisphenol-A-containing resin.")[27] See: **aluminum.** See also: **bisphenol A.**

food, organic. See: **organic food.**

food, overcooked. See: **overcooked food.**

food riots. See: **agflation.**

food security, reduced. See: **global warming.**

food thermometers. "Using a food thermometer is the only sure way of knowing if your food has reached a high enough temperature to destroy foodborne bacteria," the U.S. Department of Agriculture advises. In fact, they feel so strongly about this that they've even created a delightful anthropomorphic food thermometer character, Thermy, to deliver the catchy message that "it's safe to bite when the temperature is right!" "Most people think they know when food is 'done' just by 'eyeballing it,'" the USDA explains. "They look at it and trust their experience. Experience is good, but it sometimes can be misleading. For instance, cooking by color is definitely misleading. Meat color—pink or brown—can fool you! Think about this . . . 1 out of every 4 hamburgers turns brown in the middle *before* it has reached a safe internal temperature, according to recent USDA research." Because it's essential to make certain that the *interior* of your food—as well as the outside—has been heated sufficiently to eliminate all pathogens that could sicken or kill you and your family, Alaska's Food Safety and Sanitation Program strongly recommends that you invest in a long-stem metal probe thermometer that's easy to plunge deep into whatever you're cooking.[28]

Ironically, however, using a long-stem metal probe thermometer can actually *cause* the inner portions of your kitchen masterpieces to become contaminated. The reason is that there are more likely to be dangerous germs on the *outside* of the food you purchase than on the inside. Therefore, unless you're positive you've cooked the outside of your food long enough, and at a high enough temperature, to kill every last microbe, surface pathogens can be rubbed off onto your thermometer as you insert it, and you will just end up transferring germs from the surface to the innards of the dish you're preparing. Furthermore, some food thermometers contain mercury or glass; you should make sure yours doesn't, or it could break and contaminate your food, perhaps fatally.[29] And finally, warns the University of Mississippi's National Food Services Management Institute, don't ever forget to wash your food thermometer, thoroughly sanitize it (by dipping its stem into a sanitizing solution or wiping it with a sanitizing wipe), and properly air-dry it before and after every use; it's hard to imagine a better microbial breeding ground than a moist, food-soiled thermometer stem.[30] See also: **overcooked food; undercooked food; acrylamide.**

food, undercooked. See: **undercooked food.**

foods, fried. See: **acrylamide; trans fats.**

foods, starchy. See: **acrylamide.**

fossil fuels. In the aftermath of the Fukushima nuclear disaster,  Japan announced that it was abandoning plans to expand its nuclear industry, and a number of other countries, including Switzerland, Germany, and China, slapped an embargo on the construction of new or replacement nuclear power plants. Indeed, in May 2011, German chancellor Angela Merkel announced that her government intended to close down eight of her country's oldest reactors immediately, and to phase out nuclear power entirely by the year 2022.[31] Such responses to the dramatic explosions and frantic corrective procedures at the multireactor array along the tsunami-battered Japanese coast seem reasonable enough, given the widespread fears about unseen and insidious contamination from deadly radiation and the inescapable, if inexact, association in our minds between the power plants that light our cities and the atomic bombs that were designed to destroy them. Yet, paradoxically, if these and other similar energy policy revisions prevail, they will lead to the deaths of many more people than have perished in every nuclear power-plant accident in history combined, including Chernobyl, Three Mile Island, and Daiichi, even allowing for the most pessimistic estimate of the eventual toll from the cascade of system failures at all six of Tokyo Electric's malfunctioning units at its stricken nuclear power station.

This grim conclusion is based on a simple calculation: Regardless of the trivial contributions of wind and solar power, less electricity generated from nuclear power equals more electricity generated from the burning of fossil fuels, particularly coal. And as Joseph Romm, an energy expert at the Center for American Progress in Washington, D.C., succinctly stated, "There is no question. Nothing is worse than fossil fuels for killing people."[32] According to an exhaustive examination undertaken by the International Energy Agency of the entire life cycle of every significant form of large-scale commercial electric power production, from extraction of the consumed resource through post-use disposal, including deaths from accidents and long-term exposure to emissions and radiation, hydrocarbon combustion in general and coal in particular are orders of magnitude more lethal than nuclear power.[33] Specifically, calculations by Brian Wang of the Next

Big Future blog indicate that for every person killed by nuclear power generation, adjusted for the same amount of power produced, nine hundred deaths are attributable to oil, and—largely because of the fine particles emitted by coal-fired power plants—a staggering four thousand are killed by coal.[34]

Furthermore, as the Clean Air Task Force points out, "the burning of fossil fuels for energy is the primary cause of global warming. Scientists say that the Earth could warm by an additional 7.2°F during the 21st century if we fail to reduce fossil fuel emissions. As emissions escalate, so too does the potential environmental devastation, while our chances of mitigating them rapidly slip away."[35] In sum: Those eerily glowing uranium fuel rods may creep us out, but it's that cozy bituminous blaze that is doing us in. See: **nuclear energy.** See also: **coal; global warming.**

401(k) plans. Perhaps things have been a bit hard for you lately, what with economic difficulties and all. But when everything else fails, you have your 401(k) plan to see you through, right? Well, here's what Dan Solin, senior vice president of Index Funds Advisors and author of the best-selling *The Smartest Investment Book You'll Ever Read,* has to say about 401(k) plans: "These plans are a cesspool of high costs, hidden fees, conflicts of interest, poor investment choices, and deception about the real fiduciary status of advisors. As a consequence, participants have low returns, corresponding low balances and dim prospects for retirement with dignity."[36]

fracking. See: **hydraulic fracturing.**

fragrances. "One giant whiff of a perfume spray," warns Scottsdale immunologist Dr. Doris Rapp, "can create a medical emergency and cause some, who are very sensitive, to collapse or be unable to stand and walk." Indeed, Dr. Rapp adds, the significant portion of the population who have "chemical sensitivities" are "almost always extremely ill or incapacitated by exposures to innumerable scented items." And the *chemicals* in perfume products are just the tip of the iceberg, Dr. Rapp continues. Fragrances, she points out, can also "contain urine and feces. They can be toxic and cause allergies and changes in behavior." [37] The solution, Silent Menace.com advises, is simple: "Go without; you're not going to shrivel up and die. On the contrary, you'll be doing yourself and many others a big favor." [38] See also: **cosmetics.**

frankfurters. See: **hot dogs.**

fraudulent tax returns. See: **identity theft.**

french fries. "French fries are the worst item on the menu at fast food restaurants," opines Dr. Ben Kim, popular radio-show host and editor of the nutritional website Dr.BenKim .com. "Sure," he admits, "cola, processed cheese, and factory farmed meats aren't much better. But every ounce of those crunchy, salty, tasty fries [is] so harmful to health that I wouldn't be surprised if several years from now, the government and general public come to view French fries the way that we view cigarettes today." What is it that makes Dr. Kim so adamant about fries? "They are loaded with trans fats, known to cause immune system depression, cardiovascular disease, diabetes, obesity, sterility, birth defects, decreased ability to produce breast milk, loss of vision, and weakening of your bones and muscles," Dr. Kim warns. And wait, there's more. "French fries are also high in acrylamide, a carcinogen that is found in starchy foods that have been fried or baked at high temperatures," Dr. Kim points out. "The amount of acrylamide found in a large order of French fries at a fast food restaurant is at least 300 times higher than what the Environmental Protection Agency allows in a glass of drinking water." [39] See also: **acrylamide; trans fats.**

fructose. See: **high-fructose corn sugar (HFCS); sugar.**

fructosification of America, the. See: **sugar.**

fruit, canned. See: **bisphenol A.**

fruit juice. On May 5, 2001, the American Academy of Pediatrics

issued an official policy statement warning about the potential detrimental effects of fruit juice, which, it counsels ominously, can lead to "obesity, the development of cavities, diarrhea, and other gastrointestinal problems, such as excessive gas, bloating and abdominal pain." Instead of drinking fruit juice, therefore, the Academy recommends that children eat whole fruits, such as apples, oranges, and pears.[40] See: **fruits, whole; apples; oranges**; and **pears.**

fruit juice bottles. See: **bisphenol A.**

fruits, whole. "Many of us have come to believe that eating healthier

means eating lots of fruits and vegetables," writes well-known nutritionist and radio personality Dr. Ben Kim. But, he adds, "My experiences and research have led me to believe that too much fruit can be harmful to your health." The problem, of course, is that many whole fruits are high in sugar content; as a result, a high-fruit diet, Dr. Kim warns, can "lead to problems involving the hormones that regulate your blood sugar; insulin, glucagon, and growth hormone. A chronic imbalance of these hormones is a sure way to develop cardiovascular disease and diabetes." Does this mean that fruit lovers are predestined to a life plagued by ill health? Hardly, says Dr. Kim. If you make a point of eating some dark green lettuce, celery sticks, and avocado along with your fruit, he advises, "the mineral density in these green foods will help to dampen the unhealthy effect."[41] (See **lettuce; celery**; and **leafy green vegetables.**)

fuel-substitution programs, government subsidized. See: **agflation.**

fungi, extremophilic. See: **dishwashers.**

G

gamma ray bursts. See: **IK Pegasi.**

gas, intestinal. See: **fruit juice; omega-3 fish oil supplements.**

"geeks bearing gifts." See: **Trojan horse.**

"gender-bender" effects. See: **oranges.**

gendercide. See: **sex-selective abortion.**

genital disorders. See: **cosmetics.**

genital herpes. See: **sexually transmitted diseases; condoms.**

geomagnetic reversal. The discovery of ancient samples of volcanic rock magnetized in an opposite direction from the globe's current north-south orientation indicates that the planet's magnetic field gradually weakens and then abruptly switches position every 300,000 years or so. The paleomagnetic data provides clear evidence of tens of thousands of such polarity shifts in geologic history, some of them extremely sudden and short-lived. Although no apparent pattern to the frequency or duration of the events has been identified, the last reversal occurred 780,000 years ago, and thus the earth would seem to be long overdue for a potentially catastrophic flip-flop. Some alarming indications of a pending inversion have been detected in recent years, including a puzzling (and vaguely unsettling) migration of the north magnetic pole out of Canada and toward Russia at nearly forty miles per year and a 15 percent decline in the intensity of the planetary magnetic field since 1840, calculated from a careful examination of two centuries of ships' logs' entries that meticulously recorded contemporary compass recalibrations. The exact impact of what could be a very rapid collapse and somewhat more gradual reestablishment in a literally polar-opposite alignment of our terrestrial coordinates is very hard to predict, but no less authoritative a source than the Institute of Physics notes somberly that "since the earth's magnetic field protects us from potentially harmful radiation from the Sun, as it [the field] fades we could well be faced with a disaster on a global scale."[1]

geomagnetic storms. See: **severe space weather events.**

geothermal energy. The idea of tapping into the essentially limitless

thermal resources trapped deep beneath the earth's surface to heat buildings directly or to generate electricity with heat pumps is increasingly attractive as alternative energy sources, like gas, oil, coal, nuclear, and even hydropower either approach depletion or are seen to entail unacceptable levels of environmental risk. It is a pity to throw cold water, as it were, on this promising technology, but the disappointing outcome of several recent efforts to extract commercially useful amounts of geothermal energy raises some serious questions about the viability of large-scale, and even small-scale, projects designed to exploit this power source. In mid-December of 2009, AltaRock Energy abruptly canceled an effort to drill two-mile-deep boreholes into bedrock in the Geysers, a seismically active region one hundred miles north of San Francisco, although they did manage to go straight through $6 million in federal stimulus money and another $30 million in venture capital in the process.

Not everyone was unhappy with the outcome. Jacque Felber, a resident of nearby Anderson Springs, California, whose hometown is regularly jolted by quakes generated by far smaller, conventional geothermal projects in the area, was thrilled. "I'm just so relieved," he said. "I'm afraid one of these days it's going to knock my house off the hill."[2] One day earlier, a similar, and singularly ill-advised project in Basel, Switzerland, was called off after a series of relatively minor earthquakes triggered by geothermal drilling caused nearly $10 million in damage to buildings in the earthquake-prone city, which was leveled by a massive temblor in 1356. The geothermal project's director, former oilman Markus O. Haring, faced criminal charges for "reckless damage of structures," and according to a deadpan statement from Nicholas Deichmann of the Swiss Seismological Service, "As for Basel, it is clear that this project has been buried."[3]

And in a vivid demonstration that even small geothermal undertakings can have big impacts, in 2008, the town council of the picturesque village of Staufen im Breisgau on the edge of the Black Forest in southern Germany decided to expand a plan to refurbish the sixteenth-century town hall to include the installation of a twenty-first-century geothermal power system to heat the medieval structure. Seven five-hundred-foot deep geothermal holes were drilled into the ground beneath the venerable edifice, and within days, cracks began appearing in its facade and in the superstructures of sixty-eight other buildings in the town's historic center as the entire burg sank several millimeters into *terra* that was no longer very *firma*. "I have never encountered anything like this," said Robert Breder, a structural engineer hired to investigate the problem. Staufen's mayor, Michael Benitz, was equally nonplussed. "Will the earth continue to sink, or is it going to stop?" he wondered. "If it does stop now, then we will have got away lightly, but if it does continue it could turn out to be quite bad."[4]

gerontocracy. See: **fiscal child abuse.**

gherkins. See: **high-fructose corn syrup (HFCS).**

Glacier Peak. See: **Cascade Range volcanoes; lahars.**

glaucoma. See: **neckties.**

global warming. According to the *Fourth Assessment Report* issued in 2007 by the Intergovernmental Panel on Climate Change, the average temperature of the earth's surface air and ocean waters increased during the twentieth century by at least one degree Fahrenheit due to an increased concentration of atmospheric greenhouse gases, particularly carbon dioxide. In the report, the IPCC—established by the United Nations Environment Program and the World Meteorological Organization to "provide the world with a clear scientific view on the current state of knowledge in climate change and its potential environmental and socio-economic impacts"—projected a further, and far more dramatic, increase during the twenty-first century of anywhere between two and nearly twelve degrees Fahrenheit, with the large uncertainty in the estimates due to the difficulty of predicting the effects, or for that matter, the likelihood, of any serious worldwide efforts at mitigation of the principal contributing factors, most significantly the combustion of fossil fuels.[5]

Although the report presents credible evidence that the impacts of this potential climatological catastrophe—including rising sea levels, more extreme weather events, subtropical desertification, reduced food security, species extinctions, arctic melting, Gulf Stream disruption, coral die-off, and ocean acidification—are already manifesting themselves, the topic itself remains controversial. Many political leaders, religious figures, and even some serious scientists insist that these environmental changes are part of a natural planetary process that has produced long periods of both cooling and warming many times in the past millions of years of geologic time without any human influence; some even claim that an increase of carbon dioxide in the atmosphere, whether caused by humans or not, would actually benefit the world more than it would harm it.[6]

So, is global warming a hoax, and are we victims of some sort of mass hysteria, or should we be scared? Well, consider this—the scariest person in America, and arguably one of the scariest people in the entire world, is himself deeply concerned about the matter. In a recent jailhouse interview in the maximum-security prison in California where he is serving a life sentence, convicted multiple murderer and certified expert on apocalyptic behavior Charles Manson deflected a question about whether he would pose any further danger to society if he managed to win his release after a parole hearing next year by pointing to what he termed "a greater danger"—global warming. The normally hard-to-alarm homicidal leader of the notorious Manson Family sex cult broke a twenty-year silence to issue a stern warning about the existential risks facing the terrestrial ecosystem. "Everyone's God and if we don't wake up to that there's going to be no weather because our polar caps are melting because we are doing bad things to the atmosphere," the demonic prophet declared. "The automobiles and fossil fuels are destroying the atmosphere and we won't have air to breathe. If we don't change that as rapidly as I'm speaking to you now, if we don't put the green back on the planet and put the trees back that we've butchered, if we don't go to war against the problem . . ."[7]

Manson concluded his admonitory remarks at this point without specifying any of the potential consequences of mankind's possible inaction, but it's worth noting that he then went on to attack President Obama as "an idiot" and "a slave of Wall Street,"[8] thus incidentally adding considerably to his credibility as a persuasive soothsayer among conservative commentators who are normally dismissive of predictions of a coming worldwide environmental disaster. Adding even more weight to his words, Manson made it clear that he was not an evil brainwashing guru, insisting, "I don't tell people what to do. They know what to do. If they don't know what to do they don't come around me because I'm very mean. I am a very mal hombre, nasty. I'm in the bull ring. I run in the bull ring with the heart of the world."[9] He also displayed considerable ecological insight, saying of himself, in Spanish: *"La Hierba Mala No Muere"*—"weeds never die."[10] See: **global warming, attempting to mitigate.** See also: **agflation; coral reef bleaching; sea levels, rising.**

global warming, attempting to mitigate. According to many scien-

tists and politicians, recent attempts to combat the perceived threat of human-caused global warming are not only scientifically unfounded, but could also prove environmentally, economically, and geopoliti-
cally counterproductive, if not downright calamitous.

For example, Richard Lindzen, Alfred P. Sloan Professor of Meteorology at MIT, notes that "at the heart of it, we're talking of a few tenths of a degree change in temperature." And because the reported temperature rise itself is "so unspectacular," he adds, "we have developed all sorts of fear of prospect scenarios—of flooding, of plague, of increased storminess when the physics says we should see less. I think it's mainly just like little kids locking themselves in dark closets to see how much they can scare each other and themselves."[11] John R. Christy, Ph.D., Distinguished Professor of Atmospheric Science at the University of Alabama in Huntsville, agrees. "We have found that climate models and popular surface temperature data sets overstate the changes in the real atmosphere and that actual changes are not alarming," he told the House Ways and Means Committee in 2009. Indeed, he testified, "the actions being considered to 'stop global warming' will have an imperceptible impact on whatever the climate will do, while making energy more expensive, and thus have a negative impact on the economy as a whole." "The message here," he concluded, is that "if energy costs rise, the price the American economy will pay, especially the poorest among us, will be high—yet there will be virtually no impact on emissions or climate." [12]

Christy is also deeply worried about the fact that regulations restricting greenhouse gas emissions—such as, for example, rules limiting the burning of carbon-based fuels—could hit the developing world particularly hard. "I've always believed that establishing a series of coal-fired power plants in countries such as Kenya (with simple electrification to the villages) would be the best advancement for the African people and the African environment," he says. "An electric light bulb, a microwave oven and a small heater in each home would make a dramatic difference in the overall standard of living . . . [So] if you're talking about preventing energy from expanding in the Third World, you're condemning people to perpetual poverty. What's more, it's economic development that creates the cleanest environments we have. You don't find clean rivers or clean air in the poorest countries." [13]

And biochemist Arthur B. Robinson, Ph.D., a onetime colleague of Nobel laureate Linus Pauling who founded and runs the Oregon Institute of Science and Medicine, is convinced that if scientists would stop wringing their hands, they'd see that the carbon dioxide we're pouring into the air is actually helping us, not hurting us. "Human use of coal, oil, and natural gas has not harmfully warmed the Earth, and the extrapolation of current trends shows that it will not do so in the foreseeable future," Robinson declares in a paper he coauthored with his son and fellow chemist, Noah. "The CO_2 produced does, however, accelerate the growth rates of plants and also permits plants to grow in drier regions. Animal life, which depends upon plants, also flourishes, and the diversity of plant and animal life is increased. Human activities are producing part of the rise in CO_2 in the atmosphere. Mankind is moving the carbon in coal, oil, and natural gas from below ground to the atmosphere, where it is available for conversion into living things. We are living in an increasingly lush environment of plants and animals as a result of this CO_2 increase. Our children will therefore enjoy an Earth with far more plant and animal life than that with which we now are blessed." [14]

In short, as U.S. senator James Inhofe of Oklahoma, then chairman of, and still the ranking Republican member of, the Senate Committee on Environment and Public Works, declared in a memorable 2003 floor speech opposing U.S. ratification of the Kyoto Protocol—an international treaty aimed at reducing greenhouse gas emissions— "the science underlying the global warming hypothesis has been thoroughly discredited . . . One has to wonder if the alarmists are simply ignorant of geological and meteorological history or simply ignore it to advance an agenda." "As it turns out," he continued, "Kyoto's objective has nothing to do with saving the globe. In fact it is purely political. A case in point: French President Jacques Chirac said during a speech at The Hague in November of 2000 that Kyoto represents 'the first component of an authentic global governance.' So, I wonder: are the French going to be dictating U.S. policy?" [15]

Perhaps even more instructive, Inhofe opined, was a statement made by the European Union's environmental commissioner, Margot Wallström, after President George W. Bush announced, in March 2001, that he was abandoning a campaign promise to regulate the amount of carbon dioxide emitted by power plants in the United States—a commitment several EU countries had already made. "[Bush] has to realize that the eyes of the outside world are on him, and what the U.S. is going to do," she said. "This is about international relations, this is about economy [and] about trying to create a level playing field for big businesses throughout the world." [16] "To me," concluded Inhofe, "Chirac's and Wallström's comments mean two things: 1) Kyoto represents an attempt by certain elements within the international community to restrain U.S. interests; and 2) Kyoto is an economic weapon designed to undermine the global competitiveness and economic superiority of the United States." [17]

gluten intolerance. See: **cake, piece of.**

gold, failure to invest in. "The debts assumed by the Western democ-

racies will overwhelm their economies and lead to the end of our current dollar-denominated, global currency regime," predicts Porter Stansberry, president of the investment research firm Stansberry Associates. "This has profound implications for Americans' standard of living and our empire's role in the world." According to Stansberry, when he says things like this, he's often asked, "When will the crisis begin?" The question astounds him, he says, because it "assumes we ought to ignore" such matters as the collapse of the housing market, the bankruptcy of American auto companies, the failure of the world's largest insurance company (AIG), the receivership of the nation's two largest mortgage lenders, Fannie Mae and Freddie Mac, and U.S. deficits in excess of $1 trillion per year. "How high will gas prices have to get before your neighbors notice something is wrong?" he asks. "How many banks will have to go under? How high will unemployment have to rise? How many cities will have to go bankrupt? Where's your threshold?" "That's why I'm telling everyone: Don't ask, 'When will the crisis begin?'" Stansberry concludes. "Instead, ask, 'Where can I get the best deal on gold and silver bullion to protect my family's finances?'"[18] See: **gold, investing in.**

gold, investing in. "Don't believe the hype about gold," warns Larry

Swedroe, director of research for the Buckingham Family of Financial Services and the author of *The Only Guide to a Winning Investment Strategy You'll Ever Need.* "In January 1980, the price of gold hit $850, an increase of over $700 from its price just five years earlier . . . The media was filled with headlines eerily similar to today's—fears of inflation, a falling dollar, huge budget deficits and foreign policy problems. By June 1982, the price of gold had fallen to less than $300 an ounce. And more than 20 years later, in January 2002, it was still trading at less than $300." Swedroe goes on to wonder how many investors would have stayed the course, waiting patiently and persistently pouring more money into gold to maintain its weighting in their portfolios, after watching gold drop hundreds of dollars and "then do nothing for more than 20 years." The answer, of course, is virtually none. "The historical record is that gold experiences long periods of poor re-turns," Swedroe concludes. "If you're not prepared for another such spell, you shouldn't invest in gold."[19]

And, beyond its substandard historical performance record, there are many other reasons why gold is a dreadful long-term bet for investors. As the popular personal investing blog SteadfastFinances .com points out, gold, like other **commodities** (q.v.), pays no divi-dends and costs far more to store than securities. Worse still, it has extremely limited industrial uses, and, as a result, is priced only at the value speculators are willing to pay for it. Therefore, compared to other commodities that can be used as food or fuel, gold is not even a dependable inflation hedge. "If the doom and gloom soothsayers are right," the blog asks, "would you prefer to own a bag of gold coins or a fully stocked pantry with rice and beans?"[20] See: **gold, failure to invest in.**

government control, increased. See: **Nanny Statism; lightbulb ef-ficiency standards; seat belts.**

Grand Central Terminal. One of the landmarks everybody likes to
 visit when they come to New York is the magnificent Beaux Arts Grand Central Terminal building, famous throughout the world for its sweeping marble stair-cases, its sixty-foot-high arched windows, its star-studded ceiling mural, and the iconic four-sided clock that graces its information booth. But would you still want to go there if you knew (as the *Wall Street Journal* reported in November, 2007) that a stroll through its granite corridors would dose you with more radiation—because of the radioactive radon gas that naturally occurs in granite—than a similar walk through a nuclear power plant?[21] And pity the poor commuters whose train rides to and from work leave them no choice but to subject themselves twice every day to a poten-tially deadly blast of alpha radiation from the walls of this all-too-aptly named "terminal." Perhaps it's time for them to ditch the railroad and take to the family car. See: **radon; commuting by car.** See also: **com-muting by train.**

granola bars. Do you sometimes snack on a granola bar, thinking to yourself, "Hey, this is *healthy,* and I'm proud of myself for forgoing a fattening and nonnutritious chocolate bar in favor of one of these!"? Well, Charles H. Booras, M.D., founder of the Jacksonville, Florida, Medical Park, has bad news for you. Contrary to its reputation, granola is actually "a high-fat, high sugar cereal," he writes. "Many granola bars are simply high-calorie cookies! The latest version—the granola candy bars—are no better for you than a Milky Way or Snickers, and they cost more, too!" Indeed, Dr. Booras has placed granola bars—along with such obvious offenders as soda pop, bacon, doughnuts, potato chips, and fast-food "superburgers"—on his list of "The Ten Worst Foods for Your Health."[22] See also: **high-fructose corn syrup (HFCS); sugar.**

grapes. "During their long transit from the southern hemisphere, im-  ported grapes are susceptible to *Botrytis cinerea* rot, which causes the fruits to split and leak," says *Prevention* magazine. "To prevent that, farmers spray aggressively with fungicides." As a result of such practices, imported grapes arrive in the States laden with dangerous pesticides; indeed, the U.S. Department of Agriculture found fourteen different toxic chemicals on a single sample of imported grapes. *Prevention*'s advice: If you're going to buy imported grapes, make sure they're organically grown. It'll cost you more, but it'll alleviate your contamination concerns.[23]

However, there's something else you need to know: The grapes at your local market—imported or domestic, organic or nonorganic—can be hazardous to your safety *even if you have no intention whatsoever of purchasing them.* The reason, as the Accident Compensation Helpline (whose mission is "to help those who've suffered an injury through no fault of their own to claim the compensation they are legally entitled to") points out, is the "very common" occurrence of grapes falling on produce department floors and causing patrons to slip, often suffering grievous bodily harm in the process.[24] "Produce sections are notoriously dangerous," says Chicago attorney Mark Solmor, who was interviewed by the *Chicago Tribune*[25] after his client Estela Maldonado suffered damage to her head and neck as a result of slipping on what the local NBC television station dubbed a "rogue grape" at a Food 4 Less store in suburban Cicero.[26] "I've had people fall on watermelon juice, rotten grapes and cherry tomatoes," Solmor told the newspaper. "I have never actually had the proverbial banana peel, though." But grapes, he emphasized, are *particularly* problematic. "They are very stealthy," he pointed out. "They are small, they are round and they roll. They don't make a sound when they hit the floor."[27] Stay alert.

gravitational keyhole. See: **Asteroid 99942 Apophis.**

gray goo. This colorful term was originated by the pioneering nanotechnology engineer K. Eric Drexler to depict a speculative but thought-provoking end-of-the-world scenario in which an unstoppable horde of minuscule spontaneously self-duplicating robots make infinite numbers of copies of themselves, ultimately displacing everyone and everything in sight. As Drexler so vividly describes the sequence of events that produces this theoretical molecular train wreck in his spooky page-turner, *Engines of Creation,* "Imagine such a replicator floating in a bottle of chemicals, making copies of itself . . . the first replicator assembles a copy in one thousand seconds, the two replicators then build two more in the next thousand seconds, the four build another four, and the eight build another eight. At the end of ten hours, there are not thirty-six replicators, but over 68 billion. In less than a day, they would weigh a ton; in less than four days, they would outweigh the Earth; in another four hours, they would exceed the mass of the Sun and all the planets combined." Although Drexler came to regret the playful name he had assigned to his apocalyptic hypothesis, he stressed that "though masses of uncontrolled replicators need not be gray or gooey, the germ 'gray goo' emphasizes that replicators able to obliterate life might be less inspiring than a single

species of crab grass. They might be 'superior' in an evolutionary sense, but this need not make them valuable."[28] See also: **knowledge-enabled mass destruction (KMD); robots; Singularity, the.**

Great Filter, the. See: **Fermi's paradox.**

Great Mill Disaster of May 2, 1878. See: **cake, piece of.**

Greenland ice sheet, prospective melting of. See: **sea levels, rising.**

Gulf Stream disruption. See: **global warming.**

gum chewing. See: **chewing gum.**

gyms. "It's the ultimate irony," says health writer Allison Janse. "Some things you do to stay healthy might just take you down." It was bad enough, she complains, to learn that all those "sprouts you struggled to stomach are a home to salmonella" (See: **sprouts**). "Now we hear that when we go to the gym to prolong our lives, we may be picking up germs that could do us harm." The catalyst for Janse's concern was a pathogen-hunting tour of New York health clubs conducted by New York University microbiologist Philip M. Tierno Jr., Ph.D., for the ABC television newsmagazine *Primetime*, during which Tierno found "nasty germs" on a disturbing percentage of the equipment and surfaces he examined. "The gym is an unusually effective place for the transmission of germs," Tierno reported. "All those people, all that exposed skin and all that sweat, can create a perfect storm for spreading infections . . . Spas, saunas, and showers in health clubs should all be posted: 'User beware: people deposit germs here daily.'"[29] For those determined, in the face of this troubling news, to frequent the gym anyway, Janse offers the following advice: "Use a disinfecting or sanitizing wipe before you use a machine or piece of equipment"; "don't touch your eyes, ears, mouth, or nose after touching the equipment"; "consider wearing long workout pants instead of shorts"; "wear flip-flops in the shower"; and "bring your own soap for showering." Also, she reminds us in conclusion, "you can catch crabs—otherwise known as pubic lice—from a sauna."[30] See: **exercise, lack of; flip-flops**; and **showers.** See also: **face touching.**

H

HAARP (High Frequency Active Auroral Research Program). See: **tectonic nuclear warfare.**

hairdryers, pre-1990. See: **yard sales.**

hairspray. Before you perform an effortless styling touch-up with a quick spritz from that handy can of an easy-to-apply pressurized beauty product, you might want to reflect on the recent discovery by a trio of scientists in Japan of a new species of extremophile bacteria that has evolved to survive and thrive inside containers of hairspray.[1] According to Mohammad Abdul Bakir, one of the bacteriologists who isolated and analyzed the previously unknown microorganism, the newly identified bug is "an aerobic, rod-shaped, Gram-positive, oxidase-negative, catalase-positive bacterial isolate, strain FCC-01T . . . originating as a contaminant of hairspray . . . [which] represents a novel species of the genus *Microbacterium.*"[2] It has not yet been established whether the newly discovered species poses a health threat, says Dr. Bakir, although similar species do, in fact, cause infections in humans.[3] It is also not clear whether the tiny aerosol-loving microbe possesses the hairlike external appendages known as *fimbriae* and *pili* that many of its fellow prokaryotes do, but if it does sport an array of delicate flagelliform protuberances on its outer cell wall, presumably those fine filaments of protein are exceptionally well groomed.

hair-straightening treatments. See: **Brazilian Blowout, the.**

halogen torchiere floor lamps. See: **yard sales.**

hamburgers. See: **slimeburgers; high-fructose corn syrup (HFCS).**

hammertoe. See: **high-heel shoes.**

hand dermatitis. See: **hand washing.**

hand sanitizers, alcohol-based. Alcohol-based hand sanitizers

 have been touted as a convenient alternative to washing one's hands with soap and water. For example, James Scott, a professor at the University of Toronto School of Public Health who specializes in occupational hazards in the workplace, states categorically that for diseases like H1N1 flu, alcohol-based hand sanitizers are "the absolute best front-line protection."[4] But are alcohol-based sanitizers truly safe and effective? Absolutely not, warns Dr. Jay Reubens, president and CEO of SafeHands, Inc., and a "leading authority on hand-hygiene products and behavioral modification education/training."[5] Among the "serious side effects" of alcohol-based hand sanitizer use, Reubens cautions, are "dry, cracked, frequently painful skin that has been stripped of its natural oils. Worse yet, alcohol-based products can actually increase the risk of exposure to the same pathogens that they were designed to kill. Germs can get trapped in the crevices of dry skin and increase the potential risk of cross contamination. Therefore, repeated daily use of alcohol-based hand sanitizers is a threat to public safety." And wait, there's more. As Dr. Reubens points out, alcohol-based instant hand sanitizers can also ignite easily, are intoxicating or poisonous if ingested by children, and are destructive to floors and other surfaces.[6] See: **hand washing.**

hand washing. Conventional wisdom has it that frequent hand wash-

 ing can be a useful measure in preventing the spread of a whole host of communicable diseases from the common cold and swine flu to meningitis and even the dread African filoviruses, Marburg and Ebola. Perhaps so, but before adopting such a regimen, you'd be wise to consider the sobering results of a study conducted by the National Institute of Occupational Safety and Health (NIOSH) and the American Academy of Dermatology. Frequent hand washing, they determined, dramatically increases the odds of one's developing "hand dermatitis," a condition characterized by patches of red, scaly, and inflamed skin; itchy blisters; pus-filled lesions, crusting, deformed nails, infection, and severe pain. To minimize the risk of incurring this extremely unpleasant and hard-to-cure affliction, Susan T. Nedorost, M.D., associate professor of dermatology at University Hospitals Case Medical Center in Cleveland and a coinvestigator on the NIOSH-AAD study, recommends substituting alcohol-based hand sanitizers for hand-washing whenever possible, and, when hand-washing is unavoidable, using a cream-based lotion immediately afterward.[7] (See **hand sanitizers, alcohol-based; lotions and creams.**)

handbags. See: **purses.**

hand-drying machines, hot-air. Because of the danger that towels in public restrooms can become contaminated by germs, an ever-growing number of public facilities have installed hot-air hand-drying machines near bathroom sinks. Of course, hand dryers with push-button activation mechanisms defeat their own purpose, because anyone who turns on the machine without having washed their hands properly will spread microbes onto the button. But can dryers that activate *automatically,* whenever your hands get near them, make hand-drying machines desirable, or even acceptable? Charles Gerba, Ph.D., the environmental microbiologist from the University of Arizona who has become famous, through his media appearances, as America's "Dr. Germ," is adamant on the subject. "Don't use the sanitary blower to dry your hands," he says. "It could collect bacteria from the air and then deposit them on your hands."[8] Indeed, a 2008 study performed by microbiologists at the University of Westminster in London found that people who used a hot-air hand-drying machine to dry their hands had two to three times as many bacteria on their hands as they did *before* they washed them.[9]

handkerchiefs. Do you think that the handkerchief you just wiped

your nose with was safe to use just because it was recently laundered? If so, think again, warns environmental microbiologist Charles P. Gerba, Ph.D., of the University of Arizona. "Basically," he says, "if you do undergarments in one load and handkerchiefs in the next, you're blowing your nose in what was in your underwear." That's why Gerba advises that whenever you do your laundry, you should always wash underclothing last, in a separate load. And, he urges, not only should you use chlorine bleach, but, when you're done, you should run an empty wash, with *just* the bleach. "It's mouthwash for the machine,"[10] he says. See: **chlorine bleach.**

hand-me-down dime-store trinkets. See: **yard sales.**

handshakes. Since at least the fifth century BC in ancient Greece, and

possibly for even longer, the common handshake has been one of the world's most universally practiced rituals of greeting, agreement, congratulation, or parting. But, as *U.S. News & World Report* health writer Angela Haupt points out, germs passed from one hand to the other during handshakes put both the shaker and the shakee at risk of spreading or contracting the flu or something even worse. "Wave hello instead," she suggests helpfully.[11]

Hansen's disease. See: **armadillos; leprosy.**

headaches. As Fremont, California, chiropractor Dr. Hans Freericks

points out, "headaches are so common that people often think that getting one is a normal part of life and give it little thought." But, he cautions, "like a fever, they can also be a warning sign." Indeed, they can. To be specific, headaches are an early symptom of brain fractures, brain tumors, bubonic plague, cerebral hemorrhages, dengue fever, Ebola hemorrhagic fever, encephalitis, lupus, malaria, meningitis, multiple sclerosis, strokes, and typhus (among many other potentially fatal diseases and conditions). Knowing this, are you prepared to ignore the admonition, on Dr. Freericks's website, that "headaches may be an indicator that an individual needs to see a chiropractor and discover chiropractic care for themselves"?[12]

health claims. Award-winning author, educator, and food activist Michael Pollan makes it a "rule of thumb" to avoid all food products that "come bearing health claims." Why? "Because a health claim on a food product is a good indication that it's not really food, and food is what you want to eat," he writes. Packaged foods bearing labels extolling their intrinsic health-giving qualities are apt to be heavily processed, Pollan adds, "and the claims are often dubious at best. Don't forget that margarine, one of the first industrial foods to claim that it was more healthful than the traditional food it replaced, turned out to give people heart attacks." Pollan points out that when "Kellogg's can boast about its Healthy Heart Strawberry Vanilla cereal bars, health claims have become hopelessly compromised." Indeed, he observes with disgust, food manufactures actually have to *pay* the American Heart Association to obtain the organization's endorsement. "Don't take the silence of the yams as a sign that they have nothing valuable to say about health," Pollan concludes.[13]

health clubs. See: **gyms.**

healthy eating. See: **orthorexia.**

height insufficiency. See: **underheight.**

hemorrhagic bulbous eruptions. See: **bedbugs.**

hemorrhoids. See: **toilet, sitting on the.**

herpes, genital. See: **sexually transmitted diseases; condoms.**

hiccups. Known in the medical community by a pair of more formal descriptive terms, either *synchronous diaphragmatic flutter* (SDF) or *singultus,* from a Latin word whose primary meaning translates roughly as "the act of catching one's breath while sobbing," hiccups certainly seem a pretty trivial condition, and although there have been some rare cases of "persistent, protracted, or intractable" bouts lasting for several years—and in one celebrated case, for six decades— they are generally seen as little more than a brief embarrassment.[14] But as Garry Wilkes, M.B.B.S., F.A.C.E.M., of Medscape Reference emphasizes, they can also be symptomatic of a whole series of potentially life-threatening disorders, including metabolic diseases, diabetes, kidney failure, pneumonia, stroke, multiple sclerosis, meningitis, encephalitis, traumatic brain injury, and chronic myrocardial ischemia[15]—a troubling tally of lurking afflictions also cited by veteran journalist Gene Weingarten in his compelling compendium of latent maladies, *The Hypochondriac's Guide to Life. And Death.,* who observes pointedly, "Hiccups are harmless, except when they aren't. No other commonly reported symptom has quite so many potentially dire explanations." And Weingarten adds to the danger list of unsuspected pathologies an even more worrisome potential postmortem diagnosis: "Hiccups have been associated with tumors in or around the lung, in the diaphragm, the liver, the pancreas, the stomach, and even the sigmoid colon, which is down near the butt and should not, by the grace of God, have anything to do with breathing."[16] With this in mind, it is worth noting that the secondary meaning in Latin of the word *singultus* is "death rattle."[17]

High Frequency Active Auroral Research Program (HAARP).
See: **tectonic nuclear warfare.**

high-fat, high-calorie food addiction. "Scientists have finally confirmed what the rest of us have suspected for years: Bacon, cheesecake, and other delicious yet fattening foods may be addictive," writes Sarah Klein of Health .com. The basis of her widely reprinted report is a study led by Paul J. Kenny, Ph.D., a molecular therapeutics expert at the Scripps Research Institute, in Jupiter, Florida, demonstrating that "high-fat, high-calorie foods affect the brain in much the same way as cocaine and heroin." Using an addictive drug and eating too much junk food both gradually overload the "pleasure centers" in the brain, Kenny explains. As a result, these pleasure centers eventually "crash," and to achieve the same pleasure—or just to feel normal—we need ever-increasing amounts of the drug or food. In other words, we become addicts. During the study, Kenny and his coresearcher, graduate student Paul M. Johnson, studied three groups of lab rats. The first group was fed regular rat food; the second was given carefully controlled amounts of cheesecake, bacon, pound cake, sausage, frosting, Ding Dongs, and other fattening foods; and the third was allowed to pig out on a similar menu of high-fat, high-calorie selections virtually anytime they wanted to. "Not surprisingly," Health. com's Klein reports, "the rats that gorged themselves on the human food quickly became obese. But their brains also changed. By monitoring implanted brain electrodes, the researchers found that the rats in the third group gradually developed a tolerance to the pleasure the food gave them and had to eat more to experience a high." And eat more they did—even the threat of an electric shock was not enough to deter them. And, if you keep eating bacon, cheesecake, sausages, and/or Ding Dongs, Kenny and Johnson's research tells us, not much will be able to deter *you* either.[18]

high-fructose corn syrup (HFCS). "An overweight America may be

fixated on fat and obsessed with carbs," writes Kim Severson in the *San Francisco Chronicle*, "but nutritionists say the real problem is much sweeter—we're awash in sugar. Not just any sugar, but high fructose corn syrup. The country eats more sweetener made from corn than from sugarcane or beets, gulping it down in drinks as well as in frozen food and baked goods. Even ketchup is laced with it."[19] Indeed, as Kate Hopkins points out on her immensely popular Accidental Hedonist website, the list of products containing HFCS includes applesauce, barbecue sauce, Bloody Mary and margarita mixes, breads, breakfast cereals and pastries, candy bars and hard candies, cakes, cookies, chocolate milk, cottage cheese, cough syrups, crackers, cranberry sauce, frozen pizza, fruit drinks, gherkins, granola bars, jams and jellies, packaged hamburgers and hot dogs, piecrust, relish, salad dressings, sandwich spreads, smoothies, soft drinks, soups, tacos, tonic water, and yogurt, not to mention the majority of dishes served in fast-food restaurants.[20]

According to award-winning author and journalist Michael Pollan, "it's probably no coincidence that the wholesale switch to corn sweeteners in the 1980's marks the beginning of the epidemic of obesity and Type 2 diabetes in this country. Sweetness became so cheap that soft drink makers, rather than lower their prices, super-sized their serving portions and marketing budgets. Thousands of new sweetened snack foods hit the market, and the amount of fructose in our diets soared."[21] As if this weren't bad enough, there is increasing evidence that the fructose in corn syrup is metabolized differently than other sugars, making it even more detrimental to our health than it otherwise would be[22] (For more about this, see: **sugar**).

And wait, we're just warming up. All the extra corn that is being grown to make high-fructose corn syrup is proving disastrous for our environment. Modern corn hybrids demand more nitrogen fertilizer and more pesticide than any other crop, Pollan writes. "Runoff from these chemicals finds its way into the groundwater and, in the Midwestern corn belt, into the Mississippi River, which carries it to the Gulf of Mexico, where it has already killed off marine life in a 12,000-square-mile area."[23] Still want to gorge yourself on high-fructose corn syrup? Larissa Phillips, who writes the Mothership Meals food blog for the New York *Daily News,* offers the following succinct recap of reasons to reconsider: "Because it's a crappy industrial product produced through weird enzymic processes, because it gets digested by the liver instead of the stomach, because it is part of our national corn-addiction, because it is so cheap that it is responsible for Big Gulps and the ever-sweetening of things like soup and ketchup, because it is the end product in our increasingly industrialized unsustainable food system and because it is at least in part responsible for the obesity epidemic,"[24] she suggests.

high-heel shoes. "Everyone knows that high heels are bad for you," says Danielle Barkema, a biomechanist at Iowa State University, and now, thanks to a scientific study she and her department chair, Philip E. Martin, Ph.D., conducted in 2010, we know exactly *how* bad. Using a sophisticated combination of kinesiology tools including cameras, sensors, accelerometers, and a force platform, Barkema and Martin observed fifteen women as they walked in heels of different heights and succeeded in capturing "motion and force data" that, as the ISU News Service put it, "could change the way millions of women select their footwear." The study demonstrated conclusively that wearing heels led women to change their posture, altering joint positions at the ankle, knee, hip, and trunk in ways that, over time, can often lead to chronic lower back pain. In addition, the researchers found that walking in high heels placed significantly more pressure on the inner side of women's knees—a known risk factor for joint degeneration and osteoarthritis.[25]

Furthermore, writes noted orthopedic surgeon Neal M. Blitz, D.P.M., F.A.C.F.A.S, of the Bronx-Lebanon Hospital in New York, there are a couple of common foot problems associated with high-heel and pointy-toe shoes that are so serious that they frequently require surgery. One of these is the bunion, a knoblike bony prominence that is formed when the "big toe is pushed toward the little one"; and the other is the hammertoe, a condition in which a toe becomes so buck-led or crooked that its knuckle may have to be removed. Clearly, Blitz feels that a "warning" is called for. "I am not the Surgeon General, but I am a Foot Surgeon, and, in General, wearing high heels may result in the development of foot deformities," he quips.[26]

So, in sum, "killer heels" couldn't be more aptly named, and you should quit wearing them cold turkey, correct? Emphatically not, says London physiotherapist Sammy Margo. If you go straight from high heels to flat pumps, "you risk pain and strain," she cautions. "You need to ease yourself into a new shoe style, wearing them for half an hour at first, then building up."[27] See: **low-heel shoes.**

"holding it in." How many times have you desperately needed to pee,

but have opted not to do so because there's no conve-nient restroom nearby, or, if there *is* one, it's so unsanitary-looking that you don't dare set foot in it? Well, we hardly need to tell you that "holding it in" can be a miserably *uncomfortable* experience. But what you may not know is that it can actually be hazardous to your health—perhaps even fatally so. The reason, as medical research conducted at the National Taiwan University has demonstrated, is that the stress of having a full bladder increases the average person's heart rate by nine beats per minute, and constricts the flow of blood by 19 percent.[28] Either, says Chang-Her Tsai, M.D., Ph.D., one of the authors of the study, could be enough to trigger a heart attack. Next time, advises *Men's Health* magazine, "pee in the bushes."[29]

hollandaise sauce. "Bacteria love hollandaise," warns New York chef

Anthony Bourdain, author of the best-selling culinary exposé *Kitchen Confidential.* "Most likely the stuff on your eggs was made hours ago and held on station. Equally disturbing is the likelihood that the butter used in the hollandaise is melted table butter, heated, clarified, and strained to get out all the bread crumbs and cigarette butts." "Hollandaise sauce is a veritable petri dish of biohazards," he concludes.[30]

holly. Do you look forward to "decking your halls with boughs of

holly" every Christmas season? Would you *still* look forward to it if you knew that the leaves, bark, seeds, and especially the berries of this pretty (if prickly) green-and-red plant contain the deadly poison theobromine? Indeed, the berries contain so much of this toxic alkaloid that, according to chemistry and biomedical sciences consultant Anne Marie Helmenstine, Ph.D., eating as few as twenty of them can kill you.[31] Well, you might ask, I would never even consider eating a *single* holly berry, so what's the problem? Yes, but would your child? Your dog? In short, you may want to consider a different holiday decoration. See: **ipecac; mistletoe; poinsettia.**

homes, acoustically toxic. See: **wind turbine syndrome.**

hormonal abnormalities. See: **air fresheners.**

hormone imbalance. See: **fruits, whole.**

hospitalization. See: **medical errors.**

hot chocolate mixes. See: **trans fats.**

hot dogs. Almost everyone is aware that hot dogs are among the least wholesome foods a person can eat. Not only are they high in fat and sodium content,[32] but they're also full of preservative chemicals such as nitrates, which, as the Cancer Prevention Coalition points out, break down, during the cooking and digestive processes, into dangerous carcinogens that have been associated with bladder cancer, leukemia, and brain tumors.[33] But, unbeknownst to many, hot dogs present another, more immediate, safety hazard that can actually lead to a quick and agonizing death. According to a recent policy statement issued by the American Academy of Pediatrics, wieners are responsible for more choking fatalities among children than any other food, causing a startling 17 percent of all food-related childhood asphyxiations. "If you were to find the best engineers in the world and ask them to design the perfect plug for a child's airway, you couldn't do much better than the hot dog," explains the chief author of the AAP statement, Gary Smith, M.D., director of the Center for Injury Research and Policy in Columbus, Ohio. "It is the right shape and the right size to wedge itself in and completely block a child's airway. It's only a matter of minutes before permanent brain damage and death occur."

Indeed, the AAP is concerned enough about this problem to suggest that hot dogs be "redesigned" to eliminate their cylindrical, potentially windpipe-clogging contours. "Some entrepreneur can come out with the Safety Dog, some new design that is kid-friendly and fun to eat and has everything that a traditional hot dog has," says Smith. But health activist Mike Adams, editor of NaturalNews.com, is not sanguine about this recommendation. "Personally," he writes, "I think we should engage in a little *truth in advertising* and just mandate that hot dogs be reshaped into fleshy cancer tumors. That way, you really know what you're eating. If these dogs resembled the diseased animals they're sometimes made from, choking would no longer be a problem at all because *no one would eat them in the first place!*"[34] See also: **high-fructose corn syrup (HFCS).**

hot, sunny days. See: **warm, sunny days.**

hot tubs. The benefits of hot tubs seem obvious: They can facilitate

relaxation, and they provide health-improving hydro-therapy and massage. But before settling into (much less installing) a hot tub, it's important to be aware that using one can lead to a quick, sudden, and horrifying death. And we're not just talking about the very real danger that the heat of the water often causes drowsiness, which, in turn, can result in accidental drowning (the most common cause of fatalities associated with hot tubs), or about the less widely known fact that raising your body temperature to a high level can cause heat stroke, heart attack, skin burns, and even brain damage. Rather, we're reflecting on the grossly underpublicized hazard of hot-tub drain suction, which, according to Kassidy Emmerson, author of "The Hidden Dangers of Hot Tubs," "can actually pull a person's body parts—especially arms and legs—towards it. Young children and the elderly can be especially powerless to this sucking action and they can become entrapped," she writes. "Worse yet, nearly half of the incidents involved disembowelment."[35] See also: **summertime sex.**

hotel bedspreads. See: **bedspreads, hotel.**

housing, failure to invest in. "If you don't buy a house now, you're

stupid or broke," writes Marc Roth in *Bloomberg Businessweek* magazine. "Well," he goes on to add, "you may not be stupid or broke. Maybe you already have a house and you don't want to move. Or maybe you're a Trappist monk and have forsworn all earthly possessions. Or whatever. But if you want to buy a house, now is the time, and if you don't act soon, you will regret it." Roth's reasoning: Interest rates are at historic lows but cyclical trends suggest they won't stay there indefinitely. "Home buyers may never see such a chance again," Roth says. "What I'm trying to impress upon everyone is that if you are planning on being a homeowner now and/or in the foreseeable future, or if you are looking to move your family into a bigger home, then pay more attention to the interest rates than the price of the home. If you have a steady job, good credit, and the down payment, then you really are being offered the gift of a lifetime."[36] See: **housing, investing in.**

housing, investing in. Many Americans think that owning one's own

home is a "dream investment," but, according to Karen M. Pence, director of the Federal Reserve Board's housing and real estate finance research group, buying a house is a dreadful way to allocate one's capital. For one thing, she told an American Economic Association gathering in 2010, it's an "indivisible" asset. If you need to raise a little cash and you own equities or securities, she points out, it's easy to sell off a few shares of stock or a few bonds from your portfolio. But if you own a home, "you can't just slice off your bathroom and sell it on the market." Furthermore, a home is undiversified—you can make multiple investments in stocks and other securities and funds all over the world, but buying a home is making a huge bet on one single neighborhood. And to make matters still worse, the transaction costs of buying a house—real estate brokerage fees, mortgage fees, moving costs—are far higher than they are for other kinds of investments.[37] Throw in the dismal performance of real estate since the subprime mortgage crisis broke out in 2007, and you have more than enough reasons to avoid a home purchase like the plague. See: **housing, failure to invest in.**

human era, end of the. See: **knowledge-based mass destruction (KMD); Singularity, the.**

human papillomavirus [HPV] infection. See: **sexually transmitted diseases; condoms.**

human waste, untreated. See: **tap water.**

hydraulic fracturing. This relatively recent and increasingly contro-

versial natural gas production technique, usually referred to by the shorthand terms *fracking* or *hydrofracking,* relies on the subterranean injection at very high pressure of large quantities of water mixed with a variety of chemicals to create fractures in layers of gas-bearing shale rock, coal beds, and sand, many of which underlay critical watersheds in densely populated areas of the country, including the Northeast. These underground fractures provide pathways along which large volumes of the trapped gas can flow freely enough to be piped up to surface wellheads and profitably extracted.[38]

An April 2011 report prepared by three leading congressional Democrats—Henry Waxman (D-Calif.), Edmund Markey (D-Mass.), and Diana DeGette (D-Colo.)—lists 750 separate chemicals used by fourteen oil- and gas-service companies that employed fracking technology between 2005 and 2009. Twenty-nine of these chemicals are known or suspected carcinogens, and up to 75 percent of the fluids were left underground after the drilling procedure was completed. The report notes that, despite the fact that the ultimate resting place of those fluids "is not entirely predictable" (thanks to a special exemption from regulation under the Safe Water Drinking Act obtained by energy industry lobbyists in 2005), "the permanent underground injection of chemicals used for hydraulic fracturing is not regulated by the Environmental Protection Agency (EPA)."

The report also reveals that nearly 100 million gallons of the fluids—a little over 10 percent of the total volume utilized—contained at least one chemical categorized as a trade secret. According to the report, "In most cases the companies stated that they did not have access to proprietary information about products they purchased 'off the shelf' from chemical suppliers. In these cases the companies are injecting fluids containing chemicals that they themselves cannot identify." [39]

One chemical the fourteen service companies *were* familiar with was diesel fuel, 32 million gallons of which they injected into gas-bearing formations around the nation. Diesel fuel contains benzene, a highly toxic and carcinogenic compound tiny amounts of which can contaminate an entire water supply. Some other chemicals that the industry cheerfully admits using are eleven subcategories of special additives:

- acids, like hydrochloric acid;
- biocides, like glutaraldehyde and 2.2 Dibromo-3-nitrilopropionamide;

- breakers, like peroxodisulfates;
- clay stabilizers, like tetramethylammonium chloride;
- corrosion inhibitors, like methanol;
- crosslinkers, like potassium hydroxide;
- friction reducers, like sodium acrylate and polyacrylamide;
- gelling agents, like guar gum;
- iron-controlling agents, like ethylene glycol;
- and surfactants, like isopropanol.[40]

Unfortunately, even though the gas deposits subjected to these sustained blasts of toxic gunk are generally several thousand feet underground, and typical household or farm water wells are only a few hundred feet deep, it turns out that contamination of what the Environmental Protection Agency classifies as Underground Sources of Drinking Water (USDWs)—long routinely and emphatically dismissed by the energy industry as never having occurred and never likely to occur—may well have happened repeatedly.

In a groundbreaking development, an incident dating back to 1984, involving Kaiser Exploration and Mining and a property owner in Jackson County, West Virginia, named James Parsons, has finally been disclosed by the EPA. "When fracturing the Kaiser gas well on Mr. James Parsons' property, fractures were created allowing migration of fracture fluid from the gas well to Mr. Parsons' water well," a 1987 agency summary of the case concluded. "This fracture fluid, along with natural gas, was present in Mr. Parsons' water, rendering it unusable." Indeed, Dan Derkics, a long-serving EPA expert, now retired, who helped prepare the Parsons report, recalls literally hundreds of suspicious cases of drinking water contamination caused by fracking. However, he says, his agency was repeatedly thwarted in its efforts to learn more about these incidents because every cash payment made by an oil and gas exploration company to settle a lawsuit brought by a property owner whose water supply has been fouled is invariably made conditional on an agreement that all details of the litigation be sealed by the court and remain strictly confidential. "I can assure you that the Jackson County case was not unique," Mr. Derkics emphasizes. "That is why the drinking water concerns are real." As Carla Greathouse, a former environmental researcher and lead author of the EPA report on the Parsons fracking contamination case laments, "I still don't understand why industry should be allowed to hide problems when public safety is at stake. If it's so safe, let the public review all the cases."[41]

hydroelectric power. At first glance, hydroelectric power seems likes  the dream energy source. As the United States Geologic Survey (USGS) points out, no fuel is burned, so there is minimal pollution; water to run hydroelectric power plants is "provided free by nature"; hydropower plays a major role in reducing greenhouse gas emissions (according to the National Hydropower Association, it "prevents the burning of 22 billion gallons of oil or 120 million tons of coal each year"[42]); operations and maintenance costs are significantly lower than those incurred in most other types of power generation; the technology is "reliable and proven over time"; and, perhaps most important of all, hydropower is renewable—rainfall replenishes the water in the reservoir, so the fuel is almost always there.[43]

But first impressions can be deceiving. As the website Alternative Energy (www.altenergy.org) points out, "When a new dam's reservoir floods the countryside, people who live in the area have to move and relinquish their former lifestyles in order to make way for the project. This is very stressful and often controversial, especially if a community has maintained a particular way of life on the same land for generations."[44]

In addition, notes the conservation organization American Rivers, "by diverting water for power, dams remove water needed for healthy in-stream ecosystems. Stretches below dams are often completely de-watered. Dams prevent the flow of plants and nutrients, impede the migration of fish and other wildlife, and block recreational use."

Furthermore, American Rivers advises, "by slowing flows, dams allow silt to collect on river bottoms and bury fish spawning habitat. Silt trapped above dams accumulates heavy metals and other pollutants."[45] Eventually, warns the Alternative Energy site, the accumulating silt "renders the dam inoperable, leaving the mess for future generations, who will either have to remove the collected debris or live with a potentially catastrophic mudflow poised to inundate the area below the dam."[46]

But by far the greatest drawback to hydroelectric power is the very real, and utterly terrifying, threat of calamitous dam failures. Consider, for example, the Johnstown Flood—one of the greatest disasters in American history—which occurred after the South Fork River dam in Pennsylvania burst, unleashing a forty-foot-high wave that killed over two thousand people.[47] Unimaginably worse was the collapse of almost thirty dams in central China during torrential downpours caused by Super Typhoon Nina in 1975. "Include the toll from this single event," writes Phil McKenna in *New Scientist*, "and fatalities from hydropower far exceed the number of deaths from all other energy sources," including fossil fuels and nuclear.[48] In sum: When it comes to hydroelectric power, the best advice may be to head for the hills! See also: **fossil fuels; nuclear energy.**

hydrofracking. See: **hydraulic fracturing.**

hydrogen peroxide. Do you keep a bottle of hydrogen peroxide in  your bathroom, kitchen, or by the washer-dryer to help sanitize your sinks or laundry, or, perhaps, to treat cuts or skin irritations? Would you continue to do so if you knew that hydrogen peroxide is highly unstable, and if the water it's dissolved in when you buy it evaporates, it can potentially explode? Are you aware that hydrogen peroxide is a powerful oxidizing agent, and that, consequently, if you accidentally spill a solution of hydrogen peroxide on your clothing, it can preferentially evaporate water until it reaches a concentration where it can cause your clothing (and you, if you're wearing it) to spontaneously ignite? (Leather items, since they often contain iron from the tanning process, will often catch fire quite quickly.) Furthermore, are you cognizant of the fact that hydrogen peroxide vapors, if inhaled, can irritate your respiratory tract and, in sufficient quantities, can cause pulmonary edema and even death, and that hydrogen peroxide vapor can spontaneously detonate at temperatures above 70 degrees Celsius (lower than the temperature to which noted environmental microbiologist Charles Gerba, Ph.D., recommends you should heat household washing machine water to ensure ridding your laundry of disease-causing organisms)? Well, now you know.[49]

hydrolyzed chicken feathers. See: **salmon, farmed.**

hygiene. If we want our children to be healthy, keeping them and their

surroundings clean and germ-free should be one of our highest priorities, right? Not so fast! As Dr. Stuart B. Levy of the Tufts University School of Medicine points out in an influential report published by the Centers for Disease Control and Prevention, an increasing body of research is demonstrating "a correlation between *too much* hygiene and *increased* allergy." Levy cites four separate academic studies that have revealed a pronounced increase in the frequency of allergies, cases of asthma, and eczema among individuals raised in environments that could be described as "overly protective" against microorganisms.[50]

Rather than safeguarding us, explain the authors of one of these studies, Professors Graham Rook and John Stanford of the Centre for Infectious Diseases and International Health at University College, London, modern society's "obsession with hygiene" is actually endangering us by denying our immune systems the opportunity to encounter—and build up defenses against—the microorganisms that normally surround us. "If humans continue to deprive their immune systems of the input to which evolution has adapted it," Rook and Stanford warn, "it may be necessary to devise ways of replacing it artificially."[51] See also: **hand sanitizers, alcohol-based; hand washing; showers.**

hyperinflation. See: **inflation; superpower collapse soup; treasury bonds, U.S.**

hyperlabelosis. See: **side-effects warning labels on prescription drugs.**

hyponatremia. See: **salt, insufficient consumption of; water, drinking too much.**

I

ice cream. See: **dairy products.**

identity theft. Are you worried that a computer-savvy hacker, an un-

scrupulous back-office corporate employee, or just some run-of-the-mill light-fingered felon is going to get hold of all of your personal information and basically take over your life? Well, you should be. According to the Federal Trade Commission, "as many as 9 million Americans have their identities stolen every year." The methods range from the sophisticated techniques of electronic piracy, like using special software for online "phishing" expeditions to ply you with deceitful spam messages and "pretexting" to impersonate you in contacts with your bank or credit card company, or "skimming" your credit card data at the checkout counter with special hidden magnetic data readers, to traditional tried-and-true forms of thievery, like engaging in a little old-fashioned pickpocketing to get information directly from your purse or wallet,[1] and even "Dumpster-diving" to retrieve what you thought was secure identification data from invoices and billing notices you carelessly discarded in your trash.[2] But regardless of the techniques employed by would-be impostors, the results of their malicious masquerades can be ruinous, as this disturbing rogues' catalog of swindles, scams, and frauds identified by the FTC amply demonstrates:

- They may open new credit card accounts in your name. When they use the cards and don't pay the bills, the delinquent accounts appear on your credit report.
- They may change the billing address on your credit card so that you no longer receive bills, and then run up charges on your account. Because your bills are now sent to a different address, it may be some time before you realize there's a problem.
- They may open a new phone or wireless account in your name, or run up charges on your existing account.
- They may use your name to get utility services like electricity, heating, or cable TV.

- They may create counterfeit checks using your name or account number.
- They may open a bank account in your name and write bad checks.
- They may clone your ATM or debit card and make electronic withdrawals in your name, draining your accounts.
- They may take out a loan in your name.
- They may get a driver's license or official ID card issued in your name but with their picture.
- They may use your name and Social Security number to get government benefits.
- They may file a fraudulent tax return using your information.
- They may get a job using your Social Security number.
- They may rent a house or get medical services using your name.
- They may give your personal information to police during an arrest. If they don't show up for their court date, a warrant for arrest is issued in your name.[3]

And even if you take the excellent advice of the Center for Financial, Legal and Tax Planning to abide by the key data-management dictates of Protect, Hide, View, and Destroy, and you zealously guard all the forms of identification you carry on your person and keep your mailbox locked, you conscientiously secure any physical copies of records in your home in burglar-proof locations and all electronic documents under coded file names, you diligently access your various accounts only in private settings and in password-protected formats, and you meticulously shred all paper copies of any sensitive transactions and communications before disposing of them—even then, you are still vulnerable to the threat posed by the huge volume of hard-to-secure data in our increasingly wired society.[4] As Gunter Ollmann, a senior researcher at the Georgia-based cybersecurity firm Damballa points out, noting the easy availability on the web of cheap ($400–$700) credit card hacking programs like Zeus, "Interested in credit card theft? There's an app for that." Patrick Peterson of the online security division of Cisco agrees. "There used to be only a small number of clever criminals who would pull off these attacks," says Peterson.

"Now there is a much lower barrier of entry. It [Zeus] represents a sea change in innovation, beyond anything we've seen before."[5]

IK Pegasi. In the constellation of Pegasus, not far from the "Great

 Square of Pegasus" that shines brightly in northern hemisphere skies every autumn, there is a faint double star designated "IK Pegasi." From the vantage point of Earth, IK Pegasi is barely visible to the naked eye on a dark night, but it has the potential to be of very great import to the inhabitants of our planet. The explanation of why is a bit complicated, but it's definitely worthy of your attention. The smaller of the two stars that make up the IK Pegasi system, IK Pegasi B, is what is known as a white dwarf star; that is, it's a star that has reached the end of its evolutionary cycle and whose own gravity has caused it to collapse upon itself until it's almost unimaginably dense. Indeed, estimates are that IK Pegasi B is probably not much bigger than the earth, but that it has almost a third again as much mass as our sun.[6] An interesting fact about white dwarf stars is that there's an upper limit to how much mass they can have—it's called the Chandrasekhar limit after the Nobel Prize–winning Indian scientist who discovered it— before they explode as a "Type Ia supernova" that, among other things, obliterates the star in a matter of a few seconds, makes it shine (albeit briefly) with a brightness equal to or greater than all the other stars in the galaxy put together, and showers everything within cosmic range with an extraordinary burst of gamma radiation.[7] The Chandrasekhar limit is approximately 1.4 times the mass of our sun; in other words, IK Pegasi B is almost—but not quite—massive enough to qualify. But, you might ask, who cares? It may be *almost* at the Chandrasekhar limit, but it *isn't,* right? And even if it were, why should it matter to me?

Well, to answer your first question, IK Pegasi A, and its companion star, IK Pegasi B, revolve around each other in a remarkably close orbit—so close that, under conditions well within the realm of probability, matter from IK Pegasi A could be sucked by gravitation into IK Pegasi B, thus pushing it over the Chandrasekhar limit and causing it to "go supernova."[8] And the answer to your second question is that the IK Pegasi binary system is 150 light-years away, a mere 5 percent of the minimum "safe distance" Rochester Institute of Technology astrophysicist Michael Richmond, Ph.D., estimates a Type Ia supernova would have to be from Earth before the gamma radiation it produced would be too weak to cause "significant damage" to (if not the total obliteration of) life as we know it.[9]

The good news is that the majority of scientists believe that it will take quite a while—perhaps thousands or even millions of years—before IK Pegasi B accumulates enough matter to detonate, and that by the time it does, the IK Pegasi double star system, which is steadily moving away from our solar system, may have traveled far enough from us to prevent Armageddon.[10] (Nonetheless, suggests a prizewinning report submitted to the European Southern Observatory by a team led by Svetlana Yordanova Tzekova of the People's Astronomical Observatory of Yambol in Bulgaria, "people of the future must find a way to protect themselves . . . and abandoning Earth isn't a solution, as the deadly radiation will reach much further than the solar system."[11]) The bad news is that, because radiation from the double star system—even though it's traveling at the speed of light—takes 150 years to get here, its white dwarf component could have *already* blown up, and we just don't know it yet. So the next time you look up at the Great Square of Pegasus, pray that you don't see an extremely bright "new" star right next to it. If you do, then you—and the rest of us—are doomed.

impotence. See: **erectile dysfunction.** See also: **bicycle saddles; meat-induced impotence; smoking.**

incandescent lightbulbs. "Current incandescent bulbs on store shelves are obsolete and highly inefficient—only 10% of the energy consumed by each bulb is for light with 90% wasted on unnecessary heat," wrote U.S. representative Fred Upton, a Michigan Republican, in 2007. "Today's incandescent bulbs employ the same technology as the bulbs Thomas Edison first created over 120 years ago." Upton's concerns about such wastefulness led him to author lightbulb efficiency standards that were included in the Energy Independence and Security Act of 2007 that passed both houses of Congress and was signed into law by then-president George W. Bush. "By upgrading to more efficient light bulbs," Upton proclaimed after the bill was passed, "we will help preserve energy resources and reduce harmful emission [*sic*], all the while saving American families billions of dollars in their electric bills—and the benefits will be as easy as a flip of the switch." [12]

But what kind of "more efficient light bulb" can, and should, American families trade in their energy- and money-wasting incandescent bulbs for? Well, according to the New York State Energy Research and Development Authority (NYSERDA), the best choice is an Energy Star–qualified compact fluorescent lightbulb (CFL). "CFLs are 75% more efficient and last up to 10 times longer than incandescents, and come with a 2 year warranty!" NYSERDA raves. Indeed, NYSERDA is so excited about compact fluorescent lightbulbs that they can hardly contain themselves. "One CFL will save you up to $70 in energy costs over its lifetime!" the Agency exclaims. "If you begin by changing the five most used incandescents in your house to ENERGY STAR CFLs, you would save up to $50 annually. Imagine the savings you would see if you switched out all your light bulbs!" [13] See: **lightbulb efficiency standards; compact fluorescent lightbulbs (CFLs).**

income inequality. David A. Moss, Ph.D., the John G. McLean Pro-

fessor of Economics at the Harvard Business School and a leading academic analyst of the history of economic policy, recently made a startling discovery when he was struck by the eerie similarities in a pair of unrelated graphs—one charting the relationship between levels of financial regulation and the volume of bank failures and the other depicting long-term trends in income inequality. "I could hardly believe how tight the fit was—it was a stunning correlation," says Moss. "And it began to raise the question of whether there are causal links between financial deregulation, economic inequality and instability in the financial sector. Are all of these things connected?"

The data he uncovered were indeed startling. In 1928, the year immediately preceding the 1929 market crash that triggered the Great Depression, the top 10 percent of earners received 49.29 percent of all income, and the top 1 percent got 23.94 percent of total receipts. In 2007, the year before the 2008 market meltdown that led to the current Great Recession, the top 10 percent of the earners pocketed 49.74 percent of the gains, and the top 1 percent took home a 23.5 percent share of the winnings.[14] Moss also found that bank failures, which were widespread at the outset of the Depression, declined sharply after 1933, when tough new financial regulations were enacted under Franklin Roosevelt, and then began to mount once again after that regulatory structure was largely dismantled during the Reagan administration.

Moss further discovered that as bank failures soared in the 1920s— and again in the 1980s and 1990s—so did income inequality, and he wondered, "Is there a connection especially between extreme inequality and economic growth? . . . Do we see more risk taking at excessive levels? Deregulation feedback loops?" Commenting on the potentially devastating impact of the huge and growing gap between the rich and the poor in America, Federal Reserve governor Sarah Bloom Raskin pointed to what she saw as the clear contribution of basic income inequity to overall economic distress. "This inequality is destabilizing and undermines the ability of the economy to grow sustainably," she declared, noting that "growing levels of income in-equality are associated with increases in crime, profound strains on households, lower savings rates, poorer health outcomes, diminished levels of trust in people and institutions—these are all forces that have the potential to drag down economic growth."[15]

incompetent doctors. See: **doctors, incompetent.**

incorrect evacuation posture. See: **toilet, sitting on the.**

industrial farms. See: **meat, eating; chicken; eggs; farmers' markets.**

inflation. Although to conservative economists inflation is usually a dirty word, most mainstream practitioners of the aptly named "dismal science" agree that a modest continuous rise in prices and the slight ongoing decline in the purchasing power of money that goes with it have an overall beneficial effect on an economy. The gradual erosion in the real monetary value of wages lowers inherently inflexible labor costs without triggering job action; the steady reduction in the net worth of portfolios of corporate earnings held in cash reserves encourages companies to instead invest those profits in factory expansions and new production; and the flexibility to lower interest rates in a mildly inflationary environment provides central banks with the critical tool they need to keep the economy on an even keel, avoiding both bubbles and slumps. Perhaps most importantly, a widespread public perception that prices will always go up by a little bit all the time encourages consumers to buy now rather than later, which in turn leads to greater production of goods, more employment, and a higher level of general prosperity—the exact opposite of the conditions that prevail in a deflationary environment, when falling prices persuade potential purchasers to put off their shopping trips and hoard their increasingly valuable stores of money.

The problem with this rosy scenario is that once inflationary expectations fully take hold, prices start to rise much more rapidly, and pretty soon prudent, prompt purchasing strategies turn into panic buying, leading to irrational valuations of inherently speculative assets, like Internet stocks and high-end real estate. Similarly, the inherent decline in the value of money makes creditors reluctant to offer loans at anything other than usurious rates, and a lack of confidence in the integrity of the basic unit of exchange—the dollar—leads to misallocations of resources into unproductive investments like gold.[16] In the most extreme cases, as in modern-day Zimbabwe, "hyperinflation" rates in excess of 1 trillion percent make any economic activity other than simple barter transactions—say, offering an egg instead of cash for a billion-dollar haircut—impractical.[17]

Is it possible that such a scenario could unfold in the United States? Some economists believe that, as a consequence of the Zero Interest Rate Policy (ZIRP) and quantitative easing strategies the U.S. Federal Reserve has pursued in recent years, out-of-control inflation is virtually inevitable—perhaps sooner rather than later. For example, Peter Schiff, president of Euro Pacific Capital, Inc., and a former candidate for U.S. senator from Connecticut, states flatly that the rising costs of energy, food, and other commodities "aren't transitory." The best evidence of this, says Schiff, is the fact that Ben Bernanke thinks that they are, and "since he's always wrong, you can pretty much take it to the bank that inflation's going to get worse." "Bernanke abdicates any responsibility for rising prices," Schiff adds. He believes inflation "has nothing to do with all the money he's printing, so that means he's just going to keep printing more." The inevitable result, says Schiff: "The dollar will most certainly collapse."[18]

And Marc Faber, the renowned Swiss entrepreneur, investment analyst, and publisher of *The Gloom, Boom & Doom Report,* is, if possible, even more pessimistic. "The problem with government debt growing so much is that when the time will come and the Fed should increase interest rates, they will be very reluctant to do so and so inflation will start to accelerate," he says. "I am 100 percent sure that the U.S. will go into hyperinflation."[19] All in all, a fine (if pricey) kettle of fish, but at least it's not stagflation. See: **stagflation.**

influenza. See: **flu pandemic.**

ink-jet printers. Because laser printers have been shown to emit nanoparticles and pollutants that can cause allergies, chronic lung diseases, and cancers, many indoor-air-pollution experts have recommended that, if you have to have a printer in your office or home, you invest in an ink-jet model instead. However, before you purchase one, you should know that a study conducted by a group of Japanese scientists in 2007 found that an enclosed room in which an ink-jet printer had been operated contained an elevated level of pentanol vapors,[20] which, in sufficient quantities, can cause coughing, sore throats, painful eye and skin irritations, and even unconsciousness.[21] See: **laser printers.**

insect parts. See: **pillows and mattresses.**

insect proliferations, crop-damaging. See: **white-nose syndrome.**

insulin resistance. See: **salt, insufficient consumption of.**

Internet sex. See: **cybersex.**

intestinal gas. See: **omega-3 fish oil supplements.**

intimacy-related heart attacks. See: **sexual activity.**

investments, domestic. "I am 100% convinced that anybody who
 has their wealth in U.S. dollars will be just as broke as
the people who had their money with Madoff," says
Peter Schiff, CEO and chief global strategist of Euro
Pacific Capital, Inc. His reasoning: "There is no doubt
in my mind that [the U.S. government's policy of low
interest rates and stimulus spending] is going to destroy the economy and destroy the currency. Absolutely none whatsoever."[22] So
what can you do to protect yourself? Get rid of all your dollar-denominated holdings and put your money into more fundamentally
sound currencies like the Swiss franc or the Singapore dollar, Schiff
advises. Invest in precious metals and in foreign dividend-paying
stocks.[23] "You need to invest where wealth is being created, not where
it's being destroyed,"[24] he urges. And, he says, you'd better do all this
immediately. "I don't know how much time you have,"[25] he warns.

investments, overseas. Jack Bogle, founder of the Vanguard Group,
 doesn't invest in foreign markets, and he suggests you
shouldn't either. "There are risks out there," he told
Morningstar.com's Christine Benz in an October 2010
interview, "unseen risks, currency risks, sovereign
risks . . . Each nation has its own kind of idiosyncrasies.
Great Britain is in poorer shape than the U.S. Japan seems still to be in
the same troubled shape it was in almost two decades ago now. They
have never recovered from that big boom. So, I say, don't do it."[26] See:
investments, domestic.

ipecac. Ipecac syrup is a medicine that causes vomiting, so it's long
 been considered *the* home remedy when it's suspected
that a child or other family member has swallowed a
dangerous toxic substance and it becomes necessary
to empty his or her stomach out immediately. Indeed,

Rose Ann Soloway, R.N., associate director of the American Association of Poison Control Centers in Washington, wrote in 2000 that "syrup of ipecac is the most important thing to have in your household in the event of a poisoning."[27]

However, a recent study funded by the U.S. Health Resources and Services Administration has demonstrated conclusively that vomiting alone does not reliably remove poisons from people's stomachs. Worse still, ipecac also has unpleasant or dangerous side effects, including, in many cases, causing the *exact same symptoms* as the toxic substance the patient swallowed in the first place. For example, when researchers at the University of Rochester reexamined cases of children who ate six or fewer holly berries and experienced vomiting and diarrhea as a result, it was found that every single one of them had been given ipecac as an antidote. The researchers' conclusion: It was the ipecac that caused the vomiting, and that the holly berries, at least in very small quantities, might not, as the *New York Times* put it, be "quite as deadly as portrayed."[28] As a result of such studies—and also because ipecac is frequently abused by bulimics and anorexics—the American Association of Pediatrics now urges parents, if they have syrup of ipecac in their family medicine chests, to dispose of it immediately.[29] See: **holly.**

Israel acute paralysis virus. See: **colony collapse disorder.**

J

jaw, overuse of. See: **chewing gum.**

jet lag, social. See: **daylight saving time.**

Johnson's baby oil, role of in condom breakdown. See: **condoms.**

joint degeneration. See: **high-heel shoes.**

juice bottles. See: **bisphenol A.**

July effect, the. This descriptive term refers to the negative effect on health care in teaching hospitals caused by the annual departure during the month of July of seasoned medical residents in training and their simultaneous replacement by newly assigned and far less experienced interns. According to a recent in-depth review of data collected by thirty-nine separate clinical research teams over the period from 1989 to 2000, the midsummer turnover of one hundred thousand doctors-in-training in the United States and thirty-two thousand in Europe—typically about 20 percent to 30 percent of the entire hospital staff—leads to a spike in patient deaths of about 8 percent during this key yearly changeover period.[1] The sobering results of this systemwide investigation were reported in the *Annals of Internal Medicine* by Dr. John Q. Young, the associate program director for the residency training program in psychiatry at the University of California, San Francisco, who concluded, "Our study is a signal that there is increased risk at this time. That's the bottom line, and it's something patients should be aware of."[2]

Seeking to convey the severity of this extensive and abrupt substitution of medical personnel, Dr. Young emphasized that "this changeover is dramatic, and it affects everything. It's like a football team in a high-stakes game, and in the middle of that final drive you bring out four or five players who never played in the pros before and don't know the playbook, and the players that remained get changed to positions they never played before, and they never practiced together. That's what happens in July."[3]

junk-food addiction. See: **high-fat, high-calorie food addiction.**

K

ketchup. See: **high-fructose corn syrup (HFCS); ketchup, relish, and mustard containers; Baconator triple.**

ketchup, relish, and mustard containers. "It's the rare eatery that regularly bleaches its condiment containers," note the editors of *Pre-*

vention magazine. Furthermore, adds Kelly Reynolds, Ph.D., an environmental scientist at the University of Arizona, "the reality is that many people don't wash their hands before eating." The upshot, *Prevention* warns, is that no matter how diligent you are about your personal hygiene, "the guy who poured the ketchup before you may not have been, which means his germs are now on your fries." Squirt hand sanitizer on the outside of the condiment bottle or use a disinfectant wipe before you grab it, Dr. Reynolds suggests. And by the way, she says, holding the bottle with a napkin won't help. Napkins are porous, so microorganisms can pass right through.[1] See: **hand sanitizers, alcohol-based.**

kidney disease. See: **salt; water filters.**

kidney failure. See: **dogs; hiccups; smoking.**

kitchen countertops, "natural stone." In August 2007, *Consumer*

Reports told its readers that "natural stone" kitchen countertops were the wave of the future, with the number of installations—especially among the affluent—rising significantly for five years in a row.[2] What the magazine failed to say, however, is that those who opt for these trendy new kitchen surfaces are running the risk of significantly shortening their life spans. The reason: "Natural stone" kitchen countertops are made of granite, a substance that emits a continuous stream of radioactive radon gas into its immediate surroundings. And radon, according to the U.S. Surgeon General, is the second leading cause of lung cancer in the United States today. (Only smoking causes more lung cancer deaths.)

Indeed, Stanley Liebert, a Charlton, New York, expert in home radon detection, confirms that he's encountered more than one granite kitchen countertop with the power to "heat up your Cheerios a little."[3] Because different varieties of granite emit differing amounts of radiation, says Liebert, some granite countertop colors are more potentially troublesome than others. "We're seeing higher results in reds, pinks, purples. However, you've got to test them all."[4] Good advice.

To determine how radioactive *your* kitchen counters are, contact the American Association of Radon Scientists and Technologists (aarst. org) to find a certified technician. And then what? Well, the *New York Times* asked Dr. Lynn Sugarman of Teaneck, New Jersey, what *she* did when she found out that her "richly grained cream, brown and burgundy granite countertops" were emitting gamma rays at ten times the expected level. "I had them ripped out that very day," she replied.[5] See also: **radon; Grand Central Terminal.**

kitchen sinks. If the University of Arizona's Charles P. Gerba, Ph.D.,

 is to be believed (and, since he's one of the world's most noted environmental microbiologists, why shouldn't he be?), the phrase "Everything but the kitchen sink" should be expanded to read "Everything but the kitchen sink has fewer germs in it than the kitchen sink." "Bacteria couldn't ask for a better place to grow," says Gerba, "Especially the cracks in sinks." At the request of the *New York Daily News,* Gerba measured pathogen levels in various locations around a randomly chosen Sheepshead Bay, Brooklyn, household, and found that the kitchen sink was indeed "the mother lode."[6] "The kitchen sink is the arrival zone," he says. "You are continually bringing germ organisms in there on your food supply, and they colonize your sink and sponges and rags, and grow by the billions overnight."[7] Indeed, notes Gerba, "if an alien came from space and studied bacterial counts in the typical home, he would probably conclude he should wash his hands in the toilet, and pee in your sink." To make matters worse, Gerba says, ordinary soap and water won't kill dangerous pathogens, and wiping with a sponge only serves to spread the bacteria to whatever surfaces the sponge touches, including faucet handles and countertops.[8]

So what can you do to protect yourself and your family against contracting a foodborne illness? "Clean your kitchen sink with an antibacterial product after preparing or rinsing food, especially raw fruits and vegetables, which carry lots of potential pathogens like salmonella, campylobacter, and *E. coli*," suggests NYU professor Philip M. Tierno Jr., Ph.D., author of *The Secret Life of Germs*.[9] And, adds Cheryl L. Mudd, a microbiologist with the U.S. Agricultural Research Service's Food Safety Laboratory, "you should also disinfect it twice a week with a solution of one tablespoon of chlorine bleach and one quart of water. Scrub the basin, then pour the solution down the drain."[10] (An important proviso, courtesy of Gerba's frequent colleague, Allison Janse: "Whenever you disinfect, wear gloves, open windows, turn on ceiling fans, and send the kids out to play or in a room away from the chemicals."[110]) See: **antibacterial and antiviral products; chlorine bleach.**

kitty litter. Because most types of kitty litter are largely composed of a type of clay—bentonite—that contains measurable amounts of the radioactive isotope potassium-40, any feline who frequents the cat box would experience a radiation exposure "of about 0.1 micro roentgen per hour above background"—high enough to set off radiation monitors, but probably unlikely to represent a significant nine-lifetime dose.[12] (It is worth noting, however, that any *human being* regularly exposed to kitty litter has but one life, and that a U.S. National Academy of Science report has concluded that no dose of radiation, however small, is safe, and that the effect of all the radiation a person is exposed to throughout his or her lifetime is cumulative.[13] Indeed, to paraphrase Brenda Holloway's 1964 Motown classic, "every litter bit hurts.") See: **banana equivalent dose.**

knowledge-enabled mass destruction (KMD). *Knowledge-enabled*  *mass destruction* is a term coined by Sun Microsystems cofounder Bill Joy to describe intelligent machines—which advances in molecular nanotechnology may soon give us the power to create— that are so powerful they could destroy civilization, or even wipe out human life itself. As Canadian political scientist and disarmament expert Dr. Sean Howard explains: "Processes of self-replication, self-repair and self-assembly are an important goal of mainstream nanotechnological research. Either accidentally or by design, precisely such processes could act to rapidly and drastically alter environments, structures and living beings from within. *In extremis,* such alteration could develop into a 'doomsday scenario,' the nanotechnological equivalent of a nuclear chain-reaction—an uncontrollable, exponential, self-replicating proliferation of 'nanodevices' chewing up the atmosphere, poisoning the oceans, etc." [14]

Ray Kurzweil, the noted author, computer scientist, and futurist, takes the threat of knowledge-enabled mass destruction very seriously indeed. "Once the basic technology is available," he writes in *The Age of Spiritual Machines*, "it would not be difficult to adapt it as an instrument of war or terrorism . . . Nuclear weapons, for all their destructive potential, are at least relatively local in their effect. The self-replicating nature of nanotechnology makes it a far greater danger." [15] See also: **gray goo; Singularity, the.**

Kyoto Protocol. See: **global warming, attempting to mitigate.**

L

La Palma mega-tsunami. See: **Cumbre Vieja mega-tsunami.**

lactose intolerance. See: **dairy products.**

lahars. According to the U.S. Geological Survey, *lahar* is an Indonesian word that describes rapidly flowing and gravity-driven mixtures of rock, mud, and water that thunder down the slopes of volcanoes, destroying or burying everything in their paths. Lahars, which look and behave like torrents of wet concrete, have been known to travel distances of more than sixty miles at speeds exceeding forty miles per hour—much too fast for a person to outrun. Close to a volcano, says the USGS, lahars "have the strength to rip huge boulders, trees, and houses from the ground and carry them down valley. Further downstream they simply entomb everything in mud. Historically, lahars have been one of the most deadly volcanic hazards." [1]

The bad news is that literally hundreds of thousands of North Americans—including those dwelling in such major metropolitan areas as Seattle, Tacoma, Portland, and Vancouver—live in the shadow of active volcanoes with the potential to produce murderous torrents of unstoppable sludge. Among the most hazardous, according to the U.S. Geological Survey, are Mount Rainier, Mount Hood, Mount Baker, Mount St. Helens (whose 1980 eruption produced a catastrophic lahar that buried twenty-three square miles in up to six hundred feet of mud and rock[2]), Lassen Peak, and Mount Shasta, all of which have been classified by the USGS as "very high threat volcanoes" that are "significantly undermonitored" for eruptive activity.[3]

And wait, it gets worse: Although most lahars are caused by eruptions, they can also be triggered by less cataclysmic—and far more commonplace—events such as regional earthquakes, precipitation, glacial melting, routine volcanic venting of hot water or steam, or, in the rather ominous words of the USGS, "the unceasing pull of gravity on the volcano." Furthermore, says Dan Dzurisin, a geologist with the Cascades Volcano Observatory in Vancouver, Washington, "There's no guarantee there would be any advance warning."[4] See also: **Cascade Range volcanoes; Mount Rainier; Cascadia Subduction Zone.**

Large Hadron Collider. Commonly called the LHC, the Large Hadron Collider is the world's biggest and most powerful high-energy particle accelerator, or atom smasher, as the experimental devices are also popularly known. Occupying a 3.8-meter-wide (12 feet) concrete-lined tunnel some 27 kilometers (17 miles) in diameter buried up to 175 meters (575 feet) beneath the French-Swiss border near Geneva, the machine consists of a series of supercooled, super-conducting magnets designed to propel counterrotating beams of protons and neutrons into each other with an energy of 7 trillion electron-volts to velocities approaching the speed of light. The resulting subatomic collisions should, in theory, yield data providing answers to a number of pressing questions in contemporary physics, among them: Can the mysterious mass-conveying particle known as the Higgs boson or "God particle" be created and identified beyond reasonable doubt? Are the three basic atomic forces merely manifestations of a single effect as predicted by the Grand Unification Theory?

Why is there apparently (and happily) more matter than antimatter in the universe, a condition that appears to violate the principle of super-symmetry? Are there extra unseen dimensions of space-time? Is the relative weakness of gravity explained by the existence of other, unde-tected parallel universes that it is leaking into? And does the so-called dark matter predicted by string theory really exist?

Although uninformed observers have expressed an understand-able but groundless fear that full-scale operation of the LHC might precipitate an atom-bomb-like nuclear detonation, as a practical mat-ter the risks posed by the futuristic contraption, while in fact dire, are far more subtle. Simply summarized, they can be boiled down to a quartet of quite basic, but rather profound concerns:

First, will the extremely high energies attained by the particle collisions produce one or more tiny black holes—concentrated zones of collapsed space that will ultimately expand to consume the immediate vicinity and, eventually, the entire planet? Although this possibility has been pooh-poohed by as distinguished a physicist as Stephen Hawking, who insists that similar collisions involving cosmic rays in the earth's upper atmosphere have been taking place for billions of years with no deleterious effect, as a practical mat-ter any such resulting high-altitude microscopic black holes would have immediately rocketed off into space instead of coming to rest in, say, the French countryside, and in any case, the equations used to calculate the probability of such a catastrophe may themselves be seriously flawed.

Second, could particle collisions within the LHC accidentally trigger a **vacuum metastability event** (q.v.), tipping the known universe into a new, lower-energy state and, in the process, instantly annihilating the earth and everything else in our particular sector of space-time? Again, scientists—including the Large Hadron Collider's own "Safety Assessment Group" (LSAG)—fall back on the cosmic ray argument: If the universe is stable enough to have survived cosmic ray collisions for billions of years, they say, it's surely stable enough to survive the lower-energy jolts produced by the LHC. In other words, as Dutch science journalist Maarten Keulemans puts it, "The Universe cannot be a barrel of gunpowder, since nature constantly throws all kinds of burning fuses into it." But, adds Keulemans, "as some physicists have pointed out, there is also a possibility nature simply hasn't found the right fuse yet. And here on Earth, we're experimenting with all kinds of new fuses—for example, we're doing and planning particle accelerator experiments with . . . elements that are so unstable that they don't exist in 'real' nature."

Third, if dark matter is found and created, will it turn out to be the dreaded theoretical particle known as the "strangelet," an all-too-real version of Kurt Vonnegut's famous and catastrophic Ice-Nine, one tiny nucleus of which, by progressively contacting and infecting conventional matter, gradually but inexorably converts the earth into a large hot glob of lifeless weirdness?

And fourth, and in some ways, most alarming, if the theory proposed by Holger Bech Nielsen of the Niels Bohr Institute in Copenhagen and Masao Ninomiya of the Ukama Institute in Kyoto is correct, are the surprising series of unforeseen but serious accidents and odd mishaps that have plagued both the LHC and smaller predecessor devices at Brookhaven in Long Island and Fermilab in Batavia, Illinois, and the sudden and inexplicable cancellation of the United States Superconducting Supercollider in Texas in 1993 after several billion dollars were already spent on its construction, the results of a desperate attempt by scientists in the far future to halt all efforts to research Higgs bosons, whose production, in meaningful amounts, might conceivably annihilate everything? In that regard, the authors of this modest volume wish to stress that they have not deliberately included this seemingly far-fetched but thought-provoking notion in a cynical attempt to enlist the support of future generations of dedicated physicists in a campaign to increase the sales of their book by exploiting a basic principle of relativity first elucidated by Einstein, who wrote, "For those of us who believe in physics, the separation between past, present, and future is only an illusion." [5]

laser printers. "Millions of laser printers are charging indoor air with

an unfiltered mix of particulate matter, nano particles and pollutants [such as] volatile organic compounds, ozone, and . . . even heavy metals," reports nano-Control, an international foundation that studies the impact on human health of emissions from office machines like laser printers and copiers. "Inhaled nano particles are so tiny that they even reach the blood and the inner organs. They are blamed for toxic and allergic reactions in the lungs, for heart diseases and cancer . . . If you suffer permanently from any kind of cold symptoms like sneezing, sniffing, cough, sore throat, asthma or inflammation of the eyes or the skin for no apparent reason, it might be that pollution from your laser printer or photocopier is responsible." What can you do about this? Make sure that if there's a laser printer in your office, it's housed in a separate, well-ventilated, and otherwise unoccupied room, nano-Control advises. Or, better still, replace it with an ink-jet.[6] See: **ink-jet printers.**

Lassen Peak. See: **Cascade Range volcanoes; lahars.**

lateral femoral cutaneous nerve, compression of. See: **seat belts; skinny jeans.**

latex. See: **condoms, allergic reactions to.**

laughing or crying while eating. Laughing or crying while eating is

a choking hazard, warns the Childcare Network, and, if you have children, you should discourage them from doing so.[7] Indeed, most of us can probably remember choking or gagging when someone made us laugh while we were chewing or swallowing, and such recollections should be enough to remind us to look out for our fellow diners—no matter what their age—and refrain from saying anything funny or sad during breakfast, lunch, or dinner.

laundry. " 'Clean clothes' is a whopper of an oxymoron," writes

Health magazine, in the process of revealing that the average load of wet laundry is so pathogen-laden that it actually qualified for the publication's list of "The Germiest Places in America."[8] The culprits, explains noted University of Arizona microbiologist Charles P. Gerba, Ph.D., are our undergarments. "There's about a tenth of a gram of poop in the average pair of underwear," he says. "If you wash a load of just underwear, there will be about 100 million *E. coli* in the wash water, and they can be transmitted to the next load of laundry."[9] The result? "Anytime you transfer underwear from the washer to the dryer," concludes Gerba, "you're going to get *E. coli* on your hands."[10] So how should we respond to this underreported health menace? Well, for starters, suggests Linda Cobb, host of the television series *Talking Dirty with the Queen of Clean,* "let's just say it together, EEEEWWW!!" But Cobb has more practical advice, as well: "Run your washer and dryer at 150 degrees, and wash whites with chlorine bleach (not color-safe), which kills 99.99 percent of bugs. Transfer wet laundry to the dryer quickly so germs don't multiply, wash underwear separately, and dry for at least 45 minutes. Wash your hands after laundering, and run a cycle of bleach and water between loads to eliminate any lingering bugs."[11]

To be even safer, Philip M. Tierno Jr., Ph.D., director of clinical microbiology and immunology at New York University's Langone Medical Center, recommends you forgo the dryer altogether, since, he warns, "a dryer does not normally create a hot enough environment" to kill the bacteria that may be clinging to garments. Instead, he suggests, consider letting your clothing dry naturally, in the sun. "The ultraviolet radiation kills germs," says Tierno. "It's just as effective as bleach."[12] See: **chlorine bleach.**

leafy green vegetables. "Can salad really be bad for you?" ask Sarah

Klein, Amanda Tian, Jacqlyn Witmer, and Caroline Smith DeWaal in an influential report they coauthored for the Center for Science in the Public Interest about the "FDA Top Ten"—the ten riskiest foods regulated by the U.S. Food and Drug Administration. The answer, you may be astonished to hear, is yes. "While nutritionists shudder at the thought," they write, "it is sadly the case that nutritious greens can also be highly contaminated with pathogens." Incredibly, in the ten years leading to the publication of the CSPI report in 2009, more foodborne illness outbreaks were linked to salads and/ or thirteen of the leafy greens that are commonplace among their ingredients—iceberg lettuce, romaine lettuce, leaf lettuce, butter lettuce, baby leaf lettuce (immature lettuce or leafy greens), escarole, endive, spring mix, spinach, cabbage, kale, arugula, or chard—than to any other food.

How do these supposedly healthy vegetables become contaminated? It's a combination of things, write Klein, Tian, Witmer, and DeWaal: contact with wild animals, contact with manure, runoff of polluted water, unsanitary harvesting, or unsafe processing or food handling practices. Because of the industrialization of food production and the mass transport of foodstuffs around the world, there are many more opportunities for produce to become contaminated, and to be shipped far and wide once it has been. And, the authors warn, "once contaminated, leafy greens can support, grow, and spread pathogens until consumed." A short-term, partial solution, the authors note, can be the large-scale application of chlorine washes just after harvest. But our salads will never *really* be safe, they conclude, until the U.S. Congress enacts legislation "to give consumers farm-to-fork protection."[13] See: **chlorine washes.** See also: **lettuce.**

leftovers. See: **doggie bags.**

Legionnaires' disease. See: **faucets, hands-free.**

legs, crossing. See: **crossing your legs.**

lemon wedges. In a research study published in the December 2007 issue of the *Journal of Environmental Health*, New Jersey microbiologists Anne LaGrange Loving and John Perz surreptitiously tested a random sampling of the lemon wedges used by twenty-one different restaurants to garnish beverages ranging from sparkling water, diet sodas, and iced tea to martinis, Bloody Marys, and whiskey sours, and discovered that fully 69.7 percent of wedges were contaminated with a broad variety of pathogenic microbes that had the potential to cause infectious diseases in humans. Among the likely sources for these germs, according to Loving and Perz, were "the fingertips of a restaurant employee via human fecal or raw-meat or poultry contamination," workers who may have handled the lemons "before they even arrived at the restaurant," airborne spores "landing on the fruit or on the knife used to cut the lemon," or any combination of these factors.[14]

"People need to know that [restaurant] lemons have bacteria on them that can make them sick," concludes Loving, who notes that she first conceived of the study after she noticed a waitress with dirty fingernails delivering a drink to a table.[15] *Men's Health* magazine editor Heather Loeb agrees. "Tell the waiter you prefer your drink sans fruit," she advises. "Why risk it?"[16] (Note: In the concluding paragraph of their report, Loving and Perz suggest that other beverage garnishes, such as olives, limes, celery, and cherries, might have the same potential for contamination as lemons do. Be forewarned.[17])

leprosy. "You would think that after all these years many of the mis-
placed fears and naïve beliefs about leprosy—or as it has been more recently known, Hansen's disease—would have become extinct," writes Dennis DiClaudio in his meticulously researched, if provocatively titled, *The Hypochondriac's Pocket Guide to Horrible Diseases You Probably Already Have.* "Unfortunately, that's not the case," he adds, and he sets out to clear up some of the more common misunderstandings for us. First of all, you can't catch leprosy simply by being gazed at, or being near, an infected person. "You would have to touch an infected person or inhale some of his or her respiratory droplets, which are let loose in the air when he or she coughs," he explains. Second, says DiClaudio, leprosy sufferers are no longer, for the most part, forced to live in isolated colonies. "Now they're free to live and work wherever they please," he tells us. "There are a few thousand victims living in the United States today, and several new cases are reported every year. In fact, one might be sitting next to you on the subway tomorrow." And third, leprosy does not make your body parts fall off. "What a bunch of nonsense that is," DiClaudio assures us. It's the nerve damage *caused* by leprosy, which "leads to small wounds that go unnoticed until they are gangrenous," that results in your body parts growing disfigured and eventually falling off, he says. "Technically, it's not the leprosy."[18] For some tips on how to avoid contracting this ancient, but more-common-than-you-might-expect, affliction, see: **armadillos.**

lettuce. According to the Environmental Working Group's 2012 re-

port *Shopper's Guide to Pesticides,* lettuce is among the "dirty dozen" foods on which pesticide residues have been most frequently found. Therefore, they advise, individuals wanting to avoid pesticide-associated health risks may choose to steer clear of lettuce—unless, of course, it is grown organically.[19] (See: **organic food.** See also: **leafy green vegetables.**)

leukemia, acute lymphotic. See: **candlelight dinners.**

lice, pubic. See: **gyms.**

lightbulb efficiency standards. Republican congressman Fred

Upton of Michigan felt so strongly about the wasteful-ness of old-fashioned incandescent bulbs that, with important input from environmental groups and from the lightbulb industry itself, he authored new bulb efficiency standards to encourage the development and sales of more efficient lighting solutions. Indeed, as detailed in our entry on **incandescent lightbulbs** (q.v.), Upton's standards were included in the Energy Independence and Security Act, which was signed by President George W. Bush in 2007, and became the law of the land. "This common sense, bipartisan approach partners with American industry to save energy as well as help foster the cre-ation of new domestic manufacturing jobs," an ebullient Upton bragged at the time. And, he added, the legislation also held the promise of "saving American families billions of dollars" in electric-ity costs.[20]

But hardly had the ink dried on the bill before at least some observers began to realize that Upton's lightbulb guidelines were a threat to the very freedoms that differentiate the United States from so much of the rest of the world. "These are the kinds of regulations that make the American people roll their eyes," opined U.S. represen-tative Marsha Blackburn of Tennessee. "It is typical of a 'big Wash-ington' solution to a non-existent problem. In this case it manifests itself as an overreach into every American home."[21] Rush Limbaugh was even more vocal on the subject. "The government ought to have not a damn thing to say about the lightbulb I buy. It's none of their business, especially when this is based on a total, freaking hoax," he told his national radio audience.[22] But perhaps it was Minnesota representative Michelle Bachmann who summed up the problems with the lightbulb standards most succinctly. "Fundamentally, it is an issue of freedom," Bachmann said in 2008. "It's about whether people are able to make even the most basic decisions anymore or whether Big Brother will control every aspect of their lives."[23] Confronted with such reasoning, Upton has rethought his radical stance on energy efficiency. Indeed, in 2011, in his new role as chairman of the House Energy and Commerce Committee, he worked conscientiously to ease the way for the repeal of his own lightbulb standards.[24] See also: **Nanny Statism.**

linguistic toxicity. See **side-effects warning labels on prescription drugs.**

lip pursing. See: **pursing your lips.**

liquefied animal feces. See: **tap water.**

litter, alluvial. See: **beach, a day at the.**

Long Valley, California. See: **supervolcanoes.**

lotions and creams. Because frequent **hand washing** (q.v.) can lead to a painful condition called hand dermatitis, Susan T. Nedorost, M.D., associate professor of dermatology at University Hospitals Case Medical Center in Cleveland, recommends that, when there's no alcohol-based hand sanitizer available and you're forced to wash your hands, you should use a cream-based lotion immediately thereafter.[25] But, according to the Environmental Health Association of Nova Scotia (EHANS), slathering creams or lotions on your hands—or anywhere else on your body, for that matter—presents its own set of hazards. For one thing, the association warns in its

Guide to Less Toxic Products, many widely sold lotions and creams contain mineral oil and petrolatum, two petroleum products that, despite their recognized ability to help keep skin "moist and smooth," can be "contaminated with potentially carcinogenic polycyclic aromatic hydrocarbons (PAHs)." Propylene glycol and lanolin are also frequently used as moisturizing ingredients in lotions and creams, the EHANS guide tells us. "Propylene glycol is a recognized neurotoxin and is known to cause contact dermatitis at very low concentrations," while "lanolin is an animal product that can be contaminated with pesticides" and "may also cause allergies," the guide says. "TEA [triethanolamine], a skin irritant and immune system toxicant, is also a common ingredient in lotions," EHANS continues, as are such "estrogen-mimicking parabens" as methylparaben and propylparaben, which are frequently added as preservatives. And finally, EHANS reminds us, hand lotions "work mainly by covering dry skin with oil, which can clog pores."[26] In sum, unless you're incredibly diligent about checking out every ingredient listed on the label, the best advice for consumers when it comes to lotions and creams might just be "Hands off!" See also: **hand sanitizers, alcohol-based.**

low sperm count. See: **antibacterial and antiviral products; bisphenol A; microwave ovens.**

low-heel shoes. Surely flat shoes are better for your feet and legs than

high heels, right? Wrong, says Mike O'Neill, consulting podiatric surgeon for the British Society of Chiropodists and Podiatrists. Flat shoes can "strain the achilles tendon that runs from the back of the heel, and also the calf muscles in the back of the leg," he warns. Pain can develop in as little as two weeks.[27] In addition, O'Neill advises, "If you wear shoes such as ballet pumps for a long time, the back of the shoe tends to wear down, and you end up shuffling along like an old lady wearing slippers." Shuffling can ruin your posture, he cautions.[28] Furthermore, says Sammy Margo, a spokeswoman for the Chartered Society of Physiotherapists, because flat shoes offer no shock absorbency and little heel support, there is an added risk of developing a painful

heel condition called plantar fasciitis if you wear them constantly.[29]
See: **high-heel shoes.** See also: **flip-flops.**

Lyme disease. See: **tick-borne diseases.**

M

magazines, waiting room. See: **doctors' offices.**

maggot therapy. Also known as maggot debridement therapy
(MDT), larval therapy, and biodebridement, this
unique medical intervention employs a form of bio-
therapy consisting of the deliberate introduction of
live, disinfected fly larvae into nonhealing skin and soft
tissue to clean out the wound and promote healing.[1]
"With the spread of resistance to antibiotics and the rise of 'superbugs'
such as MRSA, antibiotics are no longer considered the panacea they
once were," reports Peta Bee in the *Sunday Times.* Instead, she writes,
the tiny grubs—which are proving strikingly effective in the treatment of antibiotic-resistant infections—are "squirming their way back
into mainstream medicine."[2] As Dr. Steven Holland, head of the im-
munopathogenesis unit of the National Institute of Allergy and Infectious Diseases (NIAID) and chief of their Laboratory of Clinical
Infectious Diseases, observed, "When surgeons clean a wound, they
cut away the dead tissue—but sometimes they can't tell the difference
between what's alive and what's dead. A maggot knows what's alive
and what's dead because it only eats dead tissue." Larvae of the green
blowfly have proven among the most effective debriding agents and
are currently marketed under the brand name Medical Maggots. Are
they cost-effective? Ask Vickie Anderson, an NIAID nurse who con-
siders the miniature miracle workers a very economical option indeed
for treating nonhealing wounds. "Thousands of dollars' worth of care
was able to handle what millions of dollars of care could not," Anderson reported, emphasizing that a container of five hundred to one
thousand disinfected maggots would set a hospital back a mere sev-
enty dollars.[3]

Of course, as Peta Bee's *Sunday Times* article acknowledges, "there is a glaring downside to maggot therapy, and one that may prove an impenetrable barrier to its mainstream use—namely the 'yuck' factor." Yet, she adds, "researchers who have been investigating the medical benefits insist that, for the good of our health, we should disregard it."[4] Indeed, in an effort to make the larval treatment process less off-putting, dressings containing maggots are usually opaque to prevent patients from seeing the hungry grubs at work, and can be applied so as to minimize the somewhat disconcerting tickling sensation the wormlike creatures cause as they nibble on necrotized flesh.[5] Perhaps such techniques have their limits, however. As one subject of the therapy noted, "When they would eat and clean, you could kind of feel them as they got down to where they needed to go."[6] See **superbugs.**

makeup. See: **cosmetics.**

mall Santas. See: **Santa Claus.**

malware. This shorthand term for "malicious software" is generally used to describe the entire repertory of furtive, invasive, and destructive programming code, including computer viruses, worms, Trojan horses, spyware, adware, rootkits, backdoors, keyloggers, and bots. The proliferation on a "seemingly insane trajectory," as Symantec chief executive Enrique Salem aptly described it, of software specifically designed to disrupt the operations and compromise the privacy of computer systems has clearly flabbergasted even the highly sophisticated security firms who battle its purveyors on a daily basis.[7] In the second half of 2007 alone, Symantec, creator of the popular Norton AntiVirus program, disclosed, "out of 54,609 unique applications deployed in Microsoft Windows PCs, 65% were malicious." The Silicon Valley–based company concluded gloomily in that same year that "the release rate of malicious code and other unwanted programs may be exceeding that of legitimate software applications."[8] In 2010, those fears were confirmed when Symantec discovered 286 million new and unique threats from malware, or about nine per second.[9]

Another security provider, Spain's Panda Software, reported receiving more than three thousand novel samples of malware per day in 2007, a tenfold increase over 2006, and described the troubling phenomenon as a "malware epidemic."[10] Finland's F-Secure Corporation stated that "as much malware was produced in 2007 as in the previous 20 years altogether."[11] And, after conducting a survey of billions of websites, in which 4.5 million pages were subjected to "in-depth analysis," Google researchers found that roughly 10 percent of them—450,000 in all—were capable of launching "drive-by downloads" of malicious software.[12] As Nir Zuk, the chief technology officer at the firewall company Palo Alto Networks recently warned, "We're seeing an inflection point where the attackers are extremely smart, and they are using completely new techniques. Every piece of content that you receive can attack you."[13]

manicures. See: **nail salons.**

margarine, stick. See: **trans fats; health claims.**

margarita mixes. See: **high-fructose corn syrup (HFCS).**

Marianna Fault. On January 21, 2009, Dr. Haydar al-Shukri, director of the Arkansas Earthquake Center at the University of Arkansas at Little Rock, announced the discovery of a previously unknown fault line located near the town of Marianna in eastern Arkansas. The fault, which is unrelated to the nearby, and better-known, New Madrid Seismic Zone, has produced earthquakes in the past that measured 7.0 or more on the Richter scale, al-Shukri said, and is likely to do so again. A 7.0 quake is similar in magnitude to the one that struck Haiti in 2010, and, since a major natural gas pipeline runs near the newly discovered fault, the result, al-Shukri warned, "is going to be a major disaster."[14] (See also: **New Madrid Seismic Zone.**)

marionette lines. See: **chewing gum; drinking from a straw; pursing your lips; sleeping on your side.**

market volatility, extreme. See: **flash crash.**

mascara. In addition to the long-term health concerns raised by the

presence of toxic substances such as heavy metals, aluminum, and phthalates in mascara (See: **cosmetics**), users need to be alert to a more immediate and disquieting problem: After a container of mascara has been opened, it can become contaminated with *Pseudomonas aeruginosa,* a bacterium highly resistant to therapy. According to Carol Barczak of the Environmental Health Association of Nova Scotia, *Pseudomonas aeruginosa* can "attack an eyeball scratched by inadvertent damage by the applicator brush." And, even if you're impeccably careful during the application process, she advises, you may still be at risk: The pathogen can also infect eyes "scratched by microscopic abrasions from soft contact lenses."[15] "Blindness can result," she warns. Furthermore, states environmental blogger Marina Hanes, "some brands of mascara also test their products on bunnies. Do you really want to support companies that use animal testing?"[16]

mass extinction. The rapid disappearance of thousands of species of

plants and animals in the few centuries since the beginning of the Industrial Revolution is well on its way to becoming the "sixth mass extinction event" in the history of our planet, and the first global evolutionary catastrophe caused exclusively by humans. "The speed at which species are being lost is much faster than any we've seen in the past—including those related to meteor collisions," warns Daniel Simberloff, an ecologist and expert in biological diversity at the University of Tennessee.[17] According to a major survey conducted recently by the American Museum of Natural History's Center for Biodiversity and Conservation, 70 percent of the scientists who analyzed the available data on what legendary paleoanthropologist and conservationist Richard Leakey has dubbed "the Sixth Extinction"[18] agreed that in the next three decades as many as half of all the species on Earth will die in one of the speediest wholesale exterminations of life-forms in the planet's four-and-a-half-billion-year history.[19]

The elimination of countless irreplaceable and, in many cases, as yet undiscovered genotypes of flora and fauna will not just constitute an epic botanical and zoological tragedy, but—because of the key roles these animals, plants, and other life-forms play in healthy and functioning ecosystems—it will also impose a huge economic cost. According to the inaptly named spokesman of the UN Environmental Program, Nick Nuttall, "the annual financial loss of services [these] eco-systems provide" (e.g., providing water, storing carbon, and stabilizing soil) is about $64 billion a year, adding up to a "cumulative loss by 2050 of land-based natural capital of around $125 trillion."[20] Indeed, warns noted Stanford University biologist Paul Ehrlich, "in pushing other species to extinction, humanity is busy sawing off the limb on which it is perched."[21] (Humanity may, however, derive some admittedly small comfort from the realization that the potential impact of an orbiting near-Earth-object could very well let us off the hook, so to speak, when it eradicates all remaining life on the planet and in the process coincidentally erases any evidence of prior gross ecological misbehavior on the part of Homo sapiens. See: **Asteroid 99942 Apophis** and **Comet Catalina.**)

mattresses. See: **pillows and mattresses.**

McDonald's Crispy Chicken Bacon Ranch Salad. See: **salads, fast-food.**

McNuggets. See: **Chicken McNuggets.**

MDVP. See: **bath salts.**

meat, eating. "Our patterns of meat consumption have become in-creasingly dangerous for both individuals and the planet," writes Michael Specter in *The New Yorker.* "According to the United Nations Food and Agriculture Organization, the global livestock industry is responsible for nearly twenty per cent of humanity's greenhouse-gas emissions. That is more than all cars, trains, ships and planes combined." Cattle consume nearly a tenth of all the world's freshwater, Specter adds, and fully 80 percent of all agricultural land is devoted to the production of meat. "The ecological implications are daunting," he says, "and so are the implications for animal welfare: billions of cows, pigs, and chickens spend their entire lives crated, boxed, or force-fed grain in repulsive conditions on factory farms. These animals are born solely to be killed, and between the two events they are treated like interchangeable parts in a machine, as if a chicken were a spark plug, and a cow a drill bit."

Furthermore, observes Specter, the human health consequences of meat consumption, and our reliance on factory farms, are "almost as disturbing" as the threats meat production poses to the environment and to the well-being of livestock.[22] For example, according to a 2007 American Public Health Association report, U.S. industrial food animal producers "generate in excess of 335 million tons of dry manure waste each year." Disposal of this waste, which "often contains pathogens, including antibiotic-resistant bacteria, dust, arsenic, dioxin and other persistent organic pollutants," frequently leads to soil saturation, "with the excess running off into streams and shallow aquifers"—in other words, into the water we drink every day.[23] And, concludes Specter, by the very act of eating animals, "humans have exposed themselves to SARS, avian influenza, and AIDS, among many other viruses. The World Health Organization has attributed a third of the world's deaths to the twin epidemics of diabetes and cardiovascular disease, both greatly influenced by excessive consumption of animal fats."[24] Fruits and vegetables, anyone?

meat-induced impotence. According to People for the Ethical Treat-ment of Animals (PETA), medical evidence indicates that meat-eating causes impotence, "because meat clogs up the arteries going to all organs, not just to the heart." The organization also makes reference to many of the other health problems associated with eating meat, including increased risk of heart disease, cancer, and strokes.

"But," they conclude, "it seems that many men care more about their virility than their longevity, so we're appealing to them on their terms." [25] See also: **erectile dysfunction.**

Medea hypothesis, the. Worries about possible asteroid impacts (see, for example, **Asteroid 99942 Apophis**) may be moot, according to paleontologist Peter Ward, professor of biology and earth and space sciences at the University of Washington, whose specialty is the study of mass extinctions, since, in his opinion, the optimistic model of the earth as a self-sustaining, life-preserving biosphere proposed in 1970 by the British scientist James Lovelock—his once-derided but now widely accepted "Gaia Hypothesis"—is dead wrong. In his book *The Medea Hypothesis: Is Life on Earth Ultimately Self-Destructive?*, which takes its name from the vengeful mother in Greek mythology who killed her own children, Ward makes the case that our planet's organisms are not altruistic participants in some sort of balanced and harmonious feel-good ecological cooperative, but vicious and destructive competitors hell-bent on each other's annihilation, consistently exhibiting behavior that is "inherently selfish and ultimately biocidal."

Ward theorizes that this pattern of wholesale depredation actually emerged with life itself when the earliest bacteria polluted the earth's primordial atmosphere with toxic methane and, later on, oxygen, which was lethal to the anaerobic life-forms that predominated at the time. Plants then appeared and removed so much carbon from the air that they managed to trigger two colossal ice ages, and in the aeons that followed, four of the five major extinction events were caused not by volcanic eruptions or meteor impacts, but by the actions of living things. "Life seems to be actively pursuing its own demise," Ward argued in a recent article in *New Scientist,* "moving earth ever closer to the inevitable day when it returns to its original state: sterile." [26] On the bright side, of course, the Medea hypothesis suggests that any guilt we humans feel about being the likely cause of the impending death of our beloved home planet may be, at least partially, misplaced. Indeed, if Ward is correct, our much-touted capacity for wreaking terrestrial havoc apparently pales in comparison to the billion-year bloodbath unleashed by our fellow multicellular life-forms.

medical errors. Although it is difficult to arrive at anything like an

exact number of people who die each year as the result of avoidable medical errors, the best estimates of the carnage range from just under fifty thousand to almost one hundred thousand annual preventable deaths in the United States, which, just to err on the side of optimism and assume that the correct figure is on the lower end of the scale, would represent an equivalent toll of fatalities from the catastrophic crash of a full-size passenger jet every other day. The root causes of this grim calculus are manifold and, though hard to cure in an environment subject to immense legal and financial pressures, are nevertheless well recognized: poorly trained or overworked physicians, novel and complex procedures, low nurse-to-patient ratios, sloppy or nonexistent documentation, miscommunication, the hectic atmosphere of the emergency room, sleep deprivation among interns, and confusing and often illegible prescriptions of potent drugs with similar-sounding names but very different effects, to name just a few of a whole host of likely sources of negative medical outcomes.[27] With these disquieting statistics in mind, the soundest advice appears to be to steer clear of the health care establishment whenever possible, and while this is clearly not an option for the gravely injured or seriously ill, certainly anyone who can take preventive steps to avoid a potential hospitalization would be well advised to do so. One such strategy that many think offers the promise of wellness preservation is the practice of meditation. See: **meditation.**

medicine cabinets. According to *Prevention* magazine, the worst

place to keep your medicine is—believe it or not—your medicine cabinet! "It's not uncommon for the temp in a steamy bathroom to reach 100°F—well above the recommended storage temperatures for many common drugs," the magazine warns. "The cutoff for the popular cholesterol drug Lipitor, for instance, is around 77°F." A better spot to store your meds, *Prevention* advises, is someplace cool and dry, such as (if you have one) the pantry.[28] See also: **tooth-brushes, keeping in medicine cabinet.**

meditation. The increasingly popular practice of meditation would seem to contribute meaningfully to the maintenance of a general level of good health as well as providing a wholesome and risk-free alternative to potentially addictive drug therapies for the reduction of stress and the management of pain, but troubling evidence to the contrary has been recently published in academic literature by a pair of researchers. J. L. Craven, for example, noted disturbing indications of detrimental psychiatric effects among regular meditators, including "uncomfortable kinesthetic sensation, mild dissociation, feelings of guilt . . . and psychosis-like symptoms, grandiosity, elations, destructive behavior, and suicidal feelings."[29] And in a clinical study of twenty-seven long-term meditators conducted by D. H. Shapiro Jr., 62.9 percent reported at least one adverse effect and 7.4 percent suffered profoundly adverse effects, among them "relaxation-induced anxiety and panic, paradoxical increases in tension, less motivation in life, boredom, pain, impaired reality testing, confusion and disorientation, feeling 'spaced out,' depression, increased negativity, being more 'judgmental,' and, ironically, feeling addicted to meditation."[30]

Further, among untrained or improperly supervised students of intensive meditative practices typical of various Asian spiritual traditions, particularly Qi Gong, accounts of followers developing severe and chronic mental or physical disorders have become sufficiently widespread to warrant their inclusion in a separate category in the *DSM-IV*, the standard reference work regularly consulted by mental health professionals, under the heading of "Qi-Gong Psychotic Reaction."[31]

mega-tsunamis. Mega-tsunamis are extremely large tsunamis, capa- ble of crossing entire oceans at jet-airplane speed and wreaking almost unimaginable destruction. There is no official scientific definition of the term (which originated in the popular media), but it is most frequently used to describe waves literally hundreds of feet high—

far higher, even, than the utterly devastating wall of water that struck northeastern Japan in the wake of the March 2011 quake there. Unfortunately, many geologists believe that the northwest coast of North America, and the entire eastern seaboard of the United States, are among the most likely areas in the world to be struck by a mega-tsunami. See: **Cumbre Vieja mega-tsunami; Oregon–Washington–British Columbia mega-tsunami.**

memory loss. See: **candlelight dinners; water filters.**

menus. "Have you ever seen anyone wash off a menu?," asks *Preven-* *tion* magazine. "Probably not. A recent study in the *Journal of Medical Virology* reported that cold and flu viruses can survive for 18 hours on hard surfaces," the magazine points out. "If it's a popular restaurant, hundreds of people could be handling the menus—and passing their germs on to you." The solution: Make it a rule never to let a menu touch your plate or your cutlery, and wash your hands as soon as possible after you place your order. And once they're clean, the *Prevention* editors remind us, the restroom door handle can recontaminate them on the way out. "Palm a spare paper towel after you wash up and use it to grasp the handle," they suggest. "Yes, other patrons may think you're a germ-phobe—but you'll never see them again, and you're the one who won't get sick." [32]

meralgia paresthetica. See: **seat belts; skinny jeans.**

metallogeusia. See: **pine nuts.**

methicillin-resistant *Staphyloccus aureus* (MRSA). See: **superbugs.**

methylenedioxypyrovalerone (MDPV). See: **bath salts.**

microwave oven door handles. "The microwave oven door handle is one of the germiest items in the workplace, so wash your hands after you touch it and before you eat that pizza you just nuked," advises Allison Janse in *The Germ Freak's Guide to Outwitting Colds and Flu,* the indispensable health manual she authored in 2005 in collaboration with University of Arizona microbiologist Charles P. Gerba, Ph.D. "The microwave kills germs on the *inside,* but you're on the outside."[33] See also: **microwave ovens.**

microwave ovens. Because microwave ovens are so convenient and

energy-efficient, says the U.S. Department of Agriculture's Food Safety and Inspection Service, they "can play an important role at mealtime." But, the department warns, "special care must be taken when cooking or reheating meat, poultry, fish, and eggs to make sure they are prepared safely." The problem is that microwave ovens tend to cook food "less evenly" than conventional ovens do and, therefore, "can leave 'cold spots,' where harmful bacteria can survive." For this reason, the USDA advises, "it is important to use a food thermometer and test food in several places to be sure it has reached the recommended safe temperature to destroy bacteria and other pathogens." Failure to do so, they caution, could result in a bout of foodborne illness for you and your loved ones.[34] (Note: The Illinois Department of Public Health can provide you with a handy list of the "recommended safe cooking temperatures" for a variety of foods, ranging from the commonplace [beef and poached eggs] to the highly exotic [ostrich and rhea]. Visit the IDPH website at http://www.idph .state.il.us/about/fdd/safecooktemp.htm to obtain your copy.[35])

But, you may ask, what about the *radiation* from microwave ovens? Isn't it at least as dangerous as the potential of contracting a disease borne by unevenly cooked food? Well, theoretically it is. Indeed, the U.S. Food and Drug Administration points out, microwave radiation can cause painful burns, cataracts, or even—because it "can alter or kill sperm"—temporary sterility. "But these types of injuries," they assure us, "can only be caused by exposure to large amounts of microwave radiation, much more than the 5mW limit for microwave oven leakage." And, in the FDA's experience, "most ovens tested show little or no detectable microwave leakage."[36] But, of course, such tests are typically conducted only under optimal conditions. And, says Professional Laboratories, Inc., a leading manufacturer of home environmental testing equipment, "slamming the oven door, dirt or food particles caught in the door seals and hinges, or basic wear and tear all cause the oven door to slightly separate from the oven enclosure. Once this happens, invisible, but highly dangerous microwave radiation leaks through the small space and this can cause irreversible damage and injury to you and your family." [37] "Every year," they report ominously, "millions of people use microwave ovens and put themselves at risk." [38]

Thankfully, Professional Laboratories, Inc., just happens to manufacture and distribute the Pro-Lab "Detecto Card" Microwave Oven Leakage Detector, which can be yours for a modest $9.95.[39] All you have to do is place a cup of water in your microwave oven, turn the oven on, and hold the Detecto Card in front of the door. "If just a smile face is visible, no radiation leakage is present," Professional Laboratories, Inc. assures us. But if, however, a "skull and cross bones appear, it could be extremely dangerous." "Do not use the oven and contact a qualified kitchen appliance technician," the company cautions.[40] See also: **microwave oven door handles.**

microwave popcorn. See: **trans fats.**

milk. According to Rick North, project director of the Campaign for Safe Food at the Oregon Physicians for Social Responsibility and former CEO of the Oregon division of the American Cancer Society, milk producers treat their dairy cattle with recombinant bovine growth hormone (rBGH)—also known as recombinant bovine somatotropin (rBST)—to boost milk production. Unfortunately, while the dairy companies may be making more milk, they are also increasing the chances that their cows will develop udder infections (which can lead to pus being present in the milk you buy). What's more, North says, injecting cows with rBGH also leads to higher levels of a hormone called insulin-like growth factor (IGF-1) in milk, which, when consumed in sufficient quantities by humans, has been linked to breast, prostate, and colon cancers. "When the government approved rBGH, it was thought that IGF-1 from milk would be broken down in the human digestive tract," North reports. But several studies have shown that an ingredient called casein in milk inhibits this process. As a result, North says, rBGH has been "banned in most industrialized countries," but not in the United States. That's why Liz Vaccariello, editor in chief of *Prevention* Magazine, urges you to make sure any milk you find in a U.S. store is clearly labeled "rGBH free," "rBST free," "produced without artificial hormones," or "organic" before you buy it and offer it to your family.[41] See also: **dairy products.**

mineral oil, role of in condom breakdown. See: **condoms.**

mistletoe. Mistletoe (not to mention the kissing that takes place under it) is one of our most revered holiday traditions. But, according to chemistry and biomedical sciences consultant Anne Marie Helmenstine, Ph.D., it's also one of the most potentially dangerous. The reason: Several varieties of mistletoe contain a poison called phoratoxin, which, as Dr. Helmenstine explains on the About.com website, can cause "blurred vision, nausea, abdominal pain, diarrhea, blood pressure changes, and even death." And, she says, most of the *other* varieties of mistletoe—the ones that don't contain phoratoxin—contain a *different* poison, tyramine, that produces many of the same symptoms. "All parts of the mistletoe plant are poisonous," Dr. Helmenstine cautions, "so if your child or pet eats mistletoe, it's a good idea to seek medical advice."[42] Of course, you can avoid this problem altogether by choosing alternative plants to decorate your home at holiday time. (And by the way, about that kissing: Even if you *do* decide to risk hanging a sprig of mistletoe above your door next Christmas, Dr. Tim Sly of Ryerson University's School of Occupational and Public Health in Toronto warns that close physical contact with others during flu season is just not worth the risk. "If there's mistletoe dangling between you and a friend," he recommends, "eschew the smack on the lips with a fake peck on the cheek instead."[43]) See: **holly; poinsettia.**

mixflation. See: **biflation.**

mobile phones. See: **cell phones, radiation hazards of; phones, biohazards of.**

money. "Money is the root of all evil," the old saying goes, and it's literally true—in a profoundly disturbing way you may never have considered. Because so many people handle the same bills and coins, the currency you use every day is an ideal spreader of the germs that cause infectious diseases. Indeed, in a study conducted at Switzerland's Central Laboratory of Virology at the University Hospitals of Geneva, researchers found that samples of flu virus placed on Swiss franc notes remained virulent and dangerous for as long as seventeen days.[44] And when scientists at the North-Eastern Hill University in Shilong, India, examined Indian banknotes, they found germs that can cause, among other things, tuberculosis, meningitis, tonsillitis, peptic ulcers, throat infections, and genital tract infections.[45]

But luckily, frequent—if not life-threatening—illnesses as a consequence of routine daily financial transactions are not a foregone conclusion. To prevent them, urges *Health* magazine's senior editor Frances Largeman-Roth, you should carry an alcohol-based hand sanitizer with you, and rub it on your hands after every encounter with legal tender.[46] And the *Wall Street Journal's* Anna Maria Andriotis and Aleksandra Todorova offer an even simpler solution: "If you don't mind making the credit-card companies richer, paying by credit card instead of cash could lower your risk of catching a bug." This isn't because of any special properties of plastic, they explain—it's because your credit card typically passes through fewer hands than cash, reducing the odds that an infected individual will have transmitted his or her germs onto it. "But don't throw away your bottle of sanitizing gel just yet," Andriotis and Todorova caution. Once they do arrive on your charge card, "viruses can still stay alive there for up to an hour or so."[47] See: **hand sanitizers, alcohol-based.** See also: **wallets.**

money market funds. See: **underinvesting.**

mood swings, severe. See: **birth-control pills; cosmetics.**

Morbidity and Mortality Weekly Report. See: **petting zoos.**

Mount Baker, Mount Hood, Mount Newberry, Mount Shasta, and **Mount St. Helens.** See: **Cascade Range volcanoes; lahars.**

Mount Rainier. "Mount Rainier provides a scenic backdrop to much of western Washington State," writes *National Geographic's* Brian Handwerk, "and more people have moved into its associated valleys. But the mountain's serene, snow-covered summit belies an ominous fact: Rainier's status as an active volcano."[48] Indeed, as the History Channel points out in a recent documentary about Rainier, the mountain's Indian name "Tahoma" alludes to "a giant slumbering in a cave"—a giant that "might suddenly awake." And when it does, the network warns, "local residents will learn they have been living under a time bomb." "It's flat out gonna happen some day," says Steve Bailey, the emergency management director of Pierce County, where Rainier is located. "The history of the mountain is clear on that."[49]

And when it does erupt, the results will be devastating beyond imagination. In the immediate vicinity of the volcano, according to a U.S. Geological Survey report, residents can expect pyroclastic flows or surges, which will propel avalanches of poison gases and debris, heated to a temperature over five hundred degrees Fahrenheit, down the mountainside at speeds as high as two hundred miles per hour. "Pyroclastic flows can destroy all structures and kill all living things in their paths by impact, burial, and incineration," the Survey report points out. The local populace will also be at risk of being struck by "ballistic projectiles"—searingly hot boulders "thrown on ballistic arcs, like artillery shells" from the crater of the erupting Rainier. Molten lava will flow down the mountainside annihilating everything in its path "either by fire, impact, or burial." Depending on which way the wind is blowing, Seattle and Tacoma to the west, or, more likely, Yakima to the east, could be buried under tons of volcanic ash with the potential to ruin crops, collapse roofs, cause life-threatening respiratory problems, and bring auto and airplane traffic to a standstill.[50]

But the gravest threat to all area residents will be presented by arguably the least recognized of all volcanic hazards: deadly mudflows called **lahars** (q.v.). Mount Rainier is capped by more glacier ice than the rest of the Cascades volcanoes combined, and, as a result, when Rainier erupts, "35 square miles of snow and ice [will be] available for melting almost instantaneously," says Penn State volcanologist Barry Voight. This is all it will take to trigger what the History Channel calls "a disaster of biblical proportions." A mammoth surge of boiling water will churn down Rainier's flanks, the network reports, shearing off slabs of ice and picking up boulders, devouring wet soil from the valley sides, and "growing in size and power as it heads towards the half dozen towns below the mountain." [51] The turbulent wall of sludge will have the consistency of wet concrete—concrete that can travel at 40 mph or more—and, by the time it reaches Tacoma and Seattle, geologist Geoff Clayton told *Seattle Weekly,* the raging torrent will have "wiped out Enumclaw, Kent, Auburn, and most of Renton, if not all of it."

Furthermore, warned Clayton, a lahar could spawn tsunamis on Puget Sound and Lake Washington, inundating Seattle from both sides.[52] All in all, predicts the History Channel, the eruption of Mount Rainier has the potential to kill eighteen thousand people, injure thirty-one thousand more, and destroy billions of dollars' worth of agricultural, residential, and commercial property. In short—unless, say, a megathrust earthquake generated by the Cascadia Subduction Zone, or an impact from Asteroid 99942 Apophis or Comet Catalina, or an Atlantic tsunami caused by the collapse of the Cumbre Vieja volcano in the Canary Islands occurs first—it will rank as the worst natural disaster in U.S. history.[53] And here's a final—truly scary— footnote provided by the PBS series *Savage Planet:* "Mount Rainier has an active hydrothermal system, which acts like an acidic sauna that essentially steams the mountain's rocky interior into soft, gooey clay. The rock eventually becomes so weak that it can collapse under it own weight"—a collapse that could trigger one or more "non-eruptive" lahars every bit as deadly as the one described above. And, because there would be no signals of an impending eruption to alert local residents, the surging walls of mud would strike with, at most, a few minutes' warning.[54] See also: **Cascadia Subduction Zone; lahars; Cascade Range volcanoes; Asteroid 99942 Apophis; Comet Catalina; Cumbre Vieja mega-tsunami.**

mouth touching. See: **face touching.**

MRSA infections. See: **superbugs; maggot therapy; summertime sex.**

mucormycosis (zygomycosis). As if being walloped by one of the worst tornadoes in U.S. history wasn't bad enough, eight of the victims of the killer EF-5 twister that flattened the city of Joplin, Missouri, in May 2011 ended up contracting mucormycosis (formerly known as zygomycosis), an uncommon but deadly fungal infection caused by microscopic spores in bits of soil and wood splinters that lodged in the deep cuts, lacerations, and puncture wounds they suffered during the devastating storm. According to Dr. Benjamin Park, chief of the epidemiology team in the Centers for Disease Control's Mycotic Diseases Branch, "Skin infection usually occurs following traumatic inoculation of the fungal spores into the skin. It is a very aggressive and severe infection and often has a case–fatality ratio of 50% or higher." And in fact, as Jacqueline Lapine, spokesperson for the Missouri Department of Health and Senior Services, reported, three of the patients who fell ill from the mysterious infection later died.

Describing his experience with the unexpected outbreak, Dr. Uwe Schmidt, an infectious disease specialist at Freeman Health System in Joplin where more than 1,700 storm survivors were treated, recalled that about a week after their wounds had been attended to—often in makeshift clinics—some patients returned with serious fungal infections. "We could visibly see mold in the wounds," Dr. Schmidt remembered. "It rapidly spread. The tissue dies off and becomes black. It doesn't have any circulation. It has to be removed."[55] And while Dr. Park of the CDC stressed that mucormycosis is "very rare,"[56] the unfortunate outbreak in Joplin may be a wake-up call for all of us. The reason, as the CDC points out on its website, is that "these fungi are common in the environment"—especially in soil and decaying wood—and "there is no vaccine available." "To help prevent an infection," the CDC advises, you should "wear protective clothing, such as gloves, pants and long-sleeved shirts, if you are handling decaying wood."[57]

MUDsex. See: **cybersex.**

mussels. "I don't eat mussels in restaurants unless I know the chef
 personally," advises famously outspoken chef Anthony
Bourdain, author of *Kitchen Confidential: Adventures in
the Culinary Underbelly.* "More often than not, mussels
are allowed to wallow in their own foul-smelling piss in
the bottom of a reach-in." [58]

mustard containers. See: **ketchup, relish, and mustard containers.**

mutual funds. "Get out of mutual funds right now," urges Motley Fool
 financial editor Jordan DiPietro. "Why? Because they're
a terrible investment. The main reason? Funds charge
management fees, marketing fees, and because they
have extremely high turnover, they have higher trading
fees as well," he explains. "Take a look at your average
mutual fund—the expense ratio (how much you pay to hold that fund
per year) is probably at least 1%. That modest-looking fee can strip
away more than 40% of your savings over a 60-year period. This type
of investment will absolutely sink your portfolio, period." What you
need to do instead, according to DiPietro, is invest in individual stocks
instead of funds. "Think this is too time-consuming, that all the volatility may keep you up at night, or that you don't trust particular companies? Nonsense!" [59] See: **stocks, individual, focusing on.**

Mycobacterium avium, See: **showers.**

myrocardial ischemia, chronic. See: **hiccups.**

N

nail salons. Nail salons can be a "haven for bacterial and fungal infections, as well as a transmission point for more serious infectious diseases," warns Lifescript.com, the popular women's health website.
"Accidental cuticle cuts are common and one dirty instrument or lax

hygiene practice from a nail technician could cause you serious health issues" including "infections, allergic reactions, loss of nails, and even hepatitis." And bacteria from footbaths can lead to foot sores and boils.

Does all this mean you should never go to a nail salon? Not necessarily. But if you *do* decide to go, says Lifescript, "the burden is on you to protect yourself." First and foremost, you should check that the salon's and each technician's beauty certifications are displayed and current. (And make sure you're seeing the original licenses, and not photocopies!) It's essential that you "pay close attention to the sterilization of the instruments (nail clippers, cuticle scissors, razors and blades)" and that you make certain they are "either freshly unwrapped, or have been newly removed from heat (autoclave) or chemical sterilization." Indeed, if you prefer, you can "bring in your own nail file, clippers, polish, and other equipment to ensure that the tools the technician uses on your hands and feet are clean." You should ask your technician how long she's been working, and, if you don't like the answer, change technicians. In short, concludes Lifescript, it's important to "keep your eyes peeled for potential health hazards. If you see anything disturbing, speak up or walk out—and alert authorities." [1]

Nanny Statism. The *Nanny State* is a term coined in 1965 by former British member of Parliament and chancellor of the exchequer Iain Macleod to describe government institutions and practices designed to protect individuals from themselves—policies that Macleod perceived as overprotective and intrusive. Citing recent developments including rules barring excessive salt content in packaged foods in New York State, regulations designed to protect schoolchildren from eating unhealthy lunches in Chicago, enhanced U.S. Transportation Security Agency airport screening procedures, and a ruling requiring those wishing to set off fireworks in San Diego to obtain a permit, author and frequent national radio commentator Paul Joseph Watson warns that there can no longer be any doubt that a twenty-first-century version of the "Nanny State" is "kicking into high gear"— a "rampant authoritarian assault on all levels of society" that "betrays the decline and fall of America." "The state is deliberately being extreme in its smothering takeover of society so as to shock and awe Americans into obeying without question," Watson writes. "The move is akin to how a stallion horse is castrated and gelded in order to alter their behavior by making them docile."

Particularly galling to Watson is a New York State Department of Health ruling that summer camps need to have medical staff available if games, such as dodgeball and tug-of-war, that "pose a significant risk of injury" are among the activities they make available to attendees. "This is all part of the process of the state replacing the parents as guardians of the children," Watson says, "and it is designed to ensure that kids become nothing more than drug-addled, dependent slobs with no energy and no life experience, perfectly molding them to grow up as obedient, video-game playing, *Clockwork Orange*–style droogs." [2]

Rhodes College economics professor Art Carden, writing in *Forbes,* cites government limits on the use of tobacco and trans fats as the basis of a considerably more nuanced call for the end of creeping Nanny Statism. "A simple *reductio ad absurdum* shows that regulations aimed at protecting people from themselves are morally absurd," he points out. "Why stop with trans fats? Why not activities that could pose more of a threat to our individual health and well-being? If we are going to try to control smoking and trans fats because they are dangerous, should we not also try to control risky sexual behavior? Letting the authorities into your living room or your kitchen puts them only a few steps from your bedroom, and I for one won't be surprised when they try to invite themselves in." [3]

Denver Post columnist David Harsanyi, who famously coined the phrase *Twinkie fascists* to describe "the finger-wagging activists" who advocate increased government control over food choices,[4] worries that nannyism is a serious threat to the constitutional liberties upon which the United States was founded. "[It's] a dangerous slippery slope," he warns. "The more government feels comfortable subverting our right to live as we wish—while not hurting others—simply to create a more agreeable society, the state will feel increasingly comfortable sabotaging our rights on all fronts." [5]

nanotechnological weapons. See: **knowledge-enabled mass destruction (KMD).**

natural gas, extraction of. See: **hydraulic fracturing.**

"natural stone" kitchen countertops. See: **kitchen countertops, "natural stone."**

near-earth object. See: **Asteroid 99942 Apophis, Comet Catalina, Torino Impact Hazard Scale.**

near-earth supernovae. See: **IK Pegasi.**

neckties. Are you a man (or, for that matter, a woman) who frequently

wears a necktie? Do you like to tie it so that it looks neat and crisp, and avoids the impression of sloppiness that an overloose knot might create? If so, according to separate research studies conducted at the New York Eye and Ear Infirmary,[6] the University of Glasgow's College of Medical and Life Sciences,[7] and the Gangnam Severance Hospital in Seoul, South Korea,[8] you are significantly increasing your chance of contracting glaucoma, an eye condition that can lead to blindness. Indeed, your very life may be at stake. "If you wear your necktie too tight, you'll have less blood flow in the jugular vein, as well as in the carotid artery," explains Tae-Sub Chung, M.D., one of the scientists who conducted the Gangnam Severance Hospital research. Changes in blood flow in the carotid artery and the jugular vein can raise pressure in the eye, a well-known risk factor for glaucoma and the eventual loss of eyesight, and they can also be a contributing factor in arteriosclerosis. And, adds Dr. Chung, "in severe cases, you could have a stroke."[9] Casual Fridays, anyone? See also: **neckties, doctors'.**

neckties, doctors'. Even if physicians survive the potentially life-

threatening risks to their *own* health they incur by wearing **neckties** (q.v.), a research study conducted at New York Hospital, Queens, demonstrates their neckwear may be a dangerous catalyst for spreading disease to *others*. The study team was led by Steven Nurkin, an

Israeli medical student working on assignment at the hospital who observed that physicians' ties would often come into contact with their patients or their bedding. The doctors would routinely scrub down after seeing a patient, Nurkin said during an interview with Reuters, but then, he noticed, they would frequently adjust their ties, an action that, he realized, could immediately recontaminate their hands. So, Reuters reports, Nurkin and his colleagues "swabbed 42 neckties worn by physicians who regularly saw patients and 10 neckties worn by security personnel. They then dabbed the swabs onto laboratory plates and identified the microorganisms that grew." The results: "Twenty of the clinicians' neckties carried pathogens, including Staphylococcus aureus, Klebsiella pneumoniae, Pseudomonas aeruginosa, and Aspergillus. In contrast, the tie of only one security guard carried a single pathogen, S. aureus." And compounding the problem, Nurkin says, is the fact that neckties are cleaned less often than other articles of clothing.

So what can be done to reduce the risk of necktie-spread disease outbreaks? Nurkin suggests that bow ties, or, at least, tie tacks that "hold ties tight to a physician's shirt" might be a step in the right direction. Doctors might also consider decontaminating their ties with a "high quality detergent spray that wouldn't ruin the tie" or even using a "necktie condom."[10] And with the fear of antibiotic-resistant **"superbugs"** (q.v.) mounting with each passing day, sentiment is growing for an outright ban on physicians' neckwear. The British Medical Association is already on record supporting such a prohibition,[11] and U.S. politicians are paying attention. "What your doctor wears around his or her neck can literally make you sick," says Bronx (New York) legislator Jeffrey D. Klein, who, as of this writing, was busy helping shepherd a "hygienic dress code" through the New York State Senate. "By making commonsense changes to the way that our health professionals dress in a clinical setting, we can prevent suffering, lower costs, and most importantly save lives."[12]

necrotic (flesh-eating) pneumonia. See: **superbugs.**

netsex. See: **cybersex.**

New Madrid Seismic Zone. A wide area spanning parts of Missouri,

Arkansas, Tennessee, Kentucky, and Illinois, the New Madrid Seismic Zone is the most seismically active area of the United States east of the Rocky Mountains. The zone was named for New Madrid, a small Missouri town within its boundaries that was totally destroyed by an earthquake in 1812 that also inflicted severe damage on nearby St. Louis. "Strong earthquakes in the New Madrid seismic zone are certain to occur in the future," states a fact sheet from the U.S. Geological Survey. "There is a 9-in-10 chance of a magnitude 6 to 7 temblor occurring in the New Madrid Seismic Zone within the next 50 years."[13] And, points out University of Memphis geologist Michael Ellis, there's close to a 10-percent chance the quake could be as bad as the one that wiped New Madrid from the globe.[14] Indeed, in a 2008 report, the U.S. Federal Emergency Management Agency warned that an earthquake event in the New Madrid Seismic Zone has the potential to produce "the highest economic losses due to a natural disaster in the United States."[15] See also: **Marianna Fault.**

New Smyrna Beach, Florida. Are you planning a vacation trip to

Florida's New Smyrna Beach anytime soon? It would hardly be surprising if you were; indeed, New Smyrna's miles of white sand and consistent surf breaks have led to its winning multiple successive titles in the *Orlando Sentinel*'s "Florida's Best Beach" competition.[16] But, before embarking, here's an important fact for you to consider: New Smyrna Beach holds the dubious distinction of being the world's leader—by quite a wide margin—in shark attacks per square mile.[17] Indeed, University of Florida ichthyologist George Burgess, who maintains the authoritative International Shark Attack File database, says that, whether they realize it or not, "most people who have swum in and around New Smyrna have been within 10 feet of a shark."[18] In 2008 alone, there were a record twenty-eight separate shark attack incidents documented there, three of them occurring in three successive days. It's no wonder the city has earned the title "Shark Attack Capital of the World."[19]

"newfangled" plumbing. See: **faucets, hands-free.**

nitrates. See: **hot dogs.**

nonoxonol-9. See: **condoms.**

nonreusable shopping bags. See: **single-use shopping bags, paper vs. plastic.**

nose touching. See: **face touching.**

nuclear energy. Is nuclear energy the answer to the twin problems of global warming and deadly pollution? Certainly, there are convincing arguments for it. "Look at it this way," says Patrick Moore, an early organizer of Greenpeace and a former antinuclear activist. "More than 600 coal-fired electric plants in the United States produce 36 percent of U.S. emissions—or nearly 10 percent of global emissions—of CO_2, the primary greenhouse gas responsible for climate change. Nuclear energy is the only large-scale, cost-effective energy source that can reduce these emissions while continuing to satisfy a growing demand for power."[20] In addition, Scott Peterson of the Nuclear Energy Institute reminds us, "nuclear plants do not emit pollutants that contribute to haze or smog."[21] Furthermore, even counting the catastrophic nuclear-plant failures following the Japanese earthquake and tsunami in 2011, nuclear power is far safer, per terawatt hour of electricity generated, than fossil fuel plants, once deaths from pollution and mining accidents are taken into account. According to calculations by the respected science and technology blog Next Big Future, the annual world death rate per terawatt hour generated for coal is 136; for oil, it's 36, and for nuclear, it's a paltry 0.04. "Japan should have had sealed backup diesel generators or updated some of their designs," says Next Big Future. "However, nuclear still compares very, very well to the other energy sources."[22]

All this notwithstanding, there are numerous reasons to think twice—or maybe many, many times—before turning to nuclear energy to solve the world's problems. First, there is the simple matter of cost. "Reactors are extremely expensive to build," writes Daniel Indiviglio in *The Atlantic.* "It can sometimes take decades to recoup initial costs. Since many investors have a short attention span, they don't like to wait that long for their investment to pay off." By contrast, says Indiviglio, investments in fossil fuel plants are relatively economical. "So it's hard for energy companies to sell a future source of nuclear energy when present sources are doing the trick for cheap."[23] To counter this problem, the nuclear industry is lobbying for taxpayer-backed loans. "The Congressional Budget Office estimates the likely default rate of these loans at over 50 percent," writes Dr. Joseph Romm, former deputy assistant U.S. secretary of energy. "If you liked nationalizing banks and insurance companies, you'll love nationalizing nuclear utilities!"[24]

But nonaffordability is only the tip of nuclear waste dump. As energy systems engineering expert Kelly Kissock, Ph.D., director of the University of Dayton's Industrial Assessment Center, observes in a summary he prepared for a *New York Times* educational supplement, major accidents may be extremely rare, but the consequences, when one does occur, are utterly calamitous: "widespread and long-lasting radiation pollution affecting several generations." Moreover, he notes, "nuclear power plants make attractive targets for terrorists." (It's hard to imagine similar concerns about terrorists assaulting a windmill or a solar array.) Another well-known concern cited by Kissock is "the spent fuel from nuclear power plants," which, he points out, "remains toxic for thousands of years," and for which the United States has yet to find an "operational long-term" repository.[25] (The scores of centuries it takes for nuclear waste materials to decline to levels deemed safe "mock[s] the meager ingenuity and constancy of a species whose entire recorded history amounts only to some 6,000 years," Jonathan Schell, prizewinning author of the antinuclear classic *The Fate of the Earth,* has written.[26])

And worse still is the issue of nuclear proliferation. "The process of turning uranium into fuel for nuclear reactors can be easily modified to produce uranium for nuclear bombs," Kissock warns. "Pakistan's and India's nuclear bombs were made this way," he cautions, and Iran, which the U.S. State Department has officially labeled "the most active state sponsor of terrorism,"[27] seems poised to follow suit. As Kissock hardly needs to remind us, the potential use of such weapons—either by nation-states or militant groups—is too horrific even to contemplate. "Instead of investing in nuclear power, which just trades one set of problems for another, let's invest in renewable energy sources like wind and solar energy," Kissock urges. "They may cost a little more now, but they don't cause any harm—and they don't run out."[28]

Jonathan Schell has a modest proposal of his own to offer, an approach to the nuclear power conundrum that he regards as "perhaps more in keeping with the peculiar nature of the peril." "Let us pause and study the matter," he suggests. "For how long? Plutonium, a component of nuclear waste, has a half-life of 24,000 years, meaning that half of it is transformed into other elements through radioactive decay. This suggests a time-scale. We will not be precipitous if we study the matter for only half of that half-life, 12,000 years. In the interval, we can make a search for safe new energy sources, among other useful endeavors. Then perhaps we'll be wise enough to make good use of the split atom."[29] See: **wind turbine syndrome; solar energy; fossil fuels; geothermal energy;** and **hydroelectric power.**

nuclear warfare, tectonic. See: **tectonic nuclear warfare.**

nurses with artificial nails. If you visit a medical center, or have to go

to the hospital, and the nurse assigned to you has artificial nails, demand another nurse *immediately*. Why? Because, as research conducted in Michigan by the Ann Arbor Veterans Affairs Medical Center and the University of Michigan Medical School has demonstrated, nurses wearing artificial nails are far more likely than those who are not to have harmful bacteria and yeasts lurking on their nails. Before washing their hands, 73 percent of the nurses with fake nails examined by the Michigan researchers had harmful pathogens present on their nails, compared with only 32 percent of nurses with "native" nails. And even *after* washing with an antimicrobial soap or a waterless alcohol-based gel, the fake-nail-adorned practitioners continued to be more likely, by a 68 percent to 26 percent margin, to be harboring dangerous microbes and yeasts.[30] There is no escaping the conclusion reached by the scientists who conducted the study: The use of artificial fingernails by health care workers has the potential to "contribute to the transmission of pathogens to patients."[31] Steer clear.

nurse-to-patient ratios, low. See: **medical errors.**

NutraSweet. See: **aspartame.**

O

ocean acidification. See: **coral reef bleaching; global warming.**

olfactory sensation, temporary loss of. See: **copying machines.**

olives, black. See: **acrylamide.**

omega-3 fish oil supplements. The supposed health benefits of omega-3 fatty acid supplements have been widely and highly touted. For example, the Mayo Clinic cites multiple studies "demonstrating that fish oil supplements lower triglycerides; reduce the risk of heart attacks, dangerous abnormal heart rhythms, and strokes in people with known cardiovascular disease; slow the buildup of atherosclerotic plaques ('hardening of the arteries'); and can even moderate high blood pressure." However, before beginning an omega-3 fish oil supplement regimen, potential users should know that, according to the Nutritional Supplement Educational Centre, "fish oil harbors possible side effects such as belching, nausea, diarrhea, bloating, and intestinal gas." Other "not so desirable" side effects, the Centre reports, are "a fishy body odor and/or 'fish breath,'" increased cholesterol levels, and increased difficulty in controlling one's blood sugar levels.[1]

orange juice. See: **fruit juice; oranges.**

oranges. A study of oranges conducted in 2005 by the United Kingdom's Government Pesticides Residues  Committee found that virtually every one tested was laced with potentially harmful pesticides.[2] Among the chemicals found were several suspected of causing cancer and "gender-bender effects"; indeed, two of them—carbofuran and methidathion—are so toxic that they have been classified as "highly hazardous" by the World Health Organization. If that isn't enough to convince you to avoid oranges—and orange juice—perhaps this will: A 2009 study conducted at the University of Rochester's Eastman Institute for Oral Health found that the acid contained in oranges decreased the hardness of tooth enamel in the subjects tested by a staggering 84 percent. "The acid is so strong that the tooth is literally washed away," said Eastman's Yan-Fang Ren, D.D.S., Ph.D., whose team conducted the survey. "We do not yet have an effective tool to avert the erosive effects," Ren added."[3] See: **scurvy.**

order flow toxicity. See: **flash crash.**

Oregon–Washington–British Columbia mega-tsunami. "Could a natural disaster like the tsunami that hit the countries around the Indian Ocean [in 2004] happen here in Oregon?" the Oregon Department of Geology and Mineral Industries (DOGAMI) asks its community education director, James Roddey, in an interview posted on its official website. "In a word, yes," Roddey replies. "We have a similar active fault offshore [the **Cascadia Subduction Zone,** q.v.], so we will someday experience an earthquake and tsunami similar to the one that . . . hit Southeast Asia. We can expect a magnitude 9 earthquake and resulting tsunami that would devastate the Pacific Northwest coast from Cape Mendocino to British Columbia."[4]

Coastal geologist Dr. George Priest, also with DOGAMI, and Jay Wilson, earthquake and tsunami program coordinator with Oregon Emergency Management, have some specific advice to offer about how to survive this threat. "Within 10 to 30 minutes after the start of the earthquake," says Priest, "the first of several large tsunami waves will strike the coast. People must realize that strong shaking at the coast means that it is vital to evacuate immediately inland or to high ground."[5] And, suggests Ward helpfully, "Do not linger or return to the beach to watch for the tsunami."[6] See also: **mega-tsunamis.**

organ decimation. See: **carpeting, old.**

organic food. According to Lee M. Silver, professor of molecular bi-

ology and public affairs at Princeton University, "the enormous premium" consumers pay to purchase organic foods is "based on mythology, not fact." For example, Professor Silver warns, organic certification rules ban only *synthetic* chemicals, leaving organic farmers "free to use many chemicals on their crops, including pyrethrin (with the formula $C_{21}H_{28}O_3$) and rotenone ($C_{23}H_{22}O_6$), which is a potent neurotoxin long used to kill fish and recently linked to Parkinson's disease." Organic food advocates, he adds, "operate under the pre-scientific delusion that substances produced by living organisms, such as pyrethrin and rotenone, aren't really chemicals, but just organic 'botanical' constituents of nature. Even the poison strychnine can be defined as 'organic,' although it's too lethal for use by organic farmers."[7] And, as if that weren't bad enough, a recent blind-taste study conducted by the *Times* of London concluded that, in three of Britain's most popular supermarket chains, organic produce scored worse than nonorganic in every single price category. In short, the *Times* concluded, "organic food is a waste of money."[8]

organotins. See: **polyvinyl chloride (PVC).**

orthorexia. Orthorexia—from the Greek *ortho* meaning "correct"

and *orexis* meaning "hunger"—is a term coined by Steven Bratman, M.D., author of *Health Food Junkies,* to describe a clinical disorder in which healthy eating becomes a dangerous obsession—on occasion, even a deadly one. As Dr. Bratman describes them, orthorexia victims—whose numbers, he says, are growing as America becomes a more nutrition-conscious society—become fixated, not on the *quantity* of food eaten (as in anorexia or bulimia), but on the *quality* of the food. "What starts as a devotion to healthy eating," he warns, "can evolve into a pattern of progressively more rigid diets that not only eliminate crucial nutrients and food groups, but ultimately cost [orthorexics] their overall health, personal relationships, and emotional well-being."[9] On the "Fatal Orthorexia" page of his website, Orthorexia.com, Bratman relates the painful story of a woman named Kate who died of heart failure brought on by orthorexia-induced starvation. "Whatever the motivation, there's nothing healthy and natural about starving yourself to death!" he concludes. "If you feel any of this applies to you, please seek help from an eating disorders specialist."[10]

osteoarthritis. See: **high-heel shoes.**

overcooked food. According to the World Health Organization (WHO), food should not be cooked "for too long or at too high a temperature."[11] WHO's principal reason for issuing this advice was the discovery in 2002 that a chemical called acrylamide, a proven carcinogen and neurotoxin that has been linked in clinical studies to an increased risk of cancer,[12] Alzheimer's,[13] and heart attacks[14]—is formed when many staples of our diet, especially carbohydrate-rich foods and those high in starch content—are fried, toasted, roasted, or baked.[15] Indeed, says the U.S. Public Health Service, concentrations of acrylamide in food "typically increase with temperature"—in other words, the higher the temperature reached, the higher the level of the toxic compound you and your family will be exposed to.[16] See: **undercooked food.** See also: **acrylamide; food thermometers.**

overheight. Health-conscious women have long known the impor- tance of keeping off those excess pounds of body weight, but what about those extra inches of body height? According to a new in-depth study published in the prestigious British medical journal *The Lancet Oncology,* being too tall carries the kind of cancer risks most people would have associated with being too fat. The exhaustive analysis by researchers at University of Oxford of nearly a decade's worth of clinical data on more than 1 million women led to the startling discovery that for every four-inch increase in height over five feet one inch, the likelihood that a woman would develop cancer increased by around 16 percent. The authors of the study were unable to identify any specific reason for this peculiar statistic, but they speculated that the unexpected susceptibility of taller-than-average individuals to the development of malignancies might be attributable to the effects of higher levels of growth hormone or even the simple fact that a person of larger stature has more cells in her body and is hence prone to more potentially harmful mutations.[17] They also pointed to earlier studies in Asia, Australasia, Europe, and North America that found the same surprising results among the inhabitants of those areas and concluded matter-of-factly: "Cancer incidence increases with increasing adult height for most cancer sites. The relation between height and total cancer relative risks is similar in different populations."[18]

As Oxford epidemiologist Jane Green, the lead author of the study noted, "The interest in this study is in giving us a clue about how cancers might develop. It's the similarity for many different kinds of cancers, in people with many different risk factors and in many different populations, that makes us think it's something very fundamental in cancer development."[19] All of this is clearly sobering news indeed for all vertically endowed members of the fair sex, but a word of caution: Women planning to add some shrinking exercises to their slimming regime should be aware that *insufficient* height also poses a number of additional equally grave health threats. See: **underheight.**

oxalic acid. See: **spinach.**

ozone. See: **room air purifiers; coal.**

P

pancake mixes. See: **trans fats.**

paper bags. See: **single-use shopping bags, paper vs. plastic.**

parabens. See: **deodorant sprays, antiperspirant; lotions and cream.**

parasites. See: **tap water; sushi, sashimi, and ceviche.**

parsley. "If you've always followed a healthy lifestyle, you may be
 surprised to find that some of the wonderful green seasonings you've made a habit of adding to your salads are downright dangerous," advises the invaluable website Pregnancy-Info.net. "Take a simple herb like parsley, for instance. Parsley, in particular the parsley seeds, should be avoided during pregnancy, since the herb may lead to birth defects and abortion." The uterus is a muscle, the website goes on to explain, and, since parsley is a potent muscle stimulant, it can cause powerful muscle contractions, which, in turn, may cause a fetus to abort.[1] In sum, if you're having a baby, or even thinking about having one, and are looking for a source of vitamin C, other foods—such as oranges—or a vitamin-C supplement, may be better choices than parsley. (See **oranges; vitamin C supplements.**)

Path of Risk, the. See: **Asteroid 99942 Apophis.**

pathogens, extremophilic. See: **dishwashers; hairspray.**

pathogens, self-replicating. See: **gray goo.**

peaches. "Being pretty as a peach comes at a price," writes *Men's*
 Health magazine's Jim Gorman. "The fruit is doused with pesticides in the weeks prior to harvest to ensure blemish-free skin." By the time the typical peach arrives in your produce department, samples taken by the U.S. Department of Agriculture indicate that it can be coated with up to nine different pesticides, Gorman says. And while apples tote a wider *variety* of pesticides, he adds, "the sheer amount and strength of those on peaches sets the fuzzy fruit apart. On an index of pesticide toxicity devised by Consumers Union, peaches rank

highest."[2] And, as if that weren't bad enough, *Prevention* magazine warns us that peach fuzz can trap pesticides, making them far harder to clean than virtually any other fruit.[3] Oh, and by the way, peach *pits* can be hazardous to your health, too. Anne Marie Helmenstine, Ph.D., reminds us that the seeds of all members of the rose family—including peaches—contain cyanide, which, as you probably already know, is a lethal poison.[4] Take care that you, your kids, or your pets don't swallow any. See also: **apples; apricots; bowl of cherries.**

pears. The health risks associated with pears—a fruit very high in

sugar content that also ranks near the top of the list of foods most frequently polluted by cancer-causing and hormone-damaging pesticides—have been well documented, here and elsewhere. And, to make matters worse, evidence is accumulating that pears are dangerous, not only to those who eat them, but also to the men and women who cultivate them, and even to the people who live near the orchards where they grow. For proof (as if proof were needed), one need look no further than St. Johns Park in Worcestershire, England, where the Worcester City Council has found it necessary to erect a plastic barrier, accompanied by bright orange warning signs, to prevent visitors from walking under the pear trees there and being struck by the heavy, fleshy fruits that commonly drop from them when they ripen. "It's a smashing year for very leafy fruits and there are some sizeable pears and not everyone is going to be passing thinking that a pear might fall on them, especially children," explained Ian Yates, the Council's parks and cemeteries manager, who added that the barrier and signs seemed a far better alternative than cutting down the pear trees.[5]

pelvic floor prolapse. See: **toilet, sitting on the.**

pentanol vapors. See: **ink-jet printers.**

perfume sprays. See: **fragrances.**

persistent organic pollutants. Generally referred to as POPs, PBTs  (persistent bioaccumulative and toxic substances), or TOMPs (toxic organic micro pollutants), this classification of profoundly harmful, and nearly indestructible, compounds includes pesticides that are currently in use or were formerly widely used, and products and by-products of a number of industrial processes.[6]

According to the U.S. Environmental Protection Agency, POPs are associated with serious—and, in many cases, fatal—human health problems, including cancer, neurological damage, birth defects, sterility, and immune and reproductive system defects,[7] and recent studies have also linked them with diabetes and other metabolic disorders.[8] The twelve POPs most hazardous to human health—the so-called Dirty Dozen—identified by the United Nations Industrial Development Organization in 1995 include aldrin, chlordane, dichlorodiphenyl-trichloroethane (DDT), dieldrin, endrin, heptachlor, hexachlorobenzene, mirex, polychlorinated biphenyls (PCBs), polychlorinated dibenzo-p-dioxins, polychlorinated dibenzofurans, and toxaphene. Since then, carcinogenic polycyclic aromatic hydrocarbons (PAHs), brominated flame retardants, and organometallic compounds like tributyltin (TBT) have been added to this dubious honor roll of lethal detritus.[9]

What all of these compounds have in common, in addition to a challenging orthography and mouth-numbing phonemes, are a pair of properties that make them particularly hazardous. First, they all possess unique qualities of semivolatility, low water solubility, and resistance to environmental degradation which make it possible for them to travel imperviously through the air on dust particles over global distances and turn up in places like Antarctica, where they were never used; indeed they are (as the International POPs Elimination Network has dubbed them) "Poisons with Passports." Second, they also all display a high degree of lipid solubility, which means they are able to penetrate the protective membranes of human and animal cells and then to become concentrated, or bioaccumulate, in the fatty tissues of living organisms, where they can cause diseases and disorders directly, or contribute to them indirectly as they get passed along, or biomagnified, in the food chain when the contaminated organism in question, say a pig or a chicken or a cow, is consumed by another organism, such as, just to cite one possible example among many, you.[10]

As Joseph DiGangi, a biochemist and molecular biologist who was the lead author of a recent International POPs Elimination Network (IPEN) report on noxious flame retardants in recycled foam carpet padding, summed up the problem, "You can think of them [POPs] as among the world's worst chemicals: substances which cannot be managed because they travel long distances and build up in the food chain, so even if you live in a place where there is no production, you are still exposed to them in your food and other sources. And they are toxic."[11] And Dr. David Carpenter, professor of environmental health and toxicology at the State University of New York, Albany, sounded a similar alarm. "We have not really appreciated how dangerous these substances are to human health," Dr. Carpenter warned. "The diseases that most people die of, diabetes, heart disease, cancer, these are the chronic diseases of old age. All of these diseases are aggravated, increased, we're more susceptible to them when we're exposed to these compounds, and now we're reaping the grim harvest to the exposure that we all have to these compounds."[12]

pesto sauce. See: **pine nuts.**

petting zoos. During the nearly two decades from 1988 to 2005, more than 1,500 outbreaks of serious infections, including *E. coli*, *Salmonella*, cryptosporidiosis, and *Coxiella burnetti* were reported among attendees at petting zoos and similar close-animal-contact exhibition sites in Europe and the United States:

- In 1988, one individual died after such a visit to a farm in Wisconsin; there were seven cases of *E. coli* infections at a similar site in Leicestershire, UK;
- In 1995, there were forty-three cases of cryptosporidiosis at a rural farm in Wales and another thirteen at one in Dublin, Ireland;
- In 1999, 781 people were infected with either *E. coli* or

Campylobacter jejuni after mingling with farm animals at the Washington County Fair in upstate New York;

- In 2000, nearly one hundred individuals came down with E. *coli* infections after a one-on-one with the cows at dairy farms in Pennsylvania and at the Medina County Fair in Ohio;
- In 2001, there were another 115 cases of E. *coli* among visitors to two other Ohio farm fairs, this time in Lorain County and Wyandot County;
- In 2002, seven children were sickened by E. *coli* from a trip to a petting zoo in Ontario, Canada, and nearly eighty more took home the same unexpected souvenir from their outing at the Lane County Fair in Oregon;
- In 2003, twenty-five visitors were infected with E. *coli* at the Fort Bend County Fair in Texas, including five who took home an additional epidemiological kewpie doll as a complication: the rare blood disorder, thrombotic thrombocytopenic purpura;[13]
- And in a brief period from the late fall of 2004 to the summer of 2005, there were three significant outbreaks of E. *coli* at petting zoos across the United States, including 108 cases in North Carolina, 63 in Florida, and 2 in Arizona, and nearly two dozen of them were diagnosed as belonging to the more severe kidney-damaging "hemolytic-uremic syndrome" version.[14]

With this in mind, it might on the whole be a better idea to forgo those up-close and personal sessions with Bossy, Porky, Bambi, Francis, Billy, and Dolly and instead friend them on Snoutbook or maybe share a few bleats, honks, oinks, or grunts on Critter.com. After all, as the Centers for Disease Control noted at the time of the most recent outbreak in an edition of its sprightly publication *Morbidity and Mortality Weekly Report,* "The National Association of State Public Health Veterinarians recognizes the benefits of human-animal contact. However, infectious diseases, rabies exposures, and other human health problems have occurred in animal contact settings . . . These incidents have substantial medical, public health, legal, and economic effects."[15]

phishing. See: **identity theft.**

phones, biohazards of. According to Melissa Breyer, senior editor of

the Care2 News Network's "Healthy & Green Living" section, our hands and our mouths are our "top germ transmitters." So it probably won't surprise you to learn that our home, office, and mobile phones are among the very germiest items we ever come in contact with.[16] To make matters worse, the heat generated by using a mobile phone makes it a cinch for bacteria to thrive and multiply; indeed, as the handy web-service how2instructions.com points out, "cell phones have tested positive for hepatitis and staph viruses."[17] The solution, writes Allison Janse—who wrote *The Germ Freak's Guide to Outwitting Colds and Flu* in collaboration with well-known University of Arizona pathogen-sleuth Charles P. Gerba, Ph.D.—is to "disinfect your phone" once a day.[18] When you do, you might want to heed Janse's advice that anytime you use disinfectants, you should "wear gloves (and a mask if you're sensitive to chemicals), open windows, turn on ceiling fans, and send the kids out to play in a room away from the chemicals."[19] And, of course, you should also keep in mind that all modern telephones contain sensitive electronic components and, as the website Simply Good Tips phrases it, "liquid is not friendly to their inner workings." Too much moisture, the website stresses, "can cause damage to your phone that could be permanent."[20] See also: **cell phones, radiation hazards of.**

phoratoxin poisoning. See: **mistletoe.**

photocopiers. See: **copying machines.**

phthalates. See: **air fresheners; cosmetics; mascara; polyvinyl chloride (PVC); rubber duckies; sex toys.**

piece of cake. See: **cake, piece of.**

pillows and mattresses. Did you know that, after five years of using

a pillow, "10% of the weight of that pillow is made up of dust mites and dust mite feces," and that "every ten years the weight of an average mattress doubles because of the same thing"? Well, it's true, says Philip

M. Tierno Jr., Ph.D., director of clinical microbiology and diagnostic immunology at Tisch Hospital, NYU Medical Center, and author of *The Secret Life of Germs: Observations and Lessons from a Microbe Hunter.* And wait, it gets worse. Unless your pillow and mattress are spanking new, Tierno told the *Today* show's Matt Lauer during a 2006 interview, they're likely to be harboring not only the mites and their waste, but also "human skin cells; bodily secretions and excretions; animal hair and dander; bacteria and fungi; perspiration; insect parts; food particles; and cosmetics, lotions, and oils."

"Is it harmful to us?" Lauer asked, as if the question even needed asking. "Absolutely," Tierno replied. "You're inhaling that eight hours per day, every day of your life." If you have allergies or asthma, "this can exacerbate both of those, and it can actually even cause, according to some researchers, allergies later on." In other words, Lauer concluded, "the monster may not be under your bed, but actually in it." Tierno agreed, but pointed out that, luckily for us, there *is* a solution: purchasing an impervious outer covering for each of our pillows and mattresses. "What's in your pillow stays there," he noted, and "what's outside stays out."[21] See also: **airplane cabins.**

pine nuts. Pine nuts are frequently heralded as a useful source of thia-

mine, vitamin B_1, and protein. In addition, they are an essential ingredient in pesto sauce, one of the world's most beloved Italian delicacies. But did you know that eating even a single pine nut can lead to a bizarre affliction called "pine mouth," a syndrome that—for weeks after you take that first fateful nibble—makes almost any kind of food you eat taste "bitter, metallic, and inedible"?[22] Well, now you know. The official name of this extremely unpleasant condition is *metallogeusia,* and it was first described by Dr. Marc-David Munk, a professor of emergency medicine at the University of New Mexico in Albuquerque who contracted pine mouth himself after grabbing a handful of pine nuts at a local salad bar and eating them raw.

The Nestlé Research Centre, in collaboration with the Belgian Poison Control Centre, has hypothesized that one particular species of Chinese pine nuts, *Pinus armandii,* might be at the root of this affliction.[23] But Dr. Munk suggests that the condition might just as likely come from eating pine nuts that have been stored improperly. "We know from agricultural research that pine nut oil can go rancid quickly," he says.[24] And Dr. Beverly Cowart, clinical director of the Monell-Jefferson Chemosensory Clinical Research Center in Philadelphia, suggests that a fungus growing on the pine nuts might be the culprit.[25]

Considering the doubt still surrounding the origins of pine mouth, compounded by the difficulty an untrained shopper might have in differentiating between a Chinese and, say, a Belgian, French, or Swiss pine nut, it might be a good idea to forgo pine nuts altogether, and to substitute a traditional tomato sauce for the pesto you were planning to heap on your next plate of spaghetti. See: **tomato-based sauces.**

pink slime. See: **"slimeburgers."**

pizza dough. See: **trans fats.**

pizza topping. See: **tomato-based sauces.**

plantar fasciitis. See: **flip-flops; low-heel shoes.**

plastic bottles. See: **bisphenol A; bottled water.**

plastic shopping bags. See: **single-use shopping bags, paper vs. plastic.**

plumbing, "newfangled." See: **faucets, hands-free.**

pneumonia, flesh-eating. See: **superbugs.**

poinsettia. Maybe you're a would-be holiday season celebrant who is eager to make your home a vibrant welcoming place, but who is also only too aware of the dangers of allowing toxic plants like **holly** or **mistletoe** (qq.v.) into your environment. And maybe you've also heard that poinsettia, with its magnificent red leaves, is a safer alternative to these two lovely but problematic traditional Christmas plants. Well, the good news is you're right. According to chemistry and biomedical sciences consultant Anne Marie Helmenstine, Ph.D., writing on About.com, poinsettia *is* a less risky seasonal decorating bet than either holly or mistletoe. But the bad news is, it's not *totally* safe. To quote Helmenstine: "If you eat a few leaves, you may feel ill or vomit. Rubbing the sap from the plant into your skin can give you an itchy rash."[26] Safe *enough*? You decide. See: **holly; mistletoe.**

pointy-toe shoes. See: **high-heel shoes.**

polka-related injuries. "For millions, polka dancing is a source of great pleasure," writes Polkaholics.com. "However, it also makes extraordinary demands on the body. The accumulated stress nights of partying puts on polka dance enthusiasts' bodies often produces injuries and pain that could last weeks, months, or possibly a lifetime. Refusing to sit at the sidelines and recuperate from their injuries, some polka lovers try to dance through their pain. This can result in even more serious injuries involving joints or muscles called up to compensate for damaged body parts."

Unfortunately, as Polkaholics.com points out, most of the things folks do to seek relief from chronic polka-related pain—whether it be "aching, sharp, dull, burning, stabbing, pounding, throbbing or shooting"—actually end up making things even worse. Take surgery, for example. "The unpredictable yet permanent impact surgery can have on your body makes this a risky, last resort alternative in most cases," Polkaholics.com says. "Despite the invasive nature of surgery and its complications, its success rate is low." Well, then, what about drug therapies? "Many commonly prescribed drugs can be just plain hard to swallow," Polkaholics.com advises. "Long term use of analgesics and anti-inflammatories can cause health problems like digestive disorders and liver damage."

With unattractive options like an operation or taking pharmaceuticals, the website says, it's not difficult to understand why many victims of polka-related injuries turn to "alternative medicine doctors and healers" to find "the relief they need to get back on the dance floor." But from this quarter, too, they're likely to be disappointed. "All too often, people seeking pain management and relief in alternative medicine therapies fall victim to self-proclaimed healers who misrepresent their qualifications and competency," Polkaholic.com laments. "No one would consider flying in a plane with a pilot whose license was revoked. Or being represented by a lawyer who couldn't pass the bar exam." Yet, the site notes, thousands of polka-pain sufferers "unwittingly submit to treatments by unregulated alternative healers." The likely result of your choosing such a course? "A mistake that might relieve you of your money but not your pain."[27]

Since World War II, the popularity of polka music across the United States has undeniably declined. Victor R. Greene, the author of *A Passion for Polka: Old-Time Ethnic Music in America*, attributes this trend, at least in part, to "the American elite," who, he argues, have tended to regard polkas as "part of the mediocre, distasteful culture of beer-drinking, half-literate white working-class slobs."[28] But isn't it just as likely that polka-related injuries—and the many obstacles society places in the path of those striving to overcome them—are to blame?

polytetrafluoroethylene (PTFE). See: **dental floss.**

polyvinyl chloride (PVC). Polyvinyl chloride (PVC), the New Jersey State Office for Prevention of Developmental Disabilities states categorically,  is "a toxic plastic that is dangerous to our health and the environment." "PVC contains dangerous chemical additives including phthalates, lead, cadmium, and/or organotins," the agency warns on its website,[29] and these toxic additives, which have been linked to cancer, reproductive and immune system damage, and asthma, among other ailments,[30] "can leach out or evaporate into the air over time, posing unnecessary dangers" to you and your family.[31] One of the biggest problems with polyvinyl chloride is its ubiquity. According to the Center for Health, Environment and Justice, the litany of products containing PVC includes apparel, automotive dashboards and upholstery, baby oil, building materials including pipes and flooring, cell phones, children's car seats, cleaning products, computer keyboards, credit cards, dishwasher and refrigerator racks, food packaging, mouthwash, plastic utensils, shampoo, shower curtains, suntan lotion, tablecloths, toys, wall coverings, and even waterbeds.[32]

And, ironically, once polyvinyl chloride is in the environment, there's no safe way to get rid of it, laments CEHJ's founder, Lois Marie Gibbs, the legendary anti–toxic waste crusader whose efforts on behalf of Love Canal victims led to the creation of the U.S. Environmental Protection Agency's Superfund in 1980. "You can't burn it," she writes, "it just changes to dioxin, another very toxic pollutant. You can't bury it—chemicals leak out into the surrounding soil and groundwater. You can't recycle it—it contaminates the recycling process." So what's to be done? "As consumers we need to send a strong message to corporations who are resisting the effort to eliminate PVC and let them know we will not purchase their products," Gibbs urges. "And, we need to enlist all levels of government to pass strong policies to phase out PVC." Furthermore, she concludes, "we must move quickly. Generating as much as seven billion pounds of PVC waste each year cannot continue . . . PVC wastes will live beyond the lifetime of everybody on this planet—a terrible legacy to leave for future generations."[33]

"Pompeiization." See: **Yellowstone National Park.**

portfolio diversification. Perhaps the one piece of advice you're likely to hear from any financial manager is "Diversify. Don't put all your eggs in one basket." But is this *good* advice? "No!" warned the late Philip Fisher, heralded by Morningstar.com as "one of the great investors of all time."[34] "Fear of having too many eggs in one basket has caused [investors] to put far too little into companies they thoroughly know and far too much in others about which they know nothing at all." And making investments without sufficient background knowledge, Fisher explained, can be *far* riskier than inadequate diversification. So what should investors do instead? Focus on individual stocks. "Take extreme care to own not the most, but the best," Fisher advised. "A little bit of a great many can never be more than a poor substitute for a few of the outstanding."[35] See: **stocks, individual, focusing on.**

potato chips. See: **acrylamide; trans fats.**

potatoes, baked. See: **acrylamide.**

potted plants. Do you have a potted plant outside your front door?

 Have you considered the possibility that if there were a fire in your home, and you had to rush out quickly, you could trip over it and die? Well, you could. Indeed, the chances are great enough that the city of Stoke-on-Trent, England, has ordered residents living in council flats there to throw the potted plants on their porches away. "While we can sympathize with those people who want to add decor to their building," explains Stoke city councillor John Daniels, "safety has to be the paramount concern."[36] And to make matters worse, the soil in the pot containing your plant could actually *cause* the fire that leads to your fatal stumble. That's because the material in the plastic pots plants are sold in commonly contains little, if any, real dirt. "What you find is a mixture of peat and vermiculite," warns the Wisconsin Department of Agriculture, Trade, and Consumer Protection. "When peat is dry, it burns easily." Indeed, a discarded cigarette butt is hot enough to ignite it, and, once lit, it can smolder for hours at a temperature high enough to melt the pot itself and set anything flammable in the immediate vicinity ablaze.[37] Still not convinced that your potted plant is a hazard? Then ask the residents of the 159-unit condominium at 23 Millrise Drive SW in Calgary, Alberta. On March 18, 2010, a massive fire there caused by a cigarette thrown into a planter left three hundred of them homeless.[38] See also: **welcome mats.**

poultry litter. See: **salmon, farmed.**

pound cake. See: **high-fat, high-calorie food addiction.**

power-plant waste (PPW). See: **coal.**

pregnancy, unwanted. See: **abstinence; birth-control pills; condoms; romance novels.**

premenstrual syndrome (PMS). See: **aspartame.**

prescription drugs, side-effects warning labels on. See: **side-effects warning labels on prescription drugs.**

pretexting. See: **identity theft.**

prophylactic devices. See: **condoms.**

prune juice. See: **acrylamide.**

Pseudomonas aeruginosa. See: **mascara.**

pulmonary anthrax. See: **runny nose.**

pulmonary edema. See: **hydrogen peroxide.**

puppies. See: **dogs.**

purses. Charles P. Gerba, Ph.D., the well-known University of Arizona microbe hunter, says the outside of purses—especially the bottoms—are among the "germiest objects" he's ever tested, largely because purses tend to pick up illness-causing bacteria from just about every surface they're placed on. "Remember, you're going outside. You're shopping. You're going to the restroom. You're going to the theater. Well, every time you put [your handbag] down, you're picking up a germ. If I was a germ, I'd be looking for a purse all the time because you're going to take me home to your family." And, to make matters worse, says Dr. Gerba, when you get home, you're as likely as not to walk into the kitchen and plunk your purse down "right on your counter, next to your sink where you're going to make dinner."[39] The folks at the purse-security website HandbagProtection.com are plenty worried about this, too. "Would you set a floor mop on your kitchen counter?" they ask rhetorically. "Of course not—floors are filthy and you don't want to spread germs and bacteria to your food preparation areas. That's exactly what happens when you set your purse on the floor, come home and place it on your table and counter."[40] Purses are basically "subways for microorganisms," Dr. Gerba says. "I'm afraid to touch them. You know, I know too much. I'll never become a purse snatcher, believe me."[41]

So what can you do to make your purse less of a hazard for you and yours? Well, HandbagProtection.com has one answer: For a mere $6.95, they'll sell you a "Purse Protector," a clever, portable, and surprisingly attractive little gadget you can slip around the edge of a table, desk, or counter and then hang your purse from so it won't ever come in contact with all the nasties on the floor or, for that matter, with any *clean* surface that you're trying to keep germ-free (To learn more, visit http://www.handbagprotection.com).[42] TV's most popular medical guru, Dr. Mehmet Oz, has some good advice on this subject, too: "Leave your purse at your door so you don't contaminate your home with what your bag picked up from the environment outside," he advises.[43] And, finally, some words of wisdom from Dr. Gerba himself: "To be on the safe side," he says, "it's probably a good idea to wipe purse bottoms down with a disinfectant wipe once a day."[44]

pursing your lips. Don't purse your lips! According to Melanie Vas-

seur, founder and chief chemist of the Fresh and Age-less Skin blog, doing so habitually will lead to wrinkles and lines around the mouth, which, Ms. Vasseur reminds us, are "often the first signs of aging on the face." (Luckily, if you have already pursed your lips for too long and have developed wrinkles in the lip and mouth area, it's not too late to reverse the trend. Vasseur Skincare, Ms. Vasseur's own company, manufactures a product called Gold Serum that, she says, uses "plant placenta DNA and RNA, nature's building blocks" to "heal and repair the skin" and "lessen your mouth area wrinkles over time."[45])

PVC. See: **polyvinyl chloride.**

Q

Qi Gong Psychotic Reaction. See: **meditation.**

quantitative easing. See: **biflation; inflation; stimulus spending, inadequate; stimulus spending, overzealous.**

quitting smoking. The hazards of smoking are universally known. (For a comprehensive review of specific conditions and diseases associated with tobacco smoke, see our entry on **smoking.**) But here's a far less publicized fact that should concern you deeply if you're a smoker thinking about kicking the nicotine habit: The act of *quitting* smoking is also highly risky and dangerous. For one thing, the drug Chantix (known generically as varenicline), widely prescribed to help patients withdraw from tobacco, has, according to the Institute for Safe Medication Practices, been linked to a wide array of health and safety problems including accidents and falls; potentially lethal heart rhythm disturbances; heart attacks; seizures; blurred vision and transient blindness; severe skin reactions; and a host of psychiatric disturbances including suicides or attempted suicides, psychosis, paranoia, hallucinations, and "homicidal ideation" (not to mention other potentially dangerous forms of hostility and aggression).[1]

Second, a Johns Hopkins University study published in the *Annals of Internal Medicine* in 2011 found that people who quit smoking "have a 70 percent increased risk of developing type 2 diabetes in the first six years without cigarettes as compared to people who never smoked." The Johns Hopkins team suspects that the elevated diabetes is related to the weight gains that are typically associated with a withdrawal from nicotine addiction.[2] (Of course, putting on significant poundage can present health problems above and beyond any diabetes concerns. The more weight you gain, writes Dr. Susan Jebb, the former head of the UK Association for the Study of Obesity, the greater your risk of cardiovascular disease; colon, prostate, and breast cancer; joint problems and back pain; and breathing or sleeping difficulties.[3])

Third, you're undoubtedly aware of the severe withdrawal symptoms that accompany most attempts to stop smoking—particularly when smokers attempt to quit "cold turkey." These include dizziness, light-headedness, insomnia, restlessness, anxiety, irritability, and hostility, not to mention depression that, the British National Health Service warns, can in rare cases become so severe that those attempting to stop using tobacco consider or actually attempt suicide.[4] As you may also have heard, nicotine patches, which provide a steady, controlled dose of nicotine to those who wear them, can ease some of these symptoms.[5] But before resorting to the use of nicotine patches—or nicotine gum, lozenges, inhalers, or pills—you'd be wise to consider this advice from the renowned British antismoking guru, Allen Carr: "Nicotine patches and other forms of NRT [nicotine replacement therapy] don't replace nicotine—they *are* nicotine. All these products do is help keep many smokers physically and psychologically addicted to the substance that's causing their problems in the first place."[6]

quivering, internal. See: **wind turbine syndrome.**

R

rabies exposures. See: **petting zoos.**

radioactive waste. See: **nuclear energy.**

radon. Learning that you may have deadly radon in your basement

must seem a little like being told that there could be a kill-crazy Klingon in your closet—it calls to mind some sort of far-fetched extraterrestrial threat from a dated science-fiction movie. Alas, radon is no futuristic fantasy. It is a nearly omnipresent element produced by the natural decay, first into radium and then into radon gas, of trace amounts of uranium present in almost all soils. Measurable, and often potentially lethal, concentrations of the colorless, odorless, tasteless, and highly radioactive noble gas have been detected, usually in basements, in about one in every fifteen residential structures in all fifty states. The Environmental Protection Administration estimated in

2003 that incidental inhalation of radon was responsible for twenty-one thousand deaths per year, and the Centers for Disease Control's National Center for Injury Prevention and Control produced a handy table for assessing the impact of radon exposure on both smokers and nonsmokers.

Using a standard level of radiation intensity found in any given home based on the volume of picocuries emitted per liter of air (pCi/L), the CDC came up with a pair of compelling lists of comparative risks. For smokers, who already inhale significant quantities of radon in cigarette smoke, inhabiting a dwelling with a level of 20 pCi/L would pose a risk of dying equal to 250 times the risk of drowning; at 10 pCi/L, it would equal 200 times the risk of dying in a house fire; at 8 pCi/L, 30 times the risk of dying in a fall; at 4 pCi/L, 5 times the risk of dying in a car crash; and at 2 pCi/L, 6 times the risk of dying from poison. And even for nonsmokers, the hazards were sobering: at 20 pCi/L, 35 times the risk of drowning; at 10 pCi/L, 20 times the risk of dying in a home fire; at 8 pCi/L, 4 times the risk of dying in a fall; at 4 pCi/L, the same risk as that of dying in a car crash; and at 2 pCi/L, the same risk as that of dying from poison.

Happily, a number of simple test kits, including charcoal canisters, alpha tracks, electret ion chambers, continuous monitors, and charcoal liquid scintillation detectors are available that can sample basement air over a two-day period and accurately establish a home's radon level, and there are some fairly straightforward and reasonably inexpensive mitigation procedures that can be undertaken.[1] Unhappily, one must actually go into the basement to attach these devices to the wall or ceiling and then, if the results turn up positive, to install some ventilators and make a few other alterations. And it is in basements that the astonishingly deadly hantavirus found in rodent droppings is most likely to lurk. Through December of 2010, there have been 560 cases of hantavirus pulmonary syndrome (HPS) reported in the United States, with a staggering 36 percent mortality rate.[2] According to the New York Department of Health, "typical symptoms include high fever, muscle aches, cough, and headache. After several days, respiratory problems worsen rapidly. The lungs may fill with fluid and victims may die of respiratory shock." And unlike radon, there is no test for either hantavirus or HPS.[3] As the department's

Peter Constantakes noted following the sudden death from HPS in June of 2011 of a chiropractor on the east end of Long Island who had recently cleaned his basement, "It's undetectable until a person gets sick."[4] See: **Grand Central Terminal; kitchen countertops, "natural stone."**

rainforest destruction. See: **coffee.**

"Rapture of the Nerds." See: **Singularity, the.**

rBGH; rBST. See: **milk.**

reading on the toilet. It's hard for the editors of *Encyclopedia Paranoiaca*—or our colleagues at the Cassandra Institute—to imagine that anyone might choose to read a serious and important work such as ours on the toilet. But, you may have wondered, if you *did* happen to do so, would it be dangerous? The sad answer, according to David Gutman, M.D., the founder and lead physician of American Hemorrhoid Specialists, is yes. "You shouldn't be reading on the toilet. Bowel movements should be quick," he says. The reason? Sitting on the toilet too long can lead to the development of hemorrhoids, which as Dr. Gutman is only too happy to remind us, "can cause bleeding, itching, pain, and the protrusion of tissue through the rectum." "Hemorrhoids are derived from anatomical structures called anal cushions—like small balloons—embedded within the wall of the anal canal," Dr. Gutman explains. Unnecessarily prolonged toilet sitting "can increase pressure on these anal cushions, causing them to become stretched out and irritated." And voilà, you've got hemorrhoids.

Dr. Gutman, whose motto is "sensitive care for a sensitive condition," understands only too well what a problem it will be for some folks to give up the habit of perusing their favorite newspaper, magazine, or novel on the "porcelain throne," and he has a solution to offer. "What I would recommend," he says, "is once they are done with the movement—if they insist on wanting to stay and read—they should wipe, flush, put the toilet-seat cover down, and sit on that. It's almost like sitting on a chair."[5] (Now you know why the American Hemorrhoid Specialists website calls Dr. Gutman a "visionary."[6]) **See also: toilets, ceramic.**

refrigerator racks. See: **polyvinyl chloride (PVC).**

relaxation-induced anxiety. See: **meditation.**

relish. See: **high-fructose corn syrup (HFCS).** See also: **ketchup, relish, and mustard containers.**

relish containers. See: **ketchup, relish, and mustard containers.**

research studies. Are individuals—or governments—horribly mis-guided when they base nutritional, health, or policy decisions on the results of "scientific research"? Well, documentary filmmaker and former science writer Tom Naughton is so skeptical about the way research studies are funded, conducted, manipulated, and reported on—all for the purpose of advancing one agenda or another—that he's concocted a fantasy describing how he'd go about "convincing the American public" that celery (which he labels "a harmless food I don't like very much and wouldn't mind giving up") causes "premature death." First of all, working "in cahoots" with a few "prominent health organizations," he would solicit research studies showing that, say, "75% of all heart attack victims consumed celery in the previous year." (This assertion would be easy to prove, because it's almost undoubtedly true; it just happens to be completely irrelevant to whether eating celery is "dangerous" or not.) Then he'd mount a major campaign to persuade the news media to "trumpet" the celery-death connection. "Given the current state of nutrition and health journalism, this wouldn't be a difficult task," Naughton says. Soon the press would be "full of headlines warning people to cut celery from their diets. *Time* magazine would run a major article titled 'Sorry, It's True . . . Celery Is A Killer.' (Subtitle: 'Party Trays Will Never Be the Same.')"

Next, Naughton proclaims, would come "the really fun part." After a decade or so, he says, he'd conduct "a large epidemiological study comparing celery consumption with death rates. And I can already guarantee the result: people who eat a lot of celery tend to die younger. This would, of course, prove that celery is a health hazard, right? Of course not. All it would prove is that health-conscious people had heeded the warnings and were dutifully avoiding celery." Or, to look at it from the opposite point of view, it would demonstrate that people who deliberately disregarded "the dire warnings about celery" were what the medical profession calls nonadherers—folks who tend to ignore health warnings of *any* kind and, as a result, also eat all kinds of *truly* unhealthy stuff, or smoke a couple of packs a day, or never get any exercise.

"Finally, for the big punch line, I'd get to announce that the whole thing was a joke," Naughton concludes. *"'Fooled ya, folks! There is not and never has been anything dangerous about eating celery. Ha-ha.'* But by then, no one would believe me. I'd be accused of being a flack for Big Celery."[7] (Ironically, it turns out that eating celery actually *may* increase your risk of premature death. Based on scientific research conducted by the U.S. Food and Drug Administration, the Environmental Working Group has placed celery on its "Dirty Dozen" list of foods so contaminated with pesticides that, unless they're grown organically, you'd be well advised to shun them entirely.[8] See: **celery.**)

restrooms, airplane. See: **airplane cabins.**

restrooms, unsanitary-looking, excessive fear of. See: **"holding it in."**

reusable shopping bags, environmental impact of. Taking along

your own rugged, long-lasting, earth-friendly carryall on a shopping trip looks like an easy way to avoid contributing to the colossal annual U.S. trash mountain of 100 billion lightweight plastic nonbiodegradable disposable baggies, but on closer inspection these feel-good bags turn out to be pretty sad sacks. For one thing, the vast majority of the inexpensive heavy-duty reusable bags many retailers provide for their customers are made in China, under lax regulatory supervision, from polypropylene, a durable plastic that takes nearly thirty times more energy to manufacture than the flimsy throwaways they are meant to replace, and almost ten times as much power as is consumed in the production of old-fashioned paper sacks processed from often recklessly harvested trees in polluting pulp mills. Even nonsynthetic bags made from canvas, hemp, jute, or cotton require a surprising amount of water to fabricate, and they are often treated with ecologically damaging caustic chemical dyes. In any case, several studies have shown that fewer than half, and possibly less than 10 percent, of the heavyweight reusable bags are actually reused, as opposed to being left in closets, forgotten in car trunks, stuffed into the back of kitchen cabinets, or worse still, simply thrown out, ending up in landfills, where their greater bulk guarantees that they will languish for a few centuries longer than their less substantial counterparts. Furthermore, when pondering a decision on whether or not to get in the habit of transporting your purchases in some sort of reusable gunnysack, there may in fact be another far more compelling reason to "bag it."[9] For details, see: **reusable shopping bags, health hazards of.**

reusable shopping bags, health hazards of. Personal carrier bags made of natural fibers or durable plastic are often referred to as "the bag for life" because their widespread adoption by shoppers could reduce oil consumption and cut back on carbon production, but they should perhaps more properly be termed "the bag for death." Wegmans Foods, a major chain of supermarkets, recently replaced 725,000 bags of two different designs after a consumer group discovered that the toxic totes contained high amounts of lead,[10] and lululemon, a Canadian athletic retailer, recalled its reusable bags because of "environmental concerns . . . over [their] proper disposal due to lead content."[11]

Equally disturbing were the results of a 2010 joint study by the University of Arizona and Loma Linda University which found that reusable shopping bags were often carriers of more than just food items—half of the bags they examined contained fecal coliform bacteria and 12 percent had traces of the deadly *E. coli* strain. The study concluded that "reusable grocery bags can be a breeding ground for dangerous foodborne bacteria and pose a serious risk to public health," and recommended that users of the potentially lethal satchels be urged to wash and bleach them regularly, to refrain from using them to carry gym clothes, and to avoid leaving them in car trunks where high temperatures might cause meat and produce to spoil.[12] A similar alarm was sounded by Dr. Richard Summerbell, research director at Toronto's Sporemetrics and former chief of medical mycology at the Ontario Ministry of Health, who reported discovering mold and bacteria concentrations in reusable carrier bags over 300 percent above safe levels.[13] The bottom line on those so-called green bags?—a bright red warning light.

right to live as we wish, subversion of. See: **Nanny Statism.**

rinsing your mouth out after brushing your teeth. According to Dr.
 Phil Stemmer, B.D.S., you should "fight the urge" to rinse your mouth out after cleaning your teeth. "Rinsing washes away the protective fluoride coating left by the toothpaste, which would otherwise add hours of protection," explains Dr. Stemmer, the founder and clinical director of the Fresh Breath Centre in London. "I try to avoid drinking any fluids for at least half an hour after brushing—it's a strange sensation at first, but you quickly get used to it. And I don't even wet my toothbrush under the tap before brushing as this can dilute the effect of the toothpaste. There's plenty of moisture in your mouth without adding excess water."[14]

rising sea levels. See: **sea levels, rising; global warming.**

robots. The popular Hollywood-generated images of malicious au-
 tomatons like the cyborgs in the *Terminator* movies, the galaxy-gobbling Borg of the *Star Trek* series, and the honey-voiced homicidal supercomputer in *2001: A Space Odyssey* have contributed to a general level of dread about the prospect in the near future of our effective replacement by various forms of artificial intelligence. But do we really need to worry about those cute little self-propelled vacuum-cleaning Roombas evolving into uncontrollable, world-dominating, death-dealing Doombas?

Well, yes, according to a number of experts in the fast-growing field of cognitive robotics. In 2008, Hans Moravec of the Robotics Institute of Carnegie Mellon University predicted that by 2040 "we will finally achieve the original goal of robotics and a thematic mainstay of science fiction: a freely moving machine with the intellectual capabilities of a human being."[15] And, as David Bruemmer of the Idaho National Laboratory has noted, "The somewhat shocking realization is that if someday AI [Artificial Intelligence] can reach a level comparable to human intelligence, there is no reason why it will not continue to sail past it."[16]

Sadly, it may already be too late to stop this imminent technological Götterdämmerung, particularly if, as seems likely, coming generations of superintelligent, servo-motor-actuated, sensor-equipped data-processing units develop the ability to make copies of themselves. Colin McGinn, professor of philosophy at the University of Miami, described the looming threat succinctly: "Self-replication is perhaps the biggest hazard presented by advanced computer technology . . . Victor Frankenstein refused to give his monstrous creation a bride for fear of this reproductive potential. Maybe we should be thinking hard now about the replicative powers of intelligent machines. If the 20th century was the century of nuclear weapons, then the 21st might be the century of self-breeding aliens of our own devising."[17] See also: **gray goo; Singularity, the.**

Rocky Mountain spotted fever. See: **tick-borne diseases.**

romance novels. Do you enjoy reading romance novels? If you do,

you may think that doing so is, at worst, a harmless diversion. But according to British "relationship psychologist," author, and television personality Susan Quilliam, women who read "bodice rippers" are putting themselves at serious risk of an unwanted pregnancy or contracting a sexually transmitted disease. Citing—among other things—a research survey that found only 11.5 percent of romantic novels mention condom use,[18] Quilliam reports, in the July 2011 issue of the *Journal of Family Planning and Reproductive Health Care,* that she has found a "clear correlation" between the frequency of romance reading and a negative attitude toward condoms. Romantic fiction, she explains, influences readers to "suspend rationality" and forsake contraception in favor of being "swept up by the moment as a heroine would," and she and her colleagues are seeing the sad consequences every day "in our clinics and therapy rooms." "Sometimes the kindest and wisest thing we can do for our clients is to encourage them to put down the books—and pick up reality," she concludes.[19]

Richard McComb, in an article about Quilliam and her work in the Birmingham (England) *Sunday Mercury,* summarizes this sorry syndrome dramatically and succinctly: "How many times does a half-naked shepherd don a condom in a pulse-racer before ravishing a divorcee on a rain-lashed Yorkshire hillside?" he asks. "It just doesn't happen. The next thing you know is the heroine's got a dose of chlamydia and a bun in the oven."[20]

room air purifiers. Room air purifiers are often recommended as a means of removing dangerous particulate matter from the air in our homes and offices. But are they safe to use? Categorically not, says a team of researchers at the University of California at Irvine. The reason? They produce ozone—some intentionally (their manufacturers claim that ozone reacts with particle molecules to improve air quality), and some as a by-product of the ionization process they use to "clean the air."[21] In either case, the ozone spewed out by these machines is more hazardous than any substances they may remove. As the California Air Resources Board puts it: "Ozone can harm the cells in the lungs and respiratory airways . . . It causes symptoms including coughing, chest tightness, and shortness of breath. In persons with asthma, ozone can worsen asthma symptoms, and one study indicates that ozone may contribute to the development of asthma. Ozone impairs breathing. Elevated exposures to ozone can cause permanent lung damage, and repeated exposure can even increase the risk of dying among persons already in poor health." And that's not all! "In addition to its impacts on health," the Board reports, "ozone can also damage materials such as rubber, fabrics, plastics and other indoor furnishings."[22] See also: **air fresheners.**

rubber duckies. Rubber duckies may indeed (to quote Ernie's im- mortal *Sesame Street* paean) "make bath time lots of fun." But, according to Philip M. Tierno Jr., Ph.D., the director of clinical microbiology and immunology at the New York University Langone Medical Center, they also pose a serious health risk to children—and their parents, too—because they accumulate bacteria at an alarming rate from the filthy bathwater they spend so many hours floating in. When Tierno, who has famously called the water in our tubs "a bacterial soup" (see: **baths**), examined a selection of kids' bath toys, he discovered that virtually every one was covered with "sky-high counts" of fecal bacteria, such as *E. coli* and *Streptococcus,* as well as *S. aureus* (which causes skin infections and far worse) and several other germs and viruses. When kids play with these toys, Tierno told the *Today* show, they often put them in their mouths or use them to squirt water on themselves or each other, so the opportunity for disease is hard to understate. And of all the "tubby toys" he tested, warned Tierno, rubber ducks and other squeaky toys were by far the most hazardous, because they have holes in them that "trap water inside and let germs thrive." When he cut these open, he said, "they looked liked sewer pipes, caked with black chunks of bacteria, filth kids could be ingesting."[23]

And, as if Tierno's findings aren't scary enough, consider this: Illness-bearing microbes are hardly the only health hazard associated with rubber duckies and their bathtub toy brethren. Rick Smith, the executive director of Environmental Defence Canada, had his own son's favorite duckie tested by the STAT Analysis Laboratory in Chicago and discovered that it contained lead, bromine, chlorine, and chromium—all known toxins. Perhaps worse still, the tests confirmed that the duckie's characteristic "pleasant rubberiness" was attributable to chemicals called phthalates (pronounced THAL-ates)— compounds that, according to the Environmental Working Group, are known to disrupt the human endocrine system and to cause reduced sperm counts, testicular atrophy, and structural abnormalities in the reproductive systems of male test animals, and that have also been linked to liver cancer. Smith found all this so worrisome that he decided to make his son's plaything the iconic "bête noire" of *Slow Death* by *Rubber Duck: The Secret Danger of Everyday Things,* the best-selling book he coauthored with environmentalist Bruce Lourie.[24] In sum, isn't it time to follow the advice imparted in another one of Ernie's iconic *Sesame Street* songs and "Put Down the Duckie"?

runny nose. If a teenage friend—or, worse, your own son or  daughter—has a runny nose, it could be a warning sign that she or he is using cocaine or other illicit drugs, cautions SAMHSA—the U.S. government's Substance Abuse and Mental Health Services Administration.[25] What's more, even if the runny-nosed individual in question proves not to be a substance abuser, he or she could be displaying early symptoms of asthma, cystic fibrosis, measles, nasal cancer, pneumonia, pulmonary anthrax, a skull fracture or traumatic brain injury, whooping cough, and/or a whole host of other dangerous diseases and conditions.[26] In this context, it's easy to see why California physician Erich Rosenberger, M.D., urges caution when confronted with an unexplained runny nose. "If you aren't sure what the cause is," he writes, "give a call to your doctor or a nurse."[27]

S

"safe sex." The helpful website Dating Aid defines *safe sex* as "a term that describes a sexual practice where there isn't any contact that involves fluids passing between partners. No exchange of blood, semen, vaginal fluids, or saliva." The site goes on to observe that "this is almost impossible, unless all kinds of physical contact is [sic] avoided in sexual activities" or "total abstinence is practiced."[1] Have fun! See: **abstinence; cybersex.**

safety card, airline. See: **airplane seat pockets.**

salad. See: **leafy green vegetables.**

salads, fast-food. "Offering a salad entrée is the latest marketing push for fast-food and quick-serve chains," reports the Physicians Committee for Responsible Medicine (PCRM). But, the organization says, an analysis by their nutrition experts demonstrates that "many fast-food salads are not any more healthful than a greasy burger." For example, PCRM found that "McDonald's Crispy Chicken Bacon Ranch Salad" with dressing has a hefty fifty-one grams of fat and 660 calories while a Big Mac has thirty-four grams of fat and 590 calories. Surprisingly, this salad entrée also has just as much cholesterol, eighty-five milligrams, as the Big Mac. "Indeed," PCRM cautions, "all six of McDonald's entrée salads are packed with fat and cholesterol, mainly from chicken and cheese." As a result the organization gave each of them their lowest health rating. Other particularly "artery-clogging salads" earning this dubious accolade include Wendy's Chicken BLT and Subway's Meatball Salad. "We did not expect these new salad entrées to be so loaded with fat and cholesterol," says Brie Turner-McGrievy, M.S., R.D., the clinical research coordinator at PCRM. "Americans thinking about getting in shape should steer clear."[2]

salmon, farmed. According to David Carpenter, M.D., director of the Institute for Health and the Environment at the University at Albany, SUNY, whose major research study on the contamination of fish was published in 2004 in the journal *Science,* nature didn't intend for salmon to be crammed into pens and raised on a diet consisting of soy, poultry litter, and hydrolyzed chicken feathers. As a result, he says, farmed salmon contain less vitamin D than wild-caught salmon, and are laced with far more contaminants, including carcinogens, PCBs, brominated flame retardants (just what you were hoping to get along with your seafood meal, right?), and pesticides. "You can only safely eat one of these [farmed] salmon dinners every 5 months without increasing your risk of cancer," Dr. Carpenter warns. "It's that bad." (By the way, if the fish you're buying is labeled "fresh Atlantic salmon," it's farmed. As Liz Vaccariello, editor in chief of *Prevention* points out, "There are no commercial fisheries left for wild Atlantic salmon.")[3]

salt, excessive consumption of. Although sodium, together with po-

tassium, magnesium, and calcium, belongs to a class of four critical electrolytes essential for healthy bodily function, and in the form of sodium chloride is a key dietary component, excessive salt consumption is now generally linked to a startling array of serious medical problems, including hypertension, stroke, cardiovascular disease, left ventricular hypertrophy, duodenal and gastric ulcers, gastric cancer, kidney disease, and osteoporosis. The alarming increase in the incidence of these conditions would seem to suggest that a major campaign to reduce overall salt consumption is in order, and in fact a recent study conducted jointly by researchers at the University of California, San Francisco, Stanford University, and Columbia University and published in the *New England Journal of Medicine* comes to exactly that conclusion. The statistics the scientists include in their report are indeed dramatic. According to their data, a per capita decrease in our average salt intake of just half a teaspoon per day could prevent between forty-four thousand and ninety-two thousand deaths from all causes annually in the United States alone.[4] "That, dear reader," enthuses *New York Times* health writer Jane Brody, "would be a very big bang for a relatively small buck."[5] See: **salt, insufficient consumption of.**

salt, insufficient consumption of. Early in 2010, researchers at the

University of California, San Francisco, Stanford University, and Columbia University announced the results of a joint study, concluding that reducing American's dietary salt levels would have an immediate beneficial effect. But Dr. Michael Alderman, professor of medicine and epidemiology at the Albert Einstein College of Medicine, is anything but convinced. The researchers' recommendations, he argued, were "based on the assumption that there would be no other effects of reduced sodium, but that's not so."[6] Specifically, Alderman points out, cutting back on salt can produce such undesirable side effects as insulin resistance, a dangerous condition in which the body's insulin loses its effectiveness in lowering blood sugar, and hormone imbalances, and he is far from alone in expressing such concerns.

Also urging us, in effect, to take these conclusions with more than a grain of salt are a pair of British physiologists, Dr. Markus Mohaupt, who found that pregnant women suffering from pre-eclampsia could be at risk from reduced sodium intake, and Bill Keatinge, who warns against a low-salt diet among the elderly during hot weather, cautioning that "heat stress causes loss of salt and water in sweat, which thickens the blood and can lead to an *increased* [emphasis added] risk of heart attack and stroke." Their doubts are echoed by Dr. David McCarron, a professor in the Department of Nutrition at the University of California at Davis who in 2007 urged the government of the United Kingdom to reconsider its national campaign to restrict salt consumption, comparing it to the previous decade's ill-advised program of hormone replacement therapy that ultimately led to a spike in breast cancer, stating in no uncertain terms, "Your policy on salt could be the next major public health disaster."[7]

It has also been suspected that a perennial sodium deficit could contribute to dysautonomia, a rare but severe and little-understood neurological disorder, and can cause hyponatremia (dangerously low sodium levels), a potentially grave nutritional complication which can result in muscle cramps, nausea, vomiting, dizziness, shock, coma, and death.[8] See: **salt, excessive consumption of.**

Santa Claus. "Santa Claus long ago displaced the Virgin Mary and  baby as the most unmistakable Christmas iconography," writes Dr. Nathan J. Grills, a public health fellow in the Department of Epidemiology and Preventative Medicine at Monash University in Melbourne, Australia. But, as Grills laments in a *British Medical Journal* article entitled "Santa Claus: A Public Health Pariah?," there has not been a commensurate increase in rigorous research on the effect of Santa on public health in general, and, specifically, on the infectious disease risk of Santa impersonators. Noting that a survey of members of the Amalgamated Order of Real Bearded Santas (AORBS), an international association of "real bearded gentlemen dedicated to the joy of being Santa," found that "Santa is sneezed or coughed on up to 10 times a day," Grills points out that the potential for mall Santas, in their asymptomatic phase, to propagate an infectious disease is only too clear. "Unsuspecting little Johnny gets to sit on Santa's lap, but as well as his present he gets H1N1 influenza," Grills writes. "Santa continues on his merry way and gives the present to a few more 100 kids before coming down with influenza himself. This then becomes a contact tracer's nightmare."[9]

And that's hardly the only health issue involving "Jolly Old Saint Nick." In 2007, for example, acting U.S. surgeon general Rear Admiral Steven K. Galson bemoaned Santa's bulk, and urged that he be portrayed as slimmer and more fit. "It is really important that the people who kids look up to as role models are in good shape, eating well and getting exercise," he told the *Boston Herald*. "It is absolutely critical. Santa is no different."[10] And Westaff, a company that supplies "quality caring Santas" to stores and other clients, has noted that Saint Nick's traditional booming "ho, ho, ho" greeting can be terrifying to small children. (Westaff has suggested to its trainees that they might want to try a gentle "ha, ha, ha," instead.)[11] In sum, for the sake of your child's physical and emotional well-being, shouldn't you consider giving Santa Claus a wide berth the next time the holidays roll around?

sashimi. See: **sushi, sashimi, and ceviche.**

saunas. See: **gyms.**

sausage. See: **high-fat, high-calorie food addiction.**

school lunches, unhealthy. See: **Nanny Statism.**

scurvy. You may consider scurvy more a historical curiosity than a current threat, but if so, you're sadly misguided. Indeed, scurvy is once again becoming common, warns the National Association for Scurvy Awareness and Prevention, principally because of the lack of fresh fruits and vegetables in the modern diet. Scurvy is characterized by weakness and aching joints and muscles, bleeding of the gums and other spontaneous hemorrhaging, loosening of the teeth, anemia, drying up of the skin and hair, general debility and immobility, and severe depression. If scurvy is left untreated, it frequently results in death. Luckily, however, this horrible disease *can* be prevented—for example, by eating an ample supply of foods rich in vitamin C, such as oranges and parsley, or by taking a vitamin C supplement.[12] (See **oranges, parsley,** and **vitamin C supplements.**)

sea levels, rising. Of all the effects of global warming, perhaps the

scariest is that increasing temperatures have the potential to cause sea levels to rise—perhaps dramatically. "Thermal expansion has already raised the oceans 4 to 8 inches," writes Stefan Lovgren of *National Geographic.* "But that's nothing compared to what would happen if, for example, Greenland's massive ice sheet were to melt." According to Lovgren, "the complete melting of Greenland" would cause sea levels to rise by twenty-three feet. But, he says, many scientists believe that the early stages of that process will cause at least a three-foot rise within the next hundred years. "The consequences would be catastrophic," warns Jonathan Overpeck, director of the Institute for the Study of Planet Earth at the University of Arizona in Tucson. A three-foot rise, he says, would "destroy whole nations and their cultures that have existed for thousands of years." Indeed, Overpeck's computer models show that island countries such as the Maldives in the Indian Ocean would be entirely submerged, and the Nile Delta and parts of Bangladesh would be rendered uninhabitable, turning tens of millions of their inhabitants into homeless refugees. In addition, a three-foot sea-level rise would swamp every U.S. East Coast city from Boston to Miami, and wreak havoc all along the Gulf Coast. "No one will be free from this," Overpeck concludes.[13] See also: **global warming.**

seat belts. Seat belts save lives, right? Well, according to internation-

ally renowned transport expert John G. U. Adams, a professor emeritus at University College London, they don't, and he's compiled traffic fatality data from seventeen different countries to support his point, which is that seat belts merely move deaths from inside cars to outside them because—as a consequence of making drivers feel safer—they encourage more risk taking, which, in turn, leads to an increase in the number of accidents. In short, Adams asserts, "protecting car occupants from the consequences of bad driving encourages bad driving." Seat belt proponents argue that there's no way to know how many—if, indeed, *any*—of the accidents upon which Adams's figures are based were caused by drivers' subconscious feelings of invulnerability, and, even if they were, whether it was seat belt use that led to such emotions. Therefore, they say, Adams's statistics are meaningless. In response, Adams admits that a comparison of road accident death statistics "does not prove that seat belt legislation has failed." "But," he maintains, "it strongly suggests it." [14]

And now, to add insult to injuries, comes word that seat belts may not only contribute to accidents, but are actually hazardous in their own right. Melissa Dahl reports on Today.com that if you're in an accident while you're wearing a tightened seat belt, you could develop a condition called meralgia paresthetica, or as it's more popularly known, "tingling thigh syndrome." [15] Meralgia paresthetica, the Johns Hopkins Hospital explains on its website, occurs when your lateral femoral cutaneous nerve becomes compressed, and it can cause "a terrible burning sensation" in your outer thigh which, in some cases, is so severe that surgery is required. [16]

Of course, whether or not you should wear a seat belt is not even your choice in most U.S. states, since "Click it or ticket" seat belt enforcement is the law of the land in the vast majority of them. [17] This worries nationally syndicated automotive columnist Eric Peters a great deal. Whether or not he buckles up, Peters argues in an article published by the National Motorists Association, is "none of the government's business—just as my diet, exercise habits, and other personal choices that may somewhat increase (or decrease) my exposure to risk/danger are likewise none of the government's business, either. Or yours, for that matter." "The premise that 'society' is responsible for the costs of each individual's personal choices is socialistic," Peters continues. "If we go that way, there will be no limit to the Nanny State." [18] See also: **Nanny Statism.**

seat pockets, airplane. See: **airplane seat pockets.**

self-replicating pathogens. See: **gray goo.**

self-replicating robots. See: **robots.**

semen quality, decline in. See: **food containers, plastic.**

severe space weather events. Periodic eruptions of solar flares can produce spectacular auroral displays often called "the Northern Lights" (or, in the southern hemisphere, "the Southern Lights"), but these immense geomagnetic storms pose a grave and ever-growing threat to our increasingly wired, technology-dependent world. The most recent significant such space weather event took place on March 13, 1989, and it triggered the total collapse within ninety seconds of the entire northeast Canadian Hydro-Quebec power grid, leaving millions of people without power for more than nine hours. In August of the same year, another much weaker solar outburst fried microchips at the Toronto Stock Exchange, halting all trading of securities. Six years later, the Canadians took one more hit when a pair of their communications satellites in geosynchronous orbit were disabled by a potent shock wave of charged solar particles. One of them—the $290 million Anik E2—took six months to repair at a cost of almost $70 million.[19] And by far the most powerful solar storm ever recorded—the "Carrington Event" of September 1, 1859, which struck at the very dawn of the modern telecommunication age—knocked out much of the North American telegraph system. The pylons that held the transmission wires emitted sparks, many telegraph operators suffered nasty electric shocks as they tapped on their keys, and sheets of telegraph paper spontaneously caught on fire.[20]

A National Research Council report concluded that if a storm of similar intensity—a "space weather Katrina"—were to strike our vastly more elaborate twenty-first-century infrastructure, the geomagnetic tsunami would short out hundreds of giant electrical transformers, overload computer networks, cripple critical communication and navigation satellites, and even touch off severe electric-resistance-induced corrosion in gas and oil pipelines. The short-term social and economic costs of such a disruption would be in the $4- to $10-billion range, with a final price tag for total restoration of the affected systems of some $1 trillion to $2 trillion after a global recovery project that would likely take four to ten years to complete.

And, according to Tom Bogdan of the Space Weather Prediction Center at the National Oceanic and Atmospheric Administration (NOAA), it's only a matter of time before an astrophysical tempest of the severity of the colossal 1859 solar whopper zaps the earth with energies equivalent to a billion hydrogen bombs[21]—a sobering prediction strongly seconded in a study by the National Academy of Sciences that noted matter-of-factly: "Such extreme events, though rare, are likely to occur again in the future."[22] Jane Lubchenco, also of NOAA, concurred with this bleak forecast of an approaching turbulent period in cosmic meteorology, stating flatly, "This is not a matter of if, it is a matter of when, and how big."[23]

sex. See: **sexual activity; sexually transmitted diseases.** See also: **abstinence; birth-control pills; condoms; cybersex; "safe sex"; summertime sex.**

sex-selective abortion. In 1990, the economist Amartya Sen con-

cluded that based on his study of reported sex ratios in India, China, and much of the developing world, a staggering total of more than 100 million women were, in effect, "missing." At that time, Sen—winner of the 1998 Nobel Prize in Economics—attributed these grim statistics to a combination of gender-based discriminatory factors, including the inferior health care, nutritional resources, and educational opportunities provided to girls, as well as the gruesome but fairly common practice of female infanticide. Two decades later, thanks to the widespread availability even in Third World countries of cheap and effective early sex-determination tests and simple and relatively safe abortion procedures, that tally of the missing has grown to at least 160 million.[24] According to an estimate by the medical journal *The Lancet,* in India alone there were 10 million "missing female births" in the past twenty years, emphasizing that "missing" meant "aborted."[25]

In the aftermath of the sudden proliferation of prenatal ultrasound gender screening clinics in India in 1979, which were touted by the All India Institute of Medical Sciences as a simple and effective method for the identification and elimination of female fetuses, the proportion of females to males in the overall population of India has declined from around 975 girls for every 1,000 boys to about 915 girls per 1,000 boys. According to Sah George, India's most vocal campaigner against this form of "gendercide," by the late 1980s, "every newspaper in Delhi was advertising for ultrasound sex determination. Clinics from Punjab were boasting that they had 10 years experience in eliminating girl children and inviting parents to come to them." [26]

A similar phenomenon was observed in China when the adoption by the government in 1979 of the controversial—and highly effective—"one-child" policy coincided with the introduction of sex testing to produce in the next two decades "a steady increase in the reported sex ratio (of male live births to female live births) from 1.06 to 1.17." Even without similar draconian population control laws, other Asian nations exhibited equally lopsided ratios: In Taiwan the ratio was 1.19, in Singapore it was 1.18, and in South Korea it was 1.12. A report in the *New England Journal of Medicine* concluded that "sex-selective abortion after ultrasonography undoubtedly accounts for a large proportion of the decline in female births," and goes on to note somberly that "the scarcity of females has resulted in the kidnapping and trafficking of women for marriage and increased numbers of commercial sex workers, with a potential rise in HIV infection and other sexually transmitted diseases." [27]

sex toys. A study of sex toys conducted by Greenpeace Netherlands in 2006 examined eight different types of dildos and vibrators purchased at random in a variety of local stores selling erotic products. Seven of the eight were found to contain phthalates, including di-2-ethyl hexyl phthalate (DEHP), disodecyl phthalate (DIDP), and diisononyl phthalate (DINP), in concentrations ranging from 29 percent to 51 percent. Among the harmful health effects of these insidious and ubiquitous chemicals commonly found in plastics are hormone disruption affecting female estrogen levels and damage to the male reproductive system.[28] How can you tell if your favorite pleasure-time plaything is laced with the stuff? Well, the UK's Ethical Sextoys provides a quartet of simple questions for a bit of "fourplay":

- Does the toy have a noticeable "chemical" smell?
- Does it feel oddly soft and pliable?
- Is it made from a jellylike substance?
- Is it really, really cheap?[29]

If the answer to any of those penetrating questions is yes, ditch that tainted lustbuster! And you might consider replacing it with one of the ecologically pure—and libidinally sublime—offerings available on Ethical Sextoys' stimulating website (http://www.ethicalsextoys .co.uk), such as the "Hand blown, crafted glass Dildo by Phalix," "Metal dildos from NJoy & Dai Do," "Beautifully smooth ceramic dildos from Lovemoiselle," the "Nookii Ooh La La Rabbit Vibrator," a set of "Feelz Toys Desi Love Balls," a "Rocks Off/Rock Chick G-Spot Clitoral Vibrating Massager," some "Manzzz Toys/Ringo Vibrating Cock Rings," a "Nookii Bomber Jacket Penis Sleeve," or maybe "a Butt plug made from cool metal and vibrating silicone."[30] After all, as "relationship and sexpert" author Olivia Devinne has observed compellingly, "Imagine lying in a post-orgasmic glow—you don't want to worry about bad chemicals in your body from your sex toy."[31]

sexual activity. According to *Discover* magazine's Patrick Morgan,
 "there are certain things you're not supposed to do during sex and having a heart attack is one of them."[32] The problem is that, according to new research conducted by Issa Dahabreh, M.D., and Jessica Paulus, Sc.D., of Tufts University's Clinical and Translational Science Institute in Boston, you are 2.7 times more likely to suffer an "acute cardiac event" during or shortly after having sexual activity than you are at other times. The good news is that the better shape you get yourself into, the more you improve your chances of surviving your lovemaking sessions. Indeed, according to Tufts' Paulus, a program of regular physical activity can reduce your risk of intimacy-related heart attacks by 30 percent. The bad news is that the Tufts study also found that people are fully 3.5 more times likely to have a heart attack or to

suffer a "sudden cardiac death" during or shortly after vigorous exercise than they are when they're sedentary. In other words, working out to reduce your risk of dying during intercourse is even more dangerous than the sexual act itself.[33] See also: **abstinence; exercise, lack of; "safe sex"; sexually transmitted diseases.**

sexual activity, lack of. See: **abstinence.**

sexually transmitted diseases. Commonly abbreviated to STDs, this
 term is gradually being replaced by a new, broader label, "sexually transmitted infections" (STIs), which experts now prefer because it includes individuals who are "infected," and, through sexual activity, may potentially infect others, without showing signs of "disease." In a simpler time, STDs and STIs were called venereal diseases (VD), a word derived from, appropriately enough, the possessive case, *Veneris,* of *Venus,* the Latin name of the Roman goddess of love. Her son, Cupid, fires the arrows of desire that trigger romances, but in the two millennia since the chubby little cherub began practicing his seductive archery, his darts have ended up imparting to their targets a whole lot of far worse things than the pangs of love. Here, courtesy of the Centers for Disease Control and Prevention, is the latest list of STDs, which annually are responsible for an estimated 340 million new cases of highly transmittable and only partially curable contagions:

- Bacterial infections:
    Bacterial vaginosis (BV)
    Chlamydia trachomatis (chlamydia)
    Haemophilus ducreyi (chancroid)
    Klebsiella granulomatis (granuloma)
    Lymphogranuloma veneris (LGV)
    Neisseria gonorrhoeae (gonorrhea)
    Pelvic inflammatory disease (PID)
    Treponema pallidum (syphilis)
- Fungal infections:
    Candidiasis (yeast infection)

- Viral infections:
    Hepatitis (A, B, C, D, and E)
    Herpes simplex (herpes simplex virus)
    Human immunodeficiency virus (HIV-AIDS)
    Human papillomavirus (HPV)
    Mollussum contagiosum virus (MCV)
- Parasites:
    Pthirus pubis (crab louse)
    Sarcoptes scabiei (scabies)
- Protozoal infections;
    Trichomonas vaginalis (trichomoniasis)[34]

If you don't find the very length of this list, and the sheer number of STD cases being contracted each year, sobering enough, consider this: A recent survey by the National Coalition of STD Directors (NCSD) found that 69 percent of STD programs experienced funding cuts from 2008 to 2009. "In other words," warns NCSD board member Dr. Will Wong, "the burden of STDs is becoming worse in this country at the same time that the resources we need to fight these illnesses continue to shrink. None of this bodes well for the future health of our nation and our communities."[35]

Ain't love grand?

See also: **condoms; romance novels.**

sexually transmitted infections (STIs). See: **sexually transmitted diseases.**

shampoo. See: **polyvinyl chloride (PVC).**

shark attacks. See: **New Smyrna Beach, Florida.**

shark, fermented. See: **Chicken McNuggets.**

shopping bags. See: **reusable shopping bags, environmental impact of; reusable shopping bags, health effects of; single-use shopping bags, paper vs. plastic.**

shopping carts. Grocery-store shopping carts are teeming with germs, warns noted University of Arizona microbiologist Charles P. Gerba, Ph.D., whose team of researchers has taken samples from shopping carts throughout the United States. "[Eighty] percent of the carts have *E. coli* on them in some parts of the country," he says. Indeed, Gerba and his associates found that shopping cart handles are more befouled by bacteria and fecal matter than the average public toilet, and, he advises, mothers who let their kids ride in shopping carts are often the principal culprits. "You're putting your broccoli right where the kid's butt was," Gerba points out. And that's hardly the only problem. According to the Centers for Disease Control, the carts are often also frequently contaminated with bacteria from leaking packages of meat or poultry.[36] To combat this hazard, Gerba suggests patronizing supermarkets that offer sanitary wipes for cart handles. Or, he says, "bring your own wipes."[37]

short stature. See: **underheight.**

shower curtains. See: **polyvinyl chloride (PVC).**

showers. Taking regular showers would seem to contribute significantly to health and hygiene, but according to Leah Feazel and Norman Pace, researchers at the University of Colorado at Boulder, a study of forty-five showerheads in nine cities, including New York, revealed that the water propelled from 40 percent of the nozzles they investigated displayed microbe counts of the respiratory pathogen *Mycobacterium avium,* a close relative of the bacterium that causes tuberculosis, that were one hundred times greater than background levels. The high pressure and elevated temperatures associated with hot showers produce a cloud of tiny germ-laden mist droplets, resulting in a potentially lethal aerosol that is capable of penetrating deep into the lungs of the hapless bather.[38] See: **baths.**

side, sleeping on your. See: **sleeping on your side.**

side-effects warning labels on prescription drugs. Caution: Read-

ing this entry may cause anxiety, hysteria, confusion, irritation, apathy, agitation, disorientation, nervousness, flatulence, and a transient or persistent pain in the neck. A paper published in 2011 in the *Archives of Internal Medicine* by Dr. Jon Duke of Indiana University reported that the average prescription drug label lists 70 possible side effects, and one medication had a warning statement calling attention to a total of 525 potential adverse reactions.[39] In an earlier research report published in 2006, Dr. Jerry Avorn and Dr. William Shrank of the Harvard Medical School coined the term *linguistic toxicity* to describe the glut of confusing and often contradictory warnings, and later that year, the Food and Drug Administration issued a guidance statement to the pharmaceutical industry expressing its view that "exhaustive lists of every reported adverse event, including those that are infrequent and minor, commonly observed in the absence of drug therapy or not plausibly related to drug therapy should be avoided." Nevertheless, Dr. Duke found that in the intervening five years following the issuance of the new FDA guidelines, the average number of side effects listed on drug labels increased by more than 25 percent.

Jim Murrell, a fifty-four-year-old telecommunications consultant quoted by journalist Gina Kolata in a recent *New York Times* article, succinctly summed up the exasperating and in some cases dangerous quandary faced by users of prescription drugs. "I took a medication that had the side effect of drowsiness," Mr. Murrell recounted. "I read a little further and saw it had another side effect. Insomnia. One medication had diarrhea as a side effect and it also had constipation. It makes no sense."[40] And as Dr. Catherine Cheng of the University of California, San Francisco, noted in a commentary on Dr. Duke's study, patients aren't the only ones suffering from the universal side effect of severe hyperlabelosis. According to Dr. Cheng, the surfeit of cautionary statements "may induce information overload and reduce physician comprehension of important safety warnings."[41]

sidelines, sitting on. See: **underinvesting.**

silence of the yams, the. See: **health claims.**

single-use shopping bags, paper vs. plastic. According to the United
 States Environmental Protection Agency (EPA), the
appropriate answer to the routine cash-register checkout question, "Paper or plastic?" is a resounding "Neither!" Widespread use of the much-maligned disposable
plastic shopping bag, which in the last three decades
has come to represent about 80 percent of all the bags provided by
grocery and convenience stores, has some clearly negative environmental consequences, but the humble brown paper bag is apparently
not much better.[42] True, as Vincent Cobb, a Chicago-based entrepreneur and founder of the website Reusablebags.com (since renamed
reuseit.com) reports, the number of "T-shirt"–style lightweight plastic
sacks produced each year is indeed "absolutely staggering"—probably
between 500 billion and a trillion—and what Cobb terms "the true
costs of the free bags" are significant. Obviously, many of the flimsy
totes are dumped in landfills (where they leach toxins into the soil and
water), and they also end up clogging storm drains, festooning trees,
choking livestock, and forming huge floating masses of marine-life-
threatening plastic debris that have been found everywhere in the
earth's oceans from the Arctic Circle to the Falkland Islands.[43]

On the other hand—or in the other hand—as the Film and Bag
Federation, a trade group within the Society of the Plastics Industry,
emphasizes, paper bags cost four times as much to manufacture as
their plastic counterparts, and the pulp-and-papermaking process
used in their fabrication consumes almost twice as much energy and
generates 70 percent more air pollution and fifty times more water
pollution.[44] Keith Christman, the managing director of plastic markets for the American Chemistry Council (ACC), a trade association
that promotes the interests of the plastic industry, notes that the contrast in bulk between the two types of grocery sacks "was illustrated
vividly at a hearing where a stack of 500 paper bags was two feet high
and heavy and a pile of 500 plastic bags was two inches high." "It requires seven times as many trucks to move an equivalent number of
paper bags," Christman adds helpfully.

That said, paper bags are made from a renewable resource—
trees—rather than the nonrenewable oil and gas required to manufacture and polymerize the key ethylene component of plastic bags,

and 20 percent of paper bags are recycled, versus about 1 percent of plastic bags, although Donna Dempsey of the Progressive Bag Alliance, yet another hardworking industry support group, insists that "people might not be aware that plastic bags are not only recycled into millions of pounds of decking, piers, posts, and fencing, but they are also being recycled back into other [plastic] bags,"[45] a point echoed by Laurie Kusek, a spokesperson for one more dedicated industry promoter, the American Plastics Council, who rightly makes much of the fact that "many, many plastic bags are reused as book and lunch bags as kids head off to school, as trash can liners, and to pick Fido's droppings off the lawn."[46]

To be fair, with paper bags there's also a lot more to recycle, since two thousand paper bags weigh almost ten times as much as the same number of plastic bags, and even though plastic bags in theory could last a thousand years as opposed to about three decades for paper bags, most landfills are sealed, so neither paper nor plastic ever degrade very much,[47] and in any case, as SaveThePlasticBag.com declares resoundingly on their informative website, "Paper bags decomposing in landfills emit methane, a greenhouse gas. The last thing we want in our landfills is anything that decomposes. The fact that plastic bags last a thousand years in a landfill is a good thing!" SaveThePlasticBag.com (which takes care to point out that it is not, and never has been, "connected with or funded by the American Chemistry Council [ACC], even indirectly") also cites warnings from the pest control companies Orkin and Terminix, as well as from the EPA, that stacks of old paper bags provide excellent shelter sites for disease-spreading—and, presumably, plastic-shunning—cockroaches.[48]

So, as we weigh our options and struggle to choose between these two equally iniquitous satchels, perhaps we should conclude, as Vincent Cobb did, that since paper and plastic bags both do considerable damage to the environment, the only really responsible way for shoppers to respond to the inevitable bagger's query is to produce from a purse or a pocket a neatly folded, handsome, durable, reliable personal shopping bag. "We want to make it cool to carry reusable shopping bags," he declared.[49] (Incidentally, if you're interested in buying a "practical, stylish, and innovative" reusable shopping bag "made from post-consumer recycled plastic bottles," Mr. Cobb will happily sell you one from his proprietary reuseit™ (formerly ACME Bags™) line of products.[50] To learn more, simply point your trusty browser to: http://www.reuseit.com/store/bags-totes-shopping-bags-c-238_239.html.) See: **reusable shopping bags, environmental impact of; reusable shopping bags, health hazards of.**

Singularity, the. In 1993, mathematician and computer scientist Vernor Vinge made the prediction that the time would soon arrive when computers would achieve levels of thinking and reasoning power comparable with or superior to those of the human intellect. He dubbed that epochal moment "the Singularity," stating flatly, and ominously, "Within thirty years, we will have the technological means to create superhuman intelligence. Shortly after, the human era will be ended."[51] Although our theoretical overthrow by our very own cybernetic creations is often ridiculed (author Ken MacLeod has dubbed the idea of the Singularity "the Rapture of the Nerds"[52]), the probability, or even possibility, that the capability of increasingly sophisticated data processors to devise and execute various strategies could soon exceed the practical capacities of the human brain is no laughing matter.[53]

Even if the computers are "friendly," they could engender an inadvertent catastrophe based on a simple programming error like the one described by Professor Nick Bostrom of the University of Oxford: "When we create the first superintelligent entity, we might make a mistake and give it goals that lead it to annihilate mankind, assuming its enormous intellectual advantage gives it the power to do so. We could mistakenly elevate a subgoal to the status of a supergoal. We tell it to solve a mathematical problem, and it complies by turning all the matter in the solar system into a giant calculating device, in the process killing the person who asked the question."[54]

Eliezer Yudkowsy of the Singularity Institute postulated a similar sequence of events in which a somewhat more ambiguously motivated form of AI (artificial intelligence) "absorbs all unused computing power on the then-existent Internet in a matter of hours, uses this computing power and smarter-than-human design ability to crack the protein folding problem for artificial proteins in a few more hours, emails separate rush orders to a dozen online peptide synthesis labs, and in two days receives via FedEx a set of proteins which, mixed together, self-assemble into acoustically-controlled nanodevices..."[55]

Software pioneer and Sun Microsystems cofounder Bill Joy takes a far darker view of things, emphasizing the very real possibility of the malicious application of our newfound wizardry: "The 21st-century technologies . . . are so powerful that they can spawn whole new classes of accidents and abuses . . . We have the possibility not just of weapons of mass-destruction (WMD) but of knowledge-enabled mass destruction (KMD), this destructiveness hugely amplified by the power of self-replication. I think it is no exaggeration to say that we are on the cusp of the further perfection of extreme evil."[56] See also: **gray goo; knowledge-enabled mass destruction (KMD); robots.**

sippy cups. See: **bisphenol A.**

sitting down. Are you sitting down while you're reading this? If so, you'd be well advised to stand up. A recent study published in *Circulation,* a journal of the American Heart Association, found that every hour per day, on average, that you spend in a sedentary position increases your risk of a cancer-related death by a whopping 9 percent, and of a cardiovascular disease–related death by an absolutely terrifying 18 percent. The truly bad news, the American Heart Association's synopsis of the study points out, is that these grim figures apply even if you're in great physical shape, have impeccable dietary habits, don't smoke, and make a point of getting regular and strenuous exercise during the rest of your day. David Dunstan, Ph.D., of the Baker IDI Heart and Diabetes Institute in Melbourne, Australia, who directed the study, cautions that although the research he and his team conducted focused on TV watchers, his results apply to sitting in general, wherever it might occur, including the workplace. "Modern society has come to mean a lot of us simply shift from chair to chair throughout the day: seat in the car, the office, the couch at home," he told the *Sydney Morning Herald.*[57] His advice: "Avoid sitting for prolonged periods."[58]

Despite the fact that your life may well depend upon following this recommendation, you can be forgiven for wondering how anyone holding down a full-time office job could possibly do so. Well, Dr. Dunstan himself sets a good example. "I've introduced a stand-up desk into my work routine," he says, "and I have become conditioned to being able to stand for a predominant part of the day." [59] Stand-up desks can be pricey ($2,000 or or more per unit), but Hugh Wilson, who wrote a piece about Dr. Dunstan for the *Daily Mail,* has found a clever and practical money-saving solution. "To type, I stand in front of a computer perched on a chair resting on a table," he says.[60] James A. Levine, M.D., Ph.D., director of the Non-Exercise Activity Thermogenesis (NEAT) Laboratory at the Mayo Clinic—whose own work strongly corroborates the Australian finding that habitual sitting can be life-threatening—recommends building even more motion into your desk-work activities than a mere stand-up desk can provide, so he's helped design the Steelcase Walkstation, a treadmill desk at which, according to the *Sydney Morning Herald,* "one can use a computer, talk on the phone, read, etc., all the while strolling at a sedate two-or-so kilometres an hour." Levine uses one himself and has introduced them (and stationary bicycle desks, too) to a range of workplaces, mostly in the United States, the *Herald* reports.[61]

Another solution favored by Dr. Levine is swapping out your desk chair for an exercise ball. "Sitting on this kind of large, inflatable ball requires you to shift slightly from side to side to keep your balance," he says, thereby keeping you in constant—if subtle—motion. Sitting on an exercise ball also "engages more muscles (especially those in your abdomen and back) than sitting in a regular chair does," Levine advises.[62] See: **stand-up desks; exercise ball, using in place of a desk chair to counter the health risks of too much sitting.**

Sixth Extinction, the. See: **mass extinction.**

skin, inflamed. See: **hand washing.**

skin, premature aging of. See: **smoking.**

skinny jeans. "Skinny jeans" may look sexy, but according to New Orleans neurologist Dr. John England, the increasing number of women who have taken to wearing them are running the risk of suffering from a nerve condition called meralgia paresthetica, or, as it's more popularly known, "tingling thigh syndrome." The condition occurs when constant pressure—in the case of skinny jeans it's rendered by the skintight denim—cuts off your lateral femoral cutaneous nerve, causing a numb, tingling, or burning sensation along the thigh.[63] Sometimes, merely swearing off restrictive clothing is all it takes to remedy "tingling thigh syndrome," the Johns Hopkins Hospital advises. But, unfortunately, an injection of a corticosteroid may occasionally also be needed to reduce swelling. And in truly stubborn cases, the Hospital warns, a procedure known as "sensory nerve surgery" may be required to relieve the compression surrounding the nerve.[64]

sleeping on your back. "Snoring," writes noted otolaryngologist Craig Schwimmer, M.D., founder and medical director of the Snoring Center in Houston Texas, "is a HUGE issue in people's lives. It causes arguments, lost sleep, less sex and ruins many a relationship." Furthermore, says Schwimmer, because snoring disturbs sleeping patterns and deprives the snorer, and his or her partner, of appropriate rest, it can lead to serious health and safety issues such as "higher risk of automobile and workplace accidents, decreased job performance and higher rates of cardiovascular diseases like high blood pressure, heart attack and stroke."[65]

But here's some surprising good news: If you snore frequently and want to stop, the solution may be as simple as changing your sleeping position. A study of 2,077 snorers conducted by sleep researchers at the Loewenstein Hospital-Rehabilitation Center, in Raanana, Israel, showed that almost 54 percent of them reduced or eliminated their snoring problem by sleeping on their sides instead of on their backs.[66] The reason, the *New York Times* reports, is that when you sleep on your back, the base of your tongue can collapse into the back of your throat, "narrowing the airway and obstructing breathing."[67] But, you may ask, how can you train yourself not to sleep on your back? Well, Earl V. Dunn, M.D., of the University of Toronto's Sunnybrook Medical Centre Sleep Laboratory recommends what he calls "getting on the ball"—literally. "Sew a tennis ball onto the back of your pajamas," he advises. "That way, when you roll over on your back, you hit this hard object," and unconsciously, you'll roll off your back onto your side.[68] See: **sleeping on your side; sleeping on your stomach; sleeping on your back, sewing a tennis ball to the back of your pajamas to discourage yourself from.**

sleeping on your back, sewing a tennis ball to the back of your pajamas to discourage yourself from. Because scientific research, including a notable study at the Loewenstein Hospital-Rehabilitation Center, in Raanana, Israel, has demonstrated that sleeping on one's side rather than one's back significantly reduces the odds that you'll snore, a growing number of doctors and sleep experts, such as (to name just two) the University of Toronto's Earl V. Dunn, M.D., and Rochelle Zak, M.D., of the New York Presbyterian Hospital Sleep-Wake Disorders Center, recommend sewing a tennis ball—or, in Dr. Zak's case, several tennis balls—to the back of your pajamas or nightshirt so that the discomfort caused by the ball(s) whenever you roll onto your back will unconsciously get you to turn right back onto your side again.[69] But, according to otolaryngologist and author Steven Y. Park, M.D., this is not a good idea at all. Leaving aside the issue of what your tennis ball antisnoring getup will do for your sex life, Dr. Park notes that wearing it "only just annoys" snorers (who find it so uncomfortable that they never fall asleep in the first place, or, if they do, wake up each time they roll over onto their backs) or "they just sleep on top of it."[70] Indeed, a study conducted by a team of seven scientists led by Drs. Douglas McEvoy, Peter G. Catcheside, and Jeremy D. Mercer of the Adelaide Institute of Sleep Health in Australia, confirms Dr. Park's opinion—fully 94 percent of the snorers for whom the "Tennis Ball Technique" was prescribed abandoned it before the researchers had a chance to conduct their follow-up survey. The reasons the patients gave ranged from "the tennis ball was too uncomfortable," "the tennis ball moved around," and "the tennis ball did not prevent me from sleeping on my back," to more serious complaints such as "backaches," "shoulder problems," and "skin irritations." Many snorers, the researchers reported, cited two or more of these reasons.[71] See: **sleeping on your stomach.**

sleeping on your side. If you sleep on your side or bury your face into

a pillow," warns Kristie Leong, M.D., "you're a perfect set-up for sleep lines"—unsightly wrinkles that form most commonly around their chin and lower cheeks. "At first," Dr. Leong advises, "sleep lines are only there when you wake up and disappear in a few hours, but over time as elastin and collagen in the skin decline, they become permanent lines and wrinkles." If you want "to keep your skin looking youthful," she cautions, you should "retrain yourself to sleep on your back."[72] See: **sleeping on your back; sleeping on your stomach.**

sleeping on your stomach. "Sleeping facedown can exaggerate the

arch at the base of your spine and cause strain," warn David L. Katz, M.D., and Debra L. Gordon, M.S., coauthors of *Stealth Health: How to Sneak Age-Defying, Disease-Fighting Habits into Your Life Without Really Trying.* "Our advice?" they write. "Sew or tape a tennis ball to the front of your nightgown or nightshirt. We guarantee your stomach-sleeping days will be over."[73] See: **sleeping on your side; sleeping on your back; sleeping on your back, sewing a tennis ball to the back of your pajamas to discourage yourself from.**

"slimeburgers." Eager to find a more cost-effective use for fatty beef

trimmings that were traditionally converted into pet food and cooking oil because of their elevated risk of contamination by *E. coli* and *Salmonella* bacteria, Beef Products, Inc., of South Dakota developed an ingenious method of disinfecting the slaughterhouse residue by injecting the leavings with ammonia, then forming the sterilized mush into blocks or chips that could be mixed with more desirable portions of the butchered cattle for eventual use as an inexpensive bulking and flavoring agent in hamburgers. Even though a study financed by Beef Products itself acknowledged that the trimmings in

question "typically included most of the material from the outer surfaces of the carcasses" and contained "larger microbiological populations," and in spite of the fact that the resulting product was declared
by Dr. David M. Theno, a food safety consultant, to have "no functional value" and was famously described as "pink slime" by USDA
microbiologist Gerald Zirnstein, who added, "I do not consider the
stuff to be ground beef, and I consider allowing it in ground beef to be
a form of fraudulent labeling," the process was approved by both the
United States Department of Agriculture and the Food and Drug Administration. Beef Products, Inc.'s "ammonia-treated meat product"
soon found its way into the ground beef sold by several major grocery-
store chains, into beef patties produced by Cargill, into the hamburgers served at Burger King, McDonald's, and other fast-food restaurants,
and into meals included in the federal school lunch program, but the
very high levels of alkalinity required to properly sterilize the meatlike
scraps led to "potential issues surrounding the palatability of a pH 9.5
product" and to complaints about ammonia "aroma." These concerns
appear to have caused Beef Products to periodically reduce the concentration of the disinfectant—some samples measured as low as 7.75
on the pH scale, well below the minimum "target" levels—and, possibly as a consequence, there have been at least fifty occasions since
2005 when *E. coli* and *Salmonella* were found in Beef Products meat,
including a pair of recent episodes when two twenty-seven-thousand-
pound batches of the company's contaminated products were recalled.
In a written statement, the company restated its commitment to ham-
burger safety, but conceded that "like any other responsible member
of the meat industry, we are not perfect."[74]

smog. See: **coal.**

smoking. With all the publicity that the health hazards of smoking—

and of inhaling secondhand smoke—have received in
recent years, it may not surprise you to learn that, according to the Centers for Disease Control, "the adverse
effects from cigarette smoking account for an estimated
443,000 deaths, or nearly one of every five deaths, each
year in the United States," or that "more deaths are caused each year by

tobacco use than by all deaths from human immunodeficiency virus (HIV), illegal drug use, alcohol use, motor vehicle injuries, suicides, and murders combined." But chances are that you're not fully aware of all the *specific* ways that cigarette smoke can harm you. Therefore, as a public service, the *Encyclopedia Paranoiaca* is proud to present, conveniently alphabetized for easy reference, the following list of diseases and other serious health problems which tobacco smoke has been proven to cause, promote, or increase the risk and/or severity of:

Abdominal aortic aneurysms, acute myeloid leukemia, asthma, atherosclerosis (arteriosclerotic vascular disease), bladder cancer, blood vessel damage, bronchitis, cancer of the esophagus, cancer of the larynx, cancer of the oral cavity, cancer of the pharynx, cancer of the uterus, cataracts, cervical cancer, chronic coughing, chronic wheezing, Crohn's disease, coronary heart disease, dental cavities, emphysema, erectile dysfunction, fetal growth restriction, gallstones, Grave's disease, heartburn, high blood pressure, infertility, irritability, kidney cancer, kidney failure, liver disease, low birth weight, lower respiratory tract infections, lung cancer, macular degeneration, middle ear infections, miscarriages, nasal sinus cavity cancer, osteoporosis, pancreatic cancer, peptic ulcers, periodontal disease, peripheral vascular disease, pneumonia, premature aging of the skin, preterm delivery, stillbirths, stomach cancer, sudden infant death syndrome (SIDS), strokes, thromboangiitis obliterans (Buerger's disease), thyroid disease, and underweight newborn children.[75]

Care for a smoke? See: **smoking bans; quitting smoking; Nanny Statism.**

smoking bans. Although smoking bans are anathema to smokers, the tobacco industry, restaurant and bar owners, and at least some civil libertarians, there's little question that they've helped save some lives. Indeed, according to Thomas R. Frieden, M.D., M.P.H., the director of the Centers for Disease Control in Atlanta, a 2009 research report commissioned by his agency confirms that "eliminating smoking in workplaces, restaurants, bars, and other public places is an effective way to protect Americans from the health effects of secondhand smoke, particularly on the cardiovascular system."[76]

But what Frieden fails to mention is the fact that *another* scientific study, conducted in 2007 by economists Scott Adams and Chad Cotti at the University of Wisconsin, Milwaukee, demonstrates conclusively that state and local smoking bans have had an unintended, and profoundly disturbing, side effect: a dramatic increase in the number of fatal alcohol-related automobile crashes. "Although an increased accident risk might seem surprising at first," Adams and Cotti write, "our evidence is consistent with two mechanisms—smokers driving longer distances to a bordering jurisdiction that allows smoking in bars, and smokers driving longer distances within their jurisdiction to bars that still allow smoking, perhaps through non-compliance or outdoor seating."

Some of the increases in DUI fatalities Adams and Cotti found were truly startling. For example, after the state of Delaware enacted a smoking ban in 2002, fatal accidents in bordering Delaware County, Pennsylvania, rose by more than 26 percent. And when Boulder County, Colorado, put a similar ban in place, the number of fatal accidents in Jefferson County, between Boulder and Denver, jumped a whopping 41 percent. Nationwide, the study found that communities that passed smoking bans between 2000 and 2005 averaged a sobering 13 percent increase in alcohol-related fatalities the following year.[77]

"When smokers turn to an alternative substance or attempt to find a substitute behavior, the effect can sometimes be more damaging than the original ban," comments TotalDUI.com, a lawyer-sponsored website that bills itself as "the #1 stop for DUI news." Policy makers must "pay attention" to Adams and Cotti's study and consider the "possible consequences" before enacting more anti-smoking legislation, the website warns. "It could be a matter of life and death."[78]

And, in an article entitled "Smoking Bans: The Silent Killer," Gawker.com's Alex Pareene advocates a more proactive response: "Clearly we should reinstitute smoking everywhere and then ban cars, nationwide," he suggests.[79] See: **smoking.** See also: **Nanny Statism.**

smoking cessation. See: **quitting smoking.**

smoothies. See: **high-fructose corn syrup (HFCS); Sonic straw-berry smoothie.**

snoring. See: **sleeping on your back.**

soap and water. See: **hand washing; bar soap.**

social jet lag. See: **daylight saving time.**

socks and stockings with elastic tops. "Socks and knee high stock-ings with elastic tops can reduce the circulation of blood from your legs back to your heart," advises Dr. Michael M. Warren, Ashbel Smith Professor of Surgery in the University of Texas Medical Branch's Division of Urology. "This can produce swollen legs and circula-tion trouble," he cautions.[80] Dr. Dan Rutherford, B.Sc., M.B., Ch.B., M.R., C.G.P., F.R.C.P., the former medical director of the respected British health website Netdoctor, agrees. You should be *especially* care-ful not to wear "socks or tights that are too restrictive" while flying, he warns. "It's very dry in planes and there is a likelihood of passengers becoming dehydrated. With dehydration, the blood becomes thicker than usual and, therefore, more prone to clotting."[81] See also: **cross-ing your legs.**

soda bottles. See: **bisphenol A.**

soda, diet. See: **diet soda.**

solar energy. Solar photovoltaic cells are often hailed as a clean and  safe alternative to power plants employ-ing fossil fuels or nuclear energy technol-ogy. Well, "clean" they may be, but "safe" is quite another story. According to Solar EnergyUses.info, the materials used in many solar systems "can create health and safety hazards for workers and anyone else coming into contact with them." In particular, the website informs us, the manufacturing of photovoltaic cells often entails human contact with hazardous materials such as arsenic and cadmium, and "even relatively inert silicon, a major material used in solar cells, can be hazardous to workers if it is breathed in as dust." Furthermore, cautions SolarEnergyUses .info, "hazardous fumes released from photovoltaic modules attached to burning homes or buildings could injure fire fighters."[82]

But these problems pale in comparison with the threat of *accidents* associated with solar power—particularly those resulting from falls and electrocutions during the installation and maintenance of rooftop solar panels. "Installing solar panels combines three of the most injury-prone jobs—roofing, carpentry and electrical work—making it particularly risky," notes Jill Replogle in *Fair Warning,* a nonprofit online magazine that provides public interest journalism on issues relating to health, safety, and corporate conduct. "At the same time, there are no federal or California workplace safety rules—and few, if any, rules in other states—that specifically apply to solar installers."[83]

The sad result has been a rash of fatal mishaps: If you have a stomach for the harrowing details, you'll find them in an article by Australian blogger Gavin Atkins entitled "Green Deaths: The Forgotten Dangers of Solar Panels." "Because of our propensity to put panels on roofs," concludes Atkins, citing statistics compiled by respected San Francisco futurist Brian Wang,[84] "solar is in fact, far more dangerous than many forms of power generation, three times more dangerous than wind power and more than 10 times more dangerous than nuclear power, by comparison to the amount of power produced." Indeed, he laments, "the fifty actual deaths from roof installation accidents for 1.5 million roof installations is equal to the actual deaths experienced so far from Chernobyl."[85] See: **fossil fuels; nuclear energy; wind turbine syndrome.**

solar flares. See: **severe space weather events.**

Sonic strawberry smoothie. A Sonic strawberry smoothie sounds healthy, doesn't it? Indeed, Sonic says that downing one is like "drinking the strawberry patch" and their menu lists it as a "balanced choice." But, according to a 2011 report issued by the Physicians Committee for Responsible Medicine (PCRM), Sonic's smallest-size strawberry smoothie contains 542 calories and ninety-nine grams of sugar. "That's more sugar than can be found in five Twinkies," the report says. As a result, PCRM has officially ranked the Sonic strawberry smoothie as one of the "worst 'healthy' fast-food items" available in the United States.[86]

soup, canned. See: **bisphenol A.**

South Sister. South Sister is an active volcano in the Oregon portion

of the Cascades Range. For details of the many potential hazards South Sister presents to the countryside surrounding it (including the growing city of Bend, Oregon), see: **Cascade Range volcanoes; lahars.**

soy. Food products made from processed soybeans, particularly tofu

and soy milk, have long been touted for their supposedly manifold health benefits, but recent research suggests that instead of singing "Soy to the World," we should be saying "Soyonara" to the edible bean of the celebrated legume, *Glycine max*. Tofu and soy milk's apparently undeserved reputations as a commendable comestible and a praiseworthy potation rest primarily on a pair of soy's allegedly health-promoting and disease-preventing ingredients, omega-3 fatty acids and isoflavones. But sad to say for soy, it turns out that the omega-3 acids it contains are of the short-chain alpha-linolenic variety, rather than the highly prized longer-chain type found in fish oil and oily fish, and have negligible value as antioxidants. Worse still, the isoflavones in soy, which were long thought by some nutritionists and clinicians to be helpful in the prevention and treatment of cancer, may actually be carcinogens themselves as well as endocrine system disruptors.

The prime source of this unfortunate news was an exhaustive survey of clinical research on soy, published in 2006 in the American Heart Association's journal *Circulation,* indicating that soy had little or no demonstrable beneficial effect on reducing cholesterol levels or blood pressure, on lessening vascular symptoms of menopause, or on slowing postmenopausal bone loss. Furthermore, the survey team, led by Frank M. Sacks, M.D., of the Harvard University School of Public Health, not only failed to turn up clear evidence of any positive impact on cancer prevention or treatment, but also called attention to two separate clinical studies suggesting that soy might actually play a role in the stimulation of breast cancer tumors.[87]

But the proverbial soy-free icing on top of the wheat-flour cake is provided by Kaayla T. Daniel, Ph.D., author of *The Whole Soy Story: The Dark Side of America's Favorite Health Food*, who minces few words in summarizing the case against soy: "Hundreds of epidemiological, clinical and laboratory studies link soy to malnutrition, digestive problems, thyroid dysfunction, cognitive decline, ADD/ADHD, reproductive disorder, even heart disease and cancer. Most at risk are babies given soy formula, vegetarians who eat soy as their main source of protein and adults self medicating with soy foods and supplements." In the helpful media kit prepared by her publisher, Dr. Daniel delivers a final memorable beaning to the edible oilseed of the humble plant in a talking point that lays out yet another not-so-hidden danger of soy consumption, namely "the Flatulence Factor." Labeling soybeans as "the King of the Musical Fruits," she refers to "containment devices such as 'gas-tight pantaloons' and odor-absorbing cushions and panties" as well as "fraternity house recipes for maximum gas production," and derides the soy industry for "trying to give status to flatus."[88] See: **omega-3 fish oil supplements.**

spam. See: **botnets; identity theft; malware; zombie armies.**

Spanish Flu Epidemic of 1918. See: **flu pandemic.**

spas. See: **gyms.**

sperm alteration. See: **microwave ovens.**

sperm count, decreased. See: **antibacterial and antiviral products; bisphenol A; rubber duckies.**

spinach. Is spinach valuable for nutrition, as common wisdom has always taught us? Absolutely not, cautions British physician Joan E.

Bamji and her chemist husband, Nariman S. Bamji. Indeed, spinach is actually *unhealthy* because it contains oxalic acid, a chemical that absorbs the vital calcium that all of us—especially children—need to grow and maintain strong bones and teeth (not to mention having properly functioning muscles and nervous systems). "Is it not possible," the Bamjis speculate, "that the intense dislike of spinach shown by most children is nature's way of protecting them from its harmful effects?" (Of course, those unfortunate enough to have had their calcium supply depleted by eating spinach can attempt to compensate by seeking out calcium-*rich* foods such as milk, cheese, and other dairy products.[89] See: **milk; dairy products.**) See also: **leafy green vegetables.**

Splenda. See: **sucralose.**

splinters. If you get a splinter from a piece of decaying wood, you could be at risk of contracting an often deadly malady called mucormycosis (or, as it was formerly known, zygomycosis) that is caused by a fungus that thrives in rotting organic matter.[90] For more about this threat, and how to avoid it, see: **wood, decaying.**

sponges. According to microbiologist Philip M. Tierno Jr., Ph.D., of the New York University Langone Medical Center, the common household sponge is, along with its close cousin, the dishrag, "the dirtiest thing in your kitchen." Why? Because when you use it to clean up kitchen liquids after preparing meat or poultry, you sop up *E. coli* bacteria and other disease-causing organisms left over from the raw food right with them. The sponge's damp, porous environment serves as a perfect breeding ground in which the microbes can flourish and multiply until there are literally billions of them. Then, when you use the sponge to wipe off other surfaces in the kitchen, warns Dr. Tierno, "you cross-contaminate your countertops, your refrigerator, and other appliances in the kitchen." What's to be done? Dr. Tierno suggests soaking your sponge in a solution of bleach and water after using it, and, in addition, microwaving it for one to two minutes each week.[91] Indeed, a December 2006 research study, published in the December 2006 issue of the *Journal of Environmental Health,* found that microwaving kitchen sponges and other scrubbing pads for one to two minutes at full power can reduce levels of bacteria, including *E. coli* and other common causes of food-borne illness, by more than 99 percent.[92] See: **chlorine bleach; sponges, microwaving; microwave ovens.**

sponges, microwaving. In 2006, a study was published demonstrat-

ing that microwaving sponges could rid these notoriously germ-ridden kitchen items of 99 percent of the pathogens they harbor (See: **sponges**). But, according to *Consumer Reports,* the practice has a hazardous downside: If the sponge dries out during the microwaving process, it can burst into flame, destroying your microwave oven and filling your house with filthy, foul-smelling smoke (assuming, that is, that the fire doesn't spread quickly enough to burn it to the ground).[93] Furthermore, some sponges contain metallic fibers that spark dangerously when microwaved; others contain chemicals or detergents that emit toxic fumes when heated[94]; and almost *all* sponges, even if they don't catch fire, can give you a nasty burn if you try to handle them too soon after zapping them.[95]

Instead of microwaving, *Consumer Reports* recommends washing your sponge in the dishwasher (but only if your machine has an "NSF rating," which means it gets hot enough, at least during the sanitize cycle, to kill bacteria). Or, they suggest, "use wet paper towels and soap to clean up spills and countertops after working with especially risky foods like raw chicken and ground beef. Toss them in the trash and wash your hands when you're through and you'll be reducing your risk of cross contamination in the kitchen, with no risk of smoke and fire." See: **sponges, washing in dishwasher; dishwashers; hand washing.**

sponges, washing in dishwasher. Washing sponges in the dishwasher

"cleans only the outer surface," warns food sciences professor Susan Brewer of the University of Illinois, so you can't trust the dishwasher to sanitize them.[96] See: **sponges, microwaving.** See also: **dishwashers.**

spring mix. See: **leafy green vegetables.**

springwater. See **bottled water.**

sprouts. "Billy, don't you dare eat those awful sprouts! Why don't you

let Mommy cook you a nice well-done cheeseburger?" may become the new mealtime exhortation following the recent widespread occurrence of *E. coli* infections in Europe originally blamed on Spanish cucumbers but ultimately traced to contaminated bean sprouts grown on an organic farm in Germany. Although very serious and often fatal food-borne illnesses are usually associated in the public mind with undercooked or spoiled meat products, outbreaks of bacterial disease attributed to this healthy-seeming, feel-good vegetarian menu item are in fact so common they are often referred to by health investigators as "sproutbreaks," and epidemiologists in the United States expressed amazement that it took their German colleagues so long to identify the culprit. "I'm just staggered," said William E. Keene, a senior epidemiologist of the Oregon Public Health Division. "This is basic outbreak investigation 101 . . . You always rule out raw milk, you always rule out ground beef, you always rule out sprouts. It just happens in the beginning steps."[97]

Because the sprouts are typically grown from seeds that germinate in conditions of high humidity, a few "bad seeds" infected with *E. coli* and *Salmonella* can easily contaminate an entire batch. Furthermore, like all fresh produce whose high nutritional values depend on their being eaten raw, sprouts are generally not cooked before being served and hence, by definition, they are not sterile. (It is only by subjecting foods to high heat that bacteria can be reliably killed—even the most thorough washing and rinsing of vegetables will not do the job.)[98]

Many growers attempt to eliminate any plant pathogens by soaking sprout seeds in a chlorine solution, but in the United States the Food and Drug Administration does not require this sterilizing step, and as a recent report from the Centers for Disease Control found, "The U.S. sprouting industry produces several hundred thousand tons of sprouts of different varieties each year. No methods to reduce or eliminate contaminations of seed in the field, to effectively decontaminate seeds before sprouting, or to clean the sprouts themselves are in place."[99] Since 1996, sprouts have been responsible for at least thirty bacterial outbreaks, and federal food safety experts warn that children, the elderly, pregnant women, and people with compromised immune systems should not eat uncooked sprouts. "If you're concerned about your risk of food-borne illness, don't eat sprouts," Dr. Keene cautioned. "They're essentially a dangerous kind of food."[100] See: **chlorine washes.**

spyware. See: **malware.**

stagflation. Although classical economic theory had always held that

high inflation rates tend over time to lead to higher rates of employment, the sudden spike in producer prices caused by the "Oil Shock" of the 1970s yielded precisely the opposite result, and governments were confronted with the unhappy prospect that the very policies they pursued to restrain runaway inflation were having the perverse effect of simultaneously increasing persistent unemployment. Although this first encounter in modern times with what soon became known as "stagflation"—high across-the-board inflation combined with stagnant or nonexistent economic growth—was generally attributed to the specific circumstances of a huge jump in the cost of petroleum caused by the Arab Oil Embargo, there's compelling evidence that a similar dynamic may be contributing to the stubborn jobless figures that have accompanied, and continued to linger after, "the Great Recession" of 2008.

According to one theory, proposed by Eduardo Loyo of Harvard's Kennedy School of Government, in addition to being set in motion by a simple "supply-push" inflationary insult (like a nasty surprise at the gas pump), stagflation can be initiated by the prevalence of a disruptive "demand-pull" upward push on prices—for example, a general debasement of the inherent value of money (such as the one that led to the current skyrocketing price of gold) brought about by an unsustainable accumulation of national debts denominated in fiat (paper) currencies like the dollar or the euro.[101]

Another explanation for stagflation is offered by political economist Jonathan Nitzan, who ascribes the alarming phenomenon to what he terms "differential accumulation," a process through which dominant corporations with overweening pricing power and potent political influence (a category overrepresented by major firms in the arms and energy industries) tend to maximize their profits and capitalizations both directly through mergers and acquisitions and indirectly by exploiting periods of competitive stress to increase their size and overall market share.[102]

Can a solution to this devastating economic crisis be found in the long run? It's an open question, though it's worth remembering that the great economist John Maynard Keynes was fond of noting that "in the long run, we are all dead."[103]

stand-up desks. "Standing desks are in," writes *Time* magazine's

Bryan Walsh. "Once the province of a few dynamic individuals like Winston Churchill, Ernest Hemingway and Donald Rumsfeld (O.K., two out of three ain't bad), the stand-up desk is spreading to the world of corporate drones." The reason, of course, is the growing body of medical evidence that days filled with too many uninterrupted hours of sitting can greatly increase your chances of a premature death (See: **sitting down**). But, according to Alan Hedge, Ph.D., C.P.E., the director of the Human Factor and Ergonomics Research Group at Cornell University, switching to a stand-up desk is likely to cause more problems than it solves. Standing to work, he says, has long been known to be unhealthy: It's "more tiring, it dramatically increases the risks of carotid atherosclerosis (ninefold) because of the additional load on the circulatory system, and it also increases the risks of varicose veins." Furthermore, Dr. Hedge cautions, "the performance of many fine motor skills also is less good when people stand rather than sit." And, when people do computer work at their standing desks, Dr. Hedge advises, they have to extend their wrists farther than they commonly do when seated, which can lead to musculoskeletal disorders such as carpal tunnel syndrome. According to *Time*'s Walsh, Hedge told him that the use of stand-up desks tends to decline rapidly after about a month. Most likely, Walsh theorizes, this is because people basically can't stand using them.[104] See also: **sitting down;**

exercise ball, using in place of a desk chair to counter the health risks of too much sitting.

STDs. See: **sexually transmitted diseases.**

sterility. See: **french fries; microwave ovens.**

stimulus spending, inadequate. According to Nobel Prize–winning

economist Paul Krugman, the U.S. Federal Reserve has been alarmingly passive and overcautious in using policies such as quantitative easing and stimulus spending to try to overcome the unemployment problems that threaten to destroy life in America as we have known it through the better part of six decades. "As recently as two years ago," Krugman writes in the *New York Times*, "anyone predicting the current state of affairs (not only is unemployment disastrously high, but most forecasts say that it will stay very high for years) would have been dismissed as a crazy alarmist. Now that the nightmare has become reality, however—and yes, it is a nightmare for millions of Americans—Washington seems to feel absolutely no sense of urgency. Are hopes being destroyed, small businesses being driven into bankruptcy, lives being blighted? Never mind, let's talk about the evils of budget deficits." [105] See: **stimulus spending, overzealous.**

stimulus spending, overzealous. "We have to stop stimulating,"

implores Peter Schiff, CEO and chief global strategist of Euro Pacific Capital, Inc., and a 2010 candidate for the retiring Thomas Dodd's seat in the U.S. Senate. If we don't, he predicts; "we're going to have runaway inflation and recession simultaneously." The reason the economy is so "screwed up," Schiff explains, is that the U.S. Federal Reserve's reckless dependency on policies such as quantitative easing and stimulus spending are destroying "the savers, producers, and the investing class that built this country." "We're abandoning capitalism and embracing socialism," Schiff concludes. "That's a recipe for disaster . . . Millions of more Americans are going to lose their jobs, and all

of us are going to lose our freedoms and our rights."[106] Not a pretty picture. See: **stimulus spending, inadequate.**

STIs (sexually transmitted infections). See: **sexually transmitted diseases.**

stocks. "Do not buy stocks," advises former Morgan Stanley invest-

ment banker Paul G. Farrell, now a MarketWatch.com columnist. "Not for retirement. Not in the coming decade. Don't. Huge risks. Wall Street is a loser. Stocks are Wall Street's ultimate sucker bet. And it'll sucker you again. You'll lose, worse than in the last decade. Wake up before Wall Street banks trigger the next meltdown, igniting mass bankruptcy." Farrell's sobering advice is based on several arguments. Chief among them are that stock prices no longer reflect corporate profits, but have become purely an artifact of insider Wall Street manipulations; that Wall Street has not ceased its dangerous trades in derivatives but has merely found new ways to disguise them; that the Federal Reserve Bank imposed no penalties on bankers for their complicity in triggering the 2008 financial crisis, thereby emboldening them to make "bigger and riskier bets in the future because they will get away with it next time, too"; and that "America's new era, featuring no growth, deflation and a jobless recovery, will continue for years."[107] See: **underinvesting.** See also: **stocks, individual, focusing on.**

stocks, individual, focusing on. "Why would you 'focus' on any in-

dividual stocks?" asks Dan Solin, senior vice president of Index Funds Advisors. "The expected return of an individual stock is about the same as the index to which it belongs, but with significantly greater risk because of 'idiosyncratic' or company-specific risk. You are better off sticking to a globally diversified portfolio of low cost index funds."[108] Howard Gold, MoneyShow.com's editor-at-large, outlines the perils of individual stock picking even more starkly in his January 2008 article "Today's Hot Tip: Don't Buy Stocks!" "Owning individual stocks can be dangerous to your financial health," he warns. "Yes, you can hit an occasional home run with a Google or Master-

Card. But it's hard to find anywhere near the diversification you can get from a broad-based mutual fund . . . And without that broad diversification, you're taking on much more risk."[109] See: **portfolio diversification; mutual funds; investments, overseas.**

stomach, sleeping on your. See: **sleeping on your stomach.**

stoves, gas. In a massive study involving forty-seven thousand patients, Dr. William J. Rea, director of the Environmental Health Center in Dallas, Texas, found that "the most important sources of indoor air pollution responsible for generating illness" were gas cooking stoves, gas hot-water heaters, and gas-powered furnaces.[110]

strangelets. See: **Large Hadron Collider.**

strawberries. Strawberries are sweet, juicy, and delicious. But unfortunately, as *Prevention* magazine's Josie Glausiusz points out, they are also "delicate and prone to disease, including fungal attacks that can turn them to mush during transit and storage." "With apples and peaches, a lot of spraying is cosmetic to get blemish-free fruits," says Richard Wiles, senior vice president for policy at the Environmental Working Group. "With berries, you're just trying to get them across the finish line into the store before they go bad." Of course, the process of getting those berries "across the finish line" means that they're likely to be doused with toxic pesticides by the time they reach your market.[111] And, as the invaluable healthy-living website *Nourishing Words* reminds us, all the little bumps on each berry make it almost impossible to wash those hazardous chemicals off. No wonder the Environmental Working Group has given strawberries the dubious honor of appearing on its "Dirty Dozen" list of foods it's inadvisable to buy unless they're organically grown.[112] See: **organic food.**

street canyons. If you had a choice between walking down a street lined with small buildings and another lined with tall ones, which would you choose? Well, Kian Fan Chung, M.D., D.Sc., F.R.C.P., professor of respiratory medicine at Imperial College, London, suggests that, if you want to minimize the amount of respiratory-health-threatening pollution you breathe in, you should make a point of picking the one with the smaller structures. "I would avoid 'street canyons,' where tall buildings line the street and create valleys where particles build up," Professor Chung advises.[113]

strokes. See: **abstinence; birth-control pills; diet soda; exercise, lack of; neckties; salt, excessive consumption of; smoking; water filters; yoga.**

stumbles, fatal. See: **potted plants; welcome mats.**

subprime mortgage bubble. See: **housing, investing in; zombie banks.**

subtropical desertification. See: **global warming.**

sucralose. One "late summer day in 1975," Burkhard Bilger wrote in a May 2006 issue of *The New Yorker*, a young Indian chemist named Shashikant Phadnis was working on an insecticide development project at Queen Elizabeth College in London when he stumbled upon what seemed like an extremely promising compound. "It was a fine crystalline powder," Bilger reported, "easy to imagine spraying over a field, and its molecules were full of chlorine atoms, like DDT." According to Bilger, Phadnis was told to test the powder "but he misunderstood; he thought that he needed to taste it. And so, using a small spatula, he put a little of it on the tip of his tongue. It was sweet—achingly sweet." And thus was born the nonnutritive artificial sweetener known as sucralose.

"It wasn't of any use as an insecticide," Phadnis's Queens College adviser, Leslie Hough, told Bilger. "That was tested." But it certainly has proved useful as a sugar substitute. "When mixed with fillers and sold in bright-yellow sachets, it's known as Splenda," Bilger informs us.[114] Despite its pesticide-manqué origins, Splenda was approved by the U.S. Food and Drug Administration (FDA) in 1998,[115] and, principally because of lingering health concerns about aspartame (marketed in the United States as NutraSweet and Equal) and because, unlike aspartame, it doesn't break down when heated and thus can be used in cooking and baking, it has become America's most widely used artificial sweetener.[116]

But, leaving aside issues of how you feel about dropping the residue of a failed insect-killer experiment into your morning cup of coffee, is sucralose safe to use? Researchers at the Duke University Medical Center don't think so. Their study, published in the prestigious peer-reviewed *Journal of Toxicology and Environmental Health*, found evidence that Splenda reduces the amount of beneficial bacteria in the intestines by 50 percent, increases the pH level in the intestines, contributes to increases in body weight, and affects P-glycoprotein in the body in such a way that crucial health-related drugs and nutrients could be rejected.[117] In short, it's really bad for you.

But, as the *New York Times* reported soon after the results were announced in 2008, there's a catch: "The Duke study was financed by the Sugar Association, the lobbying group for the natural-sugar industry and a chief competitor to and legal adversary of Splenda." Dr. Mohamed B. Abou-Donia, one of the lead researchers of the study, during which rats were fed sucralose and observed over a twelve-week period, assured the *Times* that the Sugar Association had "no input" into his group's conclusions. But McNeil Laboratories, the makers of Splenda, sticking by their advertised claim that Splenda will not cause weight gain and "may be used as part of a healthy diet," dismissed the work by Dr. Abou-Donia and his colleagues as "the Sugar Association-funded rat study." At last report, the Sugar Association was suing McNeil for false advertising (including unsubstantiated health claims), and McNeil was countersuing the Sugar Association for defamation.[118]

Meanwhile, best-selling author and health guru Andrew Weil, M.D., who has recommended that using aspartame isn't worth the risk, suggests you give sucralose a similar wide berth.[119] "You'd be wise to consume moderate amounts of sugar rather than any artificial sweeteners," he advises. "Why use them," he concludes, "if safety concerns exist?"[120] See: **sugar; aspartame.**

sudden cardiac death. See: **exercise, lack of; sex.**

sugar. Over the past twenty years, the Centers for Disease Control

have reported a dramatic increase in obesity in the United States—a rise that, according to the CDC, presents "a major risk factor for cardiovascular disease, certain types of cancer, and type 2 diabetes."[121] The most prevalent explanation is that Americans eat too much and don't exercise enough, and certainly these are important factors. But, according to Robert H. Lustig, M.D., a renowned pediatric endocrinologist at the University of California, San Francisco, the major reason we're becoming fat at such an alarming rate is our excessive consumption of sugar. According to Lustig, sugar is not simply a substance representing "empty calories" with no nutritional value that causes us to gain weight when we eat too much of it—something, of course, that we tend to do because it tastes so good.[122] (Indeed, that claim is correct as far as it goes, and it's the reason, says Gary Taubes, author of a much-discussed *New York Times Magazine* article about Lustig, that organizations such as the Department of Agriculture and the American Heart Association now recommend that we cut back on our sugar consumption.)

An even bigger problem, says Lustig, is that sugar is actually a toxin, a poison that, as Taubes puts it, has "unique characteristics, specifically in the way the human body metabolizes the fructose in it, that may make it singularly harmful, at least if consumed in sufficient quantities."[123] As Lustig himself explains, white sugar is sucrose, which is half glucose—a "good carbohydrate" that he calls "the energy of life"—and half fructose. "Fructose," he says "is the really bad actor. Fructose is like 'alcohol without the buzz.'" It forces the liver to kick more fat into the bloodstream and also generates more insulin resistance than other foodstuffs, making "the brain think it is hungry," and, therefore, leading us to eat even more.[124] Indeed, writes Taubes, insulin resistance is "now considered the fundamental problem in obesity, and the underlying defect in heart disease and in the type of diabetes, type 2, that is common to obese and overweight individuals. It might also be the underlying defect in many cancers."[125]

Adding to the problem is the fact that the majority of sugar we now eat is in the form of **high-fructose corn syrup (HFCS)** (q.v.), a food additive which, unlike refined sugar, contains more fructose than glucose, and, since the early 1980s, has been packed into more and more of our sodas and fruit drinks, baked goods, and fast and processed foods. In short, fructose is harder and harder to avoid, and we're consuming more of it than ever—a phenomenon Lustig calls "the fructosification of America." [126] But, as individuals, and as a nation, we must cut back. If we don't, and Lustig is right, concludes Taubes, we are, indeed, "in trouble." [127]

So what does Lustig think we should do? First of all, he says, "get rid of every sugared liquid in the house. Bar none. Only water and milk. There is no such thing as a good sugar beverage. Period." Second, we should eat our carbohydrates—particularly our fructose—with fiber; in other words, choose carrots, not doughnuts. ("When God made the poison," Lustig says, referring to naturally occurring sugar in fruits and vegetables, "He packaged it with the antidote.") Third, "wait 20 minutes for second portions, to get that satiety signal." And fourth, "buy your screen time minute for minute with physical activity"—in other words, if you want to watch TV for an hour, exercise for an hour." [128] See: **carrots; exercise, indoor; exercise, outdoor; milk; water, bottled; water, tap.**

suicide, financial. See: **underinvesting.**

summertime sex. Ah, those languid nights, that romantic June

moon, those balmy ocean breezes— surely this is just the perfect time for a little aquatic hanky-panky with your fa- vorite mermaid or merman. Well, we hate to be poolside party poopers and beach-going wet blankets, but there are some good reasons to throw cold water on your hydraulic lovemaking. For one thing, condoms are not designed to be used in conditions of total immersion and, as a spokesperson for Durex, a major manufacturer of prophylactic de- vices, noted, "Though the salt in sea water would not have adverse effects on condom materials, there is a strong possibility that the chemicals used in swimming pools (chlorine and ozone, for example) would." In addition, unless the pumps and filters installed in hot tubs and pools are properly maintained and regularly cleaned, the heated water they contain can become an almost perfect breeding ground for the bacteria that can cause gastrointestinal and respiratory diseases, as well as the urinary tract infections that individuals who have recently engaged in sexual intercourse are particularly vulnerable to. And a study conducted at the University of California, San Francisco, found that sperm production and motility declined measurably in men who spent prolonged periods in Jacuzzis.

Headed to the seashore for a surfside smooch? Another study, this one reported in *Environmental Science & Technology*, reported that 91 percent of the beaches they tested had detectable levels of *Enterococcus* bacteria that can cause endocarditis, diverticulitis, and meningitis as well as those pesky urinary tract infections, and 61 percent of them had traces of *E. coli*.[129] And while you're "rolling in the spray with your honey" you might end up double-dating with the MRSA "superbug." According to Dr. Lisa Plano of the University of Miami, "MRSA is in the water and potentially in the sand. This constitutes a risk to anyone who goes to the beach and uses the water."[130] Hmm—how about a friendly game of Scrabble out on the patio? See also: **hot tubs; superbugs; swimming pools, chlorinated.**

sun exposure. "There is no such thing as a safe tan," warns the Skin

Cancer Foundation. "Tanning, like sunburns, attacks the skin's DNA, producing genetic defects that may cause skin cancer . . . It is safe to say that both burning and tanning play major roles in skin cancer."[131] So what should we do to reduce our risk? The Skin Cancer Foundation is very clear about this: If you have to go outside, especially between 10 A.M. and 4 P.M., they urge, "seek the shade," and "cover up with clothing, including a broad-brimmed hat and UV-blocking sunglasses . . . Wear long-sleeved shirts and long pants" and "tightly woven fabrics." In addition, they advise, "apply an ounce (two tablespoons) of sunscreen to your entire body 30 minutes before going outside." For typical, everyday outdoor activities such as shopping, walking, or "even waiting for a bus," the foundation suggests, "a broad spectrum (UVA/UVB) sunscreen with an SPF [sun protection factor] of 15 or higher" will suffice. But for extended outdoor activity, they caution, you'll need a "water-resistant, broad spectrum (UVA/UVB) sunscreen with an SPF of 30 or higher." Finally, the foundation concludes, "because skin damage occurs with each unprotected exposure and accumulates over the course of a lifetime, sun safety for children should be a priority."[132] See: **sun exposure, insufficient; sunscreens.**

sun exposure, insufficient. A 2008 study led by Harald Dobnig, M.D., of the Medical University of Graz in Austria offers a convincing demonstration of just how important it is for people to be exposed to adequate amounts of sunlight. The research, published in the *Archives of Internal Medicine,* found that those with the lowest vitamin D levels have more than double the risk of dying from heart disease and other causes over an eight-year period compared with those with the highest vitamin D levels. Dr. Dobnig and his colleagues worry that vitamin D deficiency has become a "problem of global dimension" and cite "decreased outdoor activity" as one of the principal culprits.[133] The reason being outdoors is so important, of course, is that when the sun's UV-B rays hit the skin, a reaction takes place that enables skin cells to manufacture vitamin D. "We all need a little unprotected time in the sun during the middle hours of the day when the sun is at its highest and UV-B rays can penetrate the atmosphere," Australian National University epidemiologist Robyn Lucas, Ph.D., told *U.S. News* in an interview after Dr. Dobnig's report was released. Lucas emphasized that by "unprotected," she meant without sunscreen, hats, or protective clothing; indeed, she emphasized, "sunscreen blocks out nearly all UV radiation." In support of her argument, *U.S. News* listed a quartet of conditions, in addition to cardiovascular mortality, that science has indicated "the sunshine vitamin" may protect against: "osteoporosis, and cancers of the breast, prostate, and colon." "What's more," *U.S. News* pointed out, "sunlight has other hidden benefits—like protecting against depression, insomnia, and an overactive immune system." In sum, Dr. Lucas concluded, "far more lives are lost to diseases caused by a lack of sunlight than to those caused by too much."[134] See: **sun exposure; sunscreens; baseball caps; vitamin D supplements.**

sunscreens. "A yearlong study by the Food and Drug Administration has produced sobering data indicating that a form of vitamin A, retinyl palmitate, may accelerate development of skin tumors and lesions when applied in the presence of sunlight," Sonya Lunder, M.P.H., a senior analyst for the nonprofit Environmental Working Group, writes in the *New York Times*. "That wouldn't be a problem," she adds, "if the substance weren't an active ingredient in more than 40 percent of all sunscreens available in the United States."[135] To make matters worse, the Environmental Working Group notes, a significant percentage of sunscreen products also contain the organic compound oxybenzone, which, they warn, "can trigger allergic reactions, is a potential hormone disruptor and penetrates the skin in relatively large amounts. Some experts caution that it should not be used on children."[136]

The EWG also cites three clinical studies indicating that "people wearing sunscreens tend to stay out in the sun longer, so their total dose of UV radiation, particularly harmful UVA rays, may be larger than non-users." Indeed, the group states in its 2011 report, "experts generally agree that the tendencies of sunscreen users to spend more recreational time in direct sunlight and to wear less protective clothing may exacerbate sun damage that leads to melanoma."[137]

And finally, there's the problem that wearing a sunscreen interferes with the *healthy* thing that sunlight does for us—enabling the synthesis of vitamin D in our bodies. According to renowned Boston University Medical School biophysics professor Michael F. Holick, Ph.D., M.D., he and his colleagues studied "individuals that always wore a sunscreen before they went outside," and, he told *ABC Nightly News*, "we found that, indeed, at the end of the summer, they were deficient in vitamin D."[138] "The population of the world has been brainwashed by the American Academy of Dermatology and the sunscreen industry, for 30 years, with the unrelenting message that you should never be exposed to direct sunlight because it is going to cause serious skin cancer and death," says Holick. "People are really quite surprised by the new message that sensible sun exposure, in moderation, is very important for good health." [139] See: **sun exposure.**

superbugs. A bacterium now generally referred to as MRSA, or methicillin-resistant *Staphyloccus aureus,* made its first appearance in the United Kingdom in 1961, and subsequently began turning up some twenty years later in populations of intravenous drug users in the USA. MRSA derives its name from its most lethal attribute—a near-total immunity to the widely available and previously quite effective antibiotics customarily employed to combat bacterial infections, including virtually the entire family of penicillins and cephalosporins. More recent variants of the deadly organism have started to display resistance to a dwindling list of newer intravenously administered antibiotics, including vancomycin and teicoplanin. The term *superbug,* which was coined by the media to describe the mutated strain of the familiar "staph" infection, is, alas, quite apt. According to the Centers for Disease Control, in 2005 nearly ninety-five thousand Americans were infected by MRSA and more than eighteen thousand of them died, a number that exceeded that year's death toll from AIDS. In addition, the infections, whether ultimately fatal or not, were particularly gruesome, typically leading to toxic shock, gangrene, and necrotic, or "flesh-eating," pneumonia, which often dictated the therapeutic amputation of affected body parts.

Adding to the severity of the crisis, the fact that individuals who succumb to outbreaks almost always require hospitalization presents an additional level of risk, since hospitals themselves, with their inherently infective environments, are one of the primary sources of MRSA outbreaks and offer the most fertile breeding grounds for the killer bug.[140] As a report of the Infectious Disease Society of America noted, "about 2 million people acquire bacterial infections in U.S. hospitals each year, and 90,000 die as a result. About 70% of those infections are resistant to at least one drug." [141] On the bright side, however, several physicians specializing in the treatment of infectious diseases have recently reported considerable success in treating MRSA with maggot therapy.[142] See: **maggot therapy.**

supermarkets. "Get out of the supermarket whenever possible," ad-

vises award-winning author, food expert, and University of California at Berkeley professor Michael Pollan. "You won't find any high-fructose corn syrup at the farmer's market; you also won't find food harvested long ago and far away," Pollan points out. "What you will find are fresh whole foods picked at the peak of nutritional quality. Precisely the kind of food your great-great-grandmother would have recognized as food." [143] See: **farmers' markets.**

supernovae, near-earth. See: **IK Pegasi.**

superpower collapse soup. This evocative term was coined by

Russian-born computer scientist Dmitry Orlov to describe the quandary confronting the United States as it experiences existentially threatening social and economic conditions eerily similar to those that prevailed in the Soviet Union just prior to its collapse in 1989. Orlov's "soup" is basically a time-tested recipe for national disaster whose principal ingredients include a bloated military budget, runaway energy consumption coupled with a sharp drop in oil production, a ballooning trade deficit, an unsustainable burden of foreign-held debt, and an inherently unresponsive political system. Orlov's insight, which he developed during several trips back to his native land during its distintegration in the 1980s, initially appealed to "back-to-the-land" survivalists, peak-oil collapsitarians, and dyed-in-the-wool fear-mongers and doom-and-gloomers, but his views have since gained considerable credibility among financial analysts, like the celebrated gold-bug investor James Sinclair, and social critics, most notably the New Urbanist James Howard Kunstler, who find more than a little merit in his somber prognostications.

Orlov's chilling assessment may seem easy to dismiss, but it's worth remembering that until the late 1980s the Soviet Union, though obviously a stagnant political entity, was also apparently quite stable, and its rapid dissolution came as a shock even to experienced geopolitical observers. And if Orlov is right, a catastrophic unwinding of the American polity would indeed be messy: "We should certainly expect shortages of fuel, food, medicine, and countless consumer goods, outages of electricity, gas, and water, breakdowns in transportations systems and other infrastructure, hyperinflation, widespread shut downs and mass layoffs, along with a whole lot of despair, confusion, violence and lawlessness." Ironically, the very fact that such a prophecy seems so far-fetched makes it fit neatly into a long historical series of equally dramatic unforeseen global events.[144] See: **black swans.**

supervolcanoes. A supervolcano is quite simply, to quote Armageddon
 Online.org, "the most destructive force on this planet."[145] Only six known supervolcanoes exist in the world, and when they erupt they do so with a force tens of thousands of times greater than that of "ordinary" eruptions. Supervolcanoes lie dormant for millennium after millennium as vast reservoirs of magma build up under them. Finally, the pressure becomes too great, and they unleash their fury with a force strong enough to obliterate continents. As geologist Ted Nield of the London Geological Society has noted, "When a supervolcano goes off, it produces energy equivalent to an impact with a comet or asteroid. You can try diverting an asteroid, but there is nothing at all you can do about a supervolcano." To put it bluntly, says ArmageddonOnline.org, they "threaten the survival of mankind."[146]

Unfortunately, three supervolcanoes lie within the continental United States: the Valles Caldera in New Mexico, the Long Valley in California, and virtually all of Yellowstone National Park in Wyoming. The next time any one of them erupts, it will hurl unimaginable amounts of magma thirty miles or more into the air. Within a radius of hundreds of miles, just about everything alive will be killed by falling ash, molten lava, mudslides, pyroclastic flows, the shock wave from the sheer force of the eruption, or a combination of any or all of the above. Literally tens of thousands of people will die within just a few minutes of the eruption. Even worse, so much ash will be spewed out by the supervolcano that it will block out the sun, causing global crop failures so severe that, as Dr. Nield puts it, "the very survival of the human race will be in question."

The good news is that the Yellowstone supervolcano erupts, albeit with almost clockwork regularity, only once every 600,000 years. The bad news is that the last eruption occurred over 640,000 years ago. In other words, as ArmaggedonOnline puts it, "we are overdue for annihilation."[147] See also: **Valles Caldera National Preserve; Yellowstone National Park; Asteroid 99942 Apophis; Comet Catalina.**

sushi, sashimi, and ceviche. Is it safe to eat uncooked fish? Accord-

ing to noted NYU microbiologist Philip M. Tierno Jr., Ph.D., the answer is no. "I don't care to take the risk," he says, and if you insist on making a habit of doing so, he warns, sooner or later you're likely to be subjected to gastronomic distress from *Vibrio* germs,[148] which infest the coastal waters where the seafood used in sushi is harvested or caught and, according to the U.S. Centers for Disease Control and Prevention, can cause watery diarrhea, abdominal cramping, nausea, vomiting, fever and chills.[149] ("They can be potential killers of the compromised or elderly," Tierno advises.)

Worse still, warns Tierno, if you eat sushi, you're risking "ingesting the parasitic anisakis worm,"[150] a nematode that is frequently found in unprepared cod, flounder, fluke, haddock, herring, monkfish, and Pacific salmon, and that, if not coughed or vomited out, can penetrate human intestinal tissues, causing a severe immune response that resembles appendicitis, and may require surgical removal.[151] Tierno acknowledges that a truly expert sushi chef should be able "to tell from its appearance or odor if a fish is of the right quality," and he also will *often* (italics ours) be able to "remove the anisakis parasite without spreading the germs to the rest of the fish." But, he reminds us, "expertise varies from chef to chef." "Prepare yourself for a bout of illness now and then," he concludes.[152]

swans, black. See: **black swans.**

swimming pools, chlorinated. As world-famous physician and inte-

grative medicine pioneer Andrew Weil, M.D., points out, the chlorine used to disinfect swimming pools is "widely recognized as a health hazard."[153] To bolster his point, Weil cites a scientific study led by Dr. Alfred Bernard of the Catholic University of Louvain in Brussels indicating that children who swim frequently in chlorinated pools have an increased chance of developing asthma.[154] "The Belgian researchers also found that the risks of hay fever and other allergies more than doubled with significant exposure to chlorinated pools," Weil notes, and, he adds, "among adults, exposure to chlorine in swimming pools has been linked with other health problems including bladder and rectal cancer and, possibly, an increased risk for coronary heart disease." To make matters worse, Weil warns, even those who elect to stay out of the water are not safe. An irritant called trichloramine, which is believed to "damage the cellular barrier that protects the lungs," is released when chlorinated water "reacts with urine, sweat or other organic matter from swimmers," he explains. "Blood samples showed elevated trichloramine levels even among individuals who sat at the side of pools but didn't swim."[155] See: **swimming pools, insufficiently chlorinated.**

swimming pools, insufficiently chlorinated. "I don't go to public

pools anymore, especially if there are children in them," says internationally renowned University of Arizona microbiologist Charles P. Gerba, Ph.D. "They're basically large toilets."[156] Research conducted by the Centers for Disease Control confirms that Dr. Gerba is hardly exaggerating. In fact, one out of every eight of the over 120,000 pools inspected during 2008 had to be shut down immediately because of violations that seriously threatened the public's health and safety, and, by a wide margin, unsanitary water was by far the leading problem encountered. Every year, there are fifteen to twenty disease outbreaks precipitated by fecal matter in swimming pools, the CDC reports, and at least a quarter of them are caused by bacteria, viruses, or parasites that could be eliminated by proper chlorination practices. Urine, also found commonly in public swimming pool water, is a factor, too, because it contains nitrogen that reacts with the chlorine, depleting the supply—and therefore the disinfecting power—of the chemical.[157]

So is the risk so great that pools are to be avoided at all costs? Not necessarily, says the CDC. What you need to do is to take matters into your own hands and perform a scientific test of the water before you and/or your child enter the pool. Just visit your local pool store, purchase a packet of color-coded test strips (or order a free one from www.healthypools.org), and "dip before you dive" to make certain that the chlorine level is between 1.0 and 4.0 parts per million. If it is, your odds of avoiding a nasty bout of diarrhea or swimmer's ear are greatly improved. If it isn't, tell the pool staff to correct the problem and stay out of the water until they do. If you're unsatisfied with the response, the CDC recommends, contact your local health department.[158] See: **swimming pools, chlorinated.**

swine flu. See: **flu pandemic.**

swineherd's disease. See: **dogs.**

swordfish. "My seafood purveyor, when he goes out to dinner, won't eat swordfish," writes Anthony Bourdain, former executive chef at Brasserie Les Halles in New York City, and author of the best-selling *Kitchen Confidential: Adventures in the Culinary Underbelly.* "He's seen too many of those three-foot-long parasitic worms that riddle the fish's flesh. You see a few of these babies—and we all do—and you won't be tucking into swordfish anytime soon."[159]

synchronous diaphragmatic flutter (SDF). See: **hiccups.**

syphilis. See: **sexually transmitted diseases; condoms.**

syrup of ipecac. See: **ipecac.**

T

tablecloths. See: **polyvinyl chloride (PVC).**

tacos. See: **high-fructose corn syrup (HFCS).**

talcum powder. "Talc, talcum powder or just plain baby powder—

what could be more innocent than that?" asks *Eco Friendly Digest*. "It seems like such a soft, refreshing and harmless product, after all it's used on babies, shouldn't it be safe?" The answer, unfortunately, is it *should*, but it *isn't*. "Talcum powder has been positively linked to ovarian cancer," the *Digest* advises. "To worsen the matter, the cancer doesn't show up until 20 years after the toxic exposure. Sadly ovarian cancer in some young women has been traced back to the days when as babies they were lovingly dusted with baby powder by parents who were unaware of the hazard. How scary is that?"[1] Even more worrisome than the long-term cancer risk, cautions Springfield, Missouri, pediatrician Robert W. Steele, M.D., is the serious lung damage that can result if a baby accidentally inhales the fine grains of talcum powder, which, he notes, "can cause pneumonia, inflammation (or swelling) of the airways, and even death."[2]

And, advises the Cancer Prevention Coalition, women's body powders containing talc are just as dangerous to adults as baby powder is to infants. "Researchers have found talc particles in ovarian tumors and have found that women with ovarian cancer have used talcum powder in their genital area more frequently than healthy women," the Coalition warns. "Do not buy or use products containing talc." And, they urge, "it is especially important that women not apply talc to underwear or sanitary pads."[3]

tallness, excessive. See: **overheight.**

tallness, insufficient. See: **underheight.**

tap water. So you've read about the numerous problems with **bottled**

water (q.v.), and you're ready to go back to tap water, right? Well, before you do, consider the following facts, culled from an investigative report by Charles Duhigg of the *New York Times:* (1) Since 2004, "chemical factories, manufacturing plants and other workplaces have violated water pollution laws more than half a million times." But state governments and the Environmental Protection Agency have seldom opted to prosecute. (2) "An estimated one in 10 Americans have been exposed to drinking water that contains dangerous chemicals or fails to meet a federal health benchmark in other ways." (3) Those exposures include "carcinogens in the tap water of major American cities and unsafe chemicals in drinking-water wells." (4) Since the majority of pollutants that are fouling the nation's water have no scent and no taste, "many people who consume dangerous chemicals do not realize it, even after they become sick." (5) "An estimated 19.5 million Americans fall ill each year from drinking water contaminated with parasites, bacteria or viruses." (6) In dairy states such as California and Wisconsin, "farmers have sprayed liquefied animal feces onto fields, where it has seeped into wells, causing severe infections." Tap water in Farm Belt cities in Illinois, Indiana, Kansas, and Missouri "has contained pesticides at concentrations that some scientists have linked to birth defects and fertility problems." (7) "In parts of New York, Rhode Island, Ohio, California and other states where sewer systems cannot accommodate heavy rains, untreated human waste has flowed into rivers and washed onto beaches." (8) "Drinking water in parts of New Jersey, New York, Arizona and Massachusetts shows some of the highest concentrations of tetrachloroethylene, a dry cleaning solvent that has been linked to kidney damage and cancer."[4] Drink up! See: **water filters.**

tax returns, fraudulent. See: **identity theft.**

taxis. See: **bedbugs.**

tea, a nice hot cup of. Especially in Britain, drinking a "nice hot cup of tea" has long been hailed as the perfect remedy for absolutely everything. Consider, for example, the following message, posted on the community website LiveJournal.com in response to news reports that local shopkeepers were giving out free cups of hot tea after the July 2005 London subway bombings: "You're a bit cold? Tea. Your boyfriend has just left you? Tea. Coordinated terrorist attack on the transport network bringing the city to a grinding halt? *Tea dammit!*"[5]

But a recent Iranian study published in the *British Medical Journal* has literally dashed cold water on this genteel custom. The study, conducted by researchers at the Tehran University of Medical Sciences, found that habitual hot tea drinkers were twice as apt to contract esophageal cancer as those who regularly drank lukewarm tea. Even worse, those who frequently drank *very* hot tea were eight times as likely to be suffering from the disease.[6] So how should tea-fanciers respond to this troubling news? With a nice lukewarm cup of tea, naturally. See also: **caffeine.**

tectonic nuclear warfare. The pros and cons, and the potential risks

and putative rewards, of the use of commercial nuclear plants for the generation of large-scale, base-load electric power were already being extensively debated before the cascading disaster at Japan's multireactor facility at Fukushima in March of 2011. Although the series of increasingly grave technical failures at the giant Tokyo Electric Power station was generally attributed to the effects of a huge earthquake, followed by a devastating tsunami, there now appears to be evidence of a far darker determining factor that, if valid, would certainly provide grounds for even greater concern about the possible negative impacts of this carbon-free energy source.

According to Leuren Moret, a geoscientist who formerly worked at the Lawrence Livermore Nuclear Weapons Laboratory on the Yucca Mountain nuclear waste disposal project, the meltdowns, structural failures, and radiation releases at the six badly damaged units were in fact triggered by an act of tectonic nuclear warfare employing an aerosol/chemtrails plasma weapon designed by the Alaska-based High Frequency Active Auroral Research Program (HAARP) for the express purpose of causing Chernobyl-like radiation megaleaks.[7] Ms. Moret clearly laid the blame for this nefarious and sophisticated assault at the multiple figurative feet of "an international racketeering network within the U.S. Central Intelligence Agency, the Department of Energy, and British Petroleum on behalf of City of London bankers as part of an intentional genocidal depopulation of the northern and southern hemispheres."[8]

While it might be tempting to dismiss this theory as possibly delusional, it is worth recalling that in an article in the *Japan Times* on March 23, 2004, Ms. Moret, a then-unaffiliated but clearly perspicacious scientific expert, accurately predicted the very calamity that ultimately took place. Many of Japan's fifty-two nuclear reactors "have been negligently sited on active faults, particularly in the subduction zone along the Pacific coast, where major earthquakes of magnitude 7–8 or more on the Richter scale occur frequently," she cautioned at the time. "It is not a question of whether or not a nuclear disaster will occur in Japan, it is a question of when it will occur. Like the former Soviet Union after Chernobyl, Japan will become a country suffering from radiation sickness destroying future generations, and widespread contamination of agricultural areas will ensure a public-health disaster. Its economy will never recover." Ms. Moret's Cassandra-like admonition was seconded in the same news article by noted seismologist and Kobe University professor Katsuhiko Ishibashi who observed, "I think the situation right now is very scary. It's like a kamikaze terrorist wrapped in bombs just waiting to explode."[9]

Expanding on her recent identification of the hidden cause of the breakdowns at the Japanese installations, Ms. Moret insisted that the Stuxnet virus devised by U.S. and Israeli intelligence to disable Iranian uranium enrichment centrifuges was found in computers at Fukushima, noting that "the trouble after the earthquake was the pumps and valves and controllers malfunctioned so the workers could not get the pumps working. This just adds to the HAARP earthquake and much more evidence that it was a false-flag HAARP event."[10] Ms. Moret, who is currently an environmental commissioner in the city of Berkeley, California, also reported the sighting of a strange HAARP-created vortex cloud over San Francisco on March 18, 2011, which she is persuaded was designed to trigger "a heavy rain-out of the radiation from Fukushima onto the populace, food, and ecology of the Bay Area."[11]

teething rings. See: **bisphenol A.**

telephones. See: **phones, biohazards of; cell phones, radiation hazards of.**

temporary sterility. See: **microwave ovens.**

testicular atrophy. See: **rubber duckies.**

theobromine poisoning. See: **holly.**

tick-borne diseases. Before you spread that blanket on a nice patch
of grass in a park, at the shore, or in your own backyard, and unpack that picnic basket full of scrumptious summertime treats, consider this—you may be about to become a tasty tidbit in an unplanned holiday "ticknic." On your unintentional guest list of itsy-bitsy arachnid party crashers is a whole host of colorfully named ectoparasites, like *Ixodes scapularis* (the deer tick), its California cousin *Ixodes pacificus* (the blacklegged tick), *Amblyomma americanum* (the lone star tick), *Amblyomma maculatum* (the Gulf Coast tick), *Ornithodoros turicata* (the relapsing fever tick), and the whole extended *Dermacentor* family, including *variabilis* (the American dog tick), *andersoni* (the Rocky Mountain wood tick), *Rhipicephalus sanguineus* (the brown dog tick), and *occidentalis* (the Pacific Coast dog tick).[12] While you're noshing on watermelon, fried chicken, potato salad, and corn on the cob, these minuscule moochers will be digging into their main course—you, or more precisely, a yummy meal of your blood extracted through a tiny incision in your skin made with a harpoonlike mouthpart common to hematophagous parasitic arthropods called a hypostome.[13]

And rest assured, your inconspicuous freeloaders won't arrive empty-handed—(really, with eight tiny but very flexible appendages, how could they?)—because along with their hearty appetites, these mammal-loving vectors will be bringing with them a whole seasonal smorgasbord of exotic bacteria, protozoa, and viruses and the diseases they carry, such as *Borrelia burgdorferi sensu lato* (Lyme disease), *Borrelia hermsii* (relapsing fever), *Rickettsia rickettsii* (Rocky Mountain spotted fever), *Anaplasma phagocytophilum* (ehrlichiosis), *Francisella tularensis* (tularemia), *Coltivirus* (Colorado tick fever), and *Babesia microti* and *equi* (babesiosis).

According to the Centers for Disease Control (CDC), Lyme

disease, which was named for the town in Connecticut where it was first identified in the 1970s but has since spread to every state except Hawaii, is by far the most common tick-borne malady, with 30,000 reported cases in 2009 alone, and another 8,500 suspected cases. Although the telltale symptoms of Lyme and many other bacterial infections spread by tick bites—including body and muscle aches, fever, headaches, fatigue, joint pain, rash, stiff neck, and facial paralysis[14]—are usually mild and are generally treatable with a course of antibiotics, tick-borne ailments can in some instances lead to severe heart problems, and one of them—a formerly very rare malaria-like illness called babesiosis—has recently been singled out as a particularly worrisome scourge. In the last decade, the CDC has reported a twenty-fold increase in babesiosis infections spread by deer ticks, particularly in regions of the Northeast where Lyme disease is prevalent, and because there is currently no screening test for the organisms that cause the malady, its inadvertent spread through blood transfusions is a major threat. "We are very worried about it and are doing everything in our power to address this," declared Sanjai Kumar, chief of the emerging pathogens laboratory at the Food and Drug Administration. Admittedly, Lyme disease is, well, no picnic, but babesiosis can be fatal. According to Dr. Gary Wormser, chief of infectious diseases at Westchester Medical Center in New York, many patients infected with the babesiosis parasite suffer no effects or have mild flulike symptoms, "But some people get so sick that they wind up hospitalized, put into an intensive care unit, or even dying."[15]

ties. See **neckties; neckties, doctors'.**

tingling thigh syndrome. See: **seat belts; skinny jeans.**

TinySex. See: **cybersex.**

tobacco smoke, environmental. See: **smoking.**

toes, broken. See: **flip-flops.**

tofu. See: **soy.**

toilet, reading on. See: **reading on the toilet.**

toilet, sitting on the. In a landmark 2003 research study published in

Digestive Diseases and Sciences, an Israeli physician named Dov Sikirov, M.D., found that sitting on the toilet is not only an unnecessarily uncomfortable and inefficient way to relieve oneself, but that it is also actually unhealthful, leading directly to such painful conditions as hemorrhoids, diverticular disease, and pelvic floor prolapse.[16] The problem, as David Ling writes on his informative website Toilet-RelatedAilments.com, is that "sitting obstructs the passage of waste through the colon. Elimination is difficult, requires straining and can never be complete."[17] And, over time, the extra stress, combined with our body's less-than-total ejection of pathogen-laden waste, leads to chronic pain and disease. As Dr. Sikirov's research demonstrated, squatting rather than sitting almost completely eliminates (no pun intended) the problems caused by "incorrect evacuation posture," resulting in a far more comfortable and, ultimately, more healthful experience.

So why don't we squat, rather than sit? The answer, of course, is the ubiquity—at least in Western countries—of the "porcelain throne." "By forcing unsuspecting users to depart from the correct toileting posture, the sitting toilet has caused much distress, pain and suffering," writes Ling. "The habitual use of sitting toilets is a dangerous habit, one that you would do well to abandon."[18] But if we're not going to sit on the toilet when nature calls, what *are* we to do? Well, one option is to climb up on the edge of the toilet seat and squat there, treating the opening in the toilet as if it were a hole in the ground. But as Jonathan Isbit, author of *Nature Knows Best: Health Benefits of the Natural Squatting Position,* writes, "Using a toilet in this way can dislodge the bolts that hold it to the floor. Once the seal between the toilet and the drainpipe is broken, toxic methane gas can leak into the house." Furthermore, says Isbit, "toilet bowls are not designed to bear the concentrated strain of someone squatting (especially someone heavy). They have been known to collapse, causing severe injury from pieces of jagged porcelain."

Luckily for all of us, Isbit has invented a device he calls "Nature's

Platform," a surprisingly attractive framework, hand-fashioned from high-density polyethylene and PVC plastic, reinforced with galvanized steel tubing, that sets up quickly and easily around conventional toilets and allows people to squat above them comfortably, with their intestines and colon properly aligned, all the while avoiding the risk of injury caused by toilet dislodgment or structural failure. You can acquire one by visiting Isbit's website, NaturesPlatform.com. Doing so, he assures us, will be more than just a self-serving act. "By purchasing Nature's Platform," he writes, "you are supporting the effort to re-educate the Western World, and thereby eradicate some of the most terrible diseases afflicting our society." [19]

toilets, ceramic. Did you know that, if you have a ceramic toilet, you

may be spending part of every day literally "sitting on the hot seat"? That's because, according to Paul W. Frame, Ph.D., of the Oak Ridge Associated Universities, many of the clays typically used in the manufacture of toilet-bowl ceramics contain measurable amounts of radioactive isotopes such as "potassium-40 and the various members of the uranium and thorium decay series." [20] For more information about this underpublicized threat, see: **ceramics.**

toilets, flushing of. In 1975, Professor Charles P. Gerba of the Uni-

versity of Arizona's Department of Soil, Water, and Environmental Science, conducted a famous experiment in which he measured the amount of bacteria and viruses that are sprayed around a typical bathroom each time the toilet is flushed. The results: So many microbes were contained in the aerosol spray ejected that photos of the so-called toilet plume, Gerba now recalls, "looked like Baghdad after a U.S. air attack." [21] What's worse, he discovered, the menacing cloud you create each time you flush your toilet hangs in the air for up to two hours after you pull the handle, and commonly travels as far as eight feet up and out from the toilet bowl. Toilet-flushing aerosols land on everything in your bathroom, Gerba warns, including your toothbrush, your water glass, your sink faucets, your towels, your razor—everything. So what can you do to stay healthy in the face of all this? For starters, says Gerba, always close the toilet lid before flushing. Keep your toothbrush (and, presumably, your bathroom glass and razor, too) in the medicine cabinet, and clean your bathroom sink every day using a cleanser containing chlorine bleach.[22] In addition, suggests Philip M. Tierno Jr., Ph.D., director of clinical microbiology and diagnostic immunology at New York University Langone Medical Center, you should vacate bathrooms or restroom stalls as soon as possible after flushing "to keep the microscopic, airborne mist from choosing you as a landing site."[23] See: **toothbrushes, keeping in medicine cabinet; chlorine bleach.**

toilets, flushing of, impact on the water supply. Did you know that

 25 percent of the clean, fresh, potable water that the average household uses every day is literally flushed down the toilet? Indeed, as World Toilet Organization (WTO) founder Jack Sim told *Time* magazine during a recent waste management summit in Macao, if you're one of the millions of people who tends to "flush and forget" on a regular basis, "chances are you're dumping up to 22 liters of drinkable water every day, one three- to six-liter flush at a time." And "the problem doesn't stop there," *Time* points out. "What follows—the 'forget' part of the toilet experience—is the long and costly process of sanitizing the water that was clean before you answered nature's call." In the United Kingdom alone, says Rose George, author of *The Big Necessity: The Unmentionable World of Human Waste and Why It Matters,* "the sewage system uses as much energy as what the largest coal fire station in the [country] produces."[24]

So in a world where both clean water and fossil fuels are becoming scarcer every day, what can individual citizens do to help? Well, first and foremost, the Buffalo, New York, Water Authority recommends, you should install a water-saving displacement device in the tank of your toilet. (This can be as simple as putting a plastic jug full of pebbles in the tank. The pebbles are to keep the bottle from floating and interfering with the flushing mechanism.) Second, flush only when necessary. Don't use the porcelain throne as a wastebasket for cigarette butts or disposable diapers. And, perhaps even more important, follow the old mantra "When it's yellow, let it mellow, when it's brown, flush it down."[25] (According to the Waste Not, Want Less blog, simply by adhering to this "selective flushing" policy, U.S. residents could save over a trillion gallons of freshwater every year.)[26]

It should be noted, however, that the "mellow yellow" strategy is not uncontroversial. Consider, for example, the following anonymous comment posted on the Money Smart Life blog: "My husband does not flush the toilet after a pee and I find it repulsive, it does smell, so now he puts lots of bleach in the toilet which makes it smell worse. I feel that [the water and money he saves by not flushing the toilet] is worth more than I am."[27] See also: **chlorine bleach; toilets, flushing of.**

toluene poisoning. See: **candlelight dinners; carpeting, new.**

tomato-based sauces. According to eHowHealth.com, "pizza sauce, spaghetti sauce, ketchup and barbecue sauces typically contain high fructose corn syrup, which is used to balance the tart tomatoes and bring out the flavors of spices." And, as the *San Francisco Chronicle* points out, "almost all nutritionists finger high fructose corn syrup consumption as a major culprit in the nation's obesity crisis. The inexpensive sweetener flooded the American food supply in the early 1980s, just about the time the nation's obesity rate started its unprecedented climb."[28] Of course, obesity is only the beginning of the problem—if we're obese, our risk of contracting diabetes, cardiovascular disease, and several kinds of cancers is greatly increased.[29] Maybe you should forgo the pizza and tomato-based condiments, and opt for pesto instead of tomato sauce on your pasta. See: **pine nuts.** See also: **high-fructose corn syrup (HFCS); sugar.**

tomatoes, cherry. See: **grapes.**

tonic water. See: **high-fructose corn syrup (HFCS).**

tooth erosion. See: **brushing your teeth after meals; oranges.**

toothbrushes. "Unfortunately your mouth is home to thousands of germs," notes the invaluable wellness information website iHealth360.com. "You brush your teeth to protect your teeth and mouth from harmful bacteria and those harmful germs are transferred to your toothbrush!" To make matters worse, the bacteria-filled aerosol cloud that ascends from your bathroom toilet every time you flush it may well also be regularly coating your brush with disease-causing germs (for more information, see: **toilets, flushing of**), and the moisture and humidity supplied on a regular basis by your shower or bathtub provides a perfect environment to facilitate the growth of bacteria on toothbrush bristles between brushings.[30] So what can we do to protect ourselves from a contaminated toothbrush? *Reader's Digest* offers a simple, convenient solution: "Sterilize it in the microwave before you use it." Ten seconds on high is the best setting, the magazine recommends.[31] See: **microwave ovens.**

toothbrushes, keeping in medicine cabinet. "You need to guard your toothbrush from foreign bacteria but don't stash it in the medicine cabinet," warns *SmileLink Newsletter*, a popular national online publication for dental patients. Medicine chests, the newsletter advises, are "incubators for bacteria and yeast because there is no air circulation to dry the moisture on your toothbrush."[32] See: **toilets, flushing of.** See also: **medicine cabinets; toothbrushes.**

toothpaste, antimicrobial. "Toothpaste is supposed to help clean your teeth, but what it actually does just might horrify you," writes Mike Adams, the former clinical trial tester and consumer health advocate who founded, and serves as editor in chief of, NaturalNews.com. "When tap water meets toothpaste, the triclosan [present in antimicrobial dentifrice brands] reacts freely with the chlorine in the tap water to become chloroform," a known poison which, if inhaled in high enough concentrations, can cause depression, liver problems, and cancer, and whose presence in drinking water has been linked with bladder cancers and miscarriages. "It's a chemical reaction occurring right in your mouth while you brush your teeth. And don't think you are safe once you rinse it all out of your mouth: research shows that it can remain in your mouth after brushing for up to 12 hours, and can be easily absorbed into the tongue and through mucus into the body." Children are at an even greater risk than adults, Adams warns, since "they tend to swallow their toothpaste more while brushing their teeth."[33]

Now, it's true that toothpastes containing triclosan have been shown to diminish your chances of contracting the gum disease gingivitis, and have been hailed by Slate.com as "without question the most clinically effective" tooth-cleaning products on the market.[34] And it's also true that the amount of chloroform gas produced during every brushing is, to quote World Wildlife Federation toxicology expert Giles Watson, "very low." "But," Watson cautions, "that adds up over time. The best advice," he concludes, "is to avoid products with the chemical."[35] Or, as Mike Adams puts it, "Stop giving your money to manufacturers who are poisoning and exploiting you for profit."[36] (Note: Recent studies have suggested that, in addition to reacting with chlorine to form chloroform, triclosan may interfere with the normal growth, development, and function of the brain, the immune system, and male and female reproductive organs. Furthermore, it is suspected that the presence of triclosan in our environment is contributing to antibiotic resistance in bacteria known to cause human infections. The Centers for Disease Control and Prevention calls antibiotic resistance one of the most pressing health issues facing the United States.[37] For more information, see **antibacterial and antiviral products; superbugs.**)

Torino Impact Hazard Scale. This risk-assessment scale, ranging from zero to ten, was adopted by the International Astronomical Union to categorize the likelihood, and effect, of an impact on our planet from a collision with a "near-earth object" (astronomers' name for an asteroid or comet that passes close enough to the earth's orbit to warrant concern). For example, an object rating a ten on the Torino Scale, would, in the IAU's words, be certain to collide with Earth, and, in the process, would be "capable of causing global climatic catastrophe that may threaten the future of civilization as we know it, whether impacting land or ocean."[38] (See: **Asteroid 99942 Apophis; Comet Catalina.**)

touching your face. See: **face touching.**

toxic assets. See: **zombie banks.**

toxicity, linguistic. See **side-effects warning labels on prescription drugs.**

toys with holes in them. See: **rubber duckies.**

trade deficit, ballooning. See: **superpower collapse soup.**

traffic signs. According to the late Hans Monderman, a legendary Dutch traffic engineer who died of cancer in 2008, traditional traffic safety infrastructure—warning signs, traffic lights, metal railings, curbs, painted lines, speed bumps, and so on—is (to quote Tom Vanderbilt, who profiled Monderman in the *Wilson Quarterly*) "not only often unnecessary, but can endanger those it is meant to protect." The reason, Monderman explained, is that traffic signs provide an invitation to stop thinking, to stop acting on one's own volition.[39] "The greater the number of prescriptions, the more people's sense of personal responsibility dwindles,"[40] he said. "When you treat people like idiots, they'll behave like idiots."[41]

Matthias Schulz, writing in the German magazine *Der Spiegel*, reports that seven cities and regions in Europe are giving Monderman's concept of streets without traffic signs a try and are achieving "good results." Schulz is not surprised. Some 20 million traffic signs have already been set up all over Germany, he laments, and "psychologists have long revealed the senselessness of such exaggerated regulation. About 70 percent of traffic signs are ignored by drivers. What's more, the glut of prohibitions . . . foments resentment. [The driver] may stop in front of the crosswalk, but that only makes him feel justified in preventing pedestrians from crossing the street on every other occasion. Every traffic light baits him with the promise of making it over the crossing while the light is still yellow." [42]

In the *Wilson Quarterly*, Vanderbilt tells of a trip he took with Monderman to the village of Makkinga in the Netherlands—the site of one of the traffic engineer's most successful experiments. At the entrance to the village stood a single sign, Vanderbilt writes. "It welcomed visitors, noted a 30 kilometer-per-hour speed limit, then added: 'Free of Traffic Signs.' This was Monderman humor at its finest: a traffic sign announcing the absence of traffic signs." [43] See also: **seat belts.**

trans fats. According to CNN Health, trans fats are an "artery-clogging element of partially hydrogenated oils" that, because they "increase your LDL (bad cholesterol) and lower your HDL (good cholesterol), can significantly weaken your natural defenses against coronary heart disease." "Harvard researchers have estimated that banning trans fats from the American diet could prevent some 228,000 heart attacks each year," CNN's Mara Betsch reports. In short, she says, they "act as napalm for your heart." [44]

Trans fats are found in fried foods, which are frequently cooked in partially hydrogenated vegetable oil, and, because they help prolong product shelf life, they are also a common ingredient in commercial baked goods, pizza dough, pancake and hot chocolate mixes, potato chips, microwave popcorn, and stick margarine. New York City's board of health feels so strongly about the health hazard they represent that, in 2006, they acted to make the Big Apple the first U.S. municipality to ban them from restaurants, and, since then, California and Illinois have also enacted legislation to begin phasing them out. "Nobody wants to take away your french fries and hamburgers—I love those things, too," explains New York's mayor, Michael Bloomberg. "But if you can make them with something that is less damaging to your health, we should do that." [45]

So what can individuals do to minimize their intake of trans fats? The Harvard School of Public Health suggests that you "avoid eating commercially prepared baked foods (cookies, pies, donuts, etc.), snack foods, and processed foods, including fast foods. To be on the safe side, assume that all such products contain trans fats unless they are labeled otherwise." And "since many restaurants still use partially hydrogenated oils in their fryers," Harvard's nutrition experts recommend that, when you're eating out, you should stay away from all deep-fried foods and desserts.[46] See: **Nanny Statism.**

traumatic brain injury. See: **hiccups; runny nose.**

tray tables, seat-back. See: **airplane cabins.**

treasury bonds, U.S. "Worthless confetti." That's how investment

analyst Marc Faber, renowned for advising his clients to get out of American equities one week before the stock market crash of 1987, characterizes U.S. treasury bonds,[47] and noted Boston University economist Laurence J. Kotlikoff agrees. Writing in the International Monetary Fund's *Finance & Development,* Kotlikoff worries that U.S. fiscal and monetary policies have brought the country so close to financial ruin that even "a minor trade dispute between the United States and China," which holds $843 billion in U.S. government bonds, could trigger a massive sell-off of treasury securities "that causes the public to withdraw their bank deposits." As a direct consequence, he predicts, "the Federal Reserve would have to print trillions of dollars to cover its explicit and implicit guarantees. All that new money could produce strong inflation, perhaps hyperinflation," and an ensuing "global financial meltdown."[48] Faced with this doomsday scenario, where should investors put their money? David Stockman, former director of the Office of Management and Budget, offers the following advice: "I invest in anything that [Federal Reserve chairman] Bernanke can't destroy," he suggested to Jennifer DePaul of the *Fiscal Times,* "including gold, canned beans, bottled water and flashlight batteries."[49] See: **stimulus spending, inadequate; commodities; gold; deficit hysteria; superpower collapse soup.**

Trojan horse. Sometimes known simply as a "Trojan," this increas-

ingly ubiquitous form of malicious software is designed by hackers to infect and thereby gain access to targeted computers—including yours. The reference to the storied horse that led to the fall of Troy is based on the devious inherent design of this superficially appealing type of program. Widely available on the Internet and free of charge, the typical Trojan horse masquerades as a helpful application offering some useful or beneficial service—sniffing out and eliminating viruses, for example—but instead actually performs another, hidden and sinister function, such as installing a *new* virus that allows intruders to steal data, crash the computer, or otherwise harm the affected system.

A recent study by BitDefender noted that "Trojan-type malware is on the rise," and reported that in the first six months of 2008, seven of the top ten "e-threats" were Trojan horses that "accounted for 83% of the global malware in the wild."[50] So before you fling open the gates, as it were, to your operating system and download that tempting cybergoody, you might want to heed an update of the famous admonition issued by our Institute's namesake and inspiration, the prophet Cassandra: "Beware of geeks bearing gifts." See also: **malware.**

tuna. The World's Healthiest Foods website, whfoods.com, touts tuna

as "truly a nutrient-dense food." "An excellent source of high quality protein," it explains, "tuna are rich in a variety of important nutrients including the minerals selenium, magnesium, and potassium; the B vitamins niacin, B1 and B6; and perhaps most important, the beneficial omega-3 essential fatty acids."[51] That means we should eat lots of it, right? Wrong, says noted Canadian pollution expert Bruce Lourie, who, after gorging on tuna for three days, measured his blood mercury level and, as the *Washington Post* has reported, found that it had more than doubled, to a reading "well past the level deemed safe by the U.S. government."[52] See: **omega-3 fish oil supplements.**

TV remotes. One of the first things you should do when you check

into a hotel is disinfect the TV remote, advises Allison Janse, author of *The Germ Freak's Guide to Outwitting Colds and Flu.* And while you're at it, she suggests, disinfect the phone and the refrigerator door handle, too. "While these are frequently handled, they're rarely cleaned," she points out.[53] Your home TV remote can be a dangerous source of pathogens, too, warns Philip M. Tierno Jr., the director of clinical microbiology and immunology at the New York University Langone Medical Center. "When we're in couch potato mode," he writes, the remote "readily acquires a veneer of oils and other residues from the food we're eating while we're watching television, creating a food source for germs." Clean it weekly, he urges, to "remove the bio-loads that accumulate on it."[54] Unfortunately, writes Danielle Braff in *Men's Health* magazine, it's nearly impossible to get those hard-to-reach areas around TV remote buttons truly clean. Fortunately, however, she has a nifty solution to offer. Slip a plastic sleeve protector or Ziploc bag over your home or hotel room remote before you use it, she advises.[55]

"Twinkie fascists." See: **Nanny Statism.**

U

undercooked food. According to the U.S. Department of Health and

Human Services, one of the principal causes of the food-borne illnesses that strike as many as 76 million Americans every year and kill an estimated five thousand of them is the ingestion of food that hasn't been cooked long enough, or that has been prepared at too low a temperature.[1] Indeed, says WebMD, a good general rule of thumb for cooks to follow is: "The higher the temperature reached, the more germs are killed."[2] See: **overcooked food.** See also: **food thermometers.**

underheight. It has long been accepted in the medical community

that overweight individuals face an increased risk of succumbing to cardiovascular diseases, diabetes, cancer, and other physical disabilities, and there is persuasive statistical evidence that obesity is responsible for something on the order of one hundred thousand preventable deaths annually, but another insidious though far less publicized threat to public health—height insufficiency—exacts a similar grim toll on life expectancy. People who are categorized as seriously "underheight"—for men, a vertical measurement roughly four inches shorter than a median stature of about six feet—exhibit a greater susceptibility to often fatal pulmonary and cardiovascular disorders than their taller peers, primarily due to risk factors for these conditions contributed by their smaller lungs and narrower coronary arteries. Alas, unlike their fat counterparts, who can through diet and exercise lose dozens of pounds of body weight and thereby dramatically improve their odds of surviving into old age, short people rarely succeed in adding even an inch in height.[3] See: **overheight.**

underinvesting. According to internationally recognized wealth

management expert Ed Butowsky, founder of Chapwood Capital Investment Management, folks who "sit on the sidelines," or invest in money market funds, during periods when interest rates are low are "committing financial suicide." "You subtract taxes (and there's more coming, we know that), then you subtract out inflation, you subtract out management fees, and . . . most people are losing about 4–5% per year purchasing power. Then you do that over five years, you've lost 25% purchasing power or somewhere close to that. Now you have yourself in a *real* hole. People are totally underinvesting . . . They're committing financial suicide."

How can you avoid this problem? Butowsky says the answer is simple—educate yourself about good investments (he particularly likes hedge funds because their performance doesn't echo that of other markets) and then . . . *invest!* (Butowsky points out that he and his staff specialize in helping with the educational process, should you want to avail yourself of their services).[4]

unemployment. See: **agflation; deficit hysteria; deflation; gold, failure to invest in; stagflation; stimulus spending, inadequate.**

unknown unknowns. See: **black swans; zombification.**

unnatural selection. See: **sex-selective abortion.**

unsecured financial liabilities. See: **"doom loop."**

"uranyls." See: **ceramics.**

urinary bladder distention. See: **"holding it in."**

urogenital abnormalities in baby boys. See: **food containers, plastic.**

U-turns. According to the National Safety Commission, collisions at intersections cause more fatalities than any other type of automobile accident, and, they add ominously, "drivers making U-turns are often involved in these type crashes."[5] Indeed, the government of Singapore believes U-turns are so inherently dangerous that it has banned them entirely except in places where signs specifically permitting them are posted, and U-turns are also illegal, under a sometimes bewildering variety of circumstances, in many other locations around the world. So how does the average driver know what rule applies where? "He doesn't," says National Motorists Association president James Baxter, who recommends, therefore, that to be certain of avoiding arrest, you should never make a U-turn at an intersection with a traffic signal, in the middle of a block, in an urban or residential area, or most important of all, if there is a police officer anywhere in sight. ("This is like waving a red cape at a wounded bull, regardless of legality," says Baxter.[6]) "Beginners especially don't realize how much time and space is necessary to turn around and reach the speed of fast flowing traffic," warns DrivingSchool.com. "It may be better to drive around the block, instead of risking a U-turn."[7] Baxter, perhaps a bit reluctantly, agrees. "The blocks are quite large in West Texas and Eastern Montana," he notes wistfully.[8] See: **drivers, courteous.**

V

vacuum metastability event. According to quantum field theory, a so-called false vacuum can exist in a specific portion of the universe—indeed, one may exist in the part of the universe the earth and solar system occupy. A false vacuum is so defined because it exists in a relatively high energy state—one higher than that of a "true vacuum." But that energy state, physicists warn us, is inherently unstable. If a bubble of a lower-energy "true vacuum" were formed within the false vacuum, or collided with it, the false vacuum would suddenly and catastrophically collapse into a more stable ground state through a process known as bubble nucleation. The peculiar kind of foamy thermodynamic explosion resulting from this disruptive phase-transition event is, amazingly enough, quite analogous to the spectacular soda and candy eruption that occurs when Mentos are dropped into a bottle of Diet Coke. Therefore, if we *are* unknowingly (and quite unluckily) living in what turns out to be a doomed sector of space permeated by a false vacuum, we are potentially in a quantum world of hurt, since at any moment a lethal blob of true vacuum—formed by a quantum fluctuation, or, say, a high-speed particle created by a linear accelerator such as CERN's **Large Hadron Collider** (q.v.)—could approach and/or expand at nearly the speed of light and destroy the earth in a flash of cosmic effervescence.[1]

The Harvard theoretical physicists Stanley Coleman and Frank De Luccia summed up the existential threat facing us all in the following eloquent though disturbing passage: "The possibility that we are living in a false vacuum has never been a cheering one to contemplate. Vacuum decay is the ultimate ecological catastrophe; in the new vacuum there are new constants of nature; after vacuum decay, not only is life as we know it impossible, so is chemistry as we know it. However, one could always draw stoic comfort from the possibility that perhaps in the course of time, the new vacuum would sustain, if not life as we know it, at least some structures capable of knowing joy. This possibility has now been eliminated."[2]

vaginal atrophy. See: **abstinence.**

Valles Caldera National Preserve. Nestled in the Jemez Mountains,

less that forty miles northwest of glamorous Santa Fe, New Mexico, lies Valles Caldera National Preserve, a popular, if secluded, tourist attraction whose website promises visitors that they'll see wildlife and "beautiful vistas," and that they'll learn about the preserve's "rich history and geology."[3] Perhaps the overseers of the preserve are wise to save the "history and geology" lessons until visitors actually arrive at the site, for what their website neglects to mention is that the Valles Caldera National Preserve is one of only six locations throughout the world designated as an active supervolcano. That means Valles Caldera has the potential of blowing up at any time with a force that can literally kill thousands of people instantly, and blast suffocating ash as far away as Iowa. Is it any wonder that the Discovery Channel calls it "the sleeping monster in the heart of New Mexico"? (For up-to-date information, visit the ongoing web discussion, "Valles Caldera Is Going to Erupt, Get Out of New Mexico," available at http://www.god likeproductions.com/forum1/message1118472/.) See also: **super-volcanoes.**

***Varroa destructor* mites.** See: **colony collapse disorder.**

Vaseline, role of in condom breakdown. See: **condoms.**

veganism. See: **vegetarianism and veganism.**

vegetables, canned. See: **bisphenol A.**

vegetables, leafy green. See: **leafy green vegetables.**

vegetarianism and veganism. In a *New York Times* article entitled "Sorry, Vegans: Brussels Sprouts Like to Live, Too," Pulitzer Prize–winning author Natalie Angier argues persuasively that it's too early to "cede the entire moral penthouse to 'committed vegetarians' and 'strong ethical vegans'" who avoid eating animals—or in the case of vegans, even using products derived from them—on the basis that killing other sentient creatures "for human food and finery is nothing less than outright murder." The time has come, says Angier, when we "might consider that plants no more aspire to being stir-fried in a wok than a hog aspires to being peppercorn-studded in my Christmas clay pot." Angier notes that the "more that scientists learn about the complexity of plants—their keen sensitivity to the environment, the speed with which they react to changes in the environment, and the extraordinary number of tricks that plants will rally to fight off attackers and solicit help from afar—the more impressed researchers become, and the less easily we can dismiss plants as so much fiberfill backdrop, passive sunlight collectors on which deer, antelope and vegans can conveniently graze. It's time for a green revolution, a reseeding of our stubborn animal minds."[4]

Luckily, if you share Angier's sentiments, there's a food regime for you to adopt that's fully consistent with her manifesto. It's called fruitarianism, and, as described on the fruitarian website, TheNew Earth.org, here's what's involved: "A Fruitarian eats lots of fruit, with some nuts and grains or the products thereof. No animals, birds, fishes, insects or humans. No cabbages, lettuce leaves or bean sprouts, no celery or root vegetables. But tomatoes and avocadoes because they're fruits. And of course mangoes and papayas, oranges and lemons, bananas . . . all the wonderful fruits which the trees and bushes offer us freely so that we can distribute their seeds. As we become more aware of, and thus respectful of life in all its forms and manifestations, we are becoming more reluctant to take life, to eat other lifeforms and to consume the aura of fear and death. We begin to ask the very fundamental question: 'Why should others die so that I can live?'"[5] Indeed.

venereal diseases (VD). See: **sexually transmitted diseases.**

Vibrio **germs.** See: **sushi, sashimi, and ceviche.**

viruses, computer. See: **malware; Trojan horse.**

visceral vibratory vestibular disturbance (VVVD). See **wind turbine syndrome.**

vitamin A supplements. According to the Harvard Medical School, "the evidence is piling up that too much vitamin A weakens bones and leads to hip fractures." In 2002, Harvard researchers found that that high vitamin A intake raises the risk for hip fracture in postmenopausal women. "The data suggest that the main culprit is *retinol*, the active form of the vitamin," the medical school reported. Retinol is found in vitamin A supplements, and also in liver, eggs, full-fat dairy products, fish liver oils, and fortified foods such as cereals and skim milk. A year later, a long-term Swedish study confirmed the Harvard results. It found that men with high blood levels of retinol had a risk for hip fracture double that of subjects with average levels.[6] The study also found that the risk of fractures among those with the highest levels of vitamin A was seven times higher than those with the lowest levels. "What these results indicate is, 'Oh my God, we have found a bone poison,'" said Laura L. Tosi, M.D., chair of the Committee on Women's Health Issues for the American Academy of Orthopaedic Surgeons, after the Swedish findings were announced.[7]

Now that you know all this, it's unlikely you'll be surprised by the Harvard Medical School's recommendation that, unless you have a health condition involving a vitamin A deficiency and are under a clinician's care, you shouldn't take vitamin A supplements. Instead, the school advises, you should "eat lots of colorful vegetables" (such as carrots and spinach) "and orange fruits" (e.g., oranges and apricots), "because they provide vitamin A from beta-carotene, plus other important nutrients. You can't get too much beta-carotene because it converts to vitamin A only as the body needs it."[8] See: **carrots; spinach; oranges; apricots.**

vitamin C supplements. "Those who think that if a little vitamin C

 is good, more must be better should think again, says a team of British researchers, who found that a supplement of 500 milligrams a day could damage people's genes," writes Jane E. Brody in the *New York Times*.

According to Brody, work by the British scientists, clinical pathologists at the University of Leicester, corroborates warnings "issued for decades" by Victor Herbert, M.D., J.D., M.A.C.P., F.R.S.M., a renowned professor of medicine at the Mount Sinai School of Medicine in New York City. In an interview before his death in 2002, Herbert said that his laboratory studies over the years had shown that "the vitamin C in supplements mobilizes harmless ferric iron stored in the body and converts it to harmful ferrous iron, which induces damage to the heart and other organs." The vitamin C naturally present in foods like oranges and orange juice, he added, presents no such problems.[9] See: **oranges; fruit juice.**

vitamin D supplements. We all need vitamin D—to keep our bones strong, to prevent rickets, to make sure our nervous systems are functioning properly, to help us maintain normal calcium, and to bolster our immune systems. According to the U.S. National Institutes of Health (NIH), there is also some specific evidence that vitamin D may help us control blood pressure, that it can reduce school-age children's chances of catching seasonal flu, and that it can make women less susceptible to multiple sclerosis.

Fortunately, our skin can synthesize vitamin D through exposure to sunlight.[10] Unfortunately, as WebMD reminds us, the cumulative effects of sun exposure "put us at higher risk of cellular damage, early wrinkling, age spots, actinic keratoses, and skin cancer—including melanoma."[11] Fortunately, sunscreen products can help prevent our skin from being damaged and limit our chances of developing skin cancer, but, unfortunately, according to the Linus Pauling Institute, they also curtail the manufacture of vitamin D in our bodies.[12] Fortunately, we can take vitamin D supplements to make up for the vitamin D we fail to get from the sun. Unfortunately, however, too much supplementary vitamin D can lead to a particularly unpleasant array of health problems including anorexia, constipation, dehydration, fatigue, heart arrhythmias, irritability, muscle weakness, polyuria, vomiting, weight loss, and more seriously, abnormally high calcium levels (hypercalcemia), which, in turn, can result in bone loss, kidney stones, and the calcification of organs like the heart and kidneys.[13]

So, how much vitamin D is "too much"? Well, according to the Vitamin D Council ("a nonprofit, tax-exempt educational corporation founded in 2003 by executive director John J. Cannell, M.D., on the conviction that humans all over the world are needlessly suffering from vitamin D deficiency"[14]), "what exactly constitutes a toxic dose of vitamin D has yet to be determined, though it is possible this amount may vary with the individual."[15] In other words, it's up to *you* to figure it out. See: **sun exposure; sun exposure, insufficient; sunscreens.**

vitamin E supplements. Perhaps you've heard that taking vitamin E

supplements can reduce your risk of heart disease, and maybe even cancer. The reasoning behind this theory is that vitamin E is a powerful antioxidant. As the University of Maryland Health Center explains, "antioxidants are substances that destroy free radicals—harmful compounds in the body that damage DNA (genetic material) and even cause cell death. Free radicals are believed to contribute to aging as well as the development of a number of health problems, including heart disease and cancer. Antioxidants provide some protection against these conditions."[16]

However, before embarking on a regimen of vitamin E supplements, you should be aware that, according to the U.S. National Institutes of Health's Office of Dietary Supplements, high doses of the supplement "can cause hemorrhage and interrupt blood coagulation in animals," and that two clinical trials—one in Finland and one in Boston—have found an "increased risk of hemorrhagic stroke" in participants taking supplemental vitamin E.[17] Edgar R. Miller III, M.D., Ph.D., of the Johns Hopkins University School of Medicine, who directed a comprehensive 2004 study on the effectiveness of vitamin E, is even more blunt about what *his* team discovered. "A lot of people take vitamins because they believe it will benefit their health in the long term and prolong life. But our study shows that use of high-dose [i.e., 400 international units or more] vitamin E supplements certainly did not prolong life, but was associated with a higher risk of death."[18] The really bad news here, as Emmy-winning national radio-show host Dean Edell, M.D., points out, is that "vitamin E capsules, used as supplements, typically contain 400 IU to 800 IU." In other words, he says, what scientists refer to as a "high dose" is what "most folks taking a vitamin E capsule consume."[19]

volatile organic compounds (VOCs). See: **carpeting, new; laser printers.**

"voudou flu." See: **zombification.**

VVVD. See: **wind turbine syndrome.**

W

waiting room magazines. See: **doctors' offices.**

walking on the side of the sidewalk closest to the curb in order to

be chivalrous. Men, when you're strolling down the sidewalk with a woman, do you walk on the side closest to the curb in order to be chivalrous? The custom arose in horse-and-buggy days to protect women from being splashed with mud and worse as carriages hurtled by and chamber pots were emptied into the street, and, even today, many etiquette experts still call for a gentleman to walk on the "pavement side" of his female companion so he can serve as a human shield between her and, say, a taxi speeding along a puddle-filled thoroughfare.[1]

But would you still make a point of being gallant if you knew that doing so would expose you to a significantly greater risk than your walking partner of contracting a potentially fatal respiratory ailment? Well, it's true. A 2005 study conducted by researchers at Imperial College in London found that people who walk near the roadside are exposed to 10 percent more soot particles than those who stay close to the building line. According to the BBC, these tiny particles, known as PM10s, can become trapped in your lungs and have been linked to respiratory diseases and cancer.[2] You'd probably be asking too much if you urged your woman friend or partner to "take it to the curbside" the next time you venture out together. But may we suggest that walking *single file,* as far from the curb at possible, might be the best "win-win" strategy for both of you?

wallets. "Wallets pick up a lot of bacteria from what goes into them,"

warn Joseph Brownstein and Radha Chitale of the ABC News Medical Unit. "Paper currency has a way of getting around, from germ-filled hand to germ-filled hand. It picks up germs, viruses and often trace amounts of illegal drugs—that's not just an urban legend; several studies have confirmed that a majority of U.S. currency contains trace amounts of cocaine. And of course, all of that ends up in your wallet." And that's just the beginning of the problem. Because men keep wallets in their pockets, Brownstein and Chitale advise, the wallet warms up till it's close to body temperature—presenting ideal conditions for bacteria to breed and multiply. "When handling the contents of your wallet, after it, wash your hands," cautions renowned NYU microbiologist Philip M. Tierno Jr., Ph.D.[3] See also: **money.**

warm, sunny days. According to Professor Jon Ayres, O.B.E., B.Sc., M.D., chair of the UK's Committee on the Medical Effects of Air Pollutants (COMEAP), warm, sunny days—particularly when there's not a lot of wind—are far from the optimum time to venture outdoors, because of the danger of pollution. The problem, he says, is the formation of *temperature inversions,* "where a warm band forms in the air. It acts like a saucepan lid that traps all the emissions below." COMEAP research has shown "a sharp rise in hospital admissions due to respiratory and cardiovascular illnesses" on warm days, reports Chloe Lambert, who interviewed Ayres for the *Daily Mail.* "A rainy day may be the best for going outside," Lambert writes, "because rain is thought to clean the air by washing out the pollutants." And, if there's a nasty wind blowing, too, all the better. "When it's windy, pollution levels are lower because the particles are blown around," Ayres told Lambert.[4] See also: **exercise, outdoor.** (Note: Venturing out on pleasant days is not only a pollution risk; it also increases your chances of skin damage—or worse—caused by dangerous ultraviolet rays from the sun. For more details, see: **sun exposure.**)

warthog rectum, unwashed. See: **Chicken McNuggets.**

washing. See: **hand washing; baths; showers; hygiene.**

water, bottled. See **bottled water.**

water, drinking too little. "Most people don't drink enough water when they exercise," warns the popular men's health and lifestyle website, AskMen.com.[5] The Mayo Clinic's medical staff agree. "You need adequate fluids before, during and after exercise to help prevent dehydration," whose symptoms include dizziness, nausea, headaches, and, in severe cases, "delirium and unconsciousness," they advise.[6] Indeed, cautions University of Wisconsin clinical professor Benjamin Wedro, M.D., "organ failure and death will eventually occur" if dehydration remains unaddressed.[7] "You can usually reverse mild to moderate dehydration by drinking more fluids,"[8] the Mayo Clinic suggests. In other words, if you feel yourself getting dizzy, nauseous, or headachy during your exercise routine, you'd be wise to drink up before the delirium and unconsciousness set in. See: **water, drinking too much.**

water, drinking too much. "Everyone knows that drinking *too little* water will cause dehydration, which leads to dizziness, nausea, headaches, and, if it's particularly bad, death," writes Dennis DiClaudio in his impeccably researched, if disturbingly titled, *The Hypochondriac's Pocket Guide to Horrible Diseases You Probably Already Have.* "But the new news," he continues, "is that drinking *too much* water will cause hyponatremia, which leads to dizziness, nausea, headaches, and, if it's particularly bad, death." "Yes," DiClaudio notes, "the symptoms are exactly the same, and that can make things a little confusing while you're doubled over in pain and vomiting behind the basketball net, wondering what the hell you're supposed to do about it. But if you'd just have done what you were supposed to do in the first place and drank *just the right amount* of water, you wouldn't be in this situation."[9] See: **water, drinking too little.**

water filters. Home water filtration systems are, of course, designed to take the impurities out of tap water and make it safe to drink, wash, and cook with. But, ironically, a study at the University of North Carolina Environmental Quality Institute has found that many water filtration systems actually make tap water *more* dangerous by allowing water to build up, sit dormant in, and react with or corrode metal faucets and water pipes. What makes this a particularly serious problem is that the water filtration systems *themselves* frequently contain brass, which is a copper-and-lead alloy. The water that builds up actually leaches the lead out of the brass, where it contaminates the water you eventually bathe in or drink.[10] Lead, of course, is extremely toxic; lead poisoning is a known cause of gout, colic, abdominal pain, kidney dysfunction, memory loss, high blood pressure (which, in turn, increases your chances of having a heart attack or a stroke), seizures, miscarriages, learning disabilities and other developmental disorders, and even comas and death.[11] See: **tap water; bottled water.**

water fountains. "The moist surface area on the typical water foun-

tain is an ideal breeding ground for bacteria and viruses," warns University of Arizona environmental microbiologist Charles P. Gerba, Ph.D., and, to make matters worse, "everybody who has a cold or diarrhea has to drink a lot of water. The sick people hang around here." In fact, Gerba's research has shown that water fountain spigots often have twice the amount of bacteria as a toilet seat—more than two thousand microbes on a water fountain compared to less than one thousand microbes on an average toilet seat. "I'd go back to the bottle of water," Gerba says.[12] And remember that *school* water fountains are likely to be just as germ-ridden, if not more so, than office and mall fountains. "So pack your kids' lunch each day with a bottle of water and an instant hand sanitizer,"[13] suggests Gerba's frequent collaborator, Allison Janse. See: **bottled water; hand sanitizers, alcohol-based.**

water, tap. See: **tap water.**

waterbeds. See: **polyvinyl chloride (PVC).**

watermelon juice. See: **grapes.**

weapons of knowledge-enabled mass destruction. See: **knowledge-enabled mass destruction (KMD).**

weapons of mass disruption. See: **cyberwarfare.**

wearing tight garments below the waist. See: **crossing your legs.**

weather events, extreme, more frequent. See: **global warming.**

welcome mats. When you come into your house, says *Prevention*

magazine editor Rebekah George, your welcome mat is not only welcoming you, it's also welcoming "a lot of unwanted guests." The reason, George explained during a 2009 appearance on CBS's *Early*

Show, is that over 96 percent of shoe soles have been found to have fecal bacteria on them. When you and your family wipe your feet, bacteria from the fecal matter get into the mat, and then the next person who steps on the mat carries them right into your home. To make matters worse, many people rest their shopping bags or purses on the mat, too, while they stop to ring the doorbell or fish for their keys, and then they bring the bags or purses inside and put them on your tables and countertops, creating even more opportunities for infection.[14]

And that's hardly the only reason to get rid of your welcome mat. Should your home happen to catch on fire, the mat might be set ablaze along with it, creating a wall of flames right in front of your doorway as you try to escape. And, even if it doesn't ignite, you could still stumble over it as you rush to safety. The Great Places Housing Group, a major provider of affordable homes across northern Britain, was worried enough about such issues to officially ban the welcome mats that formerly graced the doorways of tenants' flats in Knutsford, Cheshire. "Cheshire's Fire and Rescue Service . . . agree that doormats could pose extra fire risks or trip hazards," explains Guy Cresswell, Great Places' director of housing services, "and say we are justified in asking for them to be removed."[15] The city of Stoke-on-Trent, England, agrees, too—their city council has also banned welcome mats in front of flats under their jurisdiction. Isabella Hulme, a sixty-one-year-old resident of Stoke, is one of the citizens who dutifully removed her mat. "Now the floor is left with carpet glue, which is even more of a trip hazard," she complained to a *Daily Mail* reporter.[16] See also: **potted plants.**

wheat-gluten intolerance. See: **cake, piece of.**

white-nose syndrome. A recently discovered fungus, *Geomyces de-**structans,* which produces a telltale snowy fuzz around the muzzles and on the wings of infected animals, has led to the deaths in the last five years of at least 1 million hibernating bats in caves in the northeastern United States. It must be conceded that the sudden demise of a very large number of these less-than-lovable creatures would appear at first blush to be, well, nothing to go batty about, but consider this: Bats are voracious insect predators, and in Virginia, one of about a dozen states affected by the abrupt disappearance of the once-common little brown bat, or *Myotis lucifugus,* in a single year an estimated 2.4 million pounds—that's more than two hundred *tons*—of crop-gobbling and disease-carrying bugs went uneaten.[17] As the Centers for Disease Control and Prevention observed, after reporting the troubling discovery in March 2009 of a closely related bat, *Myotis myotis,* infected with white-nose syndrome in a cave in faraway France, "because bats control insect populations throughout the world, a large decrease in bat populations would result in insect proliferations that would damage agricultural crops and spread many insect-borne diseases."[18]

wind turbine syndrome. Environmentally friendly non-greenhouse-gas-emitting windmills would seem to be a safe, sustainable source of cheap electric power, but if the concerns voiced by a distinguished New York pediatrician prove to be valid, the answer to the problems posed by the worldwide energy crisis may not be "blowin' in the wind." Studies conducted by Dr. Nina Pierpont revealed that people who have lived for five years or more within earshot of the whirring, thrumming, and buzzing sounds emitted by the huge blades mounted on the towers of large-scale industrial-level wind-power installations in the United States, the UK, Ireland, Italy, and Canada were frequently found to suffer from a number of worrisome symptoms, including heart disease, vertigo, and migraines. According to Dr. Pierpont, "There are about 12 different health problems associated with wind turbine syndrome (WTS), and these range from tachycardia, sleep disturbance, headaches, tinnitus, nausea, visual blurring, panic attacks with sensations of internal quivering to more general irritability."[19]

Dr. Pierpont's controversial views were largely validated following the recent discovery by scientists in England and Australia that the bones of the human ear are surprisingly similar to those of fish and frogs, sharing a high degree of sensitivity to low-frequency infrasonic and ultrasonic sounds and vibrations, and that this inherent auricular hypersensitivity is the likely source of a potentially disabling condition they dubbed visceral vibratory vestibular disturbance, or VVVD. "What I have shown in my research," Dr. Pierpont concludes, "is that many people.... who have been living close to a wind turbine running near their homes display a range of health illnesses and that when they move away, many of these problems also go away."[20] And as Maryland environmental activist Jon Boone, Ph.D., reports, many of those who do elect to move away from their "acoustically toxic homes" typically sell their houses at a loss or simply abandon them, because "massive wind technology produces a relentless fusillade of pulsating sound, mechanical in pattern, audible to all, and intolerable to many, particularly those sensitive to infrasound vibrations."[21]

wood, decaying. Doctors in Joplin, Missouri, received a deadly reminder of the dangers lurking in decaying wood when eight survivors of the tragic tornado that struck the city in May 2011 were subsequently infected—three of them fatally—by **mucormycosis** (q.v.), an invasive and extremely aggressive fungus that thrives in rotting organic matter and that, experts surmise, became lodged under victims' skin as a result of the twister.[22] The Centers for Disease Control points out that although mucormycosis infections are rare, the fungus itself is "quite common in the environment." Just to be safe, the CDC advises, it's a good idea to "wear protective clothing, such as gloves, pants and long-sleeved shirts, if you are handling decaying wood."[23]

worms, computer. See: **malware.**

wrinkles, premature. See: **chewing gum; drinking from a straw; pursing your lips; sleeping on your side; smoking.**

wrong worst, preparation for the. See: **black swans.**

X

x factor. See: **black swans; zombification.**

X-ray computed tomography. Generally referred to by the abbreviation CT, this medical imaging system uses digital geometric processing to generate 3-D images of the human body from two-dimensional X-rays taken along the axis of rotation of a sensing apparatus.[1] Because of the large number of individual X-rays that are required to assemble the final extremely detailed photographs, the typical radiation exposure received by the examined patient is anywhere from thirty to more than four hundred times the dosage from a standard chest X-ray, and since duplicate CT scans are often performed—one with iodine contrast to record blood flow, one without—that hazardous tally can easily reach the equivalent of seven hundred chest X-rays.[2]

According to a recent pair of peer-reviewed studies published in the *Archives of Internal Medicine,* the nearly twenty thousand diagnostic CT body scans that are performed every day in the United States—over 7 million per year—are resulting in absorbed radiation doses considerably higher than the numbers that are usually cited, and the potential cancer risk from these exposures could ultimately lead to as many as twenty-nine thousand cases attributable to CT exams performed in 2007 alone.[3]

Rita F. Redberg, M.D., M.S., a professor of medicine at the University of California, San Francisco, and editor of the *Archives,* noted in a commentary accompanying the report that the question of whether CT scans will yield "demonstrable benefits through improvements in longevity or quality of life are hotly debated. What is clear, however, is that the large dosages of radiation from such scans will translate, statistically, into additional cancers. We need to do something now, not wait 10 or 20 years to see the effects. It's not like radiation exposure can be undone after we find out that it causes cancer."

Dr. Redberg also observed pointedly, "Whenever people first question the safety of a standard practice—whether it's driving without seatbelts or x-raying children's feet to assess their correct shoe size—there will be others who say things are just fine as they are. We felt these data were accurate and significant enough to raise concern in the medical community." [4]

Y

yams, silence of the. See: **health claims.**

yard sales. It may be hard to pass up the chance to browse through a  neighbor's front lawn display of tempting secondhand goodies with rock-bottom price tags, but you might want to think twice before you check out those alfresco offerings—yes, you may save a bunch of money on that informal weekend shopping expedition, but you could end up paying for your ill-considered bargain hunting with your or your child's life. After announcing a major recall of defective consumer products, U.S. Consumer Product Safety Commission chairman Hal Stratton noted that "unfortunately many products like the ones we are recalling can remain in consumer's homes for long periods of time," and he urged families planning to visit or host a yard sale to "take steps to avoid purchasing or selling a dangerous product." [1] The CPSC "Resale Round-up" list included:

- old poorly designed cribs, playpens, and baby gates that pose a risk of suffocation and strangulation;
- old infant car seats and carriers that tend to eject toddlers;
- unsteady old-style baby walkers whose tendency to slip on stairs can lead to skull fractures, broken bones, concussions, internal injuries, and cuts and bruises;

- children's jackets and sweatshirts with choke-prone drawstring neck ties;
- pre-1996 beanbag chairs with simple-to-open zipper sides that spill out tiny, easily inhaled foam pellets;
- pre-1990 hairdryers that are prone to electrocute users;
- pre-1997 high-fire-hazard-risk halogen torchiere floor lamps;
- and pre-1987 self-locking cedar chests in which tots could become trapped and suffocate.[2]

Stacy Genovese, technical director of the Good Housekeeping Institute, pointed to some other secondhand items to avoid, including plastic dishware used for cooking or storing food, most toys made before the early 1970s when the lead paint they were slathered with was finally banned, and all mattresses and pillows, which are likely to harbor bedbugs.

"There are some things that should simply never be passed on," says Don Mays, senior director of product safety planning and technical administration at *Consumer Reports,* who singles out used bicycle helmets and hand-me-down dime-store trinkets, which can be loaded with lead and cadmium. "There's no guarantee if you buy children's jewelry that it won't contain high levels of toxic materials," Mays stresses.

In other words, for all the product recalls and government warnings and regulations, it's still a case of "Sidewalk Buyer Beware!" As Scott Wolfson, director of public affairs at the CPSC, cautions, dangerous products still regularly turn up at yard sales. "There's the law," Wolfson acknowledges, "and then there's reality."[3] See also: **bedbugs.**

Yellowstone National Park. "It is little known," stated the BBC in its 2000 documentary *Supervolcanoes,* "that lying underneath one of America's areas of outstanding natural beauty—Yellowstone Park—is one of the largest supervolcanoes in the world. Scientists have revealed that it has been on a regular eruption cycle of 600,000 years. The last eruption was 640,000 years ago . . . so the next is overdue." What's worse, there have been troubling signs of activity under the park over the last several years. For example, the ground in parts of Yellowstone has, according to the BBC, bulged upward more than twenty-eight inches over the past one hundred years. "Is this just the harmless movement of lava, flowing from one part of the reservoir to another?" the BBC wonders. "Or does it presage something much more sinister, a pressurized build-up of molten lava?" Scientists aren't sure, but there's little doubt that the Yellowstone supervolcano is going to erupt again.[4] And, when it does, writes Cecil Adams, author of the popular Straight Dope column and website, "a lot of people are going to be toast. A supereruption could kill tens of millions. Within ten to fifty miles of the next Yellowstone vent, you'll be Pompeiized beneath thousands of feet of hot ash. More than half the U.S. will experience ashfall, potentially fatal if inhaled. Ash and associated toxins could devegetate a third of the lower 48 (including some of the world's most productive farmland) for years or decades, leading to mass starvation."[5]

yoga. This ancient Indian physical, mental, and spiritual discipline is enjoying growing popularity among an estimated 20 million American fitness and wellness seekers of all ages, chiefly for the widely assumed beneficial effects of its regime of exercise and meditation on aging bodies and minds. But is there a dark side to this enlightening New Age practice? Well, um,—or om—apparently so. After more than four decades spent teaching the traditional Hindu practice, noted yogi Glenn Black has come to the conclusion that "the vast majority of people" should simply shun the two-thousand-year-old regimen. "Yoga is for people in good physical condition," says Black. "Or it can be used therapeutically. It's controversial to say so, but it really shouldn't be used for a general class."

Before you chalk all this up to bad karma, it's worth noting that there is considerable medical evidence to support Black's surprisingly negative point of view. Reports of physical complications experienced by students performing very basic yoga poses ranging from relatively minor injuries to long-lasting disabilities have been published in a number of medical journals in recent years, including *Neurology,* the *British Medical Journal,* and the *Journal of the American Medical Association.* In a related and equally sobering development, the Consumer Product Safety Commission noted that the number of yoga-related emergency room admissions doubled from 2000 to 2001, and doubled again from 2001 to 2002. And a global survey of yogis, physical therapists, and doctors conducted in 2009 by a research team at Columbia University's College of Physicians and Surgeons revealed a significant number of injuries to yoga practitioners' lower backs (231), shoulders (219), knees (174), and necks (110). Perhaps most disturbing were accounts of four separate instances of yoga devotees suffering incapacitating strokes resulting in brain damage.

As Black observes ruefully, "Today many schools of yoga are just about pushing people. You can't believe what's going on—teachers jumping on people, pushing and pulling, and saying, 'You should be able to do this by now.' It has to do with their egos." And when fellow yoga teachers approach him to assist them with bodywork to help repair or mitigate traumatic joint or muscle injuries, he tells them flatly, "Don't do yoga."[6]

yogurt. See: **dairy products; high-fructose corn syrup (HFCS).**

Z

Zero Interest Rate Policy (ZIRP). See: **inflation.**

"Zeus." See: **identity theft.**

zombie armies. According to SearchSecurity.com, *zombie army* is a popular term for "a number of Internet computers that, although their owners are unaware of it, have been set up to forward transmissions (including spam or viruses) to other computers on the Internet. Any such computer is referred to as a zombie—in effect, a computer 'robot' or 'bot' that serves the wishes of some master spam or virus originator."[1] To learn more about zombie armies, and to find out what to do if you suspect your machine might be one of the many millions that have been enslaved by cyberscum, see: **botnet.**

zombie banks. *Zombie bank* is a phrase coined in 1987 by Edward

J. Kane, Ph.D.—then a professor of economics at Ohio State University—to describe financial institutions with negative assets that manage to survive only because of government bailouts.[2] Kane, an internationally renowned economic crisis management expert who now teaches at Boston College, used the term to characterize insolvent American savings and loan corporations who were at the time being kept alive by major infusions of credit from the U.S. Federal Savings and Loan Insurance Corporation (FSLIC), but it has since been applied, in 1993, to shaky Japanese banks who owed their continuing viability to government life support, and, more recently, to European and U.S. banks rescued by massive government interventions after the subprime mortgage bubble burst in 2008.[3]

A major problem with keeping zombie banks alive during a financial crisis—especially one their own ill-advised risk taking fostered in the first place—is that showering them (and, by extension, their executives and shareholders) with state largesse is hardly a guarantee that they'll begin to extend the business or personal credit necessary to jump-start the economy; indeed, capital concerns stemming from the continuing presence of overvalued toxic assets on their balance sheets provide institutions with a powerful disincentive for doing so. And so they sit on whatever cash the government gives them while the economy continues to stagnate.[4] "More and more," Nobel Prize–winning economist Paul Krugman has written, "it looks as if we're headed for the Decade of the Living Dead."[5] See also: **"doom loop."**

zombification. In a provocative paper titled "When Zombies Attack!

Mathematical Modelling of an Outbreak of Zombie Infections," published in the prestigious 2009 anthology *Infectious Disease Modelling Research Progress*, Philip Munz and Ioan Hudea of Carleton University in Ottawa and Joe Imad and Professor Robert J. Smith? (the question mark is not a typo—Smith? had it legally added to the end of his name) of the University of Ottawa applied the basic principles of epidemiology to construct a compelling mathematical model of a city with a population of 1 million struck by a classic zombie plague. Basing their analysis of the spread of the "voudou flu" on the long-accepted "Romero Rules" articulated by director George Romero in his definitive zombie motion picture, *Night of the Living Dead*—namely, that people turn into zombies twenty-four hours after being bitten, create other zombies by biting uninfected individuals, and are often initially unaware of their transformation into zombies—the paper's authors came to a startling conclusion. Traditional strategies like imposing a quarantine were surprisingly ineffective—even with an aggressive zombie isolation program, "after 7 to 10 days, everyone was dead or undead." A theoretical "cure" was also of limited value—less than 15 percent of the world's population could be saved, and by definition the treatment did not confer effective immunity, since anyone who was bitten again would be reinfected and thus rezombified. "A zombie attack is likely to lead to a collapse of civilization unless it is dealt with quickly," the authors cautioned in a chilling summary to their groundbreaking research, adding that "the most effective way to contain the rise of the undead is to hit hard and hit often . . . As seen in the movies, it is imperative that zombies be dealt with quickly, or else we are all in a great deal of trouble."

In their closing discussion, Munz, Hudea, Imad, and Smith? note that although the specific scenarios considered in "When Zombies Attack!" may not be realistic, "it is nevertheless instructive to develop mathematical models for an unusual outbreak."[6] And, according to Discovery Science Channel columnist Patrick J. Kiger, it is this aspect of the authors' work that makes their determination that a zombie outbreak is "likely to be disastrous" so troubling. "Whether real or imagined," Kiger writes, "a zombie attack is a potent metaphor. Think of the undead not as klutzy cannibals but as the X factor, the Rumsfeldian 'unknown unknown,' the totally unexpected menace that suddenly confronts us. (The Canadian researchers' mathematical modeling of zombie attacks [may] seem like an elaborate joke, but . . . its underlying purpose was to demonstrate the progression of a rapidly spreading, unfamiliar public health threat.) In recent experience we've been confronted increasingly with such X factors, ranging from AIDS to terrorism to climate change. And time and again, we've been exposed as dangerously unprepared to deal with such paradigm-shattering threats."[7] See also: **black swans.**

zombulation. As defined by "Alstry," the Motley Fool's celebrated economics blogger who coined the term, *zombulation* means "running out of savings *and* access to capital."[8] In other words, if you're a person—or, for that matter, a company or a government—who has been "zombulated," banks have lent you more money than you can possibly ever pay back, and you can't borrow any more because they've denied you access to credit. You are still, in medical terms, alive, but, for practical purposes, you have joined the growing army of the living dead.

zygomycosis. See: **mucormycosis; splinters.**

NOTES

A

1. "Abstinence," PlannedParenthood.org, retrieved from http://www.plannedparenthood.org /health-topics/birth-control/abstinence-4215.htm, January 22, 2012.
2. Joanna K. Mohn, M.D., "NJ Senate Must Pass Stress Abstinence Bill (S-868) to Best Protect Teens," retrieved from http://98.124.133.5/njfpc/html/Articles/Why%20Stress%20Absti nence.pdf, January 25, 2012.
3. George Davey Smith, M.D., D.Sc., Stephen Frankel, D.M., Ph.D., and John Yarnell, Ph.D., "Sex and Death: Are They Related? Findings from the Caerphilly Cohort Study," *British Medical Journal*, 315 (1998), 1641–1644, retrieved from http://www.bmj.com/content /315/7123/1641?tab=full, January 24, 2012.
4. Ebrahim Shah, Ph.D., Margaret May, M.Sc., Yoav Ben-Shlomo, Ph.D., Peter McCarron, M.D., Stephen Frankel, D.M., Ph.D., John Yarnell, Ph.D., and George Davey Smith, M.D., D.Sc., "Sexual Intercourse and Risk of Ischaemic Stroke and Coronary Heart Disease: The Caerphilly Study," *Journal of Epidemiology and Community Health* 56:2 (February 2002), 99–102, retrieved from http://jech.bmj.com/content/56/2/99.full, January 24, 2012.
5. Huang-Kuang Chen, Chuen-Den Tseng, Shwu-Chong Wu, Ti-Kai Lee, and Tony Hsiu-His Chen, "A Prospective Cohort Study on the Effect of Sexual Activity, Libido and Widowhood on Mortality Among the Elderly People: 14-Year Follow-Up of 2453 Elderly Taiwanese," *International Journal of Epidemiology* 36:5 (October 2007), retrieved from http://ije.oxford journals.org/content/36/5/1136.full, January 24, 2012.
6. Monique G. Lê, Annie Bacheloti, and Catherine Hill, "Characteristics of Reproductive Life and Risk of Breast Cancer in a Case-Control Study of Young Nulliparous Women," *Journal of Clinical Epidemiology* 42:12 (1989), 1227–1233, abstract retrieved from http://www.science direct.com/science/article/pii/0895435689901212, January 24, 2012.
7. "Occupational Exposure Estimates: Acrylamide," *Carex Canada* Carcinogen Database, School of Environmental Health, University of British Columbia, retrieved from http://www .carexcanada.ca/en/acrylamide/occupational_exposure_estimates/phase_2/, August 11, 2011; "Food Contaminants and Adulteration: Ask the Regulators: Acrylamide, Furan, and the FDA," FDA.gov, U.S. Food and Drug Administration, July 10, 2011, reprinted, with updates, from *Food Safety Magazine* (June–July 2007), retrieved from http://www.fda.gov /Food/FoodSafety/FoodContaminantsAdulteration/ChemicalContaminants/Acrylamide /ucm194482.htm, August 10, 2011; and Eden Tareke, Per Rydberg, Patrik Karlsson, Sune Eriksson, and Margareta Törnqvist, "Analysis of Acrylamide, a Carcinogen Formed in Heated Foodstuffs," Department of Environmental Chemistry, Stockholm, Sweden, *Journal of Agricultural and Food Chemistry* July 17, 2002, abstract retrieved from http://pubs.acs.org/doi/abs /10.1021/jf020302f, August 10, 2011.
8. Michael DiNovi, Ph.D., *The 2006 Exposure Assessment for Acrylamide,* Center for Food Safety and Applied Nutrition, U.S. Food and Drug Administration, May 2006, retrieved from http:// www.fda.gov/downloads/Food/FoodSafety/FoodContaminantsAdulteration/Chemical Contaminants/Acrylamide/UCM197239.pdf, August 11, 2011.
9. Jørgen Schlundt, quoted in "WHO to Evaluate Deep-Frying Cancer Link," ABCNews.com, June 25, 2002, retrieved from http://abcnews.go.com/Health/story?id=116887&page=1, August 11, 2011.
10. Lucy Atkins, "Is Cooked Food Dangerous?" *Guardian,* December 4, 2007, retrieved from http://www.guardian.co.uk/science/2007/dec/04/lifeandhealth.foodanddrink, August 10, 2011.

11. Richard M. LoPachin, Ph.D., and Terrence Gavin, Ph.D., "Acrylamide-Induced Nerve Terminal Damage: Relevance to Neurotoxic and Neurodegenerative Mechanisms," *Journal of Agricultural and Food Chemistry* 56:15, 5994–6003, published online July 15, 2008, abstract retrieved from http://pubs.acs.org/doi/abs/10.1021/jf703745t, August 11, 2011.

12. Marek Naruszewicz, Danuta Zapolska-Downar, Anita Kośmider, Grażyna Nowicka, Małgorzata Kozłowska-Wojciechowska, Anna S. Vikström, and Margareta Törnqvist, "Chronic Intake of Potato Chips in Humans Increases the Production of Reactive Oxygen Radicals by Leukocytes and Increases Plasma C-Reactive Protein: A Pilot Study," *American Journal of Clinical Nutrition* 89:3 (March 2009), 773–777, abstract retrieved from http://www.ajcn.org/content/89/3/773.abstract, August 12, 2011.

13. "Reduction/Mitigation of Acrylamide Content in Foods: A Summary," FoodInsight.org, International Food Information Council Foundation, April 19, 2010, retrieved from http://www.foodinsight.org/Resources/Detail.aspx?topic=Reduction_Mitigation_of_Acrylamide_Content_in_Foods, August 12, 2011.

14. "Acrylamide News: Cancer from Cooking and Fast Food," *Raw Food News,* June 1, 2005, retrieved from http://www.rawfoodlife.com/Latest_Raw_Food_News/WHO_acrylamide020625/who_acrylamide020625.html, August 10, 2011.

15. Alyse Levine, M.S., R.D., "Acrylamide: A Cancer Causing Agent in Your Food?" Nutritionbite.com, March 1, 2011, retrieved from http://www.nutritionbite.com/2011/03/acrylamide-a-cancer-causing-agent-in-your-food, August 10, 2011.

16. Cynthia Sass, M.P.H., R.D., "Coffee Warning? What You Need to Know About Acrylamide," *Shape,* retrieved from http://www.shape.com/healthy-eating/coffee-warning-what-you-need-to-know-about-acrylamide, August 11, 2011; and Cynthia Sass, M.P.H., R.D., "Acrylamide in Food," ABCNews, June 15, 2011, retrieved from http://abcnews.go.com/Health/video/acrylamide-food-13849039, August 12, 2012.

17. Mary Ann Johnson, Ph.D., quoted in Ethan A. Huff, "Potato Chips, Fries Linked to Cancer," NaturalNews.com, November 1, 2010, retrieved from http://www.naturalnews.com/030241_acrylamides_breast_cancer.html, August 12, 2011.

18. "Nuns Mug Orphan! Soon We'll All Be Fighting for Food," *Economist,* May 6, 2007, retrieved from http://www.economist.com/node/9136006, June 8, 2011; and "The Agonies of Agflation," *Economist,* August 25, 2007, retrieved from http://www.economist.com/node/9707029, June 7, 2011.

19. William Neuman, "U.N. Notes Sharp Rise in World Food Prices," *New York Times,* January 6, 2011, B1, retrieved from http://www.nytimes.com/2011/01/06/business/global/06food.html, June 8, 2011.

20. "Protect Your Family from the Hidden Hazards in Air Fresheners," Natural Resources Defense Council, September 2007, retrieved from http://www.nrdc.org/health/home/airfresheners/fairfresheners.pdf, July 10, 2011.

21. William W. Nazaroff, Beverly K. Coleman, Hugo Destaillats, Alfred T. Hodgson, De-Ling Liu, Melissa M. Lunden, Brett C. Singer, and Charles J. Wexchler, "Indoor Air Chemistry: Cleaning Agents, Ozone and Toxic Air Contaminants," Department of Civil and Environmental Engineering, University of California, Berkeley; and Environmental Energy Technologies Division, Lawrence Berkeley National Laboratory, April 2006, retrieved from http://www.arb.ca.gov/research/apr/past/01-336_a.pdf, July 10, 2011; and Liese Greensfelder, "Study Warns of Cleaning Product Risks," Media Relations Department, University of California, Berkeley, May 22, 2006, retrieved from http://berkeley.edu/news/media/releases/2006/05/22_householdchemicals.shtml, July 10, 2011.

22. Greensfelder, "Study Warns of Cleaning Product Risk."

23. Stacey Colino, "6 Germy Places: Where Bacteria and Viruses Lurk," Lifescript.com, June 22, 2011, retrieved from http://www.lifescript.com/Health/Everyday-Care/Environment/Germy_Places_Where_Bacteria_and_Viruses_Lurk.aspx, August 26, 2011.

24. Douglas Wright, "Mile-High Health Risks: 6 Places Germs Breed in a Plane," *Budget Travel,* December 13, 2010, retrieved from http://www.budgettravel.com/feature/6-places-germs-breed-in-a-plane.3506/, August 29, 2011.

25. "The Dangers of Aluminum," Global Healing Center, retrieved from http://www.globalhealingcenter.com/dangers-of-aluminum.html, May 22, 2011; and "The Effects of Aluminum Exposure," Global Healing Center, retrieved from http://www.globalhealingcenter.com/aluminum-exposure.html, May 22, 2011.

26. Christopher Exley, Ph.D., "Does Antiperspirant Use Increase the Risk of Aluminium-Related Disease, Including Alzheimer's Disease?," *Molecular Medicine Today* 4:3 (March 1,

1998), 107–109, retrieved from http://www.sciencedirect.com/science/article/pii/S13 5743109801209X, June 3, 2011; and Amy Borenstein Graves, Ph.D.; Emily White, Ph.D.; Thomas D. Koepsell, M.D., M.P.H.; Burton V. Reifler, M.D.; Gerald van Belle, Ph.D.; and Eric B. Larson, M.D., M.P.H, "The Association Between Aluminum-Containing Products and Alzheimer's Disease," *Journal of Clinical Epidemiology* 43:1 (1990), 35–44, retrieved from http://www.sciencedirect.com/science/article/pii/089543569090053R, June 3, 2011.

27. Christopher Exley, Ph.D., Lisa M. Charles, Lester Barr, Claire Martin, Anthony Polwart, and Phillippa D. Darbre, Ph.D., "Aluminum in Human Breast Tissue," *Journal of Inorganic Biochemistry* 101:9 (September 2007), 1344–1346, retrieved from http://www.sciencedi rect.com/science/article/pii/S0162013407001304, June 4, 2011; and Phillippa D. Darbre, Ph.D., "Aluminum, Antiperspirants and Breast Cancer," *Journal of Inorganic Biochemistry* 99:9 (September 2005), 1912–1919, abstract retrieved from http://www.ncbi.nlm.nih.gov/pub med/16045991, June 4, 2011.

28. "The Dangers of Aluminum."

29. Cindy Jones-Shoeman, "Avoid Overexposure to Aluminum," NaturalNews.com, October 1, 2010, retrieved from http://www.naturalnews.com/029903_aluminum_toxicity.html, June 5, 2011.

30. "The Dangers of Aluminum."

31. Jennifer Yang, "Experts Concerned About Dangers of Antibacterial Products," *Globe and Mail* (Toronto), August 21, 2009, retrieved from http://www.theglobeandmail.com/life /health/experts-concerned-about-dangers-of-antibacterial-products/article1259471/, April 11, 2011.

32. Gina Solomon, M.D., M.P.H., "Flu Protection: Hand Sanitizer Not Antibacterial Soap!," NRDC Switchboard, Natural Resources Defense Council, May 1, 2009, retrieved from http:// switchboard.nrdc.org/blogs/gsolomon/flu_protection_hand_sanitizer.html, April 11, 2011.

33. Gina Solomon, M.D., M.P.H., " 'Antibacterial' Soaps: Buyer Beware!," *Huffington Post*, April 7, 2010, retrieved from http://www.huffingtonpost.com/gina-solomon/antibacterial-soaps -buyer_b_529240.html, April 11, 2011.

34. Mehmet Oz, M.D., *The Dr. Oz Show,* syndicated television program, September 14, 2011, quoted in "Dr. Oz's Comments Linking Apple Juice and Arsenic Cause Controversy," Inside Edition.com, September 15, 2011, retrieved from http://www.insideedition.com/news /6885/dr-ozs-comments-linking-apple-juice-and-arsenic-cause-controversy.aspx, September 18, 2011.

35. "Arsenic in Apple Juice: Dr. Oz's Extensive National Investigation," Dr. Oz.com, retrieved from http://www.doctoroz.com/videos/arsenic-apple-juice, September 18, 2011.

36. "Dr. Oz Investigates: Arsenic in Apple Juice," Dr. Oz.com, September 12, 2011, retrieved from http://www.doctoroz.com/videos/dr-oz-investigates-arsenic-apple-juice. September 18, 2011.

37. Marilynn Marchione, "Dr. Oz Accused of Fear-Mongering on Apple Juice," *Chicago Tribune*, September 15, 2011, retrieved from http://www.chicagotribune.com/news/chi-ap-us-med -applejuice-ar,0,4998160.story, September 18, 2011.

38. Rene Lynch, "Apple Juice Flap: Dr. Oz Won't Back Down," *Los Angeles Times* Blogs, September 16, 2011, retrieved from http://latimesblogs.latimes.com/nationnow/2011/09/apple-juice -flap-wont-cause-dr-oz-to-back-down-.html, September 18, 2011.

39. Patty Lovera, "Putting an End to Arsenic in Our Food Supply," Dr. Oz.com, September 12, 2011, retrieved from http://www.doctoroz.com/videos/putting-end-arsenic-our-food -supply, September 18, 2011.

40. Cecil Adams, "Are Apricot Seeds Poisonous? (A Straight Dope Classic from Cecil's Store-house of Human Knowledge)," syndicated column, August 23, 1974, retrieved from http:// www.straightdope.com/columns/read/193/are-apricot-seeds-poisonous, June 20, 2012.

41. Kristie Leong, M.D., "Should You Peel an Apple?," HealthMad.com, July 23, 2009, retrieved from http://healthmad.com/nutrition/should-you-peel-an-apple-2/, December 13, 2009. Although it's beyond the purview of this book, readers may be interested in knowing that Dr. Leong, in addition to her medical practice and helpful writings about nutrition, is a jewelry designer and bead store owner who helps budding jewelry designers find markets for their handmade jewelry. For more information, consult her article "How to Market Your Handmade Jewelry Business Through Bead Stores," available on the web at http:// www.bukisa.com/articles/99700_how-to-market-your-handmade-jewelry-business-through -bead-stores.

42. "An Apple Peel a Day Might Keep Cancer Away," *Science Daily,* June 3, 2007, retrieved from http://www.sciencedaily.com/releases/2007/06/070601181005.htm, June 6, 2010.

43. Dr. Alice B. Russell, et al., *"Prunus Armeniaca,"* "Poisonous Plants of North Carolina," Department of Horticultural Science, North Carolina State University, 1997, retrieved from http://www.ces.ncsu.edu/depts/hort/consumer/poison/Prunuar.htm, July 3, 2011.

44. Cecil Adams, "Are Apricot Seeds Poisonous?," Straight Dope, August 23, 1974, retrieved from http://www.straightdope.com/columns/read/193/are-apricot-seeds-poisonous, July 3, 2011.

45. Rebecca Wood, "Healing with Food: Apricot Kernels—Bitter Is Sweet," *Be Nourished with Rebecca Wood,* retrieved from http://www.rwood.com/Articles/Apricot_Kernels_Bitter_is_Sweet.htm, July 2, 2011.

46. *Laetrile: The Commissioner's Decision,* Food and Drug Administration, U.S. Department of Health, Education, and Welfare, 1977, retrieved from http://www.cancertreatmentwatch.org/q/laetrile/commissioner.pdf, July 3, 2011.

47. Gardiner Harris, "Armadillos Can Transmit Leprosy to Humans, Federal Researchers Confirm," *New York Times,* April 28, 2011, A1, retrieved from http://www.nytimes.com/2011/04/28/health/28leprosy.html, July 16, 2011; Richard W. Truman, Ph.D.; Pushpendra Singh, Ph.D.; Rahul Sharma, Ph.D.; et al., "Probable Zoonotic Leprosy in the Southern United States," *New England Journal of Medicine,* April 28, 2011, retrieved from http://www.nejm.org/doi/full/10.1056/NEJMoa1010536, July 16, 2011; and "Armadillo," *Wikipedia,* retrieved from http://en.wikipedia.org/wiki/Armadillo, July 16, 2011.

48. "Aspartame: Discovery and Approval," *Wikipedia,* retrieved from http://en.wikipedia.org/wiki/Aspartame#Discovery_and_approval, July 28, 2011; and James S. Turner, Esq., "The Aspartame/NutraSweet Fiasco," Stevia.net, retrieved from http://www.stevia.net/aspartame.htm, July 28, 2011.

49. "Six Former HHS Employees' Involvement in Aspartame's Approval," Briefing Report to the Honorable Howard Metzenbaum (United States Senate), U.S. General Accounting Office, July 22, 1986, retrieved from http://archive.gao.gov/d4t4/130780.pdf, July 28, 2011.

50. "Products," Aspartame Information Center, 2011, retrieved from http://www.aspartame.org/aspartame_products.html, July 28, 2011.

51. M. Soffritti, F. Belpoggi, D. D. Esposti, L, Lambertini, E. Tibaldi, A. Rigano, "First Experimental Demonstration of the Multipotential Carcinogenic Effects of Aspartame Administered in the Feed to Sprague-Dawley Rats, *Environmental Health Perspectives* 114:3 (March 2006), retrieved from http://ehp03.niehs.nih.gov/article/fetchArticle.action?articleURI=info:doi/10.1289/ehp.8711, July 28, 2011; and M. Soffritti, F. Belpoggi, E. Tibaldi, D. D. Esposti, M. Lauriola, "Life-Span Exposure to Low Doses of Aspartame Beginning During Prenatal Life Increases Cancer Effects in Rats," *Environmental Health Perspectives,* 115:9 (September 2007), abstract retrieved from http://ehp03.niehs.nih.gov/article/fetchArticle.action?articleURI=info:doi/10.1289/ehp.10271, July 9, 2011.

52. "FDA Statement on European Aspartame Study," U.S. Food and Drug Administration, April 20, 2007, updated April 26, 2010, retrieved from http://www.fda.gov/Food/FoodIngredients Packaging/FoodAdditives/ucm208580.htm, July 28, 2011.

53. Andrew Weil, M.D., "Aspartame: Can a Little Bit Hurt?," Dr. Weil.com: Q&A Library, May 9, 2006, retrieved from http://www.drweil.com/drw/u/id/QAA106654, July 28, 2011.

54. Andrew Weil, M.D., *Natural Health, Natural Medicine* (Boston: Houghton Mifflin, 2004), excerpted at http://books.google.com/books?id=Wz6nx6QMGdkC&pg=PT70&lpg=PT70&dq=Andrew+Weil+%22artificial+sweeteners%22&source=bl&ots=kJzYlw3Inr&sig=0NN3o ua1Bz6Y4lPOrOfGwvJ9Xrk&hl=en&ei=8fOpTsCpF4rZgQe-qui8Cg&sa=X&oi=book_res ult&ct=result&resnum=6&sqi=2&ved=0CDkQ6 AEwBQ#v=onepage&q&f=false, retrieved July 28, 2011.

55. Weil, "Aspartame: Can a Little Bit Hurt?"

56. Russell Schweickhart, Clark Chapman, Dan Durda, Piet Hut, Bill Bottke, and David Nesvorny, "Threat Characterizations: Trajectory Dynamics," White Paper 39, figure 4, page 9, B612 Foundation, retrieved from http://www.b612foundation.org/papers/wpdynamics.pdf, July 16, 2011; "The Threat Is Out There," *Popular Mechanics,* January 1, 2007, retrieved from http://www.popularmechanics.co.za/article/the-threat-is-out-there-2007-01-01, July 16, 2011.

57. European Space Agency, "May We Deflect Asteroids?," retrieved from http://www.esa.int/gsp/ACT/mad/op/AsteroidsAndNEOs/maywedeflect.htm, June 6, 2010; David Chandler, "Asteroid Is 'Practice Case' for Potential Hazards," *MIT News,* October 13, 2007; "MIT boffins plan for asteroidal doom," *Register* (UK), October 15, 2007.

58. Rich White, quoted in "Autumn Leaves Present Driving Hazard," CarCareNews Service, retrieved from http://www.carcarenewsservice.org/articles/autumn-leaves-present-driving-hazards, June 23, 2010.
59. Matthew C. Keegan, "Catalytic Converter Hazards!," SearchWarp.com, March 3, 2006, retrieved from http://searchwarp.com/swa45303.htm, June 23, 2010.
60. Matthew C. Keegan, "Beware of the Leaves," theArticleWriter.com, November 17, 2005, retrieved from http://www.thearticlewriter.com/beware-of-the-leaves.htm, June 23, 2010.

B

1. "The 40 Deadliest Fast Food Meals," *Daily Beast,* March 24, 2010, retrieved from http://www.thedailybeast.com/galleries/2010/03/24/the-40-deadliest-fast-food-meals.html, August 29, 2011.
2. "Caloric Foods: Holey Smokes," *Daily Beast,* May 31, 2010, retrieved from http://www.thedailybeast.com/galleries/2010/05/31/caloric-foods.html, August 29, 2011.
3. "Banana Equivalent Dose," *Wikipedia,* retrieved from http://en.wikipedia.org/wiki/Banana_equivalent_dose, July 21, 2011.
4. Tyler Gustafson, "Issue Brief: Radiological and Nuclear Detection Devices," Nuclear Threat Initiative Research Library, April 19, 2007, retrieved from www.nti.org/e_research/e3_88.html, July 21, 2011.
5. Randall Patrick Monroe, "Radiation Dose Chart," *xkcd,* retrieved from http://xkcd.com/radiation/, July 21, 2011. (According to Monroe, "If you're basing radiation safety procedures on an internet PNG image and things go wrong, you have no one to blame but yourself.")
6. Ibid.
7. Patrick Moore, Ph.D., "Going Nuclear," *Washington Post,* April 16, 2006, retrieved from http://www.washingtonpost.com/wp-dyn/content/article/2006/04/14/AR2006041401209.html, August 3, 2011.
8. Ibid.
9. Patrick Moore, Ph.D., "Earth Day Outcroppings," *Washington Times,* April 21, 2006, retrieved from http://www.washingtontimes.com/news/2006/apr/21/20060421-085828-5325r/?page=all#pagebreak, August 4, 2011.
10. Patrick Moore, Ph.D., quoted in Greg Holt, "Greenpeace Co-founder Defends PVC," *ICIS Chemical Business News,* icis.com, December 14, 2007, retrieved from http://www.icis.com/Articles/2007/12/14/9087111/greenpeace-co-founder-defends-pvc.html, August 4, 2011.
11. Ibid.
12. Moore, "Going Nuclear."
13. Allison Janse with Charles P. Gerba, Ph.D., *The Germ Freak's Guide to Outwitting Colds and Flu* (Deerfield Beach, FL: Health Communications, Inc., 2005), 56.
14. "Year-Round Sun Protection," Skin Cancer Foundation, retrieved from http://www.skincancer.org/year-round-sun-protection.html, August 26, 2011.
15. Greg Allen, "Florida Bans Cocaine-Like 'Bath Salts' Sold in Stores," NPR, February 8, 2011, retrieved from http://www.npr.org/2011/02/08/133399834/florida-bans-cocaine-like-bath-salts-sold-in-stores, May 8, 2011.
16. Ibid.
17. Joe Shortsleeve, "Link Between Bath Salts and Drug Abuse?," CBSBoston.com, February 8, 2011, retrieved from http://boston.cbslocal.com/2011/02/08/local-officials-investigating-link-between-bath-salts-drug-abuse/, May 8, 2011.
18. Mehmet Oz, M.D., "A Deadly New Drug," *Dr. Oz Show,* March 7, 2011, retrieved from http://www.doctoroz.com/videos/deadly-new-drug-pt-1, May 8, 2011.
19. Ibid.
20. Joe Weber, "Bathsalts," Death+Taxesmagazine.com, February 8, 2011, retrieved from http://www.deathandtaxesmag.com/51436/legal-meth-available-everywhere/bathsalts-2/, May 8, 2011.
21. "Bathroom: Germ-free and Healthy," Safety.com, retrieved from http://www.safety.com/articles/bathroom-germ-free-and-healthy, July 11, 2011.
22. Philip M. Tierno, Ph.D., quoted in Eric Steinman, "Getting Dirty in the Bathtub: Unchecked Bacteria Abound," Care2.com, May 4, 2010, retrieved from http://www.care2.com/greenliving/getting-dirty-in-the-bathtub-unchecked-bacteria-abound.html, May 14, 2011.
23. Melissa Breyer, "Battle the Top 10 Germ Hot Spots," Care2.com, March 5, 2009, retrieved from http://www.care2.com/greenliving/battle-the-top-10-germ-hot-spots.html, May 29, 2011.

24. Mary N. Harrison, "Keeping It Clean: Cleaning Bathrooms, Sink, Bathtub, Shower, Toilet," Institute of Food and Agricultural Sciences, University of Florida, December 2005, retrieved from http://edis.ifas.ufl.edu/fy789, May 28, 2011.

25. Sally Stich, "Wipe Out Germs—Today!," *Woman's Day,* January 5, 2009, retrieved from http://find.womansday.com/search/bathtub-disinfect/, May 29, 2011.

26. Yvonne Rodenhiser, "Bath or Shower?," Yahoo Contributor Network, July 24, 2007, retrieved from http://www.associatedcontent.com/article/318885/bath_or_shower.html?cat=5, May 14, 2011.

27. Clean Ocean Action, *Beach Sweeps: 2008 Annual Report,* retrieved from http://www.clean oceanaction.org/uploads/media/2008_Beach_Sweeps_Report_01.pdf, June 7, 2010.

28. "What Are Bed Bugs. How to Kill Bed Bugs," *Medical News Today,* July 20, 2010, retrieved from http://www.medicalnewstoday.com/articles/158065.php, August 16, 2011.

29. Steven W. Hwang, et al., "Bed Bug Infestations in an Urban Environment," *Emerging Infectious Diseases* 11:4 (April 2005), Centers for Disease Control, April 2005, retrieved from http://www.cdc.gov/ncidod/EID/vol11no04/04-1126.htm, August 16, 2011.

30. Jerry Adler, "The Politics of Bedbugs," *Daily Beast,* from *Newsweek,* September 8, 2010, retrieved from http://www.thedailybeast.com/newsweek/2010/09/08/conservatives-blame-environmentalists-for-bedbugs.html, August 16, 2011.

31. "Thinking of Doing Your *Own* Pest Control or Bug Extermination? . . . You Might Want to Think Twice," NoBuggy.com, All Natural Industries, Inc., retrieved from http://www.no buggy.com/state/texas/bug_bomb_texas.html, August 17, 2011.

32. Dini M. Miller, Ph.D., "Bed Bug Prevention and Detection," Virginia Tech University, retrieved from http://www.vdacs.virginia.gov/pesticides/pdffiles/bb-millermethods.pdf, August 16, 2011.

33. "Bed Bug Safety Tips When Traveling," Bedbug.com, 2009, retrieved from http://www.bed bug.com/Page-Bedbug-tips-when-traveling_218.aspx, August 17, 2011.

34. Miller, "Bed Bug Prevention and Detection."

35. Ibid.

36. Louis Sorkin, cited in Stacey Bradford, "Bed Bug Danger: 5 Ways to Stay Safe When You Travel," CBS MoneyWatch.com, July 1, 2010, retrieved from http://moneywatch.bnet .com/saving-money/blog/family-finance/bed-bug-danger-5-ways-to-stay-safe-when-you -travel/2517/, August 16, 2011.

37. "Bed Bug Safety Tips When Traveling."

38. Miller, "Bed Bug Prevention and Detection."

39. "Bed Bug Safety Tips When Using Public Transportation (Taxi, Train or Bus)," Bedbug .com, 2009, retrieved from http://www.bedbug.com/Page-Bedbug-tips-when-using-public -transport,-bus,-train,-or-taxi_222.aspx, August 16, 2011.

40. "Bed Bug Safety Tips When Visiting Family and Friends," Bedbug.com, 2009, retrieved from http://www.bedbug.com/Page-Bedbug-tips-when-visiting-family-and-friends_195.aspx, August 17, 2011.

41. "Bed Bug Home Protection—Smart Buy," Bedbug.com, 2009, retrieved from http://www .bedbug.com/Product-Home-Protection---Smart-Buy_1.aspx, August 17, 2011.

42. Allison Janse with Charles P. Gerba, Ph.D., *The Germ Freak's Guide to Outwitting Colds and Flu* (Deerfield Beach, FL: Health Communications, Inc., 2005), 149.

43. John Tierney, "A Release Valve for Cyclists' Unrelenting Pressure," *New York Times,* June 28, 2011, D2, retrieved from http://www.nytimes.com/2011/06/28/science/28tier.html, July 2, 2011; Steven M. Schrader, Ph.D., Brian D. Lowe, Ph.D., and Michael J. Breitenstein, B.S., "Using No-nose (Noseless) Bicycle Saddles to Prevent Genital Numbness and Sexual Dysfunction," NIOSH Science Blog, Centers for Disease Control and Prevention, retrieved from http://www.cdc.gov/niosh/blog/nsb042209_bikesaddle.html, July 2, 2011; and "Workplace Solutions: No-nose Saddles for Preventing Genital Numbness and Sexual Dysfunction from Occupational Bicycling," National Institute for Occupational Safety and Health, April 2009, retrieved from http://www.cdc.gov/niosh/docs/wp-solutions/2009-131/pdfs/2009-131 .pdf, July 2, 2011.

44. Steven M. Schrader, Ph.D., Michael J. Breitenstein, B.S., and Brian D. Lowe, Ph.D., "Original Research—Erectile Dysfunction: Cutting Off the Nose to Save the Penis," *Journal of Sexual Medicine* 5:8 (August 2008), 1932–1940, retrieved from http://www.bycycleinc.com /imagesDP/2008cutnose.pdf, July 2, 2011.

45. "Workplace Solutions: No-nose Saddles for Preventing Genital Numbness and Sexual Dysfunction from Occupational Bicycling."

46. Matthew Green, "Biflation or Stagflation? It Could Be Both," *Seeking Alpha,* June 16, 2010, retrieved from http://seekingalpha.com/article/210278-biflation-or-stagflation-it-could-be -both, June 12, 2011; and "Are You Ready for Biflation," BalanceJunkie.com, September 20, 2010, retrieved from http://balancejunkie.com/2010/09/20/are-you-ready-for-biflation/, June 11, 2011.

47. Al Lewis, " 'Biflation' Bernanke," *Wall Street Journal,* February 13, 2011, retrieved from http:// online.wsj.com/article/SB10001424052748703843004576140762706032294.html, June 12, 2011.

48. Joe Brewer, "The Coming Biofuels Disaster," CommonDreams.org, June 28, 2007, retrieved from http://www.commondreams.org/archive/2007/06/28/2153, July 7, 2011.

49. Michael Pollan, "The Great Yellow Hope," *New York Times,* May 24, 2006, retrieved from http://pollan.blogs.nytimes.com/2006/05/24/the-great-yellow-hope/, July 10, 2011.

50. David Pimentel, Alison Marklein, Megan A. Toth, Marissa Karpoff, Gillian S. Paul, Robert McCormack, Joanna Kyriazis, and Tim Krueger, "Biofuel Impacts on World Food Supply: Use of Fossil Fuel, Land and Water Resources," *Energies,* September 16, 2008, retrieved from http://www.mdpi.com/1996-1073/1/2/41/pdf, July 10, 2011.

51. Pollan, "The Great Yellow Hope."

52. Sara Newmann, M.D., M.P.H., cited in Marie Suszynski, "The 11 Best Birth Control Options for Women: Birth Control Pills," EverydayHealth.com, updated July 13, 2011, retrieved from http://www.everydayhealth.com/sexual-health-pictures/the-11-best-birth-control-options -for-women.aspx#/slide-4, January 26, 2012.

53. Mayo Clinic Staff, "Combination Birth Control Pills: Risks," MayoClinic.com, November 18, 2011, retrieved from http://www.mayoclinic.com/health/combination-birth-control-pills /MY00990/DSECTION=risks, January 26, 2012.

54. Lauren Pearle, Olivia Katrandjian, Chris Cuomo, and Glenn Ruppel, "FDA to Review Safety Issues Surrounding Leading Birth Control Pill Yaz," ABCNews.com, December 6, 2011, re-trieved from http://abcnews.go.com/Health/fda-discuss-safety-issues-surrounding-leading -birth-control/story?id=15099220#.TyGHJSMfjoA, January 12, 2011.

55. Mayo Clinic Staff, "Combination Birth Control Pills: Risks."

56. Dominique Browning, "Hitting the Bottle," *New York Times,* May 9, 2011, A23, retrieved from http://www.nytimes.com/2011/05/09/opinion/09browning.html, May 21, 1011.

57. "Hazard in a Bottle—the Plastic Industry's Pyrrhic Victory," *Economist,* August 22, 2008, retrieved from http://www.economist.com/node/11991291?story_id=11991291, May 21, 2011; and Christine Dell'Amore, "BPA Linked to Heart Disease, Study Confirms," *National Geographic* News, January 16, 2009, retrieved from http://news.nationalgeographic.com/news /2010/01/100115-bpa-bisphenol-a-heart-disease/, May 21, 2011.

58. David Biello, "Plastic (Not) Fantastic—Food Containers Leach a Potentially Harmful Chemi-cal," *Scientific American,* February 19, 2008, retrieved from http://www.scientificamerican .com/article.cfm?id=plastic-not-fantastic-with-bisphenol-a, May 21, 1011.

59. Lyndsey Layton, "Alternatives to BPA Containers Not Easy for U.S. Foodmakers to Find," *Washington Post,* February 23, 2010, retrieved from http://www.washingtonpost.com/wp -dyn/content/article/2010/02/22/AR2010022204830.html, May 21, 2011.

60. Biello, "Plastic (Not) Fantastic."

61. Dell'Amore, "BPA Linked to Heart Disease."

62. Nassim Nicholas Taleb, *The Black Swan: The Impact of Highly Improbable Events* (New York: Random House, 2007); Will Davies, "All in a Flap: Beware Unknown Unknowns," *Oxonian Review,* June 3, 2007, retrieved from http://www.oxonianreview.org/issues/6-3/6-3davies .htm, April 8, 2011.

63. "Blarney Stone: Cork, Ireland," *Sacred Sites: Places of Peace and Power,* retrieved from http:// sacredsites.com/europe/ireland/blarney_stone.html, September 12, 2011; and "History of the Blarney Stone," *Authentic Ireland Travel,* retrieved from http://www.authenticireland .com/blarney+stone/, September 12, 2011.

64. "Copiously-Kissed Blarney Stone Tops List of Germ-Laden World Attractions," press re-lease, TripAdvisor.com, June 11, 2009, retrieved from http://www.tripadvisor.com/Press Center-i247-cl-Press_Releases.html, September 12, 2011.

65. Josie Glausiusz, "Fruits and Veggies to Buy Organic: Blueberries," *Prevention,* retrieved from http://www.prevention.com/dirtiestcleanest/6.html, September 19, 2011.

66. "War in the Fifth Domain: Are the Mouse and the Keyboard the New Weapons of Conflict?" *Economist,* July 1, 2010, retrieved from http://www.economist.com/node/16478792, June 26, 2011.

67. Meg Marco, "FBI: 1 Million US Computers Have Been Taken Over by Botnets," *Consumerist,* June 14, 2007, retrieved from http://consumerist.com/2007/06/fbi-1-million-us-computers-have-been-taken-over-by-botnets.html, June 27, 2011.

68. "FTC Consumer Alert: Botnets and Hackers and Spam (Oh My!)," Federal Trade Commission, June 2007, retrieved from http://www.ftc.gov/bcp/edu/pubs/consumer/alerts/alt132.shtm, June 27, 2011.

69. "Bottled Water: Pure Drink or Pure Hype," Natural Resources Defense Council, 1999, retrieved from http://www.nrdc.org/water/drinking/bw/exesum.asp, February 23, 2010.

70. Ibid.

71. Krisy Gashler, "Thirst for Bottled Water Unleashes Flood of Environmental Concerns," *Ithaca Journal* (New York), June 27, 2008, retrieved from http://www.usatoday.com/news/nation/environment/2008-06-07-bottled-water_N.htm, February 27, 2010.

72. Ibid.

73. "How to Minimize the Risk of a Child Choking," *Childcare Network: The Working Parent's Best Friend,* retrieved from http://www.childcarenetwork.net/Family-Forums/how-to-minimize-the-risk-of-a-child-choking.html, June 23, 2011.

74. Keeley Drotz, R.D., C.D., "Common High-Risk Choking Foods for Toddlers," HealthCastle.com, May 12, 2011, retrieved from http://www.healthcastle.com/common-high-risk-choking-foods-toddlers, June 23, 2011.

75. "Cherry," AgriLife Extension Service, Department of Horticultural Sciences, Texas A&M University, retrieved from http://aggie-horticulture.tamu.edu/archives/parsons/fruit/cherry.html, June 23, 2011.

76. Anne Marie Helmenstine, Ph.D., "Yes, Apple Seeds and Cherry Pits are Poisonous," About.com Guide, September 12, 2007, retrieved from http://chemistry.about.com/b/2007/09/12/yes-apple-seeds-and-cherry-pits-are-poisonous.htm, April 4, 2011.

77. Deirdre Imus, "Brazilian Blowout Craze: Is It Safe?," March 16, 2011, retrieved from http://www.foxnews.com/health/2011/03/16/brazilian-blowout-craze-safe/, April 13, 2011.

78. "Brazilian Blowout Solution Contains Formaldehyde," Health Canada Advisory 2010-182, October 26, 2010, retrieved from http://www.hc-sc.gc.ca/ahc-asc/media/advisories-avis/_2010/2010_167-eng.php, April 13, 2011.

79. Katy Muldoon, "Hazard Alert About Brazilian Blowout, Issued Months Ago in Oregon, Goes Nationwide," *Oregonian,* April 11, 2011, retrieved from http://www.oregonlive.com/today/index.ssf/2011/04/hazard_alert_about_brazilian_blowout_issued_months_ago_in_oregon_goes_nationwide.html, April 13, 2011.

80. Imus, "Brazilian Blowout Craze."

81. Charles Clover, "'Dangerous' Levels of Arsenic in 10pc of Rice," *Telegraph,* August 29, 2007, retrieved from http://www.telegraph.co.uk/earth/agriculture/food/3304831/Dangerous-levels-of-arsenic-in-10pc-of-rice.html, August 13, 2011.

82. Stephen Kirkpatrick, "Professor Warns Against Arsenic 'On Your Plate,'" *Dartmouth,* September 24, 2010, retrieved from http://thedartmouth.com/2010/09/24/news/arsenic, August 13, 2011.

83. Andrew Meharg, Ph.D., cited in "Rice Tainted by Arsenic Raises the Risk of Cancer," *Daily Mail,* March 23, 2007, retrieved from http://www.dailymail.co.uk/health/article-444222/Rice-tainted-arsenic-raises-risk-cancer.html, August 13, 2011.

84. Mary Lou Zoback, quoted in Joel Achenbach, "Under the World's Greatest Cities, Deadly Plates," *Washington Post,* February 23, 2010, retrieved from http://www.washingtonpost.com/wp-dyn/content/article/2010/02/22/AR2010022204828_2.html, June 22, 2012.

85. Phil Stemmer, B.D.S., quoted in Matthew Barbour, "Seven Daily Sins: Shower Every Day? Rinse After Brushing Teeth? These 'Healthy' Habits Could Be Devilishly Bad for You," *Daily Mail,* April 27, 2011, retrieved from http://www.dailymail.co.uk/health/article-1380504/Seven-daily-sins-Shower-day-Rinse-brushing-teeth-These-healthy-habits-devilishly-bad-you.html, April 28, 2011.

C

1. August McLaughlin, "Dangerous Effects of Caffeine," Livestrong.com, retrieved from http://www.livestrong.com/article/119148-dangerous-effects-caffeine/, August 30, 2011.

2. "Washburn 'A' Mill Explosion," Minnesota Historical Society, retrieved from http://www.mnhs.org/library/tips/history_topics/73washburn.html, April 13, 2011.

3. "Celiac Disease," Mayo Clinic Health Information, retrieved from http://www.mayoclinic.com/health/celiac-disease/DS00319, April 13, 2011.

4. Felicity Barringer, "If Quakes Weren't Enough for California, Enter the 'Superstorm,'" *New York Times*, January 16, 2011, A17, retrieved from http://www.nytimes.com/2011/01/16/science/earth/16flood.html, April 10, 2011; and Lucy Jones, "USGS: ARkStorm—California's Other 'Big One,'" U.S. Geological Survey, January 17, 2010, retrieved from http://www.outlookseries.com/A0998/Science/3956_Lucy_Jones_USGS_ARkStorm_California_other_Big_One_Lucy_Jones.htm, April 10, 2011

5. Daniel Tencer, "California's 'Big One' Could Be Massive 'Superstorm' That Floods State: Scientists," *Raw Story*, January 17, 2011, retrieved from http://www.rawstory.com/rs/2011/01/17/big-one-massive-superstorm/, April 10, 2011.

6. Barringer, "If Quakes Weren't Enough."

7. "Toluene: Knowing Its Components, Applications and Hazards," retrieved from http://www.articledashboard.com/Article/Toluene-Knowing-Its-Components-Applications-And-Hazards/840833, February 21, 2010.

8. "Carpeting," SilentMenace.com, retrieved from http://www.silentmenace.com/Carpeting.html, June 6, 2011.

9. "An Introduction to Indoor Air Quality: Volatile Organic Compounds (VOCs)," U.S. Environmental Protection Agency, epa.gov, retrieved from http://www.epa.gov/iaq/voc.html, June 6, 2011.

10. "Carpeting."

11. Ibid.

12. "The Dangers of Indoor Pollution: Introduction," SilentMenace.com, retrieved from http://www.silentmenace.com/Home_Page.php, June 6, 2011.

13. Dr. Paul Beaumont, cited in "World's Greatest Food Myth," *Sydney Morning Herald*, March 23, 2009, retrieved from http://www.smh.com.au/lifestyle/diet-and-fitness/worlds-greatest-food-myth-20090403-9myq.html, June 21, 2012.

14. "Volcano," excerpted from *Talking About Disaster: Guide for Standard Messages*, National Disaster Education Coalition, Washington, D.C., 1999, retrieved from http://www.disastercenter.com/guide/volcano.html, August 21, 2011.

15. Jessica Kowal, "Residents, Experts Eye 'Volcano in Back Yard'," *Chicago Tribune*, August 24, 2003, retrieved from http://articles.chicagotribune.com/2003-08-24/news/0308240409_1_rainier-dangerous-volcano-lahar, June 18, 2011.

16. John W. Ewert, Marianne Guffanti, and Thomas L. Murray, "An Assessment of Volcanic Threat and Monitoring Capabilities in the United States: Framework for a National Volcano Early Warning System," U.S. Geological Survey, April 2005, retrieved from http://pubs.usgs.gov/of/2005/1164/2005-1164.pdf, June 20, 2011.

17. "Volcano."

18. Robin Lloyd, "Tsunami-Generating Earthquake Near U.S. Possibly Imminent," LiveScience, January 3, 2005, retrieved from http://www.livescience.com/3775-tsunami-generating-earthquake-possibly-imminent.html, June 2, 2011; and "Largest Earthquakes in the World Since 1900," USGS National Earthquake Information Center, U.S. Geological Survey, U.S. Department of the Interior, updated 2011, retrieved from http://earthquake.usgs.gov/earthquakes/world/10_largest_world.php, June 2, 2011.

19. Yumei Wang, quoted in Ben Jervey, "Cascadia: The West Coast Fault Line That Is 'Nine Months Pregnant,'" *Good*, March 22, 2011, retrieved from http://www.good.is/post/cascadia-the-west-coast-fault-line-that-is-nine-months-pregnant/, June 1, 2011.

20. Rob Witter, Ph.D., quoted in Lori Tobias, "Big Earthquake Coming Sooner Than We Thought, Oregon Geologist Says," *Oregonian*, April 19, 2009, retrieved from http://www.oregonlive.com/news/index.ssf/2009/04/big_earthquake_coming_sooner_t.html, June 1, 2011.

21. Mike Caldwell, "Tsunami Warning, Preparedness, and Interagency Cooperation: Lessons Learned," Statement of Record Submitted to the House Subcommittee on National Security, Homeland Defense and Foreign Operations, Committee on Oversight and Government, April 14, 2011, retrieved from http://oversight.house.gov/images/stories/Other_Documents/4-14-2011_Caldwell_NatSec_Tsunami_Testimony.pdf, June 1, 2011.

22. Josie Glausiusz, "Fruits and Veggies to Buy Organic: Celery," *Prevention*, retrieved from http://www.prevention.com/dirtiestcleanest/2.html, August 31, 2011.

23. Tara Parker-Pope, "New Study Finds That Cellphone Use Changes Some Activity in the Brain," *New York Times*, February 23, 2011, retrieved from http://query.nytimes.com/gst/fullpage.html?res=9E04E5DC133CF930A15751C0A9679D8B63&pagewanted=1, April 10, 2011.

24. "Cell Phones Show Effect on Brain Activity Most Pronounced Near the Antenna; Find-

ing Is of Unknown Clinical Significance," Summary of Intramural NIH/Brookhaven National Laboratory Cell Phone Study in the *Journal of the American Medical Association*, "@ Brookhaven Today," Brookhaven National Laboratory, February 23, 2011, retrieved from http://www.bnl.gov/bnlweb/pubaf/pr/PR_display.asp?prID=1239&template=Today, April 10, 2011.

25. Nora D. Volkow, M.D., et al., "Effects of Cell Phone Radiofrequency Signal Exposure on Brain Glucose Metabolism," *Journal of the American Medical Association* 305:8 (2011), 808–813, abstract retrieved from http://jama.ama-assn.org/content/305/8/808, April 10, 2011.

26. Paul W. Frame, Ph.D., "General Information About Uranium in Ceramics," Oak Ridge Associated Universities, retrieved from http://www.orau.org/ptp/collection/consumer%20products/uraniumceramicsgeneralinfo.htm, August 22, 2011.

27. Helen Caldicott, M.D., "Unsafe at Any Dose," *New York Times*, May 1, 2011, WK10, retrieved from http://www.nytimes.com/2011/05/01/opinion/01caldicott.html, August 22, 2011.

28. Anne Marie Helmenstine, Ph.D., "Yes, Apple Seeds and Cherry Pits Are Poisonous," About.com Guide, September 12, 2007, retrieved from http://chemistry.about.com/b/2007/09/12/yes-apple-seeds-and-cherry-pits-are-poisonous.htm, April 4, 2011.

29. Mark Rieger, Ph.D., *Introduction to Fruit Crops* (Binghamton, NY: The Haworth Press, 2006), 145.

30. Kristie Leong, M.D., "Four Bad Beauty Habits That Cause Lines Around the Mouth," April 11, 2011, retrieved from http://www.associatedcontent.com/article/7918489/four_habits_that_cause_wrinkles_and.html, May 25, 2011.

31. Jim Gorman, "The 10 Dirtiest Foods You're Eating: Chicken" *Men's Health*, retrieved from http://www.menshealth.com/mhlists/foodborne_illness/Chicken.php, July 25, 2011.

32. Michael Specter, "The Extremist," *New Yorker*, April 4, 2003, retrieved from http://www.michaelspecter.com/2003/04/the-extremist/, July 27, 2011.

33. Gerald Kuester, quoted in Richard Behar and Michael Kramer, "Something Smells Fowl," *Time*, October 17, 1994, retrieved from http://www.time.com/time/printout/0,8816,981629,00.html, July 27, 2011.

34. Behar and Kramer, "Something Smells Fowl."

35. Liam Mayclem, "Dinner with Anthony Bourdain," 7x7SF.com, November 26, 2007, retrieved from http://www.7x7.com/love-sex/dinner-anthony-bourdain, September 14, 2011; and Nick Barlow, "McNuggets and Warthog Rectum," *Helsinki Times*, November 5, 2009, retrieved from http://www.helsinkitimes.fi/htimes/tv-column/8688-mcnuggets-and-warthog-rectum.html, September 13, 2011.

36. Sean O'Neal, "Anthony Bourdain," *A.V. Club*, January 8, 2008, retrieved from http://www.avclub.com/articles/anthony-bourdain.2132/, September 14, 2011.

37. "10 Questions for Anthony Bourdain," Time.com, October 31, 2007, retrieved from http://www.time.com/time/magazine/article/0,9171,1680149,00.html, September 13, 2011.

38. O'Neal, "Anthony Bourdain."

39. "The 100 Most Unhealthy Foods in the American Diet," X-Ray Vision-aries Blog, X-Ray TechniciansSchools.org, retrieved from http://www.x-raytechnicianschools.org/florida/the-100-most-unhealthy-foods-in-the-american-diet/, September 14, 2011.

40. Jennifer Lance, "Avoid Chlorine Bleach—Make Your Own Whitener or Use the Sun," *Eco Child's Play*, August 5, 2007, retrieved from http://ecochildsplay.com/2007/08/03/avoid-chlorine-bleach-make-your-own-whitener-or-use-the-sun/, July 4, 2010.

41. Ibid.

42. Sarah Klein, Amanda Tian, Jacqlyn Witmer, and Caroline Smith DeWaal, "The FDA Top Ten: The Riskiest Foods Regulated by the U.S. Food and Drug Administration," Center for Science in the Public Interest, October 6, 2009, retrieved from http://www.cspinet.org/new/200910061.html, April 2, 2011.

43. "Replacing Chlorine Wash," WorldPoultry.net, June 26, 2008, retrieved from http://www.worldpoultry.net/news/new-development-might-replace-chlorine-wash-id2672.html, April 3, 2011.

44. "Clowns 'Too Scary' for Children's Wards in Hospitals," Sky News, January 16, 2008, retrieved from http://news.sky.com/skynews/Home/Sky-News-Archive/Article/20080641300836, April 10, 2011; and Michael Holden, "Don't Send in the Clowns," Reuters.com, January 16, 2008, retrieved from http://www.reuters.com/article/2008/01/16/us-clowns-odd-idUSL1582409620080116, April 10, 2011.

45. Adam Sherwin, "Don't Send in the Clowns: They Scare the Crowd," *Sunday Times* (UK), July 8, 2006, retrieved from http://www.timesonline.co.uk/tol/news/uk/article684697.ece, April 10, 2011.

46. *The Toll from Coal: An Updated Assessment of Death and Disease from America's Dirtiest Energy Source*, Clean Air Task Force, September 2010, retrieved from http://www.catf.us/resources/publications/files/The_Toll_from_Coal.pdf, June 24, 2011.

47. "Problems of Coal: Combustion Waste," Clean Air Task Force, retrieved from http://www.catf.us/coal/problems/waste/, June 24, 2011.

48. Fred Pearce, "The Return of Killer Coal," *New Scientist* Blogs, March 12, 2008, retrieved from http://www.newscientist.com/blog/environment/2008/03/freds-footprint-return-of-killer-coal.html, June 24, 2011.

49. "Our Vision," Merchants of Green Coffee, Inc., retrieved from http://www.merchantsofgreencoffee.com/4_About_the_Merchants/issues_in_the_industry.html, August 31, 2011.

50. "Issues in the Industry," Merchants of Green Coffee, Inc., retrieved from http://www.merchantsofgreencoffee.com/4_About_the_Merchants/issues_in_the_industry.html, August 31, 2011.

51. Danielle Braff, "Eliminate Germs in Your House," Men'sHealth.com, 2010, retrieved from http://www.menshealth.com/mhlists/fight_household_germs/printer.php, July 24, 2011.

52. Alexei Barrionuevo, "Bees Vanish, and Scientists Race for Reasons," *New York Times*, April 24, 2007, retrieved from http://www.nytimes.com/2007/04/24/science/24bees.html, May 12, 2011; and Genaro C. Armas, "Mystery Ailment Strikes Honeybees," Associated Press, February 11, 2007, retrieved from http://www.washingtonpost.com/wp-dyn/content/article/2007/02/11/AR2007021100650.html, May 12, 2011.

53. Dennis vanEngelsdorp, Jerry Hayes Jr., Robyn M. Underwood, Dewey Caron, and Jeffery S. Pettis, "A Survey of Managed Honey Bee Colony Losses in the U.S., Fall 2009 to Winter 2010," *Journal of Apicultural Research* 50 (2011), 1–10, retrieved from http://ento.psu.edu/publications/vanenegelsdorp%20et%20al%202011.pdf, May 15, 2011.

54. David Derbyshire, "Why a Mobile Phone Ring May Make Bees Buzz Off: Insects Infuriated by Handset Signals," *Daily Mail* Online, May 12, 2011, retrieved from http://www.dailymail.co.uk/sciencetech/article-1385907/Why-mobile-phone-ring-make-bees-buzz-Insects-infuriated-handset-signals.html#ixzzlM8y9Tiql, May 12, 2011.

55. CCD Steering Committee, *Colony Collapse Disorder Progress Report*, U.S. Department of Agriculture, June 2010, retrieved from http://www.ars.usda.gov/is/br/ccd/ccdprogressreport2010.pdf, May 15, 2011.

56. Rick Wills, "Bee Die-off in Pa. 'Worse than We Thought,'" *Pittsburgh Tribune-Review*, February 2, 2007, retrieved from http://webcache.googleusercontent.com/search?q=cache:vZWXur_5_XToJ:www.pittsburghlive.com/xlpittsburghtrib/s_491440.html, May 31, 2012.

57. BBC News, "Bee Vanishing Act Baffles Keepers," February 27, 2007, retrieved from http://news.bbc.co.uk/2/hi/6400179.stm, May 12, 2011.

58. Michael Leidig, "Honeybees in U.S. Facing Extinction," *Telegraph*, May 29, 2011, retrieved from http://www.telegraph.co.uk/news/1545516/Honey-bees-in-US-facing-extinction.html, May 12, 2011.

59. David L. Chandler, "Comet Put on List of Potential Earth Impactors," *New Scientist*, June 1, 2005, retrieved from http://www.newscientist.com/article/dn7449-comet-put-on-list-of-potential-earth-impactors.html?full=true&print=true, June 22, 2012.

60. James Debevec, "Private Investments: Commodities," Private Investments.com, February 22, 2011, retrieved from http://www.privateinvestments.com/private-investments-commodities.html, June 22, 2012.

61. "Green Commuting," U.S. Small Business Administration, retrieved from http://www.sba.gov/content/green-commuting, July 18, 2011.

62. Yokota Fritz, "Green Transport Company: Biking Too Dangerous," *Cyclelicious*, July 6, 2007, retrieved from http://www.cyclelicio.us/2007/07/green-transport-company-biking-too.html, July 20, 2011.

63. Richard Masoner, "Air Quality District Says 'Drive a Car,'" December 5, 2007, Cyclelicious, retrieved from http://www.cyclelicio.us/2007/air-quality-district-says-drive-a-car/, July 21, 2011.

64. Adam Voiland, "6 Myths About Commuting by Bicycle," *U.S. News Health*, May 15, 2008, retrieved from http://health.usnews.com/health-news/blogs/on-men/2008/05/15/6-myths-about-commuting-by-bicycle, July 20, 2011.

65. "How to Go Green: Commuting," Treehugger.com, Discovery Communications, Inc., September 29, 2008, retrieved from http://www.treehugger.com/files/2008/09/how-to-go-green-commuting.php, July 18, 2011.

66. *Toward a Cleaner Future*, Office of Transport and Air Quality, U.S. Environmental Protection

Agency, 2005, 26, retrieved from http://www.epa.gov/oms/about/420r05011.pdf, July 17, 2011.

67. "Green Commuting."

68. "Public Transportation Reduces Our Dependence on Oil," PublicTransportation.org, American Public Transportation Association, retrieved from http://www.publictransportation .org/benefits/energy/Pages/default.aspx, July 18, 2011; and "Public Transportation Is the Responsible Environmental Choice," PublicTransportation.org, American Public Transportation Association, retrieved from http://www.publictransportation.org/benefits/environment /Pages/default.aspx, July 18, 2011.

69. Deborah S. Hildebrand, "All Aboard! Trains: The Alternative Commuting Solution," OfficeArrow.com, retrieved from http://www.officearrow.com/air-hotel-and-transportation /all-aboard-trains-the-alternative-commuting-solution-oaiur-2818/view.html, July 17, 2011.

70. "Train Companies Should Keep Freedom to Sell Alcohol on Trains," Association of Train Operating Companies, June 29, 2010, retrieved from http://www.atoc.org/media-centre/latest-press -releases/train-companies-should-keep-freedom-to-sell-alcohol-on-trains-100483, July 18, 2011.

71. Richard E. Wener, Ph.D., "Studying the Effects of Car Versus Train Travel on Physical Activity and Psychological Response of Commuters," Polytechnic University Department of Humanities and Social Sciences, 2005, funded by the Robert Wood Johnson Foundation, report retrieved from http://www.rwjf.org/reports/grr/044743.htm, July 17, 2011.

72. "Dump the Pump," PublicTransportation.org, American Public Transportation Association, 2011, retrieved from http://www.publictransportation.org/news/campaigns/dump thepump/Pages/default.aspx, July 17, 2011.

73. Allison Gendar, "Beware the City Travel Bugs! What *The News* Found and Where We Found It," *Daily News* (New York), December 22, 2003, retrieved from http://articles.nydailynews .com/2003-12-22/news/18247447_1_germs-coli-bacteria-subway-station/, July 18, 2011.

74. Rick Leventhal, "Schumer Proposes 'No Ride' List for Train Travelers," FoxNews.com, May 9, 2011, retrieved from http://www.foxnews.com/politics/2011/05/09/schumer-proposes -ride-list-train-travelers/, July 21, 2011.

75. "Public Transit = Much Safer Travel," Light Rail Now!, March 3, 2001, retrieved from http:// www.lightrailnow.org/facts/fa_00015.htm, July 21, 2011.

76. Michael P. Ehline, Esq., "The Unseen Danger of Riding the Train," eZine Articles, June 11, 2008, retrieved from http://ezinearticles.com/?The-Unseen-Danger-of-Riding-the -Train&id=1242753, July 21, 2011.

77. Michael P. Ehline, Esq., "Call Our 24-Hour Attorney Hotline Now: Train Accident," retrieved from http://www.ehlinelaw.com/pages/100075/san-bernardino-train-accident-lawyer.htm, July 21, 2011; and Michael P. Ehline, Esq., "Call Our 24-Hour Attorney Hotline Now: Southern California Train Crash Attorneys," retrieved from http://www.ehlinelaw.com/pages /3097/train-accident-attorneys-metrolink-crash-lawyers.htm, July 21, 2011.

78. Alex Johnson, "Shining a Light on Hazards of Fluorescent Bulbs," MSNBC.com, April 7, 2008, retrieved from http://www.msnbc.msn.com/id/23694819/ns/us_news-environment/t /shining-light-hazards-fluorescent-bulbs/, September 7, 2011.

79. Elizabeth Shogren, "CFL Bulbs Have One Hitch: Toxic Mercury," NPR.org, February 15, 2007, retrieved from http://www.npr.org/templates/story/story.php?storyId=7431198, September 7, 2011.

80. C. Michael Roland, Ph.D., "The Barrier Performance of Latex Rubber." *Rubber World* ("The Technical Service Magazine for the Rubber Industry") 208:3 (June 1993), retrieved from http://www.thefreelibrary.com/The+barrier+performance+of+latex+rubber.-a014089514, January 22, 2012.

81. C. Michael Roland, Ph.D., quoted in William D. Gairdner, "Condomania," February 16, 1998, Canadian Conservative Forum, retrieved from http://www.conservativeforum.org/Essay sForm.asp?ID=6071, January 22, 2012.

82. "Male Latex Condoms and Sexually Transmitted Diseases," Centers for Disease Control and Prevention, updated April 11, 2011, retrieved from http://www.cdc.gov/condomeffective ness/brief.html, January 22, 2012.

83. Stephen Genuis, M.D., "What About the Condom?," *Risky Sex* (Edmonton, Alberta: Winfield Publishing, 1992), retrieved from http://www.catholiceducation.org/articles/sexuality /se0001.html, January 22, 2012.

84. "Preventing Pregnancy: How Effective Is a Male Condom?," American Pregnancy Association, August 2003, retrieved from http://www.americanpregnancy.org/preventingpreg nancy/malecondom.html, January 22, 2012.

85. "Male Latex Condoms and Sexually Transmitted Diseases."
86. Bruce Voeller, Anne H. Coulson, Gerald S. Bernstein, and Robert M. Nakamura, "Mineral Oil Lubricants Cause Rapid Deterioration of Latex Condoms," *Contraception* 39:1 (January 1989), 95–102, abstract retrieved from http://www.contraceptionjournal.org/article/0010-7824%2889%2990018-8/abstractref, January 22, 2012.
87. Cecil Adams, "Can HIV Pass Through the Pores in Latex Condoms? (A Straight Dope Classic from Cecil's Storehouse of Human Knowledge)," May 6, 1994, retrieved from http://www.straightdope.com/columns/read/1178/can-hiv-pass-through-the-pores-in-latex-condoms, January 22, 2012.
88. Andrew Weil, M.D., "Ask Dr. Weil: Allergic to Latex Condoms?," Dr. Weil.com, July 18, 2006, retrieved from http://www.drweil.com/drw/u/id/QAA368178, January 27, 2012.
89. "Can a Latex Allergy Be Life Threatening?," Australasian Society of Clinical Immunology and Allergy, March 25, 2010, retrieved from http://www.allergy.org.au/content/view/39/253/, January 27, 2012.
90. Weil, "Ask Dr. Weil: Allergic to Latex Condoms?"
91. Lisa Johnson Mandell, "Most Dangerous Spot in the Office," AOL Jobs, March 16, 2011, retrieved from http://jobs.aol.com/articles/2011/03/16/most-dangerous-spot-in-the-office/, August 30, 2011.
92. "A Global Problem: Toner Dust and Emissions of Laser Printers and Copying Machines," nano-Control International Foundation, retrieved from http://www.nano-control.de/english.php#K53, April 1, 2011.
93. "Photocopiers: The Main Hazards," Workers Health Centre, updated May 15, 2005, retrieved from http://www.workershealth.com.au/facts011.html, September 9, 2011.
94. "The Dangers of Indoor Chemical Pollution: Photocopiers," SilentMenace.com, retrieved from http://www.silentmenace.com/Photocopiers.html, September 10, 2011.
95. John Collins Rudolf, "Under the Sea, Hot, White Reefs," *New York Times Week in Review*, June 5, 2011, WK3, retrieved from http://www.nytimes.com/2011/06/05/weekinreview/05reefs.html?ref=fishandothermarinelife, June 10, 2011.
96. C. Mark Eakin, Ph.D., quoted in "Heat Stress in Caribbean Corals in 2005 Worst on Record—Caribbean Reef Ecosystems May Not Survive Repeated Stress," National Oceanographic and Atmospheric Administration, November 15, 2010, retrieved from http://www.noaanews.noaa.gov/stories2010/20101115_coralbleaching.html, June 10, 2011.
97. Rudolf, "Under the Sea."
98. "The Importance of Coral to People," World Wildlife Fund, retrieved from http://www.worldwildlife.org/what/wherewework/coraltriangle/importance-of-coral.html, June 10, 2011.
99. P. W. Glynn, "Coral Reef Bleaching: Ecological Perspectives," *Coral Reefs* 12:1 (March 1, 1993), 1–17, retrieved from http://www.springerlink.com/content/k12w48311274206n/, June 10, 2011.
100. Eakin, "Heat Stress."
101. "Climate Accord Loopholes Could Spell 4.2°C Rise in Temperature and End of Coral Reefs by 2100," Institute of Physics, September 29, 2010, retrieved from http://www.iop.org/news/sep10/page_44805.html, June 10, 2011.
102. Michelle Lalonde, "Study Exposes Cracks in Cosmetics' Foundation," *Montreal Gazette,* May 16, 2011, retrieved from http://www.montrealgazette.com/health/Study+exposes+cracks+cosmetics+foundation/4788260/story.html, June 22, 2011; and *Heavy Metal Hazard,* Environmental Defence, May 2011, retrieved from http://environmentaldefence.ca/sites/default/files/report_files/HeavyMetalHazard%20FINAL.pdf, June 22, 2011.
103. Carol Barczac, "The Hazards of Cosmetics," *AEHA Quarterly,* Summer 1995, Environmental Health Association of Nova Scotia (formerly the Nova Scotia Allergy and Environmental Health Association), retrieved from http://www.environmentalhealth.ca/summer95cosmetic.html, June 22, 1995.
104. "Protect Your Family from the Hidden Hazards in Air Fresheners," Natural Resources Defense Council, September 2007, retrieved from http://www.nrdc.org/health/home/airfresheners/fairfresheners.pdf, June 22, 2011; and Leigh Erin Connealy, M.D., "Beauty to Die For: Health Hazards of Cosmetics and Skin Care Products Revealed," NaturalNews.com, January 20, 2006, retrieved from http://www.naturalnews.com/016898.html, June 20, 2011.
105. Noelle Robbins, "Not a Pretty Picture," *Earth Island Journal,* Spring 2011, retrieved from http://www.earthisland.org/journal/index.php/eij/article/not_a_pretty_picture/, June 22, 2011.

106. Michelle Valenzuela, "List of Foods Containing High Fructose Corn Syrup," eHow.com, retrieved from http://www.ehow.com/list_5851584_list-high-fructose-corn-syrup.html, July 16, 2011.

107. "Cough Syrup and Cavities," MySmileWay.com, Delta Dental Plans Association, retrieved from http://www.deltadentalins.com/oral_health/cough_syrup.html, July 16, 2011.

108. K. R. Aryal and H. al-Khaffaf, "Venous Thromboembolic Complications Following Air Travel: What's the Quantitative Risk? A Literature Review," *European Journal of Vascular and Endovascular Surgery* 31:2 (February 2006), 187–199, retrieved from http://www.sciencedirect.com/science/article/pii/S1078588405005411, August 6, 2011.

109. "All About Blood Clots," Health24.com, February 26, 2010, retrieved from http://www.health24.com/medical/Condition_centres/777-792-822-1852,17624.asp, August 6, 2011.

110. Ian Gurney, "A Wave of Destruction Will Destroy America's East Coast," *Daily Express*, August 10, 2004, retrieved from http://www.rense.com/general56/tsu.htm, June 29, 2010.

111. Steven N. Ward, Ph.D., and Simon Day, Ph.D., "Tsunami Thoughts," *CSEG Recorder*, December 2005, Canadian Society of Exploration Geophysicists, retrieved from http://www.es.ucsc.edu/~ward/papers/CSEG.pdf, July 4, 2010.

112. "Mega-Tsunami Threatens to Devastate U.S. Coastline," Science Daily, September 3, 2001, retrieved from http://www.sciencedaily.com/releases/2001/09/010903091755.htm, June 30, 2010.

113. Allison Janse with Charles P. Gerba, Ph.D., *The Germ Freak's Guide to Outwitting Colds and Flu* (Deerfield Beach, FL: Health Communications, Inc., 2005), 50.

114. Radha Chitale, "Ten Places Where Germs Lurk," ABC News/Health, October 26, 2008, 3, retrieved from http://abcnews.go.com/Health/ColdandFluNews/story?id=6106018&page=3, July 24, 2011.

115. Janse, *Germ Freak's Guide*.

116. "How to Maintain and Sanitize Cutting Boards," What'sCookingAmerica.net, retrieved from http://whatscookingamerica.net/CuttingBoards/AllAbout.htm, July 24, 2011.

117. Straight Dope Science Advisory Board, "What's Better, a Wooden Cutting Board or a Plastic One?," Straight Dope, February 8, 2011, retrieved from http://www.straightdope.com/columns/read/1882/whats-better-a-wooden-cutting-board-or-a-plastic-one, July 24, 2011.

118. Jane E. Brody, "Wooden Cutting Boards Found Safer Than Plastic," *New York Times*, February 10, 1993, retrieved from http://www.nytimes.com/1993/02/10/health/wooden-cutting-boards-found-safer-than-plastic.html, July 24, 2011.

119. "Cutting Boards: Wood or Plastic," Ochef.com, retrieved from http://www.ochef.com/645.htm, July 24, 2010.

120. Danny Alfaro, "Cutting Boards and Food Safety," About.com Guide: Culinary Arts, retrieved from http://culinaryarts.about.com/od/culinarytools/p/cuttingboards.htm, July 24, 2011.

121. "Metaphoria," *Adventures in Cybersex*, retrieved from http://dk-net.com/users/kevin/cybersex.html, January 26, 2012.

122. Shari Cohn, M.S.S.W., L.C.S.W., S.C., C.S.A.T., "Cybersex Addiction," 2006, retrieved from http://www.sharicohn.com/cybersex.html, January 26, 2012.

123. "War in the Fifth Domain—Are the Mouse and the Keyboard the New Weapons of Conflict?," *Economist*, July 1, 2010, retrieved from http://www.economist.com/node/16478792, June 26, 2011.

124. Robert Fry, "Fighting Wars in Cyberspace," *Wall Street Journal*, July 21, 2010, retrieved from http://online.wsj.com/article/SB10001424052748703724104575379343636553602.html, June 26, 2011.

125. Tom Gjelten, "Cyberwarrior Shortage Threatens U.S. Security," *Morning Edition*, National Public Radio, July 19, 2010, retrieved from http://www.npr.org/templates/story/story.php?storyID=128574055, June 26, 2011.

126. "War in the Fifth Domain."

D

1. "Delicious Dairy-Free Dining," NutritionMD.org, Physicians Committee for Responsible Medicine, retrieved from http://www.nutritionmd.org/nutrition_tips/nutrition_tips_go_vegetarian/dairy_free.html, August 30, 2011; and "Understanding the Problems with Dairy Products," NutritionMD.org, Physicians Committee for Responsible Medicine, retrieved from http://www.nutritionmd.org/nutrition_tips/nutrition_tips_understand_foods/dairy.html, August 30, 2011.

2. Brian Handwerk, "Daylight Saving Time 2011: Why and When Does It Begin?" *National*

Geographic News, March 13, 2011, retrieved from http://news.nationalgeographic.com/news/2011/11/110313-daylight-savings-time-2011-what-time-is-it-spring-forward-nation/, April 10, 2011; and Imre Janszky and Rickard Ljung, "Shifts To and From Daylight Saving Time and Incidence of Myrocardial Infarction," *New England Journal of Medicine* 359 (1966), abstract retrieved from http://www.uni-protokolle.de/nachrichten/text/166129/, April 10, 2011.

3. Darrell Delamaide, "Deficit Hysteria Grips Washington," MarketWatch.com, February 16, 2011, retrieved from http://www.marketwatch.com/story/deficit-hysteria-grips-washington-2011-02-16, February 21, 2011.

4. Bernard Boudreau, *Mass Production, The Stock Market Crash and the Great Depression* (Lincoln, NE: Author's Choice Press, 1996); Ben S. Bernanke, "Deflation: Making Sure 'It' Doesn't Happen Here," Remarks of the Chairman of the Federal Reserve Board Before the National Economics Club, Washington, D.C., 2002, retrieved from http://www.federalreserve.gov/boarddocs/speeches/2002/20021121/default.htm, June 12, 2011; Paul R. Krugman, "It's Baaaaaack: Japan's Slump and the Return of the Liquidity Trap," Brookings Institution, Papers on Economic Activity, 1998, 137–206, retrieved from http://www.brookings.edu/~/media/Files/Programs/ES/BPEA/1998_2_bpea_papers/1998b_bpea_krugman_dominquez_rogoff.pdf, June 12, 2011; and Mike Moffatt, "What Is Deflation and How Can It Be Prevented?," About.com, retrieved from http://economics.about.com/cs/inflation/a/deflation.htm, June 12, 2011.

5. James Bullard, "Seven Faces of 'The Peril,'" *Federal Reserve Bank of St. Louis Review,* September–October 2010, preprint dated July 29, 2010, retrieved from http://research.stlouisfed.org/econ/bullard/pdf/SevenFacesFinal Jul28.pdf, June 12, 2011; and Joe Weisenthal, "PIMCO's El-Erian: The U.S. Is on the Road to Deflation," BusinessInsider.com, August 5, 2010, retrieved from http://www.businessinsider.com/pimcos-el-erian-the-us-is-on-the-road-to-deflation-2010-8, June 12, 2011.

6. Heiner Flassbeck quoted in "U.N. Economic Think Tank Signals Deflationary Danger," Agence France-Presse, September 14, 2010, retrieved from http://www.expatica.com/ch/news/local_news/un-economic-thinktank-signals-deflationary-danger_96208.html, June 12, 2011.

7. Moffatt, "What Is Deflation"; William Buiter, "Deflation: Prevention and Cure," National Bureau of Economic Research, Working Paper No. 9623, April 2003, retrieved from http://www.nber.org/papers/w9623, June 12, 2011; Charles Hugh Smith, "Why the Fed's Zero Interest Rate Policy May Be Dangerous," DailyFinance.com, March 6, 2010, retrieved from http://www.dailyfinance.com/2010/03/06/why-the-feds-zero-interest-rate-policy-may-be-dangerous/, June 12, 2011; and Keith R. McCullough, "Is This Finally the Economic Collapse," *Fortune*, August 11, 2010, retrieved from http://money.cnn.com/2010/08/11/news/economy/economic_collapse_GDP_unemployment.fortune/index.htm, June 12, 2011.

8. "Dental Floss," *Guide to Less Toxic Products*, Environmental Health Association of Nova Scotia (EHANS), 2004, retrieved from http://lesstoxicguide.ca/index.asp?fetch=personal#lotio, August 30, 2011.

9. Christian Nordqvist, "What Is Body Odor (B.O.)? What Causes Body Odor?" *Medical News Today,* December 9, 2009, retrieved from http://www.medicalnewstoday.com/articles/173478.php, June 4, 2011; "Carboxylic Acids—Biological Importance," *Science Encyclopedia,* JRank Science and Philosophy website, retrieved from http://science.jrank.org/pages/1220/Carboxylic-Acids-Biological-importance.html, June 4, 2011; Andreas Natsch, Samuel Derrer, Felix Flachsmann, and Joachim Schmid, "A Broad Diversity of Volatile Carboxylic Acids, Released by a Bacterial Aminoacylase from Axilla Secretions, as Candidate Molecules for the Determination of Human-Body Odor Type," *Chemistry and Biodiversity* 3:1 (January 19, 2006), 1, retrieved from http://onlinelibrary.wiley.com/doi/10.1002/cbdv.200690015/pdf, June 4, 2011; and Mayo Clinic Staff, "Sweating and Body Odor: Treatments and Drugs," MayoClinic.com, December 9, 2010, retrieved from http://www.mayoclinic.com/health/sweating-and-body-odor/DS00305/DSECTION=treatments-and-drugs, June 4, 2011.

10. Stephanie Watson, "Antiperspirant Safety: Should You Sweat It?," WebMD, June 1, 2011, retrieved from http://www.webmd.com/skin-beauty/features/antiperspirant-facts-safety, June 5, 2011.

11. Susan Conova, "Estrogen's Role in Cancer," *In Vivo: The Newsletter of Columbia University Medical Center,* May 20, 2003, retrieved from http://www.cumc.columbia.edu/publications/in-vivo/Vol2_Iss10_may26_03/index.html, June 4, 2011.

12. Salynn Boyles, "Antiperspirant Chemical Found in Breast Tumors—Findings Don't Prove Link to Cancer but Deserve Closer Look," WebMD Health News, January 12, 2004, retrieved from http://www.webmd.com/breast-cancer/news/20040112/antiperspirant-chemical -found-in-breast-tumors, June 4, 2011.

13. "Aluminum and Alzheimer's Disease," Fact Sheet 406, Alzheimer's Society, September 2008, retrieved from http://www.alzheimers.org.uk/site/scripts/documents_info.php? documentID=99, June 4, 2011.

14. Linda Carroll, "Daily Diet Soda Tied to Higher Risk for Stroke, Heart Attack," Today Health, MSNBC.com, February 10, 2011, retrieved from http://today.msnbc.msn.com/id/41479869 /ns/today-today_health/t/daily-diet-soda-tied-higher-risk-stroke-heart-attack/, July 18, 2011.

15. Mitchell Elkind, M.D., quoted in Susan Conova, "Is Diet Soda Deadly?," news release, Columbia University College of Physicians and Surgeons, February 21, 2011, retrieved from http:// ps.columbia.edu/news/diet-soda-deadly, July 28, 2011.

16. Harry Wallop, "Dishwashers Harbour 'Killer Bugs'," Telegraph, June 21, 2011, retrieved from http://www.telegraph.co.uk/health/healthnews/8589765/Dishwashers-harbour-killer -bugs.html, June 23, 2011.

17. "'My Dishwasher Is Trying to Kill Me': New Research Finds Harmful Fungal Pathogens Living in Dishwasher Seals," Science Daily, June 20, 2011, retrieved from http://www.science daily.com/releases/2011/06/110620133138.htm, June 25, 2011.

18. Nina Gunde-Cimerman, quoted in Wallop, "Dishwashers Harbour."

19. Nina Gunde-Cimerman, quoted in Lesley Ciarula Taylor, "Deadly Fungus Could Be Festering in Your Dishwasher," Hamilton Spectator (Ontario), June 22, 2011, retrieved from http:// www.thespec.com/living/healthfitness/article/551598-deadly-fungus-could-be-festering-in -your-dishwasher, June 25, 2011.

20. "Professional Values and Reported Behaviours of Doctors in the USA and UK: Quantitative Survey," BMJ Quality & Safety, March 7, 2011, retrieved from http://qualitysafety.bmj.com /content/early/2011/02/07/bmjqs.2010.048173.full, April 10, 2011; and Susie Sell, "One in Five Doctors Has Worked with an Incompetent Colleague," GPonline.com, March 8, 2011, retrieved from http://www.gponline.com/News/article/1058622/One-five-doctors -worked-incompetent-colleague/, April 10, 2011.

21. Allison Janse with Charles P. Gerba, Ph.D., The Germ Freak's Guide to Outwitting Colds and Flu (Deerfield Beach, FL: Health Communications, Inc., 2005), 77–78.

22. Janse, Germ Freak's Guide, 119.

23. "Diseases from Dogs," National Center for Infectious Diseases, retrieved from http://www .cdc.gov/healthypets/animals/dogs.htm, April 10, 2011.

24. Lisa Conti, D.V.M. M.P.H., quoted in Catherine Guthrie, "The Hazards of Puppy Love," O, The Oprah Magazine, June 2008, retrieved from http://www.oprah.com/health/Is-Your-Pet -Making-You-Sick-How-Dogs-Spread-Germs, April 10, 2011.

25. Edmund Conway, "Bank of England Says Financiers Are Fuelling an Economic 'Doom Loop,'" Telegraph, November 6, 2009, retrieved from http://www.telegraph.co.uk/finance/financial crisis/6516579/Bank-of-England-says-financiers-are-fuelling-an-economic-doom-loop.html, August 6, 2011.

26. Piergiorgio Alessandri and Andrew G. Haldane, Bank of England, November 2009, based on a presentation delivered by Mr. Haldane at the Federal Reserve Bank of Chicago twelfth annual International Banking Conference on "The International Financial Crisis: Have the Rules of Finance Changed?," September 25, 2009, retrieved from http://www.bankofengland.co.uk /publications/speeches/2009/speech409.pdf, August 6, 2011.

27. Floyd Norris, "Learning to Live with Debt," New York Times, August 5, 2011, B1, retrieved from http://www.nytimes.com/2011/08/05/business/learning-to-live-with-debt.html?_r =1&pagewanted=all, August 6, 2011.

28. Brandon Carter and W. H. McCrea, "The Anthropic Principle and Its Implications for Biological Evolution," Philosophical Transactions of the Royal Society A 310:1512 (December 20, 1983), 347–363, abstract retrieved from http://rsta.royalsocietypublishing.org/content /310/1512/347, September 11, 2011; J. Richard Gott III, "Implications of the Copernican Principle for Our Future Prospects," Nature 363 (May 27, 1993), 315–319, abstract retrieved from http://www.nature.com/nature/journal/v363/n6427/abs/363315a0.html, September 11, 2011; and Jim Holt, "Doom Soon: A Philosophical Invitation to the Apocalypse," Lingua Franca 7:8 (October 1997), retrieved from http://linguafranca.mirror.theinfo.org/9710/holt .html, September 11, 2011.

29. Gott, "Implications."

30. Holt, "Doom Soon."
31. Allison Janse with Charles Gerba, Ph.D., *The Germ Freak's Guide to Outwitting Colds and Flu* (Deerfield Beach, FL: Health Communications, Inc., 2005), 16.
32. Martica Heaner, "Kick the Doughnut Habit, and Make Your Nutritionist Smile," *New York Times,* May 3, 2005, retrieved from http://www.nytimes.com/2005/05/03/health/nutrition /03cons.html, August 27, 2011.
33. Kristie Leong, M.D., "Four Bad Beauty Habits That Cause Lines Around the Mouth," April 11, 2011, retrieved from http://www.associatedcontent.com/article/7918489/four_hab its_that_cause_wrinkles_and.html, May 25, 2011.
34. Joseph D. Younger, "When Courtesy Turns Dangerous," *Car & Travel* Digital Edition, March 2010, 11, retrieved from http://www.nxtbook.com/nxtbooks/aaa_ny/ct_201003/#12, February 20, 2010.
35. Christopher Jensen, "As Convertible Tops Drop, Risk of Hearing Loss Rises," *New York Times,* January 4, 2011, retrieved from http://wheels.blogs.nytimes.com/2011/01/04/as-convert ible-tops-drop-risk-of-hearing-loss-rises/, April 10, 2011; and A. A. Mikulec, S. B. Lukens, L. E. Jackson, and M. N. Deyoung, "Noise Exposure in Convertible Automobiles," *Journal of Laryngology and Otology,* online publication, November 25, 2010, abstract retrieved from http://journals.cambridge.org/action/displayAbstract?fromPage=online&aid=7986238, April 10, 2011.
36. "Tips for Teens: The Truth About Heroin," U.S. Department of Health and Human Services and SAMHSA's National Clearinghouse for Alcohol and Drug Information, retrieved from SAMHSA's Health Information Network, http://ncadi.samhsa.gov/govpubs/phd860, February 28, 2010.

E

1. Bill Marsh, "A Hen's Space to Roost," *New York Times,* August 15, 2010, WK3, retrieved from http://graphics8.nytimes.com/packages/pdf/weekinreview/20100815-chicken-cages.pdf, August 28, 2011.
2. "Chickens Used for Food," People for the Ethical Treatment of Animals, retrieved from http://www.peta.org/issues/animals-used-for-food/chickens.aspx, August 27, 2011.
3. Peter Singer, "The Ethics of Eating," Project Syndicate, June 2006, retrieved from http://www .utilitarian.net/singer/by/200606--.htm, August 28, 2011.
4. Phyllis Entis, M.Sc., S.M.(NRCM), "Risky Eating: Raw and Undercooked Eggs," eFoodAlert .com, March 25, 2009, retrieved from http://efoodalert.blogspot.com/2009/03/risky-eating -raw-and-undercooked-eggs.html, April 4, 2011.
5. Jeanna Bryner, "Natural Viagra: Spider Bite Causes Erection," LiveScience, April 30, 2007, retrieved from http://www.livescience.com/4429-natural-viagra-spider-bite-erection.html, January 26, 2012.
6. "Spider Venom That Causes Four-Hour Long Erections 'Could Be the New Viagra,'" *Mail Online,* Science and Tech, March 8, 2011, retrieved from http://www.dailymail.co.uk/sci encetech/article-1363810/Spider-venom-cause-hour-erections-new-Viagra.html, January 26, 2012.
7. Vladimir Hernandez, "Spider Venom Could Boost Sex Life," BBC News, May 4, 2007, retrieved from http://news.bbc.co.uk/2/hi/americas/6625397.stm, January 26, 2012.
8. "Spider Venom That Causes."
9. "H1N1 Information: Prevention Tips," Carondelet Health Network, retrieved from http:// www.carondelet.org/home/h1n1-information/prevention-tips.aspx, July 23, 2011.
10. Diana Rocco, "Germs: Micro Riders on MTA Subways," My Fox NY, May 11, 2011, retrieved from http://www.myfoxny.com/dpp/news/germs-microbe-riders-on-mta-subways -20110511, July 23, 2011.
11. Charles P. Gerba, Ph.D., cited in "8 Ways to Avoid Germs (You'll Be Shocked by How Close Germs Are)," NewsMax.com Wires, January 23, 2007, retrieved from http://archive.news max.com/archives/articles/2007/1/23/123237.shtml?s=br, July 23, 2011.
12. Tatiana Morales, "Danger on the Escalator," CBS News.com, February 11, 2009, retrieved from http://www.cbsnews.com/stories/2005/02/17/earlyshow/living/ConsumerWatch /main674650.shtml, July 18, 2011.
13. James A. Levine, M.D., Ph.D., "The Extreme Dangers of Sitting," Mayo Clinic, January 20, 2011, retrieved from http://neurosynthesisarchives.wordpress.com/2011/01/20/the -extreme-dangers-of-sitting/, August 14, 2011.
14. "Exercise Ball vs. Desk Chair," Livestrong.com, retrieved from http://www.livestrong.com

/article/109461-exercise-ball-vs.-desk-chair/, August 15, 2011; and "Are Exercise Balls Safe for the Office?," Livestrong.com, retrieved from http://www.livestrong.com/article/380730 -are-exercise-balls-safe-for-the-office/, August 15, 2011.

15. Dawna Theo, "Exercise Danger Signs," retrieved from http://www.ehow.com/about_5434342 _exercise-danger-signs.html, June 5, 2010.

16. Jane E. Brody, "Dangers of Indoor Air Pollution," *New York Times,* January 28, 1981, retrieved from http://www.nytimes.com/1981/01/28/garden/dangers-of-indoor-air-pollution.html ?sec=health, February 22, 2010.

17. Mayo Clinic Staff, "Exercise: 7 Benefits of Regular Physical Activity," MayoClinic.com, July 23, 2011, retrieved from http://www.mayoclinic.com/health/exercise/HQ01676, August 28, 2011; "Exercise In-Depth Report," *New York Times,* retrieved from http://health.ny times.com/health/guides/specialtopic/physical-activity/print.html, August 28, 2011; and "The Risks of Not Taking Exercise," BBC World Service, retrieved from http://www.bbc.co .uk/worldservice/sci_tech/features/health/healthyliving/exerciserisk.shtml, August 28, 2011.

18. Anne Harding, "Heart-Attack Risk Spikes After Sex, Exercise," Health.com, March 22, 2011, retrieved from http://www.cnn.com/2011/HEALTH/03/22/health.risk.sex.work out/index.html, August 28, 2011; and Issa J. Dahabreh, M.D. and Jessica K. Paulus, Sc.D., "Association of Episodic Physical and Sexual Activity with Triggering of Acute Cardiac Events: Systematic Review and Meta-analysis," *Journal of the American Medical Association* 305:12 (March 23–30, 2011), 1225–1233, abstract retrieved from http://jama.ama-assn .org:content:305:12:1225.abstract, August 29, 2011.

19. "Particulate Matter Primer," Center for Innovation in Engineering and Science Education, re-trieved from http://www.ciese.org/curriculum/airproj/pmprimer.html, February 20, 2010.

F

1. Kim Painter, "Your Health: Hand-to-face Touch Is Crucial Link to Catching Flu," *USA Today,* September 28, 2009, retrieved from http://www.usatoday.comnews/health/painter/2009 -09-27-your-health_N.htm, July 10, 2011.

2. Allison Janse with Charles P. Gerba, Ph.D., *The Germ Freak's Guide to Outwitting Colds and Flu* (Deerfield Beach, FL: Health Communications, Inc., 2005), 22–23.

3. Claire Mitchell, "Study: Food Safety Issues at DC Farmers Markets," July 26, 2011, retrieved from http://www.foodsafetynews.com/2011/07/study-food-safety-issues-at-dc-farmers-mar ket/, August 21, 2011.

4. Joel Grover and Matt Goldberg, "False Claims, Lies Caught on Tape at Farmers Markets," NBC News Los Angeles, September 23, 2010, retrieved from http://www.nbclosangeles .com/news/local/Hidden-Camera-Investigation-Farmers-Markets-103577594.html, August 21, 2011.

5. Charles P. Gerba, Ph.D., "Transcript: 'Germy' Jobs," Online discussion, WashingtonPost.com, April 3, 2006, retrieved from http://www.washingtonpost.com/wp-dyn/content/discus sion/2006/03/31/DI2006033101212.html, May 14, 2011.

6. Lisa B. Bernstein, M.D., cited in Elizabeth Landau, "Conquering the 'Ewww' Factor of the Public Potty," CNN.com/Health, December 9, 2008, retrieved from http://edition.cnn .com/2008/HEALTH/10/03/bathroom.hygiene/index.html, July 5, 2011.

7. Eryn Brown, "Hands-Free Faucets Harbor Germs, Johns Hopkins Study Says," *Los Angeles Times,* March 31, 2011, retrieved from http://articles.latimes.com/2011/mar/31/news/la heb-hands-free-faucet-bacteria-20110331, May 15, 2011.

8. George Dvorsky, "The Fermi Paradox: Back with a Vengeance," *Sentient Developments,* August 4, 2007, retrieved from http://www.sentientdevelopments.com/2007/08/fermi-paradox-back -with-vengeance.html, September 11, 2011; and "Fermi Paradox," *Wikipedia,* updated Septem-ber 7, 2011, retrieved from http://en.wikipedia.org/wiki/Fermi_paradox, September 11, 2011.

9. Nick Bostrom, "Existential Risks: Analyzing Human Extinction Scenarios and Related Haz-ards," *Journal of Evolution and Technology* 9 (March 2002), retrieved from http://www.nick bostrom.com/existential/risks.html, April 6, 2011; and "Great Filter," *Wikipedia,* updated June 20, 2011, retrieved from http://en.wikipedia.org/wiki/Great_Filter, September 11, 2011.

10. Laurence J. Kotlikoff, as quoted in "Austerity or Stimulus? Some Economists Have Much More Extreme Views Than That," *Economist,* August 12, 2010, retrieved from http://www .economist.com/businessfinance/PrinterFriendly.cfm?story_id=16792828, February 12, 2010.

11. Laurence J. Kotlikoff and Richard Munroe, "U.S. Debt Is Child Abuse," Bloomberg Opinion, October 21, 2010, retrieved from http://www.kotlikoff.net/content/us-debt-fiscal-child-abuse, February 21, 2011.

12. Edward Wyatt and Graham Bowley, "New Rules Would Limit Trades in Volatile Market," *New York Times,* May 19, 2010, B1, retrieved from http://www.nytimes.com/2010/05/19/business/19crash.html, August 16, 2011.

13. David Easley, Marcos M. Lopez de Prado, and Maureen O'Hara, "The Microstructure of the 'Flash Crash': Flow Toxicity, Liquidity Crashes, and the Probability of Informed Trading," *Journal of Portfolio Management* 37:2, (Winter 2011), 118–128, retrieved from Social Science Research Network, http://papers.ssrn.com/so13/papers.cfm?abstract_id=1695041, August 15, 2011.

14. Edward E. Kaufman and Carl M. Levin, "Preventing the Next Flash Crash," *New York Times,* May 6, 2011, A27, retrieved from http://www.nytimes.com/2011/05/06/opinion/06kaufman.html, August 16, 2011.

15. Laura T. Coffey, "Can Your Flip-Flops Kill You?," Today Health, August 18, 2009, retrieved from http://today.msnbc.msn.com/id/32453516/ns/today-today_health/t/can-your-flip-flops-kill-you/, May 14, 2011.

16. Christopher Wanjek, "Flip-Flops Bad for Feet," LiveScience.com, June 24, 2008, retrieved from http://www.livescience.com/7520-flip-flops-bad-feet.html, July 14, 2011.

17. Mallika Marshall, M.D., cited in "The Dangers of Flip-Flops . . . in Footwear!," CBS News.com, February 11, 2009, retrieved from http://www.cbsnews.com/2100-500165_162-4200038.html, March 31, 2012.

18. Dr. Rebecca Tung, "The Hidden Dangers of Flip-Flops, Baseball Caps," Loyola University Medical Center, Maywood, Illinois, June 17, 2011, retrieved from http://www.lumc.edu/Template/luhs/newsrelease/reportdetail.cfm?autonumber=973441488, July 14, 2011.

19. Marshall, "The Dangers of Flip-Flops."

20. Coffey, "Can Your Flip-Flops Kill You?"

21. Dr. Richard Maleski, quoted in Kellie B. Gormly, "Flip-flop Flap: Wearing the Popular Sandals Can Be a Sore Issue," *Pittsburgh Tribune-Review,* June 6, 2011, retrieved from http://www.pittsburghlive.com/x/pittsburghtrib/lifestyles/fashion/s_740694.html, July 14, 2011.

22. "Pandemics and Pandemic Threats since 1900," FLU.gov, August 21, 2011, retrieved from http://www.pandemicflu.gov/general/historicaloverview.html, August 21, 2011.

23. Pat Bailey, "The Top 10: Epidemic Hall of Infamy," *UC Davis Magazine* 23:4 (Summer 2006), retrieved from http://ucdavismagazine.ucdavis.edu/issues/su06/feature_1b.html, August 21, 2011.

24. "Pandemics and Pandemic Threats Since 1900."

25. Jeffrey K. Tautenberger and David M. Morens, "1918 Influenza: the Mother of All Pandemics," *Emerging Infectious Diseases* 12:1 (January, 2006), retrieved from Centers for Disease Control, http://www.cdc.gov/ncidod/eid/vol12no01/05-0979.htm, August 21, 2011.

26. "How Dangerous Is Plastic?," RealSimple.com, retrieved from http://www.realsimple.com/magazine-more/inside-magazine/ask-real-simple/how-dangerous-plastic-10000001779534/page7.html, May 21, 2011.

27. Nena Baker, *The Body Toxic: How the Hazardous Chemistry of Everyday Things Threatens Our Health and Well-Being* (New York: North Point Press, 2008), 222–223.

28. "Food Myths: Myth #8—'I don't need to use a food thermometer. I can tell when my food is cooked,'" Food Safety and Sanitation Program, Alaska Department of Environmental Health, retrieved from http://www.dec.state.ak.us/eh/fss/consumers/food_myths.htm, August 13, 2011.

29. Ibid.

30. "Food Safety Fact Sheet, Using Food Thermometers," National Food Services Management Institute, University of Mississippi, 2009, retrieved from http://nfsmi-web01.nfsmi.olemiss.edu/documentlibraryfiles/PDF/20090319104948.pdf, August 13, 2011.

31. Patrick McGroarty, and Jan Hromadko, "Germany to Drop Nuclear Power by 2022," Dow Jones Newswires, May 30, 2011, retrieved from http://online.wsj.com/article/BT-CO-20110530-703242.html, June 24, 2011; and Bernard Keane, "BHP and the New Maths of Nuclear Reactors," Crikey, May 17, 2011, retrieved from http://www.crikey.com.au/2011/05/17/bhp-and-the-new-maths-of-nuclear-reactors/, June 24, 2011.

32. Phil McKenna, "Fossil Fuels Are Far Deadlier Than Nuclear Power," *New Scientist,* Issue 2805, March 23, 2011, retrieved from http://www.newscientist.com/article/mg20928053.600-fossil-fuels-are-far-deadlier-than-nuclear-power.html, June 24, 2011.

33. "Environmental and Health Impacts of Electricity Generation," International Energy Agency, June 2002, retrieved from http://www.ieahydro.org/reports/ST3-020613b.pdf, June 24, 2011.

34. Brian Wang, "Deaths per TWh by Energy Source," NextBigFuture.com, March 13, 2011, retrieved from http://nextbigfuture.com/2011/03/deaths-per-twh-by-energy-source. html, June 24, 2011.

35. "Problems of Coal: CO_2 Pollution from Coal," Clean Air Task Force, retrieved from http://www.catf.us/coal/problems/co2/, June 24, 2011.

36. Dan Solin, "Seven Reasons Why Your Investments Are Doomed," *Huffington Post*, February 23, 2010, retrieved from http://www.huffingtonpost.com/dan-solin/seven-reasons-why -your-in_b_470038.html, March 29, 2011.

37. Doris J. Rapp, M.D., "Dangers of Personal Care Products," in "Health Tips" section of www .drrapp.com, retrieved from http://www.drrapp.com/alerts.htm, February 21, 2010.

38. "Perfume," retrieved from http://www.silentmenace.com/Perfumes.html, February 22, 2010.

39. Dr. Ben Kim, "Acrylamide: What Is It, and Which Foods Contain It?" Dr.BenKim.com, retrieved from http://drbenkim.com/articles-acrylamide.html, August 14, 2011.

40. Vincent Iannelli, M.D., "Avoiding the Dangers of Fruit Juice," About.com Pediatrics, updated May 30, 2011, retrieved from http://pediatrics.about.com/cs/nutrition/a/fruit_juice.htm, September 18, 2011; and "The Use and Misuse of Fruit Juice in Pediatrics," American Academy of Pediatrics, *Pediatrics* 107:5 (May 2001), 1210–1213, retrieved from http://pediatrics .aappublications.org/content/107/5/1210, September 18, 2011.

41. Dr. Ben Kim, "Eating Too Much Fruit Can Be Bad for Your Health," Dr.BenKim.com, retrieved from http://drbenkim.com/articles-fruit.html, August 14, 2011.

G

1. "Look Down, Look Up, Look Out," *Economist*, May 10, 2007, retrieved from http://www .economist.com/node/9143913, April 6, 2011; Dr. Tony Phillips, "Earth's Inconstant Magnetic Field," NASA News Topics, December 19, 2003; Matt Ridley, "Magnetic North Is on the Move. Time to Panic?," *Wall Street Journal*, February 19, 2011, retrieved from http://online .wsj.com/article/SB10001424052748703584804576144674154457288.html, April 6, 2011; Barry Patrick, "Ships' Logs Give Clues to Earth's Magnetic Decline," *New Scientist*, May 11, 2006, retrieved from http://www.newscientist.com/article/dn9148-ships-logs-give-clues-to -earths-magnetic-decline.html, April 6, 2011; IOP Institute of Physics, http://www.physics .org; "Geographic Reversal," Wikipedia.org, updated May 15, 2012, retrieved from http:en .wikipedia.org/wiki/Geomagnetic_reversal, May 31, 2012.

2. James Glanz, "Geothermal Project in California Is Shut Down," *New York Times*, December 11, 2009, retrieved from http://www.nytimes.com/2009/12/12/science/earth/12quake.html, September 11, 2011.

3. James Glanz, "Quake Threat Leads Swiss to Close Geothermal Project," *New York Times*, December 10, 2009, retrieved from http://www.nytimes.com/2009/12/11/science/earth /11basel.html, September 11, 2011.

4. Mark Waffel, "Buildings Crack Up as Black Forest Town Subsides, *Spiegel* Online International, March 19, 2008, retrieved from http://www.spiegel.de/international/zeit geist/0,1518,541296,00html, September 11, 2011.

5. *Climate Change 2007: Synthesis Report: Contribution of Working Groups I, II and III to the Fourth Assessment Report of the Intergovernmental Panel on Climate Change* (Core Writing Team, R. K. Pachauri and A. Reisinger, [eds.]), IPCC, Geneva, Switzerland, 2007, retrieved from http://www.ipcc.ch/publications_and_data/ar4/syr/en/contents.html, May 30, 2011.

6. James M. Inhofe, "The Science of Climate Change," Senate Floor Statement, July 28, 2003, retrieved from http://inhofe.senate.gov/pressreleases/climate.htm, June 12, 2011; and "Ten Top Reasons to Be a Climate Change Skeptic (and Counter Arguments)," *Planet Kansas: Voice of the Kansas Sierra Club*, December–January 2008, 4–5, retrieved from http://kansas .sierraclub.org/Planet/2007-1201/Planet%20Kansas-2007-1201-4web.pdf, June 12, 2011.

7. Fiona Govan, "Charles Manson Breaks Silence to Warn of Global Warming," *Daily Telegraph*, April 19, 2011, retrieved from http://www.telegraph.co.uk/news/worldnews/northamerica/usa /8460868/Charles-Manson-breaks-silence-to-warn-of-global-warming.html, May 30, 2011.

8. Ibid.

9. Bill Hutchinson, "Convicted Murderer Charles Manson Breaks Silence: 'I Worry About Global Warming, Obama Is an 'Idiot'" *Daily News* (New York), April 19, 2011, retrieved from http://articles.nydailynews.com/2011-04-19/news/29467816_1_charles-manson -corcoran-state-prison-global-warming, May 30, 2011.

10. "Global Warming Must Be True, Charles Manson Believes in It," *Daily Mail*, retrieved from http://www.dailymail.co.uk/news/article-1378178/Charles-Manson-breaks-20-year -silence-40th-anniversary-gruesome-Sharon-Tate-murders.html, May 30, 2011.

11. Richard Lindzen, interviewed on *Larry King Live*, January 7, 2010, transcript retrieved from http://transcripts.cnn.com/TRANSCRIPTS/0701/31/lkl.01.html, July 19, 2011.

12. John R. Christy, Ph.D., Written Testimony Before the House and Ways and Means Commit-tee, February 25, 2009, retrieved from http://waysandmeans.house.gov/media/pdf/111 /ctest.pdf, July 26, 2011.

13. John R. Christy, Ph.D., Letter to U.S. Representative Richard Pombo, Chairman of the House Resources Committee, May 22, 2003, quoted in Myron Ebell, "Energy Bill Prompts Rash of Proposals," Competitive Enterprise Institute, May 28, 2003, retrieved from http://cei.org/news -letters-cooler-heads-digest/vol-vii-no-11, July 19, 2011.

14. Arthur B. Robinson, Noah E. Robinson, and Willie Soon, "Environmental Effects of Increased Atmospheric Carbon Dioxide," Oregon Institute of Science and Medicine, November 1, 2007, retrieved from http://www.oism.org/pproject/s33p36.htm, July 19, 2011.

15. Inhofe, "Science of Climate Change."

16. Margot Wallström, quoted in Stephen Castle, "European Union Sends Strong Warning to Bush over Greenhouse Gas Emissions," *Independent*, March 19, 2001, retrieved from http:// www.commondreams.org/cgi-bin/print.cgi?file=/headlines01/0319-01.htm, July 24, 2011.

17. Inhofe, "Science of Climate Change."

18. Porter Stansberry with Braden Copeland, "An Answer to the Most Popular 'End of America' Question," *Daily Wealth*, February 5, 2011, retrieved from http://www.dailywealth.com /1623/An-Answer-to-the-Most-Popular-End-of-America-Question, March 28, 2011.

19. Larry Swedroe, "Don't Believe the Hype About Gold," CBSMoneyWatch.com, September 14, 2009, retrieved from http://moneywatch.bnet.com/investing/blog/wise-investing/dont -believe-the-hype-about-gold/842/, March 27, 2011.

20. "Ten Reasons Why Investing in Gold Is a Bad Idea," SteadfastFinances.com, October 9, 2009, retrieved from http://steadfastfinances.com/blog/2009/10/09/10-reasons-why-investing -in-gold-is-a-bad-idea/, March 27, 2011.

21. Spencer Reiss, "Green with (Nuclear) Energy" (review of *Power to Save the World: The Truth About Nuclear Energy* by Gwyneth Cravens), *Wall Street Journal*, November 20, 2007, D8, re-trieved from http://online.wsj.com/article/SB119551341776798449.html, March 21, 2011.

22. Charles H. Booras, M.D., "The Ten Worst Foods for Your Health," Jacksonville Medical Park Online, retrieved from http://www.jaxmed.com/tenworst.htm, April 3, 2011.

23. "EWG's 2011 Shopper's Guide to Pesticides in Produce: Methodology," Environmental Work-ing Group, 2011, retrieved from http://www.ewg.org/foodnews/methodology/, September 12, 2011; and "Fruits and Veggies to Buy Organic: Imported Grapes," Prevention.com, re-trieved from http://www.prevention.com/dirtiestcleanest/13.html, September 12, 2011.

24. "Supermarket Accident Facts: Did You Know?" Accident Compensation Helpline, retrieved from http://www.accidenthelpline.com/accident-types/supermarket-slips/, September 13, 2011; and "About Us," Accident Compensation Helpline, retrieved from http://www.acci denthelpline.com/about-us/, September 13, 2011.

25. Cynthia Dizikes, "Grapes on Floor Blamed for Falls in Two Lawsuits," *Chicago Tribune*, March 23, 2010, retrieved from http://articles.chicagotribune.com/2010-03-23/news/ct -talk-grapes-lawsuits-0324-20100323_1_grapes-cherry-tomatoes-holt, September 2, 2011.

26. Adriana Correa, "Two Grocery Stores in a Jam over Loose Grapes," NBC Chicago, March 25, 2010, http://www.nbcchicago.com/news/local/Two-Grocery-Stores-Get-In-a-Jam-Over -Loose-Grapes-89009617.html, September 12, 2011.

27. Dizikes, "Grapes on Floor."

28. K. Eric Drexler, *Engines of Creation: The Coming Era of Nanotechnology* (New York: Doubleday, 1986); "Gray Goo," as cited in http://en.wikipedia.org/wiki/Gray_goo, retrieved April 6, 2011.

29. Philip M. Tierno, Jr., Ph.D., quoted in Allison Janse with Charles P. Gerba, Ph.D., *The Germ Freak's Guide to Outwitting Colds and Flu* (Deerfield Beach, FL: Health Communications, Inc., 2005), 102.

30. Janse with Gerba, ibid., 102–8.

H

1. Alexis Madrigal, "10 Strange Species Discovered Last Year," Wired Science, May 26, 2009, retrieved from http://www.wired.com/wiredscience/2009/05/strangespecies/, April 18, 2011.

2. Mohammad Abdul Bakir, et al., "*Microbacterium hatatnosis* sp. nov., isolated as a contaminant of hairspray," *International Journal of Systematic and Evolutionary Microbiology* 58, 654–658, retrieved from http://ijs.sgmjournals.org/cgi/content/abstract/58/3/654, April 18, 2011.

3. "New Species of Bacteria Contaminates Hairspray," Science Daily, March 9, 2008, retrieved from http://www.sciencedaily.com/releases/2008/03/080307110337.htm, April 18, 2011.

4. Jenny Hall, "Do Hand Sanitizers Really Work," University of Toronto "Research and Innovation" web pages, October 14, 2009, retrieved from http://www.research.utoronto.ca/behind_the_headlines/do-hand-sanitizers-really-work/, June 7, 2010.

5. Judy Goldstein, "Dangers found in Alcohol-Based Hand Sanitizer Use," DenverPost.com, February 5, 2009, retrieved from http://yourhub.denverpost.com/def-section/dangers-found-alcohol-based-hand-sanitizer-use/Q6ysDl4kOAFlXYeN2KrS3I-ugc, May 17, 2012.

6. Dr. Jay Reubens, quoted in Judy Goldstein, ibid. (It should be noted that Dr. Reubens feels so strongly about the dangers of alcohol-based hand sanitizers that he has set aside his successful career as a Boca Raton, Florida, dentist in order to devote his life, not only to warning the public about them, but to marketing alternative products.)

7. Chris Seper, "Heavy Hand-washing Could Irritate Skin, Researcher Says," Northeast Ohio Health and Medical Consumer News, Health and Fitness Archive Site, February 19, 2008, retrieved from http://blog.cleveland.com/health/2008/02/soap_and_water_is_said.html, December 10, 2009; and Martha Kerr, "Frequent Hand Washing May Increase Risk for Contact Dermatitis in Healthcare Workers," *MedScape Medical News*, February 6, 2008, retrieved from http://www.medscape.com/viewarticle/569856, September 12, 2011.

8. Charles P. Gerba, Ph.D., quoted in Andrew Weil, "Ask Dr. Weil: Where Are the Germs?," retrieved from http://www.drweil.com/drw/u/QAA400573/Where-Are-the-Germs.html, April 4, 2011.

9. Keith Redway and Shameem Fawdar, "A Comparative Study of Three Different Hand Drying Methods: Paper Towel, Warm Air Dryer, Jet Air Dryer," European Tissue Symposium, November, 2008, retrieved from http://www.europeantissue.com/pdfs/090402-2008%20WUS%20Westminster%20University%20hygiene%20study,%20nov2008.pdf, April 17, 2011.

10. Wendy Marston, "Scientist at Work: Charles Gerba; On Germ Patrol, at the Kitchen Sink," *New York Times*, February 23, 1999, retrieved from http://www.nytimes.com/1999/02/23/health/scientist-at-work-charles-gerba-on-germ-patrol-at-the-kitchen-sink.html?pagewanted=2, July 3, 2010.

11. Angela Haupt, "9 Holiday Health Hazards to Avoid," *U.S. News & World Report,* December 13, 2010, retrieved from http://health.usnews.com/health-news/family-health/living-well/slideshows/9-holiday-health-hazards-to-avoid, March 25, 2011.

12. Dr. Hans Freericks, "Is Your Headache an Early Warning Sign?," Discover Chiropractic website, June 2008, retrieved from http://mydiscoverchiropractic.com/headaches/is-your-headache-an-early-warning-sign, February 20, 2010. (Note: Those who, having read Dr. Freericks's advice, want to consult him directly about their headaches can reach his office at 510-797-4796.)

13. Michael Pollan, "Unhappy Meals," *New York Times Magazine,* January 28, 2007, retrieved from http://michaelpollan.com/articles-archive/unhappy-meals/, August 20, 2011.

14. Gary Wilkes, M.B.B.S., F.A.C.E.M., "Hiccups," *Medscape Reference,* updated July 19, 2010, retrieved from http://emedicine.medscape.com/article/775746-overview, September 11, 2011; and Amanda Schaffer, "A Horrific Case of Hiccups, a Novel Treatment," *New York Times,* January 10, 2006, retrieved from www.nytimes.com/2006/01/10/health/10hicc.html, September 10, 2011.

15. Wilkes, "Hiccups."

16. Gene Weingarten, "Hiccups Can Mean Cancer," excerpted from *The Hypochondriac's Guide to Life. And Death.* (New York: Simon & Schuster, 1998), 64–65.

17. D. P. Simpson, M.A., *Cassell's Latin Dictionary* (New York: Macmillan, 1977).

18. Sarah Klein, "Fatty Foods May Cause Cocaine-like Addiction," Health.com, posted on CNN Health, March 30, 2010, retrieved from http://www.cnn.com/2010/HEALTH/03/28/fatty.foods.brain/index.html, August 24, 2011; Paul M. Johnson and Paul J. Kenny, Ph.D., "Dopamine D2 Receptors in Addiction-like Reward Dysfunction and Compulsive Eating in Obese Rats," *Nature Neuroscience* 13:5, 635–641, published online March 28, 2010, abstract retrieved from http://www.nature.com/neuro/journal/v13/n5/full/nn.2519.html, August 25, 2011; and Jeff Ostrowski, "Scripps Florida: Addicted Rats 'Starved Themselves' Rather Than Give Up Junk Food in Study," *Palm Beach Post*, March 29, 2010, retrieved from http://

www.palmbeachpost.com/health/scripps-florida-addicted-rats-starved-themselves-rather -than-470310.html, August 24, 2011.

19. Kim Severson, "Sugar Coated: We're Drowning in High Fructose Corn Syrup. Do the Risks Go Beyond Our Waistline?," *San Francisco Chronicle,* February 18, 2004, retrieved from http://www.news.ucdavis.edu/in_the_news/full_text/view_clip.lasso?id=7519, July 16, 2011.

20. Kate Hopkins, "The Accidental Hedonist's Guide to Foods and Products Containing High Fructose Corn Syrup (HFCS)," Accidental Hedonist, June 1, 2008, retrieved from http:// www.accidentalhedonist.com/index.php/2005/06/09/foods_and_products_containing _high_fruct, July 16, 2011.

21. Michael Pollan, "When a Crop Becomes King," *New York Times,* July 19, 2002, retrieved from http://michaelpollan.com/articles-archive/when-a-crop-becomes-king/, July 16, 2011.

22. Gary Taubes, "Is Sugar Toxic?," *New York Times Magazine,* April 17, 2011, MM47, retrieved from http://www.nytimes.com/2011/04/17/magazine/mag-17Sugar-t.html?pagewanted=all, July 15, 2011.

23. Pollan, "When a Crop Becomes King."

24. Larissa Phillips, MothershipMeals.blogspot.com, quoted in Matthew McDermott, "Don't Eat High Fructose Corn Syrup? You're Both Snobby and a Racist," Treehugger.com, October 20, 2008, retrieved from http://www.treehugger.com/files/2008/10/avoid-high-fructose-corn -syrup-you-are-snobby-racists.php, July 16, 2011.

25. "ISU Study Finds High Heels May Lead to Joint Degeneration and Knee Osteoarthritis," Iowa State University News Service, July 28, 2010, retrieved from http://www.news.iastate.edu /news/2010/jul/highheels, July 23, 2011.

26. Neal N. Blitz, D.P.M., F.A.C.F.A.S, "Are High Heels *Really* Bad For Your Feet?," AOL Healthy Living, May 31, 2011, retrieved from http://www.huffingtonpost.com/neal-m-blitz/high -heels-dangers_b_868646.html, July 23, 2011.

27. Peta Bee, "Are Flat Shoes Bad for You," *Guardian,* May 5, 2008, retrieved from http://www .guardian.co.uk/lifeandstyle/2008/may/05/fashion.fitness, July 23, 2011.

28. Tsung-Ming Lee, M.D., F.E.S.C., Sheng-Fang Su, Ph.D., Ming-Fong Chen, M.D., Ph.D., F.A.C.C., F.E.S.C., and Chang-Her Tsai, M.D., Ph.D., "Acute Effects of Urinary Bladder Distention on the Coronary Circulation in Patients with Early Atherosclerosis," *Journal of the American College of Cardiology* 36:2 (August 2000), 453–460, retrieved from http://content .onlinejacc.org/cgi/content/full/36/2/453, January 25, 2012.

29. Adam Campbell and Brian Good, "100 Ways to Protect Your Heart," *Men's Health,* retrieved from http://www.menshealth.com/spotlight/heart/100-ways-to-live-forever.php, January 26, 2012.

30. Anthony Bourdain, *Kitchen Confidential: Adventures in the Culinary Underbelly* (New York: Bloomsbury, 2000), quoted in Allison Janse with Charles P. Gerba, Ph.D., *The Germ Freak's Guide to Outwitting Colds and Flu* (Deerfield Beach, FL: Health Communications, Inc., 2005), 119.

31. Anne Marie Helmenstine, Ph.D., "Poisonous Holiday Plants," About.com, retrieved from http://chemistry.about.com/od/toxicchemicals/tp/poisonous-holiday-plants.htm, March 30, 2011.

32. David B. Ryan, "Top 10 Worst Foods for Kids to Eat," retrieved from http://www.livestrong .com/article/70149-top-worst-foods-kids-eat/, April 23, 2011.

33. "What's Wrong with Hot Dogs?," Cancer Prevention Coalition, School of Public Health, University of Illinois at Chicago, 2003, retrieved from http://www.preventcancer.com/con sumers/food/hotdogs.htm, April 23, 2011.

34. Mike Adams, "Choking on Hot Dogs? It's Not the Shape, It's the Ingredients," NaturalNews. com, February 24, 2010, retrieved from http://www.naturalnews.com/028243_hot_dogs _choking.html, April 23, 2011.

35. Kassidy Emmerson, "The Hidden Dangers of Hot Tubs," retrieved from http://www.associated content.com/article/79928/the_hidden_dangers_of_hot_tubs.html?cat=5, June 5, 2010.

36. Marc Roth, "If You Don't Buy a House Now, You're Stupid or Broke," *Bloomberg Businessweek,* December 8, 2009, retrieved from http://www.businessweek.com/lifestyle/content /dec2009/bw2009127_753974.htm, February 20, 2011. (Incidentally, author Roth is the founder and president of Home Warranty of America, which, as *Businessweek* points out, "touches just about every part of the real estate industry since it sells through builders, real estate agents, title companies, mortgage companies, and directly to consumers." Hence, if you decide to follow Mr. Roth's advice, he's a logical person to help make your dream a reality.)

345

37. Jon Hilsenrath, "Fed Economist: Housing Is a Lousy Investment," Real Time Economics (a *Wall Street Journal* blog), January 5, 2010, retrieved from http://blogs.wsj.com/econom ics/2010/01/05/fed-economist-housing-is-a-lousy-investment/, February 20, 2011.

38. "Hydraulic Fracturing 101," Earthworks, retrieved from http://www.earthworksaction.org /FracingDetails.cfm, August 7, 2011.

39. Nicholas Kusnetz, "Fracking Chemicals Cited in Congressional Report Stay Underground," ProPublica, retrieved from http://www.propublica.org/article/fracking-chemicals-cited-in -congressional-report-stay-underground/single, August 7, 2011.

40. "Preliminary Revised Draft Supplemental Generic Environmental Impact Statement (SGEIS): Horizontal Drilling and High-Volume Hydraulic Fracturing in the Marcellus Shale and Other Low-Permeability Gas Reservoirs," New York State Department of Environmental Conservation, July 2011, retrieved from http://www.dec.ny.gov/energy/75370.html, August 7, 2011.

41. Ian Urbina, "A Tainted Water Well, and Concern There May Be More," *New York Times,* August 4, 2011, A14, retrieved from http://www.nytimes.com/2011/08/04/us/04natgas .html?pagewanted=all, August 7, 2011..

42. National Hydropower Association, cited in "Facts About Hydropower," Wisconsin Valley Improvement Company, retrieved from http://new.wvic.com/index.php?option=com_con tent&task=view&id=7&Itemid=44, June 25, 2011.

43. "Hydroelectric Power Water Use," United States Geologic Survey, February 8, 2011, retrieved from http://ga.water.usgs.gov/edu/wuhy.html, June 25, 2011.

44. "Hydroelectric Power," Alternative Energy website, retrieved from http://www.altenergy.org /renewables/hydroelectric.html, June 25, 2011.

45. "10 Ways Dams Damage Rivers," American Rivers, retrieved from http://www.americanrivers .org/our-work/restoring-rivers/dams/background/10-ways.html, June 25, 2011.

46. "Hydroelectric Power Water Use."

47. Christine Gibson, "Our 10 Greatest Natural Disasters," *American Heritage,* August–September 2006, retrieved from http://www.americanheritage.com/content/our-10-greatest-natural -disasters?page=show, June 25, 2011.

48. Phil McKenna, "Fossil Fuels Are Far Deadlier Than Nuclear Power," *New Scientist,* Issue 2805, March 23, 2011, retrieved from http://www.newscientist.com/article/mg20928053.600 -fossil-fuels-are-far-deadlier-than-nuclear-power.html, June 24, 2011.

49. Occupational Safety and Health Administration, "Occupational Safety and Health Guideline for Hydrogen Peroxide," U.S. Department of Labor, retrieved from http://www.osha.gov /SLTC/healthguidelines/hydrogenperoxide/recognition.html, May 17, 2012.

50. Stuart B. Levy, "Antibacterial Household Products: Cause for Concern," Presentation from the 2000 Emerging Infectious Diseases Conference in Atlanta, Georgia, retrieved from http:// www.cdc.gov/ncidod/eid/vol7no3_supp/levy.htm#11, March 26, 2011.

51. Graham A. W. Rook and John L. Stanford, "Give Us This Day Our Daily Germs," *Immunology Today,* March 1998, abstract retrieved from http://www.ncbi.nlm.nih.gov/pubmed/9540269, March 25, 2011.

I

1. "Fighting Back Against Identity Theft," About Identity Theft, Federal Trade Commission, retrieved from http://www.ftc.gov/bcp/edu/microsites/idtheft/consumers/about-identity -theft.html, July 26, 2011.

2. Glen Vaagen, "Garbage Cans Can Lead to Identity Theft," MyCentralOregon.com., September 27, 2010, retrieved from http://www.mycentraloregon.com/news/index.php, July 26, 2011.

3. "Fighting Back Against Identity Theft."

4. Bart A. Basi and Marcus S. Renwick, "Identity Theft: The New Financial Nightmare," Center for Financial, Legal, and Tax Planning, Inc., 2007, retrieved from http://www.taxplanning .com/identitytheft.html, July 26, 2011.

5. Jim Giles, "Cybercrime Made Easy," *New Scientist,* March 20, 2010, retrieved from http://www .allbusiness.com/government/government-bodies-offices/14207830_1.html, July 26, 2011.

6. "Great Square of Pegasus: Easy to See," EarthSky.com, June 29, 2009, retrieved from http:// earthsky.org/favorite-star-patterns/great-square-of-pegasus-wings-in-sept-equinox, August 2, 2011; and Svetlana Yordanova Tzekova, Hristo Stavrev Stavrev, and Ivan Zhivkov Dimitrov, "Report N: 310 IK Pegasi (HR 8210)," European Southern Observatory, 2004, retrieved from http://www.eso.org/public/outreach/eduoff/cas/cas2004/casreports-2004/rep-310/, August 2, 2011.

7. Jean Tate, "Chandrasekhar Limit," UniverseToday.com, September 21, 2009, retrieved from http://www.universetoday.com/40852/chandrasekhar-limit/, August 2, 2011; and Michael Richmond, "Will a Nearby Supernova Endanger Life on Earth?," December 5, 2009, retrieved from http://www.tass-survey.org/richmond/answers/snrisks.txt, August 2, 2011

8. Eugenie Samuel, "Supernova Poised to Go Off Near Earth," *New Scientist,* May 23, 2002, retrieved from http://www.newscientist.com/article/dn2311-supernova-poised-to-go-off -near-earth.html, August 2, 2011.

9. Richmond, "Will a Nearby Supernova."

10. Samuel, "Supernova Poised to Go Off."

11. Tzekova, et al., "Report N: 310 IK Pegasi."

12. Daniel J. Weiss, "Rep. Fred Upton Eats His Own: Congressman Pushes Vote to Kill His Light Bulb Efficiency Standards," Center for American Progress, July 11, 2011, retrieved from http://www.americanprogress.org/issues/2011/07/light_bulb_standards.html, September 5, 2011.

13. "Compact Fluorescent Lighting," New York State Energy Research and Development Agency (NYSERDA), retrieved from http://www.getenergysmart.org/EEproducts/Lighting/CFL .aspx, September 5, 2011.

14. Louise Story, "Income Inequalities and Financial Crises," *New York Times,* August 22, 2010, WK5, retrieved from http://www.nytimes.com/2010/08/22/weekinreview/22story.html, August 18, 2011.

15. "As Income Gap Balloons, Is It Holding Back Growth?" *All Things Considered,* National Public Radio, July 10, 2011, retrieved from http://www.npr.org/2011/07/10/137744694/as -income-gap-balloons-is-it-holding-back-growth, August 18, 2011.

16. Andrew B. Abel and Ben S. Bernanke, *Macroeconomics,* Fifth Edition (Boston: Addison-Wesley, 2003); N. Gregory Mankiw, *Macroeconomics,* Fifth Edition (New York: Worth Publishers, 2002); and Milton Freidman, "Nobel Lecture: Inflation and Unemployment," *Journal of Political Economy* 85:3 (June 1977), 451–472, retrieved from http://www.hilbertcorpora tion.com.ar/nobellecturemf.pdf, June 12, 2011.

17. "Zimbabwe: A Worthless Currency," *Economist,* July 17, 2008, retrieved from http://www .economist.com/node/11751346?story_id=E1_TTSVTPQG, June 12, 2011; Steve H. Hanke, "New Hyperinflation Index (HHIZ) Puts Zimbabwe Inflation at 89.7 Sextillion Percent," Cato Institute, May 3, 2010, retrieved from http://www.cato.org/zimbabwe, June 12, 2011; and Patrick McGroarty and Farai Mutsaka, "How to Turn 100 Trillion Dollars into Five and Feel Good About It," *Wall Street Journal,* May 11, 2011, retrieved from http://online.wsj.com/article/SB10001424052748703730804576314953091790360 .html?KEYWORDS=Zimbabwe, June 12, 2011.

18. Peter Schiff, interviewed on *RT America,* May 3, 2011, retrieved from http://ronpaulrally .org/2011/06/peter-schiff-on-rt-dollar-could-collapse-this-fall-may-3-2011/, June 13, 2011.

19. Chen Shiyin and Bernard Lo, "U.S. Inflation to Approach Zimbabwe Level, Faber Says," Bloomberg.com, May 27, 2009, retrieved from http://www.bloomberg.com/apps/news?pid =newsarchive&sid=avgZDYM6mTFA, June 13, 2011.

20. Naoki Kagi, Shuji Fujii, Youhei Horiba, Norikazu Namiki, Yoshio Ohtani, Hitoshi Emi, Hajime Tamura, and Yong Shik Kim, "Indoor Air Quality for Chemical and Ultrafine Particle Contaminants from Printers," *Building and Environment* 42:5 (2007), 1949–1954, abstract retrieved from http://www.sciencedirect.com/science?_ob=ArticleURL& _udi=B6V23-4MFJJ3G-1&_user=10&_coverDate=05%2F31%2F2007&_rdoc=1&_fmt =high&_orig=gateway&_origin=gateway&_sort=d&_docanchor=&view=c&_search StrId=1703164566&_rerunOrigin=google&_acct=C000050221&_version=1&_urlVer sion=0&_userid=10&md5=ad7051117b1ff400cf48ddd2000febbd&searchtype=a, April 2, 2011.

21. "4-Methyl-2-pentanol: Identification, Toxicity, Use, Water Pollution Potential, Ecological Toxicity and Regulatory Information," PAN Pesticides Database, Pesticide Action Network, retrieved from http://www.pesticideinfo.org/Detail_Chemical.jsp?Rec_Id=PC38071 #Symptoms, April 2, 2011.

22. Peter Schiff, commentary on *The Peter Schiff Show,* December 17, 2008, retrieved from http:// www.youtube.com/watch?v=gapZx0bJiRU, April 2, 2011.

23. Brian O'Keefe, "Peter Schiff: Oh, He Saw It Coming," *Fortune Investor Daily,* January 23, 2009, retrieved from http://money.cnn.com/2009/01/20/magazines/fortune/okeefe_schiff.for tune/index.htm, April 2, 2011.

24. Peter Schiff, interviewed by Gregg Greenberg on *TheStreetTV*, October 1, 2009, retrieved from http://www.thestreet.com/video/10605794/schiff-says-buy-foreign-stocks-gold.html #42951588001, April 2, 2011.

25. Peter Schiff, commentary on *The Peter Schiff Show*.

26. Christine Benz, "Bogle: Why I Don't Invest Overseas," Morningstar.com, October 15, 2010, retrieved from http://www.morningstar.com/cover/videoCenter.aspx?id=355647, January 30, 2011.

27. "Is Ipecac Syrup Always the Best Remedy?," WebMD, May 29, 2000, retrieved from http://www.medicinenet.com/script/main/art.asp?articlekey=51587, March 30, 2011.

28. Anahad O'Connor, "The Claim: Holly and Its Decorative Berries Can be Deadly," *New York Times*, December 22, 2008, retrieved from http://www.nytimes.com/2008/12/23/health/23real.html, March 30, 2011.

29. American Academy of Pediatrics Committee on Injury, Violence, and Poison Prevention, "Poison Treatment in the Home," *Pediatrics* 112:5 (November 2003), 1182–1185, retrieved from http://pediatrics.aappublications.org/content/112/5/1182.full, March 30, 2011.

J

1. Roni Caryn Rabin, "Perhaps July's Reputation Is Justified," *New York Times*, July 12, 2011, D6, retrieved from http://www.nytimes.com/2011/07/12/health/research/12risks.html, July 14, 2011; and Dr. John Q. Young, et al., " 'July Effect': Impact of the Academic Year-End Changeover on Patient Outcomes. A Systematic Review," *Annals of Internal Medicine*, retrieved from http://www.annals.org/content/early/2011/07/11/0003-4819-155-5-201109060-00354.full, July 14, 2011.

2. "Deaths Up, Care Levels Down, at Teaching Hospitals in July," HealthDay, Medicine Plus, U.S. National Library of Medicine, National Institutes of Health, July 11, 2011, retrieved from http://www.nlm.nih.gov/medlineplus/news/fullstory_114159.html, July 14, 2011.

3. Rabin, "Perhaps July's Reputation."

K

1. The Editors of *Prevention* magazine, *List Maker's Get-Healthy Guide: Top To-Dos for an Even Better You!* (New York: Rodale Books, 2010), excerpted in "7 Germiest Places," ABCNews.com, February 20, 2011, retrieved from http://abcnews.go.com/Health/Wellness/germiest-public-places/story?id=12952188, July 3, 2011.

2. *Consumer Reports*, August 2007.

3. Kate Murphy, "What's Lurking in Your Countertop?," *New York Times*, July 24, 2008, retrieved from http://www.nytimes.com/2008/07/24/garden/24granite.html?pagewanted=1, March 26, 2011.

4. "Granite Countertops A Health Threat?," CBS News.com, July 25, 2008, retrieved from http://www.cbsnews.com/stories/2008/07/25/earlyshow/health/main4292754.shtml, March 26, 2011.

5. Murphy, "What's Lurking."

6. Susan Ferraro, "Invisible Critters on Your Counters," *Daily News* (New York), November 1, 1998, retrieved from http://articles.nydailynews.com/1998-11-01/news/18076613_1_charles-gerba-bacteria-coli, June 26, 2011.

7. Cullen Murphy, "Something in the Water," *Atlantic*, September 1997, retrieved from http://www.theatlantic.com/past/docs/issues/97sep/water.htm, June 26, 2011.

8. Charles P. Gerba, Ph.D., cited in James Young, "What Types of Bacteria Are Found in Wet Sinks," eHow.com, December 30, 2010, retrieved from http://www.ehow.com/list_7710297_types-bacteria-found-wet-sinks.html, June 25, 2012.

9. Philip M. Tierno, Jr., Ph.D., quoted in "The Germiest Places in America," Health.com, March 12, 2008, retrieved from http://www.health.com/health/article/0,,20410740,00.html, June 25, 2011.

10. Cheryl L. Mudd, quoted in "The Germiest Places in America."

11. Allison Janse with Charles P. Gerba, Ph.D., *The Germ Freak's Guide to Outwitting Colds and Flu* (Deerfield Beach, FL: Health Communication, Inc., 2005), 24.

12. "Cat Litter," Oak Ridge Associated Universities, January 20, 2009, retrieved from http://www.orau.org/ptp/collection/consumer%20products/catlitter.htm, August 22, 2011.

13. *Health Risks from Exposure to Low Levels of Ionizing Radiation, BEIR VII, Phase 2*, National Research Council, U.S. National Academy of Sciences, 2005, cited in Helen Caldicott, M.D.,

"Nuclear Apologists Play Shoot the Messenger on Radiation," *National Times,* TheAge.com, April 26, 2011, retrieved from http://www.theage.com.au/opinion/society-and-culture /nuclear-apologists-play-shoot-the-messenger-on-radiation-20110425-1du2w.html, August 22, 2011.

14. Sean Howard, "Nanotechnology and Mass Destruction: The Need for an Inner Space Treaty," *Disarmament Diplomacy,* Issue 65, August 2002, retrieved from http://www.acronym.org.uk /dd/dd65/65op1.htm, April 6, 2011.

15. Ray Kurzweil, *The Age of Spiritual Machines: When Computers Exceed Human Intelligence* (New York: Viking Penguin, 1999), 142.

L

1. "Debris Flows, Mudflows, Jökulhlaups, and Lahars," U.S. Geological Survey/Cascades Volcano Observatory, Vancouver, Washington, retrieved from http://vulcan.wr.usgs.gov /Glossary/Lahars/description_lahars.html, June 20, 2011; and C. Driedger, A. Doherty, and C. Dixon (Project Coordinators), *Living with a Volcano in Your Backyard,* U.S. Geological Survey and National Park Service, General Information Product 19, Chapter 2: "Lahar in a Jar," updated September 13, 2010, retrieved from http://vulcan.wr.usgs.gov/Outreach/Pub lications/GIP19/chapter_two_lahar_in_a_jar.pdf, June 18, 2011.

2. Jessica Kowal, "Residents, Experts Eye 'Volcano in Back Yard,'" *Chicago Tribune,* August 24, 2003, retrieved from http://articles.chicagotribune.com/2003-08-24/news/0308240409_1 _rainier-dangerous-volcano-lahar, June 18, 2011.

3. John W. Ewert, Marianne Guffanti, and Thomas L. Murray, "An Assessment of Volcanic Threat and Monitoring Capabilities in the United States: Framework for a National Volcano Early Warning System," U.S. Geological Survey, April 2005, retrieved from http://pubs.usgs.gov /of/2005/1164/2005-1164.pdf, June 20, 2011.

4. Dan Dzurisin, quoted in Jim Gorman, "5 Natural Disasters Headed for the United States," *Popular Mechanics,* September 6, 2006, retrieved from http://www.popularmechanics.com /science/environment/natural-disasters/3852052?click=main_sr, June 18, 2011.

5. Dennis Overbye, "Gauging a Collider's Odds of Creating a Black Hole," *New York Times,* April 15, 2008, F2; Keith Hassett, "Atom Smasher Exposes Hole in Earth's Defenses," Bloomberg News, January 10, 2010, retrieved from http://www.bloomberg.com/news/2010-01-10 /atom-smasher-exposes-hole-in-earth-s-defenses-kevin-hassett.html, May 15, 2011; Maarten Keulemans, "Sorry! Er . . . I Think I Messed Up the Universe a Bit," *Exit Mundi,* retrieved from http://www.exitmundi.nl/vacuum.htm, May 14, 2011; LCH Safety Assessment Group, "Review of the Safety of LHC Collisions," European Organization for Nuclear Research (CERN), September 5, 2008, retrieved from http://lsag.web.cern.ch/lsag/LSAG-Report.pdf, May 15, 2011; and Dennis Overbye, "The Collider, the Particle and a Theory About Fate," *New York Times,* October 13, 2009, D1.

6. "Under Suspicion: Emissions of Laser Printers" and "A Global Problem: Toner Dust and Emissions of Laser Printers and Copying Machines," nano-Control, retrieved from http:// www.krank-durch-toner.de/english.html, April 1, 2011.

7. "How to Minimize the Risk of a Child Choking," Childcare Network, retrieved from http:// www.childcarenetwork.net/Family-Forums/how-to-minimize-the-risk-of-a-child-choking .html, September 4, 2011.

8. "The Germiest Places in America," Health.com, March 12, 2008, retrieved from http://www .health.com/health/article/0,,20410740_6,00.html, June 5, 2011.

9. Charles P. Gerba, Ph.D., quoted in Kim Carollo, "Dirty Laundry? How Nasty Germs Survive in Your Washer," ABC News OnCall + Wellness Center, May 27, 1910, retrieved from http://abcnews.go.com/Health/Wellness/washing-machines-loaded-bacteria-dirty-clothes /story?id=10751420, June 5, 2011.

10. "The Germiest Places in America."

11. Linda Cobb, "The Germiest Places You Will Ever Visit," *Talking Dirty with the Queen of Clean!,* retrieved from http://queenofclean.com/free-stuff/germiest-places/, June 5, 2011.

12. Philip M. Tierno, Jr., Ph.D., *The Secret Life of Germs: Observations and Lessons from a Microbe Hunter* (New York: Pocket Books, 2001), 94; and Philip M. Tierno Jr., Ph.D., quoted in Carollo, "Dirty Laundry."

13. Sarah Klein, Amanda Tian, Jacqlyn Witmer, and Caroline Smith DeWaal, "The FDA Top Ten: The Riskiest Foods Regulated by the U.S. Food and Drug Administration," Center for Science in the Public Interest, October 6, 2009, retrieved from http://www.cspinet.org/new /200910061.html, April 2, 2011.

14. Anne LaGrange Loving and John Perz, "Microbial Flora on Restaurant Beverage Lemon Slices," *Journal of Environmental Health,* December 1, 2007, retrieved from http://www.thefreelibrary.com/Microbial+flora+on+restaurant+beverage+lemon+slices.-a0172839589, May 28, 2011.

15. Anne LaGrange Loving, quoted in Frank Ellis, "Lemon with Your Drink? Restaurant Lemons Are Loaded with Germs," *Outlook,* Arizona Environmental Health Association, December 2007, retrieved from http://www.azeha.org/Dec07Newsletter.pdf, May 29, 2011.

16. Heather Loeb, "Where the Bugs Are," *Men's Health,* May 2008, 96.

17. Loving and Perz, "Microbial Flora."

18. Dennis DiClaudio, *The Hypochondriac's Pocket Guide to Horrible Diseases You Probably Already Have* (New York: Bloomsbury, 2006), 52–53.

19. "EWG's 2012 Shoppers's Guide to Pesticides in Produce: Executive Summary," Environmental Working Group, 2012, retrieved from http://www.ewg.org/foodnews/summary/. June 24, 2012.

20. Daniel J. Weiss, "Rep. Fred Upton Eats His Own: Congressman Pushes Vote to Kill His Light Bulb Efficiency Standards," Center for American Progress, July 11, 2011, retrieved from http://www.americanprogress.org/issues/2011/07/light_bulb_standards.html, September 5, 2011.

21. Marsha Blackburn, quoted in "Barton Leads Republican Effort to Repeal Light Bulb Ban," Office of Congressman Joe Barton of Texas, January 6, 2011, retrieved from http://joebarton.house.gov/NewsRoom.aspx?FormMode=Detail&ID=634, September 6, 2011.

22. "Caller Defends Rep. Upton and His Stupid Stance on Lightbulbs," transcript, *Rush Limbaugh Show,* November 10, 2010, retrieved from http://www.rushlimbaugh.com/home/daily/site_111010/content/01125109.guest.html, September 6, 2011.

23. Robin Bravender, "Conservatives Burn over Fred Upton's Light Bulb Law," Politico.com, November 12, 2010, retrieved from http://www.politico.com/news/stories/1110/45059.html, September 6, 2011.

24. Weiss, "Rep. Fred Upton Eats."

25. Chris Seper, "Heavy Hand-washing Could Irritate Skin, Researcher Says," Northeast Ohio Health and Medical Consumer News, February 19, 2008, retrieved from http://blog.cleveland.com/health/2008/02/soap_and_water_is_said.html, December 10, 2009; and Martha Kerr, "Frequent Hand Washing May Increase Risk for Contact Dermatitis in Healthcare Workers," *Medscape Medical News,* February 6, 2008, retrieved from http://www.medscape.com/viewarticle/569856, September 12, 2011.

26. *Guide to Less Toxic Products,* Environmental Health Association of Nova Scotia (EHANS), 2004, retrieved from http://lesstoxicguide.ca/index.asp?fetch=personal#lotio, August 30, 2011.

27. Peta Bee, "Are Flat Shoes Bad for You," *Guardian,* May 5, 2008, retrieved from http://www.guardian.co.uk/lifeandstyle/2008/may/05/fashion.fitness, July 23, 2011.

28. Kate Wighton, "Why Heels Are Good for You and Great for Your Sex Life," *Sun,* May 7, 2009, retrieved from http://www.thesun.co.uk/sol/homepage/woman/health/health/article2416005.ece#ixzz1Sw1Lfkrs, July 24, 2011.

29. Bee, "Are Flat Shoes Bad."

M

1. Jennifer Wenger, "Medieval Miracle Workers: Are Maggots Making a Medical Comeback?," *National Institutes of Health Record* 56:15 (July 20, 2004), retrieved from http://nihrecord.od.nih.gov/newsletters/2004/07_20_2004/story01.htm, June 26, 2011; and "Maggot Therapy," *Wikipedia,* June 13, 2011, retrieved from http://en.wikipedia.org/wiki/Maggot_therapy, June 29, 2011.

2. Peta Bee, "Nurse, the Maggots," *Sunday Times* (UK) March 12, 2007, retrieved from http://www.timesonline.co.uk/tol/life_and_style/health/features/article1499049.ece, June 29, 2011.

3. Wenger, "Medieval Miracle Workers."

4. Bee, "Nurse, the Maggots."

5. Rosemary Morgan, "Larval Therapy," *Student BMJ,* British Medical Association, August 2002, retrieved from http://archive.student.bmj.com/issues/02/08/education/271.php, June 26, 2011.

6. Wenger, "Medieval Miracle Workers."

7. Christopher Drew and Verne G. Kopytoff, "Deploying New Tools to Stop the Hackers," *New York Times,* June 18, 2011, B1, retrieved from http://www.nytimes.com/2011/06/18/technology/18security.html, June 26, 2011.

8. *Symantec Internet Security Threat Report—Trends for July–December 2007,* Vol. 13, April

2008, retrieved from http://eval.symantec.com/mktginfo/enterprise/white_papers/b-white paper_internet_security_threat_report_xiii_04-2008.en-us.pdf, June 26, 2011.

9. Drew and Kopytoff, "Deploying New Tools."

10. "Malicious Programs Hit New High," BBC News, February 8, 2008, retrieved from http://news.bbc.co.uk/2/hi/technology/7232752.stm, June 26, 2011.

11. "F-Secure Reports Amount of Malware Grew by 100% During 2007," F-Secure Corporation, December 4, 2007, retrieved from http://www.f-secure.com/en_US/about-us/pressroom/news/2007/fs_news_20071204_1_eng.html, June 26, 2011.

12. "Google Searches Web's Dark Side," BBC News, May 11, 2007, retrieved from http://news.bbc.co.uk/2/hi/technology/6645895.stm, June 26, 2011.

13. Drew and Kopytoff, "Deploying New Tools."

14. "Arkansas at Risk for Major Earthquake?," Associated Press, January 21, 2009, retrieved February 27, 2010, from cbsnews.com, http://www.cbsnews.com/stories/2009/01/21/tech/main4745993.shtml.

15. Carol Barczac, "The Hazards of Cosmetics," *AEHA Quarterly*, Summer 1995, Environmental Health Association of Nova Scotia (formerly the Nova Scotia Allergy and Environmental Health Association), retrieved from http://www.environmentalhealth.ca/summer95cosmetic.html, June 22, 1995.

16. Marina Hanes, "Eco-friendly Mascara Tips from Application to Removal," October 26, 2009, retrieved from http://www.aboutmyplanet.com/daily-green-tips/eco-friendly-mascara/, June 29, 2011.

17. Joby Warrick, "Mass Extinction Underway, Majority of Biologists Say," *Washington Post*, April 21, 1998, A4.

18. Richard Leakey and Roger Lewin, *The Sixth Extinction: Patterns of Life and the Future of Humankind* (New York: Doubleday, 1995).

19. "Official Statement on Current Mass Extinction," American Museum of Natural History, Center for Biodiversity and Conservation, May 30, 1998, retrieved from http://www.amnh.org/museum/press/feature/biofact.html, April 15, 2011.

20. Matthew Knight, "U.N. Report: Eco-systems at 'Tipping Point,'" CNN, May 10, 2010, retrieved from http://www.cnn.com/2010/WORLD/americas/05/10/biodiversity.loss.report/index.html, April 15, 2011.

21. Paul Ehrlich, quoted in "Hall of Biodiversity: The Sixth Extinction," American Museum of Natural History, retrieved from http://www.amnh.org/exhibitions/hall_tour/extinct.html, April 15, 2011.

22. Michael Specter, "Annals of Science: Test-Tube Burgers," *New Yorker*, May 23, 2011, 32.

23. "Toward a Healthy, Sustainable Food System," American Public Health Association, November 6, 2007, retrieved from http://www.apha.org/advocacy/policy/policysearch/default.htm?id=1361, June 18, 2011.

24. Specter, "Test-Tube Burgers."

25. "Does Eating Meat Really Cause Impotence?," People for the Ethical Treatment of Animals, retrieved from http://www.peta.org/about/faq/Does-eating-meat-really-cause-impotence.aspx, June 30, 2011.

26. Peter Ward, *The Medea Hypothesis: Is Life on Earth Ultimately Self-Destructive?* (Princeton: Princeton University Press, 2009); Peter Ward, "Gaia's Evil Twin: Is Life Its Own Worst Enemy?," *New Scientist*, June 17, 2009, retrieved from http://www.newscientist.com/article/mg20227131.400-gaias-evil-twin-is-life-its-own-worst-enemy.html, May 24, 2011; and Jascha Hoffman, "Killer Earth," *New York Times Magazine*, December 13, 2009, 49.

27. "To Err Is Human: Building a Safer Health Care System," Institute of Medicine, National Academy Press, November 1, 1999; Lucian L. Leape, "Error in Medicine," *Journal of the American Medical Association*. 272:23 (1994), 1851–1857, December 21, 1994.

28. Jessie Knadler, "The 16 Worst Places to Stash Your Stuff," *Prevention*, March 28, 2008, retrieved from http://today.msnbc.msn.com/id/23727879/ns/today-today_health/t/worst-places-stash-your-stuff/, July 7, 2011.

29. J. L. Craven, "Meditation and Psychotherapy," *Canadian Journal of Psychiatry* 34:7 (October 1989), 648–653, PubMed Abstract PMID 2680046, retrieved from http://www.ncbi.nlm.nih.gov/pubmed/2680046, May 31, 2012.

30. D. H. Shapiro Jr., "Adverse Effects of Meditation: A Preliminary Investigation of Long-term Meditators," *International Journal of Psychosomatics* 39:1–4 (1992), 62–67, PubMed Abstract PMID 1428622, retrieved from http://www.ncbi.nlm.nih.gov/pubmed?term=1428622, May 31, 2012.

31. American Psychiatric Association, *Diagnostic and Statistical Manual of Mental Disorders: DSM-IV*, (1994) Appendix I: "Glossary of Culture-bound Syndromes."

32. The Editors of *Prevention* Magazine, *List Maker's Get-Healthy Guide: Top To-Dos for an Even Better You*! (New York: Rodale Books, 2010), excerpted in "7 Germiest Places," ABCNews.com, February 20, 2011, retrieved from http://abcnews.go.com/Health/Wellness/germiest-public-places/story?id=12952188, July 3, 2011.

33. Allison Janse with Charles P. Gerba, Ph.D., *The Germ Freak's Guide to Outwitting Colds and Flu* (Deerfield Beach, FL: Health Communications, Inc., 2005), 75.

34. "Cooking Safely in the Microwave Oven," Food Safety and Inspection Service, U.S. Department of Agriculture, May 24, 2011, retrieved from http://www.fsis.usda.gov/fact_sheets/Cooking_Safely_in_the_Microwave/index.asp, August 7, 2011; and "Microwave Ovens and Food Safety," *Fact Sheets: Appliances & Thermometers*, Food Safety and Inspection Service, U.S. Department of Agriculture, May 24, 2011, retrieved from http://www.fsis.usda.gov/fact sheets/microwave_ovens_and_food_safety/index.asp. August 7, 2011.

35. "Recommended Safe Cooking Temperatures," *Food, Drugs and Dairies*, Illinois Department of Public Health, retrieved from http://www.idph.state.il.us/about/fdd/safecooktemp.htm, August 7, 2011.

36. "Microwave Oven Radiation," U.S. Food and Drug Administration, April 26, 2011, retrieved from http://www.fda.gov/Radiation-EmittingProducts/ResourcesforYouRadiationEmittingProducts/ucm252762.htm, August 7, 2011.

37. "What Causes Microwave Ovens to Leak?," Professional Laboratories, Inc., retrieved from http://www.prolabinc.com/microwave_leak_detector.asp, August 7, 2011.

38. "Pro-Lab Products: Microwave Oven Leakage Detector," Professional Laboratories, Inc., retrieved from http://www.prolabinc.com/products.asp. August 7, 2011.

39. "Pro-Lab Microwave Oven Leakage Detector," HealthHomeTest.com, retrieved from http://www.healthhometest.com/product_info.php?products_id=174, August 7, 2011.

40. "Microwave Oven Leakage Detector Instructions," Professional Laboratories, Inc., retrieved from http://www.prolabinc.com/instructions/detecto.html, August 7, 2011.

41. Liz Vaccariello, "The 7 Foods Experts Won't Eat," *Prevention*, November 26, 2009, retrieved from http://www.prevention.com/cda/expertblog/news.voices/faces.of.prevention?plckController=Blog&plckScript=blogScript&plckElementId=blogDest&plckBlogPage=BlogViewPost&plckPostId=Blog%3A6e8f19ea-6832-4839-b71e-62608af9b2d8Post%3A8c8413e2-61fd-40de-a549-9603f4a09c01, August 25, 2011.

42. Anne Marie Helmenstine, Ph.D., "Poisonous Holiday Plants," About.com, retrieved from http://chemistry.about.com/od/toxichemicals/tp/poisonous-holiday-plants.htm, March 30, 2011.

43. Dr. Tim Sly, quoted in "Staying Festively Flu-free," *Ryerson University News and Events*, November 25, 2010, retrieved from http://www.ryerson.ca/news/media/spotlight/holiday2010/index.html, March 30, 2011.

44. Anna Maria Andriotis and Aleksandra Todorova, "Can You Catch Swine Flue from Money?," SmartMoney.com, retrieved from http://www.smartmoney.com/spending/travel/can-you-catch-swine-flu-from-money/#ixzz1HaJdG4f9, March 24, 2011.

45. Nagesh Bhat, Surekha Bhat, Kailash Asawa, and Anil Agarwal, "An Assessment of Oral Health Risk Associated with Handling of Currency Notes," *International Journal of Dental Clinics* 2:3 (July–September 2010), retrieved from http://www.intjdc.com/index.php/intjdc/article/view/18, March 26, 2011.

46. Frances Largeman-Roth, cited in "Could Your Purse Be Making You Sick?," Today Health, MSNBC.com, retrieved from http://today.msnbc.msn.com/id/21423163/ns/today-today_health/, March 26, 2011.

47. Andriotis and Todorova, "Can You Catch Swine Flu."

48. Brian Handwerk, "Rainier Eruption Odds Low, Impact High, Expert Says," *National Geographic* News, September 25, 2003, retrieved from http://news.nationalgeographic.com/news/2003/09/0924_030925_mtrainiereruption.html. June 19, 2011.

49. *Mega Disasters: American Volcano*, History Channel, June 13, 2006, retrieved from http://www.history.com/videos/mega-disasters-american-volcano, June 19, 2011.

50. "Pierce County Volcanic Hazard," *Pierce County Natural Hazard Mitigation Plan*, Pierce County, Washington, November 2008, retrieved from http://www.co.pierce.wa.us/xml/abtus/ourorg/dem/EMDiv/MP/PC%20Volcanic.pdf, June 19, 2011.

51. *Mega Disasters: American Volcano*.

52. Frank Parchman, "The Super Flood," *Seattle Weekly*, October 19, 2005, retrieved from http://www.seattleweekly.com/2005-10-19/news/the-super-flood/, June 19, 2011.

53. *Mega Disasters: American Volcano.*
54. Micah Fink, "Mount Rainier: America's Most Dangerous Volcano," Savage Planet, retrieved from http://www.pbs.org/wnet/savageplanet/01volcano/03/indexmid.html, June 19, 2011.
55. "Aggressive Fungus Strikes Joplin Tornado Victims," Associated Press, June 10, 2011, retrieved from http://www.carthagepress.com/joplin-tornado/x41284196/Aggressive-fungus-strikes -Joplin-tornado-victims, August 2, 2011; and Timothy Williams, "Rare Infection Strikes Victims of a Tornado in Missouri," *New York Times,* June 11, 2011, page A12, retrieved from http:// www.nytimes.com/2011/06/11/us/11fungus.html?_r=3&ref=health, August 2, 2011.
56. Williams, "Rare Infection."
57. "Mucormycosis (Zygomycosis): Prevention," Centers for Disease Control and Prevention, July 28, 2011, retrieved from http://www.cdc.gov/fungal/mucormycosis/risk-prevention .html, August 1, 2011.
58. Anthony Bourdain, *Kitchen Confidential: Adventures in the Culinary Underbelly* (New York: Bloomsbury, 2000), quoted in Allison Janse with Charles P. Gerba, Ph.D., *The Germ Freak's Guide to Outwitting Colds and Flu* (Deerfield Beach, FL: Health Communications, Inc., 2005), 119.
59. Retrieved from http://www.fool.com/investing/mutual-funds/2010/08/16/this-invest ment-will-sink-your-portfolio.aspx. January 30, 2011.

N

1. "Manicure Mishaps—How Safe Is Your Nail Salon?," Lifescript.com, June 7, 2005, retrieved from http://www.lifescript.com/Body/Looks/Fix-its/Manicure_Mishaps_-_How_Safe _is_Your_Nail_Salon.aspx, March 29, 2011; Jacqueline Metcalfe, "How Clean Is Your Nail Salon?," Lifescript.com, April 2, 2007, retrieved from http://www.lifescript.com/Body/Looks /Fix-its/Risky_Business_How_Clean_is_Your_Nail_Salon.aspx, March 29, 2011.
2. Paul Joseph Watson, "Nanny State Betrays Decline and Fall of America," Alex Jones' Prison Planet, May 31, 2011, retrieved from http://www.prisonplanet.com/nanny-state-betrays -decline-and-fall-of-america.html, July 22, 2011.
3. Art Carden, "Life, Liberty and the Pursuit of Fatty Foods," Forbes.com, March 4, 2010, retrieved from http://www.forbes.com/2010/03/03/trans-fat-regulation-government-opin ions-contributors-art-carden.html, July 22, 2010.
4. David Harsanyi, *Nanny State: How Food Fascists, Teetotaling Do-Gooders, Priggish Moralists, and Other Boneheaded Bureaucrats Are Turning America into a Nation of Children* (New York: Broadway Books, 2007), 18.
5. Ibid, 11.
6. C. Teng, R. Gurses-Ozden, J. M. Liebmann, C. Tello, and R. Ritch, "Effect of a Tight Necktie on Intraocular Pressure," *British Journal of Opthalmology* 87:8 (August 2003), 946–948, abstract retrieved from http://bjo.bmj.com/content/87/8/946, May 8, 2011.
7. Mark Rafferty, Terence J. Quinn, Jesse Dawson, and Matthew Walters, "Neckties and Cerebrovascular Reactivity in Young Healthy Males: A Pilot Randomised Crossover Trial," Institute of Cardiovascular and Medical Sciences, College of Medical and Life Sciences, University of Glasgow, October 20, 2010, retrieved from http://www.sage-hindawi.com/journals/srt /2011/692595/abs/, May 7, 2011.
8. "Tight Neckties 'Increase Stroke, Glaucoma Risk,'" *Chosun Ilbo,* June 18, 2009, retrieved from http://english.chosun.com/site/data/html_dir/2009/06/18/2009061800856.html, May 7, 2011.
9. Tae-Sub Chung, M.D., quoted in "Tight Neckties 'Increase Stroke, Glaucoma Risk.'"
10. Karla Gale, "Physicians' Neckties May Harbor Bacteria," Reuters Health, May 24, 2004, retrieved from http://forums.studentdoctor.net/archive/index.php/t-124401.html, June 9, 2011.
11. Alex Berry, "Tie Ban for Doctors to Stop Spread of MRSA," *Telegraph,* December 18, 2006, retrieved from http://www.telegraph.co.uk/news/uknews/1537202/Tie-ban-for-doctors-to -stop-spread-of-MRSA.html, June 9, 2011.
12. Rick Karlin, "Your Doctor's Outfit Can Make You Sick," Capitol Confidential blog, *Albany Times Union,* May 3, 2011, retrieved from http://blog.timesunion.com/capitol/ar chives/66079/your-doctors-outfit-can-make-you-sick/, June 9, 2011.
13. Robert Roy Britt, "New Data Confirms Strong Earthquake Risk to Central U.S.," Live Science, posted June 22, 2005, retrieved from http://www.livescience.com/environment/050622 _new_madrid.html, June 5, 2010.
14. Ibid.

15. United States Federal Emergency Management Agency, "New Study Examines Impact of 7.7 Magnitude Earthquake on States in New Madrid Seismic Zone," November 20, 2008, retrieved from http://www.fema.gov/news/newsrelease.fema?id=46853, June 5, 2010.

16. New Smyrna Beach Florida Visitors Bureau website home page, retrieved from http://www.nsbfla.com/, April 8, 2011.

17. Richard Luscombe, "Surge in Fatal Shark Attacks Blamed on Global Warming," *Observer,* May 4, 2008, retrieved from http://www.howstuffworks.com/framed.htm?parent=fish/dangerous-place-shark-attack.htm&url=http://www.guardian.co.uk/environment/2008/may/04/wildlife.climatechange, April 8, 2011.

18. Stephen Regenold, "North America's Top Shark-attack Beaches," ForbesTraveler.com, April 21, 2008, retrieved from http://www.usatoday.com/travel/news/2008-04-18-shark-beaches-forbes_N.htm, April 9, 2011.

19. Pete Thomas, "Shark Attack Capital of the World, New Smyrna Beach, Fla., to Host Pro Surfing Contest," *Los Angeles Times,* March 10, 2009, retrieved from http://latimesblogs.latimes.com/outposts/2009/03/post-1.html, April 9, 2011.

20. Patrick Moore, "Going Nuclear," *Washington Post,* April 16, 2006, retrieved from http://www.washingtonpost.com/wp-dyn/content/article/2006/04/14/AR2006041401209.html, August 3, 2011.

21. Scott Peterson, "Nuclear Energy: Does It Make Sense for the Environment? YES," *New York Times,* October 10, 2005, retrieved from http://teacher.scholastic.com/scholasticnews/indepth/upfront/debate/index.asp?article=d1010, August 2, 2011.

22. "Comparing Deaths/TWh for All Energy Sources," NextBigFuture, March 13, 2011, retrieved from http://nextbigfuture.com/2011/03/deaths-per-twh-by-energy-source.html, August 3, 2011.

23. Daniel Indiviglio, "Why Are New U.S. Nuclear Reactor Projects Fizzling?," *Atlantic,* February 1, 2011, retrieved from http://www.theatlantic.com/business/archive/2011/02/why-are-new-us-nuclear-reactor-projects-fizzling/70591/, August 3, 2011.

24. Dr. Joseph Romm, "How Did $50B Worth of High-Risk, Job-Killing Nuclear Loans Get into the Stimulus?," Alternet.org, February 11, 2009, retrieved from http://www.alternet.org/environment/126464/how_did_$50b_high-risk_job-killing_nuclear_loans_get_in_the_stimulus_/, August 2, 2011.

25. Kelly Kissock, Ph.D., "Nuclear Energy: Does It Make Sense for the Environment? NO," *New York Times,* October 10, 2005, retrieved from http://teacher.scholastic.com/scholasticnews/indepth/upfront/debate/index.asp?article=d1010, August 2, 2011.

26. Jonathan Schell, "From Hiroshima to Fukushima: Rethinking Atomic Energy," *Nation,* March 15, 2011, retrieved from http://www.thenation.com/article/159238/hiroshima-fukushima, August 3, 2011.

27. "Country Reports on Terrorism 2009," Office of the Coordinator for Counterterrorism, U.S. Department of State, August 5, 2010, retrieved from http://www.state.gov/s/ct/rls/crt/2009/140889.htm, August 3, 2011.

28. Kissock, "Nuclear Energy."

29. Schell, "From Hiroshima to Fukushima."

30. Carl T. Hall, "Studies Bare Health Care Hazards: Catheters, Even Nurses' Fake Nails, Pose Risk of Infection, Experts Say in S.F.," *San Francisco Chronicle,* September 29, 1999, retrieved from http://articles.sfgate.com/1999-09-29/news/17699089_1_california-nurses-associa tion-acrylic-nails-hospital-bed, September 17, 2011; and "Harmful Bacteria Associated with Artificial Acrylic Fingernails: Is Handwashing Enough?," University of Michigan, September 28, 1999, retrieved from http://www.questia.com/googleScholar.qst?docId=5002342661, September 17, 2011.

31. Shelly A. McNeil, M.D., Catherine L. Foster, M.D., Sara A. Hedderwick, M.R.C.P., and Carol A. Kauffman, M.D., "Effect of Hand Cleansing with Antimicrobial Soap or Alcohol-Based Gel on Microbial Colonization of Artificial Fingernails Worn by Health Care Workers," *Clinical Infectious Diseases* 32:3 (February 1, 2001), 367–372, retrieved from http://cid.oxfordjournals.org/content/32/3/367.full, September 17, 2011.

O

1. Nutritional Supplement Educational Centre, "Omega 3 Side Effects," retrieved from http://www.nutritional-supplement-educational-centre.com/omega-3-side-effects.htm, February 21, 2010.

2. Geoffrey Lean, "Oranges Are Not the Safest Fruit—They All Exceed Pesticide Limits," *Indepen-*

dent, December 18, 2005, retrieved from http://www.independent.co.uk/environment/oranges-are-not-the-safest-fruit—they-all-exceed-pesticide-limits-519954.html, June 7, 2010.

3. "Orange Juice Worse for Teeth Than Whitening Agents, Study Finds," Science Daily, July 1, 2009, retrieved from http://www.sciencedaily.com/releases/2009/06/090630132007.htm, December 13, 2009.

4. "Could a Large Tsunami Strike the Oregon Coast?," Oregon Department of Geology and Mineral Industries, December 29, 2004, retrieved from http://www.oregongeology.com/sub/news&events/archives/TsunamiPR.pdf, July 1, 2010.

5. Ibid.

6. Ibid.

7. Lee M. Silver, Ph.D., "Are Organic Food Advocates in Thrall to Mythology Rather Than Science?", letter published in the *Wall Street Journal*, January 29, 2007, retrieved from http://online.wsj.com/article/SB117003142935690677.html, May 31, 2012.

8. Andrew Ellison, "Organic Food Is a Waste of Money," *Times* (London), September 5, 2009, retrieved from www.perubiotec.org/PDFs/Organic_Bogus_TIMESONLINE.pdf, May 30, 2012.

9. Steven Bratman with David Knight, *Health Food Junkies* (New York: Broadway Books, 2001).

10. Steven Bratman, "Fatal Orthorexia," Orthorexia.com, June 3, 2010, retrieved from http://www.orthorexia.com/?page_id=22, March 28, 2011.

11. "Food Safety: Frequently Asked Questions—Acrylamide in Food," World Health Organization, 2011, retrieved from http://www.who.int/foodsafety/publications/chem/acrylamide_faqs/en/index.html, August 13, 2011.

12. Lucy Atkins, "Is Cooked Food Dangerous?" *Guardian*, December 4, 2007, retrieved from http://www.guardian.co.uk/science/2007/dec/04/lifeandhealth.foodanddrink, August 10, 2011.

13. Richard M. LoPachin, Ph.D., and Terrence Gavin, Ph.D., "Acrylamide-Induced Nerve Terminal Damage: Relevance to Neurotoxic and Neurodegenerative Mechanisms," *Journal of Agricultural and Food Chemistry* 56:15, 5994–6003, published online July 15, 2008, abstract retrieved from http://pubs.acs.org/doi/abs/10.1021/jf703745t, August 11, 2011.

14. Marek Naruszewicz, Danuta Zapolska-Downar, Anita Kośmider, Grażyna Nowicka, Małgorzata Kozłowska-Wojciechowska, Anna S. Vikström, and Margareta Törnqvist, "Chronic Intake of Potato Chips in Humans Increases the Production of Reactive Oxygen Radicals by Leukocytes and Increases Plasma C-Reactive Protein: A Pilot Study," *American Journal of Clinical Nutrition* 89:3 (March 2009), 773–777, abstract retrieved from http://www.ajcn.org/content/89/3/773.abstract, August 12, 2011.

15. Cynthia Sass, M.P.H., R.D., "Coffee Warning? What You Need to Know About Acrylamide," *Shape*, retrieved from http://www.shape.com/healthy-eating/coffee-warning-what-you-need-to-know-about-acrylamide, August 11, 2011.

16. "Draft Toxicological Profile for Acrylamide," Agency for Toxic Substances and Disease Registry, Public Health Service, U.S. Department of Health and Human Services, September 2009, 153, retrieved from http://www.atsdr.cdc.gov/toxprofiles/tp203-c6.pdf, August 13, 2011.

17. Nicholas Bakalar, "Women's Cancer Risk Is Linked to Height," *New York Times*, August 2, 2011, D6, retrieved from http://www.nytimes.com/2011/08/02/health/nutrition/02risks.html, August 4, 2011.

18. Jane Green, D. Phil., et al., "Height and Cancer Incidence in the Million Woman Study: Prospective Cohort, and Meta-Analysis of Prospective Studies of Height and Total Cancer Risk," *Lancet Oncology* 12:8 (August 2011), 785–794, abstract retrieved from http://www.thelancet.com/journals/lanonc/article/PIIS1470-2045%2811%2970154-1/abstract, August 4, 2011.

19. Bakalar, "Women's Cancer Risk."

P

1. "Parsley and Other Herbal Dangers," Pregnancy-Info.net, retrieved from http://www.pregnancy-info.net/parsley-and-other-herbal-dangers.html, December 14, 2009.

2. Jim Gorman, "The 10 Dirtiest Foods You're Eating: Peaches," *Men's Health*, retrieved from http://www.menshealth.com/mhlists/foodborne_illness/Peaches.php, August 31, 2011.

3. "Fruits and Veggies to Buy Organic: Peaches," *Prevention*, retrieved from http://www.prevention.com/dirtiestcleanest/3.html, August 31, 2011.

4. Anne Marie Helmenstine, Ph.D., "Yes, Apple Seeds and Cherry Pits are Poisonous," About.com Guide, September 12, 2007, retrieved from http://chemistry.about.com/b/2007/09/12/yes-apple-seeds-and-cherry-pits-are-poisonous.htm, April 4, 2011.

5. "Council Erects Danger Sign: 'Warning Falling Pears,'" *Daily Mail*, October 3, 2006, retrieved from http://www.dailymail.co.uk/news/article-408359/Council-erects-danger-sign-Warning-falling-pears.html, June 6, 2010.

6. "What Are POPs?," International POPs Elimination Network, 2011, retrieved from http://www.ipen.org/ipenweb/generalpublic/whatpops.html, June 8, 2011.

7. "Persistent Organic Pollutants (POPs): Health Effects of POPs," U.S. Environmental Protection Agency, May 6, 2011, retrieved from http://www.clu-in.org/contaminantfocus/default.focus/sec/Persistent_Organic_Pollutants_(POPs)/cat/Health_Effects_of_POPs/, June 8, 2011.

8. "Environmental Pollution and Diabetes May be Linked," University of Cambridge News Centre, January 25, 2008, retrieved from http://www.admin.cam.ac.uk/news/press/dpp/2008012501, June 7, 2011.

9. *POPs: Persistent Organic Pollutants,* United Nations Industrial Development Organization, Vienna, Austria, November 2003, retrieved from http://www.unido.org/fileadmin/import/49004_POPs_Brochure_Final_Version.pdf, June 8, 2011.

10. "What Are POPs?"

11. Julie Scelfo, "Raising Concerns About Chemicals in Recycled Carpet Padding," *New York Times,* May 19, 2011, D2, retrieved from http://www.nytimes.com/2011/05/19/garden/tests-on-carpet-padding-show-toxins.html, June 7, 2011.

12. "POPsible Nightmare," Interview with Dr. David Carpenter, *Living on Earth,* December 15, 2006, retrieved from http://www.loe.org/shows/segments.html?programID=06-P13-00050&segmentID=2, June 8, 2011.

13. "Partial List of Outbreaks of Zoonosis Associated with Fairs and Petting Zoos," *Wikipedia,* retrieved from http://en.wikipedia.org/wiki/Zoonosis, April 8, 2011.

14. "Outbreaks of Escherichia coli O157:H7 Associated with Petting Zoos," *Morbidity and Mortality Weekly Report,* December 23, 2005, retrieved from http://www.cdc.gov/mmwr/preview/mmwrhtml/mm5450a1.htm, April 8, 2011.

15. "Compendium of Measures to Prevent Disease Associated with Animals in Public Settings," National Association of State Public Health Veterinarians, Inc. (NASPHV)," *Morbidity and Mortality Weekly Report,* March 25, 2005, retrieved from http://www.cdc.gov/mmwr/PDF/rr/rr5404.pdf, April 8, 2011.

16. Melissa Breyer, "Battle the Top 10 Germ Hot Spots," Healthy & Green Living, care2.com, March 5, 2009, retrieved from http://www.care2.com/greenliving/battle-the-top-10-germ-hot-spots.html?page=2, May 12, 2011.

17. "How to Disinfect and Clean a Cellphone," how2instructions.com, retrieved from http://www.how2instructions.com/Cleaning/Misc/How_To_Disinfect_and_Clean_A_Cellphone.html, June 2, 2011.

18. Allison Janse with Charles P. Gerba, Ph.D., *The Germ Freak's Guide to Outwitting Colds and Flu* (Deerfield Beach, FL: Health Communications, Inc., 2005), 65.

19. Ibid, 24.

20. "How to Clean Your iPhone or Other Touch Screen Phone," Simply Good Tips, September 30, 2008, retrieved from http://tips.simplygoodstuff.com/how-to-clean-your-iphone-or-other-touch-screen-phone/, August 30, 2011.

21. Philip M. Tierno, Jr., Ph.D., interviewed by Matt Lauer on *Today,* NBC News, January 11, 2006, retrieved from http://www.bing.com/video/watch/video/how-dirty-are-your-pillows/6mt8jh6, May 7, 2011.

22. Courtney Hutchison, " 'Pine Mouth': How Pine Nuts Can Ruin Tastebuds for Weeks," *Good Morning America*'s OnCall+ Wellness Center, July 7, 2010, retrieved from http://abcnews.go.com/Health/Wellness/pine-mouth-pine-nuts-leave-bitter-taste-lingers/story?id=11097222, March 20, 2011.

23. F. Destaillats, C. Cruz-Hernandez, F. Giuffrida, F. Dionisi, M. Mostin, and G. Verstegen, "Identification of the Botanical Origin of Commercial Pine Nuts Responsible for Dysgeusia by Gas-Liquid Chromatography Analysis of Fatty Acid Profile," *Journal of Toxicology* 2011, 2011, retrieved from http://www.hindawi.com/journals/jt/2011/316789/, March 20, 2011.

24. Elizabeth Weise, "Link Between Nuts, 'Pine Mouth Syndrome' Is Hard to Crack," *USA Today,* March 15, 2010, retrieved from http://www.usatoday.com/news/health/2010-03-16-Pinemouth16_ST_N.htm, March 20, 1011.

25. Hutchison, " 'Pine Mouth.' "

26. Anne Marie Helmenstine, Ph.D., "Poisonous Holiday Plants," About.com, retrieved from http://chemistry.about.com/od/toxicchemicals/tp/poisonous-holiday-plants.htm, March 30, 2011.

27. "Polka Pain Relief and Management," Polkaholics.com, 2002, retrieved from http://www.polkaholics.com/polka%20pain.htm, August 9, 2011.
28. Victor R. Greene, *A Passion for Polka: Old-Time Ethnic Music in America* (Berkeley and Los Angeles: University of California Press, 1992), 244, retrieved from http://books.google.com/books?id=bAzGNogQmM4C&pg=PA244, August 9, 2011.
29. "PVC—A Major Source of Phthalates," Office for Prevention of Developmental Disabilities, New Jersey Department of Human Services, retrieved from http://www.nj.gov/humanservices/opmrdd/health/pvc.html, August 5, 2011.
30. Chris Rauber, "Bay Area Companies Join Forces to Phase Out PVC Plastics," *San Francisco Business Times*, December 7, 2005, retrieved from http://www.bizjournals.com/eastbay/stories/2005/12/05/daily25.html, August 5, 2011.
31. "PVC—A Major Source of Phthalates."
32. "PVC: The Poison Plastic—PVC Products in Your Home," Center for Health, Environment and Justice, retrieved from http://www.besafenet.com/pvc/pvcproducts.htm, August 5, 2011.
33. Lois Marie Gibbs, "Keeping the American Promise: Achieve Safer and Healthier Future by Eliminating PVC, the Poison Plastic," in *PVC: The Poison Plastic, Health Hazards and the Looming Waste Crisis*, Center for Health, Environment and Justice, Environmental Health Strategy Center, December 2004, retrieved from http://www.besafenet.com/pvc/documents/bad_news_comes_in_threes.pdf, August 5, 2011.
34. "Great Investors: Philip Fisher: Important Don'ts for Investors," Morningstar.com, retrieved from http://news.morningstar.com/classroom2/course.asp?docId=145662&page=1&CN=com, January 29, 2011.
35. Philip A. Fisher, *Common Stocks and Uncommon Profits* (New York: Harper & Brothers, 1958), 118.
36. "Health and Safety Killjoys Ban Welcome Mats and Pot Plants—Because They're a Fire Risk," *Daily Mail*, June 25, 2009, retrieved from http://www.dailymail.co.uk/news/article-1195522/Flat-tenants-forced-throw-away-welcome-mats-pot-plants-health-safety-risk.html, April 18, 2011.
37. "Watch Out for Flaming Flower Pots," ConsumerReports.org, October 30, 2006, retrieved from http://discussions.consumerreports.org/n/blogs/blog.aspx?webtag=cr-safety&entry=42, April 24, 2011.
38. Nadia Moharib and Shawn Logan, "Massive Millrise Fire Engulfs Condos," *Calgary Sun*, March 18, 2010, retrieved from http://www.calgarysun.com/news/alberta/2010/03/18/13278506.html, April 24, 2011; and "Massive Calgary Condominium Blaze Caused by Potting Soil Catching Fire," CBC News, July 21, 2010, retrieved from http://www.cbc.ca/news/canada/calgary/story/2010/07/21/con-planter-fires.html, April 24, 2011.
39. Barbara Grijalva, "Toting Bacteria," KOLD News 13, Tucson, Arizona, August 22, 2005, retrieved from http://www.kold.com/story/3752986/toting-bacteria?nav=14RTdcr&redirected=true, September 12, 2011.
40. "Purse Protection: Keep Your Purse Clean and Safe," HandbagProtection.com, retrieved from http://www.handbagprotection.com, September 13, 2011.
41. Elisabeth Leamy, "Your Purse Could Be Making You Sick," ABCNews.com, August 8, 2006, retrieved from http://abcnews.go.com/GMA/OnCall/story?id=2283311&page=1, September 13, 2011.
42. "Purse Protection."
43. Mehmet Oz, M.D., cited in Patty Neger and Lara Naaman, "Dr. Oz's Tips on How to Disinfect Everyday Items," ABCNews.com, September 11, 2009, retrieved from http://abcnews.go.com/GMA/BeautySecrets/dr-oz-explains-germs-off-purse-make/story?id=8543211, September 13, 2011.
44. Grijalva, "Toting Bacteria."
45. Melanie Vasseur, "How to Get Rid of Lip and Mouth Wrinkles," Fresh and Ageless Skin blog, March 18, 2011, retrieved from http://freshandagelessblog.com/2011/03/18/how-to-get-rid-of-lip-and-mouth-wrinkles/, May 25, 2011; and "Gold Serum," Vasseur Skincare, retrieved from http://www.vasseurskincare.com/products/Gold-Serum.html, May 25, 2011.

Q

1. Thomas J. Moore, Michael R. Cohen, and Curt D. Furberg, M.D., Ph.D., "Strong Safety Signal Seen for New Varenicline Risks," Institute for Safe Medication Practices, May 21, 2008, retrieved from http://www.ismp.org/docs/vareniclinestudy.asp, July 7, 2011; Stephanie Saul, "F.A.A. Bans Antismoking Drug, Citing Side Effects," *New York Times*, May 22, 2008, retrieved

from http://www.nytimes.com/2008/05/22/business/22drug.html, July 7, 2011; and Duff Wilson, "Study Links Smoking Drug to Cardiovascular Problems," *New York Times,* July 5, 2011, B3, retrieved from http://www.nytimes.com/2011/07/05/business/05smoke.html, July 7, 2011.

2. "Smoking Cessation May Actually Increase Risk of Developing Type 2 Diabetes," Johns Hopkins University School of Medicine, January 4, 2010, retrieved from http://www.hopkins medicine.org/news/media/releases/Smoking_Cessation_May_Actually_Increase_Risk _of_Developing_Type_2_Diabetes, July 8, 2011.

3. Dr. Susan Jebb, "Why a Healthy Weight Is Important," BBC Health, retrieved from http://www .bbc.co.uk/health/treatments/healthy_living/your_weight/whatis_lose.shtml, July 9, 2011.

4. Timothy A. Ferenchick, M.D., "Quit Smoking Timeline: Nicotine Withdrawal Symptoms," CommittoQuitSmoking.com, June 7, 2011, retrieved from http://www.committoquitsmok ing.com/quit-smoking-timeline-nicotine-withdrawal-symptoms/, July 9, 2011; and "Patches, Gum and Other Stop Smoking Medicine," Smokefree, UK Department of Health, 2011, re-trieved from http://smokefree.nhs.uk/ways-to-quit/patches-gum-and-nicotine-replacement -therapy/, July 9, 2011.

5. "Patches, Gum and Other Stop Smoking Medicine."

6. Allen Carr, quoted in "Nicotine Patches Report," LifePrinciples.com, retrieved from http:// www.lifeprinciples.com/smokingReport.html, July 9, 2011.

R

1. "A Citizen's Guide to Radon," U.S. Environmental Protection Agency, January 2009, retrieved from http://www.epa.gov/radon/pubs/citguide.html, July 15, 2011; and "Toxicological Pro-file for Radon," Agency for Toxic Substances and Disease Registry, U.S. Public Health Service, December 1990, retrieved from http://www.bvsde.paho.org/bvstox/i/fulltext/toxprofiles /radon.pdf, July 15, 2011.

2. "Hantavirus," Centers for Disease Control and Prevention, May 17, 2011, retrieved from http://www.cdc.gov/hantavirus/surveillance/index.html, July 15, 2011.

3. "Hantavirus Pulmonary Syndrome (HPS)," New York State Department of Health, June 2011, retrieved from http://www.health.ny.gov/diseases/communicable/hantavirus/fact_sheet .htm, July 15, 2011.

4. Russell Drumm, "Rattled by Hantavirus," *East Hampton Star* (New York), June 30, 2011, re-trieved from http://easthamptonstar.com/News/2011630/Rattled-Hantavirus, July 15, 2011.

5. "How Dangerous Is It to Read on the Toilet?," Esquire.com, December 3, 2009, retrieved from http://www.esquire.com/features/answer-fella/toilet-reading-1209, August 11, 2011; and David Gutman, M.D., "How Do Hemorrhoids Develop?," American Hemhorrhoid Spe-cialists, SensitiveCare.com, retrieved from http://www.sensitivecare.com/lm_hemorrhoids .aspx?isOn=2&isAt=2&isHm=2, August 11, 2011.

6. "Meet Dr. Gutman," American Hemorrhoid Specialists, SensitiveCare.com, retrieved from http://www.sensitivecare.com/DrGutman.aspx?isOn=4, August 11, 2011.

7. Tom Naughton, "Eggs and Celery: Killer Foods," "Bad Science" Archive, *Fat Head* movie blog, April 19, 2010, retrieved from http://www.fathead-movie.com/index.php/2010/04/19/eggs -and-celery-killer-foods/, September 16, 2011.

8. Josie Glausiusz, "Fruits and Veggies to Buy Organic," *Prevention,* retrieved from http://www .prevention.com/dirtiestcleanest/index.html, September 16, 2011.

9. Ellen Gamerman, "An Inconvenient Bag," *Wall Street Journal,* September 26, 2008, retrieved from http://online.wsj.com/article/SB122238422541876879.html, April 5, 2011; U.S. In-ternational Trade Commission, Import Database, http://dataweb.usitc.gov/, accessed April 5, 2011.

10. Jeff Plungis, "Wegmans Markets Replaces Reusable Bags After Group Cites High Lead Levels," Bloomberg.com, September 10, 2010, retrieved from http://www.bloomberg.com/news /2010-09-10/wegmans-markets-replaces-reusable-bags-after-group-cites-high-lead-levels .html. April 5, 2011.

11. Karen Hawthorne, "Back to Plastic? Reusable Grocery Bags May Cause Food Poisoning," *National Post* (Canada), May 29, 2009, retrieved from http://network.nationalpost.com/np /blogs/theappetizer/archive/2009/05/20/back-to-plastic-reusable-grocery-bags-may-pose -public-health-risk.aspx, April 5, 2011; and "Reusable Bags Contain Bacteria, Mould: Study," CTV News, Toronto, November 27, 2008, retrieved from http://toronto.ctv.ca/servlet/an /local/CTVNews/20081127/reusable_bags_081127/20081127?hub=TorontoHome, April 5, 2011.

12. "Reusable Grocery Bags Contaminated With E. Coli, Other Bacteria," *UA News*, University of Arizona, June 24, 2010, retrieved from http://uanews.org/node/32521, April 5, 2011; Charles P. Gerba, David Williams, and Ryan G. Sinclair, "Assessment of the Potential for Cross Contamination of Food Products by Reusable Shopping Bags," Department of Soil, Water, and Environmental Science, University of Arizona, Tucson, and School of Public Health, Loma Linda University, Loma Linda, California, June 9, 2010, retrieved from http://uanews .org/pdfs/GerbaWilliamsSinclair_BagContamination.pdf, April 5, 2011; and "Reusable Grocery Bags Found to Be Full of Bacteria," *Washington Post*, June 25, 2010, retrieved from http:// www.washingtonpost.com/wp-dyn/content/article/2010/06/24/AR2010062406143.html, April 5, 2011.

13. Hawthorne, "Back to Plastics?"

14. Phil Stemmer, B.D.S., quoted in Matthew Barbour, "Seven Daily Sins: Shower Every Day? Rinse After Brushing Teeth? These 'Healthy' Habits Could Be Devilishly Bad for You," *Daily Mail*, April 27, 2011, retrieved from http://www.dailymail.co.uk/health/article-1380504/Seven -daily-sins-Shower-day-Rinse-brushing-teeth-These-healthy-habits-devilishly-bad-you.html, April 28, 2011.

15. Hans Moravec, "Rise of the Robots—the Future of Artificial Intelligence," ScientificAm erican.com, March 23, 2009, retrieved from http://www.scientificamerican.com/article .cfm?id=rise-of-the-robots, May 30, 2011.

16. David Bruemmer, "Humanoid Robotics—What Does the Future Hold?" Idaho National Laboratory, May 30, 2006, retrieved from http://www.inl.gov/adaptiverobotics/human oidrobotics/future.shtml, May 30, 2011.

17. Colin McGinn, "Hello, HAL," *New York Times*, January 3, 1999, retrieved from http://www .nytimes.com/1999/01/03/books/hello-hal.html?pagewanted=7&src=pm, May 30, 2011.

18. Amanda B. Diekman, Mary McDonald, and Wendi L. Gardner, "Love Means Never Having to Be Careful: The Relationship Between Reading Romance Novels and Safe Sex Behavior," *Psychology of Women Quarterly* 24:3 (June 2000), 179–188, retrieved from http://onlinelibrary .wiley.com/doi/10.1111/j.1471-6402.2000.tb00199.x/pdf, January 21, 2012.

19. Susan Quilliam, " 'He Seized Her in His Manly Arms and Bent His Lips to Hers . . . '": The Surprising Impact That Romantic Novels Have on Our Work," *Journal of Family Planning and Reproductive Health Care* 37:3 (July 2011), 179–181, retrieved from http://jfprhc.bmj.com /content/37/3/179.full, January 20, 2012.

20. Richard McComb, "Mills and Boon Is Bad for Your Sex Life," *Sunday Mercury* (Birmingham, UK), July 10, 2011, retrieved from http://www.sundaymercury.net/news/column ists/george-tyndale/2011/07/10/george-tyndale-mills-and-boon-is-bad-for-your-sex-life -66331-29024361/, January 20, 2012.

21. "Indoor Air Purifiers That Produce Even Small Amounts of Ozone May Be Risky for Health, UC Irvine Study Finds," University of California press release, May 9, 2006, retrieved from http://www.universityofcalifornia.edu/news/article/8149, February 22, 2010.

22. "Beware of Ozone-generating Indoor 'Air Purifiers,'" California Air Resources Board, March 2006, retrieved from www.arb.ca.gov/research/indoor/ozone_gen_fact_sheet-a.pdf, June 26, 2012.

23. Heather Lodge, "*Today* Show Investigation Finds Cute Little Bath Toys Can Harbor Germs," KDSK.com., March 3, 2010, retrieved from http://www.ksdk.com/news/watercoolers/story .aspx?storyid=197121&catid=71, July 4, 2011.

24. Rick Smith and Bruce Lourie with Sarah Dopp, *Slow Death by Rubber Duck: The Secret Danger of Everyday Things* (Berkeley: Counterpoint, 2009), cover and 43–46; and "Chemical Families: Phthalates," Environmental Working Group, retrieved from http://www.ewg.org/chem index/term/480, July 4, 2011.

25. "Tips for Teens: The Truth About Cocaine," U.S. Department of Health and Human Services and SAMHSA's National Clearinghouse for Alcohol and Drug Information, retrieved from SAMHSA's Health Information Network, http://ncadi.samhsa.gov/govpubs/phd640i, February 28, 2010.

26. "Runny Nose: Symptoms and Signs Index," MedicineNet.com, retrieved from http:// www.medicinenet.com/runny_nose/symptoms.htm, February 28, 2010; and "Symptoms: Runny Nose," retrieved from http://wrongdiagnosis.com/sym/runny_nose.htm, February 28, 2010.

27. Erich Rosenberger, M.D., "Does a Runny Nose Need to Be Treated?," retrieved from http:// www.helium.com/items/1335391-does-a-runny-nose-need-to-be-treated, February 28, 2010.

1. Maria Gonzales, "Safe—Or Safer—Sex in Every Relationship," Dating Aid, September 21, 2011, retrieved from http://www.datingaid.co.za/sexuality/safe-or-safer-sex-every-relation ship, January 25, 2012.

2. "Doctors Rate New Salad Entrées Hyped by Chains," Physicians Committee for Responsible Medicine, May 2003, retrieved from http://www.pcrm.org/search/?cid=615, August 27, 2011.

3. Liz Vaccariello, "The 7 Foods Experts Won't Eat," *Prevention,* November 26, 2009, retrieved from http://www.prevention.com/cda/expertblog/news.voices/faces.of.prevention?plckC ontroller=Blog&plckScript=blogScript&plckElementId=blogDest&plckBlogPage=BlogVie wPost&plckPostId=Blog%3A6e8f19ea-6832-4839-b71e-62608af9b2d8Post%3A8c8413e2 -61fd-40de-a549-9603f4a09c01, August 25, 2011.

4. Pam Belluck, "Big Benefits Are Seen from Eating Less Salt, *New York Times,* January 20, 2010, retrieved from http://www.nytimes.com/2010/01/21/health/nutrition/21salt.html, June 23, 2010.

5. Jane E. Brody, "After Smoking and Fats, Focus Turns to Salt." *New York Times,* January 25, 2010, retrieved from http://www.nytimes.com/2010/01/26/health/26brod.html, June 24, 2010.

6. Belluck, "Big Benefits Are Seen"; Brody, "After Smoking and Fats"; Kirsten Bibbins-Domingo, Ph.D., M.D., Glenn M. Chertow, M.D., M.P.H., Pamela G. Coxson, Ph.D., Andrew Moran, M.D., James M. Lightwood, Ph.D., Mark J. Pletcher, M.D., M.P.H., and Lee Goldman, M.D., M.P.H., "Projected Effect of Dietary Salt Reductions on Future Cardiovascular Disease," *New England Journal of Medicine,* 362: 590–599, published online January 20, 2010, retrieved from http:// www.nejm.org/doi/pdf/10.1056/NEJMoa0907355, April 5, 2012.

7. "New Salt Campaign Under Attack," Salt Manufacturers' Association, press release, July 10, 2005, retrieved from http://www.saltsense.co.uk/releases/rel015.php, June 26, 2012; and David McCarron, M.D., F.A.C.P., quoted in "Salt Policy Could Be 'A Disaster Waiting to Happen,'" Salt Manufacturers' Association, press release, March 7, 2007, retrieved from http:// www.saltsense.co.uk/releases/rel022.php, May 31, 2012.

8. John Tierney, "When It Comes to Salt, No Rights or Wrongs. Yet," *New York Times,* February 22, 2010, retrieved from http://www.nytimes.com/2010/02/23/science/23tier.html, June 24, 2010.

9. Nathan J. Grills, "Santa Claus: A Public Health Pariah?," *British Medical Journal* 339:b5261, December 16, 2009, retrieved from http://www.bmj.com/content/339/bmj.b5261.full, April 14, 2011.

10. Mike Underwood, "Hey, St. Nick: Put Down the Cookie," *Boston Herald,* November 30, 2007, 4, retrieved from http://www.bostonherald.com/news/regional/general/view.bg?articleid =1047979#articleFull, April 15, 2011.

11. Janet Fyfe-Yeomans and Amanda Grant, "Australian Santas Asked Not to 'Ho Ho Ho,'" FoxNews.com, November 15, 2007, retrieved from http://www.foxnews.com/story/0.2933 ,311797,00.html, April 15, 2011.

12. Kelly Sundstrom, "Common Nutritional Disorders: Scurvy," eHow.com, retrieved from http:// www.ehow.com/about_5103808_common-nutritional-disorders.html, June 26, 2012.

13. Stefan Lovgren, "Warming to Cause Catastrophic Rise in Sea Level?," *National Geographic* News, updated April 26, 2004, retrieved from http://news.nationalgeographic.com/news /2004/04/0420_040420_earthday.html, August 31, 2011; and Stefan Lovgren, "Greenland Melt May Swamp LA, Other Cities, Study Says," *National Geographic* News, April 8, 2004, retrieved from http://news.nationalgeographic.com/news/pf/54234057.html, August 31, 2011.

14. Mick Hamer, "Do Compulsory Seatbelts Save Lives?," *New Scientist,* February 19, 1981, retrieved from http://books.google.com/books?id=bvrsJuPd6SUC&pg=PA461&1pg=PA4 61&dq=Adams+seat+belts+University+College&source=bl&ots=_1WspAVOvj&sig=oOFf 9omYSIwDSeYLf91EMdYMVmU&hl=en&ei=rfVjTtvgIY2urAe7mISuCg&sa=X&oi=book _result&ct=result&resnum=5&ved=0CGUQ6AEwBA#v=onepage&q=Adams%20seat%20 belts%20University%20College&f=false, September 4, 2011; and John G. U. Adams, "The Efficacy of Seat Belt Legislation," *SAE Transactions,* 1982, 2824–2838, Society of Automotive Engineers, retrieved from http://john-adams.co.uk/wp-content/uploads/2006/SAE%20 seatbelts.pdf, September 4, 2011.

15. Melissa Dahl, "Skinny Jeans Give Thigh Nerve a Painful Pinch," Today.com, May 22, 2009, retrieved from http://www.msnbc.msn.com/id/30870617/ns/health-behavior/t/skinny -jeans-give-thigh-nerve-painful-pinch/, September 4, 2011.

16. "Meralgia Paresthetica," Johns Hopkins Hospital, HopkinsMedicine.org, retrieved from http://www.hopkinsmedicine.org/neurology_neurosurgery/specialty_areas/peripheral _nerve_surgery/conditions/meralgia_paresthetica.html, August 31, 2011.
17. "Seat Belt Laws," Governors Highway Safety Association, September 2011, retrieved from http://www.ghsa.org/html/stateinfo/laws/seatbelt_laws.html, September 4, 2011.
18. Eric Peters, "Seat Belt Laws, Helmet Laws and Nattering Busybodies," National Motorists Association, retrieved from http://www.motorists.org/seat-belt-laws/busybodies, September 4, 2011.
19. Jon Hamilton, "Solar Storms Could be Earth's Next Katrina," *All Things Considered,* National Public Radio, February 26, 2010, retrieved from http://www.npr.org/templates/story/story .php?storyId=124125001, April 10, 2011.
20. "Timeline: the 1859 Solar Superstorm," *Scientific American,* July 29, 2008, retrieved from http://www.scientificamerican.com/article.cfm?id=timeline-the-1859-solar-superstorm, April 10, 2011; and E. V. Cliver and L. Svalgaard, "The 1859 Solar-Terrestrial Disturbance and the Current Limits of Extreme Space Weather Activity" *Solar Physics* 224:407, received September 21, 2004.
21. Hamilton, "Solar Storms Could Be."
22. Executive Summary, "Severe Space Weather Events—Understanding Societal and Economic Impacts," National Research Council, 2008, National Academies, retrieved from http://www .nap.edu/catalog/12507.html, April 10, 2011.
23. Richard Alleyne, "Sun Storm May Be 'Global Katrina,'" *Telegraph,* February 27, 2011, retrieved from http://www.telegraph.co.uk/science/space/8350329/Sun-storm-may-be -global-Katrina.html, April 10, 2011.
24. Ross Douthat, "160 Million and Counting," *New York Times,* June 27, 2011, A21, retrieved from http://www.nytimes.com/2011/06/27/opinion/27douthat.html, July 2, 2011; and Amartya Sen, "More Than 100 Million Women Are Missing," *New York Review of Books* 37:20 (December 20, 1990), retrieved from http://ucatlas.ucsc.edu/gender/Sen100M.html, July 2, 2011.
25. Amanda Cunningham, "India Confronts Gender-Selective Abortion," *All Things Considered,* National Public Radio, March 21, 2006, retrieved from http://www.npr.org/templates/story /story.php?storyId=5293148, July 2, 2011.
26. "India's Unwanted Girls," BBC News, South Asia, May 22, 2011, retrieved from http://www. bbc.co.uk/news/world-south-asia-13264301, July 2, 2011; and "Case Study: Female Infanticide," Gendercide Watch, retrieved from http://www.gendercide.org/case_infanticide.html, July 2, 2011.
27. Therese Hesketh, Ph.D., Li Lu, M.D., and Zhu Wei Xing, M.P.H., "The Effect of China's One-Child Family Policy After 25 Years," Health Policy Report, *New England Journal of Medicine* 353:11 (September 15, 2005), 1171–1176, retrieved from http://www.nejm.org/doi/full /10.1056/NEJMhpr051833, July 2, 2011.
28. "How Safe Is Your Sex Toy?," Greenpeace, September 8, 2006, retrieved from http://www .greenpeace.org.uk/blog/toxics/bad-vibrations-we-expose-an-eu-sex-scandal, January 22, 2012.
29. "What Is Phthalate Free?" Ethical Sextoys, retrieved from http://www.ethicalsextoys.co.uk /phthalate-free/, January 22, 2012.
30. "EthicalSexToys.co.uk—the First and Only UK Eco Sextoy Store," retrieved from http://www .ethicalsextoys.co.uk, January 23, 2012.
31. Olivia Devinne, "Phthalates in Sex Toys and How They Are Harmful to the Body," *Ezine Articles,* February 25, 2012, retrieved from http://ezinearticles.com/?Phthalates-in-Sex-Toys -and-How-They-Are-Harmful-to-the-Body&id=5935026, January 23, 2012.
32. Patrick Morgan, "Sex Increases Risk of Heart Attack by 2.7x," *Discover* magazine's Discoblog, March 24, 2011, retrieved from http://blogs.discovermagazine.com/discoblog/2011/03/24 /sex-increases-risk-of-heart-attack-by-2-7x-significantly-less-than-its-fun-multiplier/, August 29, 2011.
33. Julie Steenhuysen, "Yes, Sex Can Kill You, U.S. Study Shows," Reuters, March 22, 2011, retrieved from http://www.reuters.com/article/2011/03/22/us-heart-exercise-idUS TRE72L6KR20110322, August 29, 2011; and Issa J. Dahabreh, M.D., and Jessica K. Paulus, Sc.D., "Association of Episodic Physical and Sexual Activity with Triggering of Acute Cardiac Events: Systematic Review and Meta-analysis," *Journal of the American Medical Association* 305:12 (March 23–30, 2011), 1225–1233, abstract, retrieved from http://jama.ama-assn .org:content:305:12:1225.abstract, August 29, 2011.
34. "Sexually Transmittable Diseases," Centers for Disease Control and Prevention, updated August 4, 2010, retrieved from http://www.cdc.gov/std/general/default.htm, January 22, 2012.

35. Dr. William Wong, "STDs: A Growing Problem with Dwindling Resources," Reproductive Health Reality Check, November 17, 2009, retrieved from http://www.rhrealitycheck.org /blog/2009/11/16/stds-a-growing-problem-with-dwindling-resources, January 22, 2011.

36. Stephanie Stahl, "Hidden Dangers of Shopping Carts," CBS3.com, Philadelphia, November 13, 2008, retrieved from http://cbs3.com/health/Shopping.Carts.Danger.2.863832.html, July 4, 2010.

37. Charles Gerba, Ph.D., "Surprising Places Germs Lurk," BottomLineSecrets.com, December 1, 2008, retrieved from http://www.bottomlinesecrets.com/article.html?article_id=46976, July 4, 2010.

38. James N. Dillard, M.D., "Household Horror," *Easthampton Star* (New York), December 3, 2009, A8.

39. Ed Silverman, "The Problem with Labeling: Too Many Side Effects," Pharmalot, May 25, 2011, retrieved from http://www.pharmalot.com/2011/05/the-problem-with-labeling-too -many-side-effects/, September 12, 2011.

40. Gina Kolata, "Side Effects? These Drugs Have a Few," *New York Times Week in Review,* June 5, 2011, WK4, retrieved from http://www.nytimes.com/2011/06/05/weekinreview/05drugs .html, September 11, 2011.

41. Christine Cheng, Pharm.D., quoted in David Jacobson, "UCSF Pharmacy Authors Call for Prioritizing Drug Label Warnings," University of California, San Francisco, June 8, 2011, retrieved from http://pharmacy.ucsf.edu/news/2011/06/08/1/, September 12, 2011.

42. "Questions About Your Community: Shopping Bags: Paper or Plastic or . . . ? ," U.S. Environmental Protection Agency, retrieved from http://web.archive.org/web/20060426235724 /http://www.epa.gov/region1/communities/shopbags.html, July 17, 2011.

43. John Roach, "Are Plastic Grocery Bags Sacking the Environment?," *National Geographic News,* September 2, 2003, retrieved from http://news.nationalgeographic.com/news /2003/09/0902_030902_plasticbags.html, July 17, 2011.

44. Ibid.

45. Irena Choi Stern, "Greening Up by Cutting Down on Plastic Bags," *New York Times,* August 5, 2007, retrieved from http://www.nytimes.com/2007/08/05/nyregion/nyregion special2/05Rbags.html, July 17, 2011.

46. Roach, "Are Plastic Grocery Bags."

47. "Questions About Your Community"; and "Planet Earth's New Nemesis?," BBC News, May 8, 2002, retrieved from http://news.bbc.co.uk/2/hi/uk_news/1974750.stm, July 17, 2011.

48. SaveThePlasticBag.com, http://savetheplasticbag.com/ReadContent461.aspx, accessed July 17, 2011.

49. Roach, "Are Plastic Grocery Bags."

50. "About reuseit Brand Products," reuseit.com, retrieved from http://www.reuseit.com/about -us/our-company/about-acme-bags, July 17, 2011.

51. Vernor Vinge, "The Coming Technological Singularity: How to Survive in the Post-human Era," Singularity Institute, 1993, retrieved from http://www-rohan.sdsu.edu/faculty/vinge /misc/singularity.html, April 6, 2011.

52. Ken MacLeod, *The Cassini Division* (New York: Tor Books, 1999).

53. John Markoff, "Scientists Worry Machines May Outsmart Man," *New York Times,* July 26, 2009, A1, retrieved from http://www.nytimes.com/2009/07/26/science/26robot.html, April 6, 2011; ArmedRobots.com (http://www.armedrobots.com/).

54. Nick Bostrom, "Existential Risks: Analyzing Human Extinction Scenarios and Related Hazards," *Journal of Evolution and Technology* 9 (March 2002), retrieved from http://www .nickbostrom.com/existential/risks.html, April 6, 2011.

55. Eliezer Yudkowsky, "Why Work Toward the Singularity?" Singularity Institute, retrieved from http://singinst.org/overview/whyworktowardthesingularity/, April 6, 2011.

56. Bill Joy, "Why the Future Doesn't Need Us," *Wired,* April 2000, retrieved from http://www .wired.com/wired/archive/8.04/joy.html, April 6, 2011.

57. Lissa Christopher, "Beware of the Chair," *Sydney Morning Herald,* March 4, 2010, retrieved from http://www.smh.com.au/executive-style/management/beware-of-the-chair -20100303-pj4g.html#ixzz1V1wIH5dI, August 14, 2011; and Paul Wallis, "Sitting Down Is Very Bad for You, Says New Australian Study," *Digital Journal,* March 3, 2010, retrieved from http://www.digitaljournal.com/article/288480?tp=1, August 14, 2011.

58. Issie Laposwki, "Hours Spent Sitting Down Linked to Risk of Death from Heart Disease, Even Among Physically Fit," *Daily News* (New York), January 12, 2010, retrieved from http://

www.nydailynews.com/lifestyle/health/2010/01/12/2010-01-12_hours_spent_watching
_tv_linked_to_risk_of_death_from_heart_disease.html, August 14, 2011.

59. Christopher, "Beware of the Chair."

60. Hugh Wilson, "Could Sitting Down Be the Death of You?," *Daily Mail*, August 10, 2010, retrieved from http://www.dailymail.co.uk/health/article-1301708/Could-sitting-death -Experts-reveal-hours-perched-chairs-having-disastrous-effect-health.html, August 15, 2011.

61. Christopher, "Beware of the Chair."

62. James A. Levine, M.D., Ph.D., "The Extreme Dangers of Sitting," Mayo Clinic, January 20, 2011, retrieved from http://neurosynthesisarchives.wordpress.com/2011/01/20/the -extreme-dangers-of-sitting/, August 14, 2011.

63. Melissa Dahl, "Skinny Jeans Give Thigh Nerve a Painful Pinch," Today.com, May 22, 2009, retrieved from http://www.msnbc.msn.com/id/30870617/ns/health-behavior/t/skinny -jeans-give-thigh-nerve-painful-pinch/, September 4, 2011.

64. "Meralgia Paresthetica," Johns Hopkins Hospital, HopkinsMedicine.org, retrieved from http://www.hopkinsmedicine.org/neurology_neurosurgery/specialty_areas/peripheral _nerve_surgery/conditions/meralgia_paresthetica.html, August 31, 2011.

65. Craig Schwimmer, M.D., M.P.H., F.A.C.S., "About the Snoring Center: Our Philosophy," Snoring Center, retrieved from http://www.snoringcenter.com/about.html, May 27, 2011; and Craig Schwimmer, M.D., M.P.H., F.A.C.S., "Is Snoring Serious?," Snoring Center, re- trieved from http://www.snoringcenter.com/about.html, May 27, 2011.

66. A. Oksenberg, E. Arons, S. Greenberg-Dotan, K. Nasser, and H. Radwan, "The Significance of Body Posture on Breathing Abnormalities During Sleep," *Harefuah*, May 2009, abstract retrieved from http://www.ncbi.nlm.nih.gov/pubmed/19630360, May 27, 2011.

67. Anahad O'Connor, "The Claim: To Reduce Snoring, Try Sleeping on Your Side," *New York Times*, April 18, 2011, retrieved from http://www.nytimes.com/2011/04/19/health/19really .html, May 26, 2011.

68. Earl V. Dunn, M.D., quoted in "Snoring: 10 Tips for a Silent Night," excerpted by the Edi- tors of *Prevention* Magazine in *The Doctors Book of Home Remedies,* Chapter 119 (New York: Bantam Books, 1991), retrieved from http://www.mothernature.com/l/The-Doctors-Book -of-Home-Remedies/Snoring_2690.html, May 27, 2011.

69. Ibid.; Rochelle Zak, M.D., cited in Andrew Taber, "Dream House," *Men's Health* Spotlight, retrieved from http://www.menshealth.com/spotlight/sleep/9-barriers.php, May 28, 2011.

70. Steven Y. Park, M.D., "Usual and Unusual Ways to Stop Snoring," DoctorStevenPark.com, August 27, 2010, retrieved from http://doctorstevenpark.com/sleep-apnea-basics/usual -and-unusual-ways-to-stop-snoring-2, May 28, 2011.

71. James J. Bignold, B.Sc., Georgina Deans-Costi, B.Sc., Mitchell R. Goldsworthy, B.Sc., Claire A. Robertson, B.Sc., Douglas McEvoy, M.D., Peter G. Catcheside, Ph.D., and Jeremy D. Mercer, Ph.D., "Poor Long-Term Patient Compliance with the Tennis Ball Technique for Treating Positional Obstructive Sleep Apnea," *Journal of Clinical Sleep Medicine* 5:5 (October 15, 2009), retrieved from http://www.ncbi.nlm.nih.gov/pmc/articles/PMC2762713/, May 28, 2011.

72. Kristie Leong, M.D., "Four Bad Beauty Habits That Cause Lines Around the Mouth," April 11, 2011, retrieved from http://www.associatedcontent.com/article/7918489/four_hab its_that_cause_wrinkles_and.html, May 25, 2011.

73. David L. Katz, M.D., and Debra L. Gordon, M.S., "Best Sleeping Positions for Your Back: Don't Sleep on Your Stomach," ReadersDigest.com, excerpted from David L. Katz, M.D., and Debra L. Gordon, M.S., *Stealth Health* (New York: Reader's Digest Association, 2005), retrieved from http://www.rd.com/health/best-sleeping-positions-for-your-back/, August 6, 2011.

74. Michael Moss with Griff Palmer, "Safety of Beef Processing Method Is Questioned," *New York Times*, December 31, 2009, A1, retrieved from http://www.nytimes.com/2009/12/31/us /31meat.html?_r=1, April 16, 2011.

75. Carl J. Brant, G.P., and Gavin Petrie, M.B., Ch.B., F.R.C.P., "Smoking: Health Risks," Netdoc- tor, February 14, 2005, retrieved from http://www.netdoctor.co.uk/health_advice/facts /smokehealth.htm, June 22, 2011; "Health Effects of Exposure to Secondhand Smoke," Smoke-free Homes and Cars Program, U.S. Environmental Protection Agency, October 13, 2010, retrieved from http://www.epa.gov/smokefree/healtheffects.html, June 22, 2011; Terry Martin, "The Effects of Secondhand Smoke on Our Health," About.com Guide, July 20, 2008, retrieved from http://quitsmoking.about.com/cs/secondhandsmoke/a/second handsmoke.htm, June 22, 2011; Terry Martin, "Respiratory Disease Statistics: The Preva-

lence of COPD," About.com Guide, July 12, 2004, retrieved from http://quitsmoking.about
.com/od/tobaccostatistics/a/COPDstatistics.htm, June 22, 2011; Mayo Clinic Staff, "Secondhand Smoke: Avoid Dangers in the Air," Mayo Foundation for Medical Education and
Research (MFMER), March 6, 2010, 2, retrieved from http://www.mayoclinic.com/health
/secondhand-smoke/CC00023/NSECTIONGROUP=2, June 22, 2011; "Diseases Caused
by Smoking," Smoking Facts and Fiction, retrieved from http://www.smoking-facts-and
-fiction.com/beverly_hansen_omalley.html, June 22, 2011; "Smoking's Impact on Health Is
Not Limited to Lung Cancer," Discovery Fit and Health, http://health.howstuffworks.com
/wellness/smoking-cessation/smokings-impact-on-health.htm, June 21, 2011; "Abdominal
Aortic Aneurysm," University of Southern California Center for Vascular Care, retrieved
from http://www.surgery.usc.edu/divisions/vas/abdominalaorticaneurysm.html, June 22,
2011; Laurie Barclay, M.D., "Fight the Fire of Crohn's Disease: Quit Smoking!," WebMD
Health News, April 16, 2001, retrieved from http://www.webmd.com/smoking-cessation
/news/20010416/fight-fire-of-crohns-disease-quit-smoking, June 22, 2011; and "Smoking and Your Digestive System," National Digestive Diseases Information Clearinghouse
(NDDIC), February 2006, retrieved from http://digestive.niddk.nih.gov/ddiseases/pubs
/smoking/, June 22, 2011.

76. Salynn Boyles, "Expert Panel: Smoking Bans Save Lives," WebMD Health News, October 15,
2009, retrieved from http://www.medicinenet.com/script/main/art.asp?articlekey=106604,
April 26, 2011.

77. Scott Adams and Chad Cotti, "Drunk Driving After the Passage of Smoking Bans in Bars,"
Journal of Public Economics 92:5–6 (June 2008), 1288–1305, retrieved from http://www.stop
thebans.com/sitebuildercontent/sitebuilderfiles/afterbandrunkdriving.pdf, April 25, 2011.

78. "Smoking Bans Contribute to Rise in Fatal DUI Crashes, Study Finds," TotalDUI.com,
retrieved from http://www.totaldui.com/news/articles/headlines/smoking-bans-and-duis
.aspx, April 24, 2011.

79. Alex Pareene, "Smoking Bans: The Silent Killer," Gawker.com, April 3, 2008, retrieved from
http://gawker.com/#!375838/smoking-bans-the-silent-killer, April 25, 2011.

80. Dr. Michael M. Warren, "Tight Clothing Can Be Hazardous to Your Health," Galveston
County Daily News, December 7, 2010, retrieved from http://galvestondailynews.com/story
/196350, August 5, 2011.

81. Dr. Dan Rutherford, B.S., M.B., Ch.B., M.R.C.G.P., F.R.C.P., "Deep Vein Thrombosis,"
Netdoctor.co.uk, updated April 3, 2011, retrieved from http://www.netdoctor.co.uk/travel
/diseases/dvt.htm, August 6, 2011.

82. "Positive and Negative Impact of Solar Energy," SolarEnergyUses.Info, retrieved from http://
solarenergyuses.info/positive-and-negative-impact-of-solar-energy/, August 14, 2011.

83. Jill Replogle, "Solar Installer's Death Points to Job Hazards in a Growing, Green Industry,"
FairWarning.org, October 12, 2010, retrieved from http://www.fairwarning.org/2010/10
/solar-installers-death-points-to-job-hazards-in-a-growing-green-industry/, August 16, 2011.

84. Brian Wang, "Deaths Per Terrawatt Hour for All Energy Sources: Rooftop Solar Is Actually
More Dangerous Than Chernobyl," NextBigFuture.com, March 14, 2008, retrieved from http://
nextbigfuture.com/2008/03/deaths-per-twh-for-all-energy-sources.html, August 14, 2011.

85. Gavin Atkins, "Green Deaths: The Forgotten Dangers of Solar Panels," AsianCorrespondent
.com, May 17, 2011, retrieved from http://asiancorrespondent.com/54571/green-deaths
-the-forgotten-dangers-of-solar-panels/, August 16, 2011.

86. "The Five Worst Supposedly 'Healthy' Fast-Food Items," Physicians Committee for Responsible Medicine, Spring 2011, retrieved from http://www.pcrm.org/health/reports/the-five
-worst-supposedly-healthy-fast-food-items, August 27, 2011.

87. Frank Sacks, M.D., et al., "Soy Protein, Isoflavones, and Cardiovascular Health," AHA Science
Advisory, American Heart Association, January 17, 2006, retrieved from http://circ.ahajour
nals.org/content/113/7/1034.full#SEC5, August 7, 2011.

88. Kaayla Daniel, Ph.D., "The Whole Soy Story: The Dark Side of America's Favorite Health
Food," blog.wholesoystory.com, 2009, retrieved from http://blog.wholesoystory.com, August
8, 2011.

89. Joan E. Bamji and Nariman S. Bamji, quoted in "Medicine: Is Spinach Dangerous?," Time
Magazine, March 30, 1953, retrieved from http://www.time.com/time/magazine/article
/0,9171,818047,00.html, June 21, 2012.

90. "Mucormycosis (Zygomycosis)," Centers for Disease Control and Prevention, August 1,
2011, retrieved from http://www.cdc.gov/fungal/mucormycosis, August 2, 2011.

91. Lisa Zamosky, "6 Daily Habits That May Make You Sick," WebMD.com, May 5, 2010, re-

trieved from http://www.webmd.com/allergies/living-with-allergies-10/6-daily-habits-that
-may-make-you-sick, July 5, 2010.

92. Anahad O'Connor, "The Claim: You Can Disinfect a Kitchen Sponge in the Microwave," *New York Times*, March 27, 2007, retrieved from http://www.nytimes.com/2007/03/27/health /27real.html, April 27, 2011.

93. "Zapping Sponges May Have Unexpected Results," ConsumerReports.org, January 30, 2007, retrieved from http://blogs.consumerreports.org/safety/2007/01/zapping_sponges.html, July 6, 2010.

94. Amy Toffelmire, "Kitchen Sponge Safety," *Courier-Post* Online, Cherry Hill Township, New Jersey, updated January 23, 2009, retrieved from http://health.courierpostonline.com/Text Item.aspx?id=4372, July 6, 2010.

95. Ibid.

96. "Must I Banish Sponges from My Kitchen to Avoid the Risk of Contamination?," ShelfLifeAd vice.com, March 8, 2010, retrieved from http://shelflifeadvice.com/content/must-i-ban ish-sponges-my-kitchen-avoid-risk-contamination, July 6, 2010.

97. William Neuman, "The Poster Plant of Health Food Can Pack Disease Risks," *New York Times*, June 11, 2011, B1, retrieved from http://www.nytimes.com/2011/06/11/bus iness/11sprouts.html?_r=1&ref=williamneuman, June 17, 2011.

98. Elisabeth Rosenthal, "My Salad, My Health," *New York Times Week in Review*, June 12, 2011, retrieved from http://www.nytimes.com/2011/06/12/weekinreview/12organic.html ?ref=elisabethrosenthal, June 17, 2011.

99. Thomas Breuer, et al., "A Multistate Outbreak of *Escherichia Coli* O157:H7 Infections Linked to Alfalfa Sprouts Grown from Contaminated Seeds," *Emerging Infectious Disease* 7:6 (Novem-ber–December 2011), Centers for Disease Control and Prevention, retrieved from http:// www.cdc.gov/ncidod/eid/vol7no6/breuer.htm, June 17, 2011.

100. Judy Dempsey and William Neuman, "Deadly E. Coli Outbreak Linked to Sprouts from a German Farm," *New York Times*, June 6, 2011, A4, retrieved from http://www.nytimes .com/2011/06/06/world/europe/06germany.html?ref=williamneuman, June 17, 2011.

101. Eduardo Loyo, "Demand-Pull Stagflation," draft working paper, John F. Kennedy School of Government, Harvard University, April 2000, retrieved from http://sims.princeton.edu/yftp /Loyo/LoyoStgfltn.pdf, June 26, 2012.

102. Jonathan Nitzan, "Regimes of Differential Accumulation: Mergers, Stagflation and the Logic of Globalization," *Review of International Political Economy* 8:2 (Summer 2001), 226-274, retrieved from http://bnarchives.yorku.ca/3/01/010800N__Regimes_of_differential_ac cumulation.pdf, June 26, 2012.

103. John Maynard Keynes, *A Tract on Monetary Reform* (London: Macmillan, 1924), 80.

104. Bryan Walsh, "The Dangers of Sitting at Work—and Standing," TIMEHealthland, April 13, 2011, retrieved from http://healthland.time.com/2011/04/13/the-dangers-of-sitting-at -work%E2%80%94and-standing/, August 15, 2011.

105. Paul Krugman, "The Feckless Fed," *New York Times*, July 12, 2010, A19, retrieved from http:// www.nytimes.com/2010/07/12/opinion/12krugman.html, February 21, 2011.

106. Peter Schiff, interviewed by Jennifer Schonberger, Motley Fool, August 9, 2010, retrieved from http://www.fool.com/investing/general/2010/08/09/peter-schiff-were-in-the-early -stages-of-a-depress.aspx, April 1, 2011.

107. Paul B. Farrell, "10 Reasons to Shun Stocks Till Banks Crash," MarketWatch.com, December 7, 2010, retrieved from http://www.marketwatch.com/story/10-reasons-to-shun-stocks-till -banks-crash-2010-12-07, February 21, 2011.

108. Dan Solin, "Worst Advice in the World for Volatile Markets," *Huffington Post*, May 11, 2010, retrieved from http://www.huffingtonpost.com/dan-solin/worst-advice-in-the -world_b_568202.html, January 30, 2011.

109. Howard Gold, "Today's Hot Tip: Don't Buy Stocks!," MoneyShow.com, April 3, 2008, retrieved from http://www.moneyshow.com/investing/articles.asp?aid=EDITOR-14440, February 19, 2011.

110. David Wimberly, "Natural Gas Is Unnatural," Alive.com, February 2002, retrieved from http://www.alive.com/859a3a2.php?subject_bread_cramb=411, July 5, 2010.

111. Josie Glausiusz, "Fruits and Veggies to Buy Organic: Strawberries," *Prevention*, retrieved from http://www.prevention.com/dirtiestcleanest/4.html, September 16, 2011.

112. E. Baron, "Sweet Poison: Non-Organic Strawberries," NourishingWords.net, June 23, 2011, retrieved from http://nourishingwords.net/2011/06/23/sweet-poison-non-organic-straw berries/, September 19, 2011.

113. Chloe Lambert, "Want to Keep Your Heart and Lungs Healthy? Don't Sit Next to the Photocopier," *Daily Mail*, March 15, 2011, retrieved from http://www.dailymail.co.uk/health/article-1366304/Want-heart-lungs-healthy-Dont-sit-photocopier.html, September 9, 2011.

114. Burkhard Bilger, "Department of Food Science: The Search for Sweet," *New Yorker*, May 22, 2006, 40, retrieved from http://archives.newyorker.com/?i=2006-05-22#folio=040, July 28, 2011.

115. "FDA Approves New High-Intensity Sweetener Sucralose," FDA Talk Paper T98-16, Food and Drug Administration, U.S. Department of Health and Human Services, April 1, 1998, retrieved from http://www.splendatr.com/Splenda%20General%20Docs/FDA%20Splenda%20Approval.pdf, July 28, 2011

116. Elaine Magee, M.P.H., R.D., "Which Artificial Sweetener Is Right for You?" WebMD, February 20, 2004, retrieved from http://www.webmd.com/diet/features/which-artificial-sweetner-is-right-for-you?page=2, July 28, 2011; and Ivan Lerner, "Artificial Sweeteners Market to Change," ICIS.com, May 19, 2009, retrieved from http://www.icis.com/Articles/2009/05/25/9217338/artificial-sweeteners-market-to-change.html, July 28, 2011.

117. Mohamed B. Abou-Donia, Emam M. El-Masry, Ali A. Abdel-Rahman, Roger E. McLendon, and Susan S. Schiffman, "Splenda Alters Gut Microflora and Increases Intestinal P-Glycoprotein and Cytochrome P-450 in Male Rats," *Journal of Toxicology and Environmental Health*, Part A, 71:21 (2008), 1415–1429, abstract and excerpt retrieved from http://www.tandfonline.com/na101/home/literatum/publisher/tandf/journals/content/uteh20/2008/uteh20.v071.i21/15287390802328630/production/15287390802328630.fp.png_v03, July 28, 2011; and Joanne Waldron, "Duke University Study Links Splenda to Weight Gain, Health Problems," October 20, 2008, retrieved from http://www.naturalnews.com/024543_health_Splenda_weight.html, July 28, 2011.

118. Lynnley Browning, "New Salvo in Splenda Skirmish," *New York Times*, September 22, 2008, retrieved from http://www.nytimes.com/2008/09/23/business/23splenda.html, July 28, 2011.

119. Andrew Weil, M.D., "Sweet and Natural?," Dr.Weil.com: Q&A Library, June 23, 2008, retrieved from http://www.drweil.com/drw/u/QAA400414/Sweet-and-Natural.html, July 28, 2011.

120. Andrew Weil, M.D., "Aspartame: Can a Little Bit Hurt?," Dr.Weil.com: Q&A Library, May 9, 2006, retrieved from http://www.drweil.com/drw/u/id/QAA106654, July 28, 2011.

121. "U.S. Obesity Trends," Centers for Disease Control, March 3, 2011, retrieved from http://www.cdc.gov/obesity/data/trends.html, July 15, 2011.

122. Robert H. Lustig, M.D., *Sugar: The Bitter Truth*, July 27, 2009, University of California Television, retrieved from http://www.uctv.tv/search-details.aspx?showID=16717, July 16, 2011.

123. Gary Taubes, "Is Sugar Toxic?," *New York Times Sunday Magazine*, April 17, 2011, MM47, retrieved from http://www.nytimes.com/2011/04/17/magazine/mag-17Sugar-t.html?pagewanted=all, July 15, 2011.

124. Lustig, "Bitter Truth."

125. Taubes, "Toxic."

126. Lustig, "Bitter Truth."

127. Taubes, "Toxic."

128. Lustig, "Bitter Truth."

129. Sally Law, "The Risks of Summer Sex," LiveScience, June 11, 2009, retrieved from http://www.livescience.com/3671-risks-summer-sex.html, January 23, 2012.

130. Robin Lloyd, "Infectious Superbug Invades Beaches," LiveScience, February 13, 2009, retrieved from www.livescience.com/3330-infectious-superbug-invades-beaches.html, January 23, 2012.

131. "The Dangers of Tanning," Skin Cancer Foundation, retrieved from http://www.skincancer.org/the-dangers-of-tanning.html, August 26, 2011.

132. "Guidelines," Skin Cancer Foundation, retrieved from http://www.skincancer.org/prevention-guidelines.html, August 26, 2011; and "Year-Round Sun Protection," Skin Cancer Foundation, retrieved from http://www.skincancer.org/year-round-sun-protection.html, August 26, 2011.

133. Harald Dobnig, M.D., Stefan Pilz, M.D., Hubert Scharnagl, Ph.D., Wilfried Renner, Ph.D., Ursula Seelhorst, M.A., Britta Wellnitz, LL.D., Jurgen Kinkeldei, D.Eng., Bernhard O. Boehm, M.D., Gisela Weihrauch, M.Sc., and Winfried Maerz, M.D., "Independent Association of Low Serum 25-Hydroxyvitamin D and 1,25-Dihydroxyvitamin D Levels with All-Cause and Cardiovascular Mortality," *Archives of Internal Medicine* 168:12 (June 23, 2008), 1340–1349, retrieved from http://archinte.ama-assn.org/cgi/content/short/168/12/1340, August 23, 2011.

134. Deborah Kotz, "Time in the Sun: How Much Is Needed for Vitamin D?," *U.S. News* Health,

June 23, 2008, retrieved from http://health.usnews.com/health-news/family-health/heart/articles/2008/06/23/time-in-the-sun-how-much-is-needed-for-vitamin-d, August 22, 2011.

135. Sonya Lunder, M.P.H, "What We Still Don't Know About Sunscreens: The Vitamin A Issue," *New York Times* Blogs, July 5, 2010, retrieved from http://roomfordebate.blogs.nytimes.com/2010/07/05/what-we-still-dont-know-about-sunscreens/, August 23, 2011.

136. "Nanomaterials and Hormone Disruptors in Sunscreens," *EWG's Skin Deep: Sunscreens 2011*, Environmental Working Group, June 23, 2011, retrieved from http://breakingnews.ewg.org/2011sunscreen/sunscreens-exposed/nanomaterials-and-hormone-disruptors-in-sunscreens/, August 23, 2011.

137. "Sunscreen and Skin Cancer," *EWG's Skin Deep: Sunscreens 2011*, Environmental Working Group, June 23, 2011, retrieved from http://breakingnews.ewg.org/2011sunscreen/sunscreens-exposed/sunscreens-exposed-9-surprising-truths/, August 23, 2011.

138. Michael F. Holick, M.D., Ph.D., quoted in Robert Bazell, "Sunscreens Can Block Vitamin D," NBC News, January 19, 2004, retrieved from http://www.msnbc.msn.com/id/4001172/ns/nightly_news/t/sunscreens-canblock-vitamin-d/, August 23, 2011.

139. "Andrew W. Saul Interviews Vitamin D Expert Michael F. Holick, M.D., Ph.D.," Doctor Yourself.com, January 19, 2004, retrieved from http://www.doctoryourself.com/holick.html, August 23, 2011.

140. "Methicillin-resistant *Staphylococcus Aureus* (MRSA) Infections," Centers for Disease Control and Prevention, April 15, 2011, retrieved from http://www.cdc.gov/mrsa/, June 26, 2011; Sally Bloomfield, "Superbugs: Managing the Risks," *Practice Nurse*, June 6, 2008, retrieved from http://www.accessmylibrary.com/coms2/summary_0286-36389612_ITM, June 26, 2011; and "MRSA: A Potted History," MRSA Action UK, May 2009, retrieved from http://mrsaactionuk.net/pottedhistoryMRSA.html, June 26, 2011.

141. "Bad Bugs, No Drugs: Executive Summary," Infectious Disease Society of America, July 2004, retrieved from http://www.idsociety.org/PrintFriendly.aspx?id=5558, June 26, 2011.

142. Jennifer Wenger, "Medieval Miracle Workers: Are Maggots Making a Medical Comeback?," *National Institutes of Health Record* 56:15 (July 20, 2004), retrieved from http://nihrecord.od.nih.gov/newsletters/2004/07_20_2004/story01.htm, June 26, 2011.

143. Michael Pollan, "Unhappy Meals," *New York Times Magazine,* January 28, 2007, retrieved from http://michaelpollan.com/articles-archive/unhappy-meals/, August 20, 2011.

144. Ben McGrath, "The Dystopians," *New Yorker,* January 26, 2009; Dmitry Orlov, *Reinventing Collapse: The Soviet Example and American Prospects*" (New Society Publishers, 2008); "Closing the 'Collapse Gap,'" *Energy Bulletin,* December 4, 2006; and James Howard Kunstler, "A Christmas Eve Story," *Energy Bulletin,* November 24, 2007; http://www.wikipedia.org.

145. "Super Volcano," ArmageddonOnline, retrieved from http://armageddononline.tripod.com/volcano.htm, July 6, 2010.

146. Ibid.

147. Ibid.

148. Philip M. Tierno, Jr., Ph.D., *The Secret Life of Germs* (New York: Simon & Schuster, 2001), 144–145.

149. "Vibrio parahaemolyticus," National Center for Zoonotic, Vector-Borne, and Enteric Diseases, Centers for Disease Control and Prevention, July 17, 2009, retrieved from http://www.cdc.gov/nczved/divisions/dfbmd/diseases/vibriop/, June 28, 2011.

150. Tierno, *Secret Life.*

151. Ingrid Koo, Ph.D., "Sushi Scares—Infectious Diseases Associated with Eating Sushi or Raw Fish," About.com, April 15, 2009, retrieved from http://infectiousdiseases.about.com/od/g/a/Sushi.htm, June 28, 2011.

152. Tierno, *Secret Life.*

153. Andrew Weil, M.D., "Dangers of Chlorine?," Ask Dr. Weil, November 6, 2009, retrieved from http://www.drweil.com/drw/u/QAA361110/dangers-of-chlorine.html, July 4, 2011.

154. Alfred Bernard, Ph.D., Marc Nickmilder, Ph.D., Catherine Voisin, M.Sc., and Antonia Sardella, M.D., "Impact of Chlorinated Swimming Pool Attendance on the Respiratory Health of Adolescents," *Pediatrics* 124:4 (October 1, 2009), 1110–1118, retrieved from http://pediatrics.aappublications.org/content/124/4/1110.full?sid=2870b722-caa5-48b0-b0f5-812c73752fd8, July 3, 2011.

155. Weil, "Dangers of Chlorine?"

156. Charles P. Gerba, Ph.D., quoted in Leo W. Banks, "They Call Him Dr. Germ," *Tucson Weekly,* October 9, 2008, retrieved from http://www.tucsonweekly.com/tucson/they-call-him-dr-germ/Content?oid=1092882, May 29, 2011.

157. "Violations Identified from Routine Swimming Pool Inspections—Selected States and Counties, United States, 2008," *Morbidity and Mortality Weekly Report* 59:19 (May 21, 2010), Centers for Disease Control and Prevention, retrieved from http://www.cdc.gov/mmwr /preview/mmwrhtml/mm5919a2.htm, July 4, 2011; and Remy Melina, "Public Swimming Pools: How Dirty Are They?," Life's Little Mysteries, July 1, 2010, retrieved from http://www .lifeslittlemysteries.com/public-swimming-pools-how-dirty-are-they--0906/, July 4, 2011.

158. Chris Wiant, "This Summer: Dip Before You Dive to Help Avoid Recreational Water Ill-nesses," HealthyPools.org, May 23, 2011, retrieved from http://healthypools.org/, July 5, 2011; and "Be an Activist Swimmer: Order Your Free Pool Test Kit," HealthyPools.org, retrieved from http://www.healthypools.org/order-pool-kit-form/, July 5, 2011.

159. Anthony Bourdain, *Kitchen Confidential: Adventures in the Culinary Underbelly* (New York: Bloomsbury, 2000), excerpted by Barnes and Noble.com and retrieved from http://www .barnesandnoble.com/w/kitchen-confidential-anthony-bourdain/1003858285, July 23, 2011.

T

1. "Talc, Talcum Powder, Baby Powder," *Eco Friendly Digest,* retrieved from http://www.eco -friendly-digest.com/talc.html, June 25, 2011.

2. Robert W. Steele, M.D., "Is Talcum Powder Safe for Babies," iVillage.com, retrieved from http://www.ivillage.com/talcum-powder-safe-babies/6-n-136821, June 25, 2011.

3. "Risks of Talcum Powder," Cancer Prevention Coalition, retrieved from http://www.prevent cancer.com/consumers/cosmetics/talc.htm, June 25, 2011.

4. Charles Duhigg, "Toxic Waters: Clean Water Laws Are Neglected, at a Cost in Suffering," *New York Times,* September 13, 2009, A1, retrieved from http://www.nytimes.com/2009/09/13 /us/13water.html, April 12, 2011.

5. "Jslayeruk," message posted on Metaquotes LiveJournal, 2005, reprinted in "Quotations About Tea," *TheQuoteGarden.com,* retrieved from http://www.quotegarden.com/tea.html, August 28, 2011.

6. "Steaming Hot Tea Linked to Cancer," BBC News, March 27, 2009, retrieved from http:// news.bbc.co.uk/2/hi/7965380.stm, August 28, 2011; and Miranda Hitti, "Hot Tea May Raise Esophageal Cancer Risk," March 26, 2009, WebMD Health News, retrieved from http:// www.webmd.com/cancer/news/20090326/hot-tea-may-raise-esophageal-cancer-risk, Au-gust 28, 2011.

7. Alfred Lambremont Webre, "Scientist: Japan Nuke 'Accidents' Are Tectonic Nuclear Warfare," March 23, 2011, retrieved from http://www.pakalertpress.com/2011/03/23/scientist-japan -nuke-%E2%80%9Caccident%E2%80%9D-are-tectonic-nuclear-warfare/, June 4, 2011.

8. Alfred Lambremont Webre, "Leuren Moret: Fukushima HAARP Nuclear Attack by CIA, DOE, BP for London Banks," Seattle Exopolitics Examiner, May 9, 2011, http://jhaines6 .wordpress.com/2011/05/11/leuren-moret-fukushima-haarp-nuclear-attack-by-cia-doe-bp -for-london-banks/.

9. Leuren Moret, "Japan's Deadly Game of Nuclear Roulette," *Japan Times,* May 23, 2004, re-trieved from http://search.japantimes.co.jp/cgi-bin/fl20040523x2.html, June 7, 2011.

10. "Scientist Leuren Moret—Japan Earthquake and Nuclear 'Accident' Are Tectonic Nuclear Warfare," ExopoliticsTV, YouTube.com, retrieved from http://www.youtube.com/watch ?v=5WxmeOqYtB0, June 6, 2011.

11. Ibid.

12. "Tick-borne Diseases," Centers for Disease Control, National Institute of Occupational Safety and Health, NIOSH Workplace Safety and Health Topics, March 30, 2011, retrieved from http://www.cdc.gov/niosh/topics/tick-borne/, July 4, 2011; and "Tickborne Diseases of the U.S.," Centers for Disease Control, March 28, 2011, retrieved from http://www.cdc.gov /ticks/diseases/, July 4, 2011.

13. "Tick-borne Disease," *Wikipedia,* retrieved from http://en.wikipedia.org/wiki/Tick-borne _disease, July 4, 2011.

14. "Tickborne Diseases of the U.S."; and "Tickborne Diseases," National Institute of Allergy and Infectious Diseases, June 17, 2008, retrieved from http://www.niaid.nih.gov/topics/tick borne/Pages/Default.aspx, July 4, 2011.

15. Laurie Tarkan, "Once Rare, Infection by Tick Bite Spreads," *New York Times,* June 21, 2011, D6, retrieved from http://www.nytimes.com/2011/06/21/health/21ticks.html, July 4, 2011.

16. Dov Sikirov, M.D., "Comparison of Straining During Defecation in Three Positions: Results and Implications for Human Health," *Digestive Diseases and Sciences* 48:7 (July 1, 2003), 1201–1205, retrieved from http://dx.doi.org/10.1023/A:1024180319005, April 8, 2011.

17. David Ling, "We Ignore Squatting at Our Peril . . . ," Toilet-RelatedAilments.com, retrieved from http://www.toilet-related-ailments.com/squatting.html, June 26, 2012.

18. David Ling, "The Astonishing Thing About Sitting Toilets That You'll Never Hear Today . . . ," Toilet-RelatedAilments.com, retrieved from http://www.toilet-related-ailments.com/, June 26, 2012.

19. Jonathan Isbit, "Nature's Platform: The Basis for a Healthier Life," NaturesPlatform.com, retrieved from http://www.naturesplatform.com/, April 29, 2011.

20. Paul W. Frame, Ph.D., "General Information About Uranium in Ceramics," Oak Ridge Associated Universities, retrieved from http://www.orau.org/ptp/collection/consumer%20 products/uraniumceramicsgeneralinfo.htm, August 22, 2011.

21. Charles P. Gerba, Ph.D., cited in "Dr. Germ: Here a germ, there a germ, everywhere a . . . wait," College of Agriculture and Life Sciences, University of Arizona, February 17, 2005, retrieved from http://ag.arizona.edu/media/archives/6.11.html, April 4, 2011.

22. "Gross! WHAT Happens When You Flush?," Netscape Home & Living, retrieved from http://channels.isp.netscape.com/homerealestate/package.jsp?name=fte/toiletgerms/toilet germs&floc=wn-nx, April 4, 2011.

23. Philip M. Tierno, Jr., Ph.D, cited in "What Can You Catch in Restrooms," WebMD, 2002, retrieved from http://www.webmd.com/balance/features/what-can-you-catch-in-restrooms, April 4, 2011.

24. Don Duncan, "Is It Time to Kill Off the Flush Toilet," Time, November 6, 2008, retrieved from http://www.time.com/time/health/article/0,8599,1857113,00.html, July 3, 2011.

25. "Water Saving Tips," Buffalo Water Authority, Buffalo, New York, 2010, retrieved from http:// www.buffalowaterauthority.com/CustomerService/ConsumerTips/WaterSavingTips, July 3, 2011; and "How to Convert Any Toilet to a Low Flush Toilet," wikiHow.com, June 1, 2011, retrieved from http://www.wikihow.com/Convert-Any-Toilet-to-a-Low-Flush-Toilet, July 7, 2011.

26. "If It's Yellow, Let It Mellow . . . ," Waste Not, Want Less Blog, January 1, 2008, retrieved from http://wastenotwantless.blogspot.com/2008/01/if-its-yellow-let-it-mellow.html, July 3, 2011.

27. Anonymous comment in response to Ben Edwards, "Save Money by Not Flushing the Toilet?," Money Smart Life Blog, October 10, 2010, retrieved from http://moneysmartlife.com /save-money-by-not-flushing-the-toilet/, July 3, 2011.

28. Kim Severson, "Sugar Coated: We're Drowning in High Fructose Corn Syrup. Do the Risks Go Beyond Our Waistline?," San Francisco Chronicle, February 18, 2004, retrieved from http://www.news.ucdavis.edu/in_the_news/full_text/view_clip.lasso?id=7519, July 16, 2011.

29. Gary Taubes, "Is Sugar Toxic?," New York Times Magazine, April 17, 2011, MM47, retrieved from http://www.nytimes.com/2011/04/17/magazine/mag-17Sugar-t.html?pagewanted=all, July 15, 2011.

30. "10 Surprising Places Where Germs Are Hiding in Your Home!," iHealth360.com, February 6, 2010, retrieved from http://ihealth360.com/uncategorized/10-surprising-places-where -germs-are-hiding-in-your-home, May 14, 2011.

31. "How to Dodge a Nasty Cold or Flu," ReadersDigest.ca, retrieved from http://www.readers digest.ca/health/sickness-prevention/how-dodge-nasty-cold-or-flu, May 14, 2011.

32. "Sanitize for Your Protection," SmileLink Newsletter, Niantic Dental Associates Edition, retrieved from http://www.nianticdental.com/nl/article.php?id=1748&type=col, July 7, 2011.

33. Mike Adams, "Toxic Chemical Triclosan Commonly Found in Anti-Bacterial Soaps, Toothpaste Products," NaturalNews.com, October 29, 2007, retrieved from http://www.natural news.com/022178.html#ixzz1J9S776BZ, April 11, 2011.

34. Seth Stevenson, "Paste Test: Which Toothpaste Should You Buy?," Slate, Oct. 7, 1998, retrieved from www.slate.com/id/3604/, April 10, 2011.

35. Giles Watson, quoted in Mark Prigg and Rebecca Lawrence, "Toothpaste Cancer Alert," London Evening Standard, April 15, 2005, retrieved from http://www.secretofthieves.com /article12triclosan.cfm, April 10, 2011.

36. Mike Adams, "Warning: Toxic Chemical Triclosan Can Turn Your Toothpaste into Chloroform," Natural News.com, February 13, 2006, retrieved from http://www.naturalnews .com/017804.html, April 10, 2011.

37. "Not Effective and Not Safe: The FDA Must Regulate Dangerous Antimicrobials in Everyday Products," Natural Resources Defense Council, April 2010, retrieved from http://www.nrdc .org/health/files/antimicrobials.pdf, April 14, 2011.

38. National Aeronautics and Space Administration, "The Torino Impact Hazard Scale," retrieved from NASA's Near Earth Object Program web pages, http://neo.jpl.nasa.gov/torino_scale.html, February 22, 2010.

39. Tom Vanderbilt, "The Traffic Guru," *Wilson Quarterly*, Summer 2008, Woodrow Wilson International Center for Scholars, retrieved from http://www.wilsonquarterly.com/article.cfm?AID=1234, August 31, 2011.

40. Matthias Schulz, "Controlled Chaos: European Cities Do Away with Traffic Signs," *Der Spiegel*, November 16, 2006, retrieved from http://www.spiegel.de/international/spiegel/0,1518,448747,00.html, August 31, 2011.

41. Vanderbilt, "Traffic Guru."

42. Schulz, "Controlled Chaos."

43. Vanderbilt, "Traffic Guru."

44. Mara Betsch, "Some Fats Help, Some Harm Your Heart," CNN Health, September 23, 2008, retrieved from http://articles.cnn.com/2008-09-23/health/moh.fats.heart_1_trans-fats-unsaturated-fats-alice-lichtenstein?_s=PM:HEALTH, June 28, 2011.

45. "Trans Fats 101," University of Maryland Medical Center, November 3, 2010, retrieved from http://www.umm.edu/features/transfats.htm, June 28, 2011; and "New York City Passes Trans Fat Ban," MSNBC.com News Services, December 5, 2006, retrieved from http://www.msnbc.msn.com/id/16051436/ns/health-diet_and_nutrition/t/new-york-city-passes-trans-fat-ban/, June 28, 2011.

46. "Shining the Spotlight on Trans Fats," Harvard School of Public Health, retrieved from http://www.hsph.harvard.edu/nutritionsource/nutrition-news/transfats/, June 28, 2011.

47. Dr. Marc Faber, "U.S. Bonds Worthless Confetti," TV interview produced by the *Gloom, Boom & Doom Report*, July 11, 2010, retrieved from http://www.youtube.com/watch?v=P9Ig58p_124, February 19, 2011.

48. Laurence J. Kotlikoff, "A Hidden Fiscal Crisis," *Finance & Development*, International Monetary Fund, September 2010, 30–32.

49. Jennifer DePaul, "David Stockman: U.S. Is in 'Race to the Fiscal Bottom,'" *Fiscal Times*, October 6, 2010, retrieved from http://www.thefiscaltimes.com/Articles/2010/10/06/David-Stockman-US-Is-in-Race-to-the-Fiscal-Bottom.aspx, February 20, 2011.

50. "BitDefender Malware and Spam Survey Finds E-Threats Adapting to Online Behavioral Trends," BitDefender.com, August 3, 2009, retrieved from http://www.bitdefender.com/news/bitdefender-malware-and-spam-survey-finds-e-threats-adapting-to-online-behavioral-trends-1094.html, January 23, 2012.

51. "Tuna," World's Healthiest Foods website, retrieved from http://www.whfoods.com/genpage.php?tname=foodspice&dbid=112, June 6, 2010.

52. Lisa Bonos, "Book Review: *Slow Death by Rubber Duck* by Rick Smith and Bruce Lourie," *Washington Post*, January 10, 2010, retrieved from http://www.washingtonpost.com/wp-dyn/content/article/2010/01/08/AR2010010801303.html, June 6, 2010.

53. Allison Janse with Charles P. Gerba, Ph.D., *The Germ Freak's Guide to Outwitting Colds and Flu* (Deerfield Beach, FL: Health Communications, Inc., 2005), 151.

54. Philip M. Tierno Jr., Ph.D., *The Secret Life of Germs: Observations and Lessons from a Microbe Hunter* (New York: Pocket Books, 2001), 96.

55. Danielle Braff, "Eliminate Germs in Your House: Remote Control—170 Channels of High-Def Filth," *Men's Health*, 2010, retrieved from http://www.menshealth.com/mhlists/fight_household_germs/printer.php, July 24, 2011.

U

1. "Bacteria and Foodborne Illnesses," National Digestive Diseases Information Clearinghouse (NDDIC), U.S. Department of Health and Human Services, May 2007, retrieved from http://digestive.niddk.nih.gov/ddiseases/pubs/bacteria/, August 12, 2011.

2. Denise Mann, reviewed by Jonathan L. Gelfand, M.D., "Germs in the Kitchen," WebMD, October 18, 2007, 2, retrieved from http://www.webmd.com/food-recipes/features/germs-in-kitchen?page=2, August 12, 2011.

3. Daniel Engber, "The Fat and the Short of It," *New York Times Magazine*, October 18, 2009, 23–24.

4. Ed Butowsky, "Are Americans Committing Financial Suicide?," Interview by Pimm Fox on *Taking Stock*, Bloomberg News, August 12, 2010, retrieved from http://www.edbutowsky.com/media-releases/how-to-avoid-financial-suicide/, January 30, 2011.

5. "The National Safety Commission Alerts," April 27, 2010, retrieved from http://alerts.nationalsafetycommission.com/2010/04/making-safe-and-legal-u-turn.html, June 11, 2011.

6. James Baxter, "How to Avoid an Illegal U-Turn Ticket," National Motorists Association Blog, February 2, 2008, retrieved from http://blog.motorists.org/how-to-avoid-an-illegal-u-turn -ticket/, June 11, 2011.
7. Dieter Fischer, "Low Risk Driving—A Skill for Life: The U-Turn," Driving School.com, retrieved from http://www.driving-school.com.au/UTurn06.htm, June 11, 2011.
8. Baxter, "How to Avoid."

V

1. Sten Odenwald, "The Decay of the False Vacuum," *Astronomy,* November 1983; retrieved from http://www.astronomycafe.net/cosm/decay.html, May 11, 2011; Allan Guth, "An Eternity of Bubbles?," retrieved from http://www.pbs.org/wnet/hawking/mysteries/html/guth_1.html, May 11, 2011; Marcelo Gleiser, Barrett Rogers, and Joel Thorarinson, "Bubbling the False Vacuum Away," *Physical Review D* 77:2 (January 16, 2008), retrieved from http://link.aps .org/doi/10.1103/PhysRevD.77.023513, May 15, 2011; and Jared Daniel, "If the Universe as We Know It Ends, When Will It Happen?," Lifeboat Foundation blog, May 28, 2010, retrieved from http://lifeboat.com/blog/2010/05/if-the-universe-as-we-know-it-ends-when-will-it -happen, May 11, 2011.
2. Sidney Coleman and Frank De Luccia, "Gravitational Effects on and of Vacuum Decay," *Physical Review* 21:12 (June 15, 1980), 3314, retrieved from www.physics.princeton.edu/~steinh /ph564/ColemanDeLuccia.pdf, May 15, 2011.
3. "Welcome to Valles Caldera," official website of the Valles Caldera National Preserve, retrieved from http://www.vallescaldera.gov/comevisit/, June 28, 2010.
4. Natalie Angier, "Sorry, Vegans: Brussels Sprouts Like to Live, Too," *New York Times,* December 22, 2009, D2, retrieved from http://www.nytimes.com/2009/12/22/science/22angi.html, August 28, 2011.
5. "How to Become a Fruitarian," TheNewEarth.org, retrieved from http://www.thenewearth .org/fruit.html, August 27, 2011.
6. "Vitamin A and Hip Fracture Risk," *Harvard Medical School Family Health Guide,* January 23, 2003, updated March 2003, retrieved from http://www.health.harvard.edu/fhg/updates /update0303c.shtml, August 19, 2011.
7. "Vitamin A: Bone Poison?," WebMD Osteoporosis Health Center, January 22, 2003, retrieved from http://www.webmd.com/osteoporosis/news/20030122/vitamin-bone-poison, August 19, 2011.
8. *Harvard Medical School Family Health Guide.*
9. Jane E. Brody, "Taking Too Much Vitamin C Can Be Dangerous, Study Finds," *New York Times,* April 9, 1998, retrieved from http://www.nytimes.com/1998/04/09/us/taking-too -much-vitamin-c-can-be-dangerous-study-finds.html, August 15, 2011; and "Prof. Victor Herbert," retrieved from http://www.victorherbert.com/, August 15, 2011.
10. "Vitamin D," MedLinePlus, U.S. National Library of Medicine, National Institutes of Health, February 24, 2011, retrieved from http://www.nlm.nih.gov/medlineplus/druginfo/natu ral/929.html, August 19, 2011; "Dietary Supplement Fact Sheet: Vitamin D," Office of Dietary Supplements, U.S. National Institutes of Health, June 24, 2011, retrieved from http:// ods.od.nih.gov/factsheets/vitamind/, August 18, 2011; and Jane Higdon, M.D, "Micronutrient Information Center: Vitamin D," Linus Pauling Institute, Oregon State University, March 2004, updated in January 2008 by Victoria J. Drake, Ph.D., retrieved from http://lpi.oregon state.edu/infocenter/vitamins/vitaminD/, August 19, 2011.
11. "The Dark Side of Sun Exposure," WebMD, reviewed by Laura J. Martin, M.D., July 21, 2010, retrieved from http://www.webmd.com/melanoma-skin-cancer/slideshow-sun-damaged -skin, August 19, 2011.
12. Higdon, "Micronutrient Information."
13. "Hypervitaminosis D: Vitamin D Toxicity," PubMedHealth, U.S. National Institutes of Health, retrieved from http://www.ncbi.nlm.nih.gov/pubmedhealth/PMH0002561/, August 19, 2011; "Vitamin D Toxicity," Vitamin D Council, August 8, 2011, retrieved from http://www.vitamindcouncil.org/about-vitamin-d/what-is-vitamin-d/vitamin-d-toxicity/, August 19, 2011; "Vitamin D," MedLinePlus; "Dietary Supplement Fact Sheet: Vitamin D"; and Higdon, "Micronutrient Information."
14. "About the Vitamin D Council," Vitamin D Council, July 15, 2011, retrieved from http:// www.vitamindcouncil.org/about-us/, August 19, 2011.
15. Vitamin D Council, "Vitamin D Toxicity."
16. "Vitamin E Overview," Online Medical Reference, University of Maryland Medical Center,

retrieved from http://www.umm.edu/altmed/articles/vitamin-e-000341.htm, August 18, 2011.

17. "Dietary Supplement Fact Sheet: Vitamin E," Office of Dietary Supplements, U.S National Institutes of Health, June 24, 2011, retrieved from http://ods.od.nih.gov/factsheets/vitamine/, August 18, 2011.

18. Dean Edell, M.D., "Vitamin E Dangerous?," HealthCentral.com, November 10, 2004, retrieved from http://www.healthcentral.com/drdean/408/60985.html, August 18, 2011.

19. Ibid.

W

1. K. Cooper Ray, "Social Primer Bill of Rites, Article 9: A Man Hugs the Curb," SocialPrimer. com, March 24, 2011, retrieved from http://www.socialprimer.com/2011/03/sp-bill-of-rites -article-nine-a-man-hugs-the-curb/, August 20, 2010; and Liz Scott, "Dating Dilemma— Should a Man Take the Curb Side of the Sidewalk?," Lemondrop.com, March 15, 2010, retrieved from http://www.lemondrop.com/2010/03/15/dating-etiquette-should-he-walk -on-the-curbside-of-the-sidewalk/, August 20, 2011.

2. "Roadside Warning over Pollution Story," BBC News, November 2, 2005, retrieved from http://news.bbc.co.uk/go/pr/fr/-/2/hi/uk_news/england/london/4400706.stm, August 20, 2011.

3. Joseph Brownstein and Radha Chitale, "10 Germy Surfaces You Touch Every Day," ABC News Medical Unit, September 5, 2008, retrieved from http://abcnews.go.com/Health/Cold andFluNews/story?id=5727571&page=1, September 2, 2011.

4. Chloe Lambert, "Want to Keep Your Heart and Lungs Healthy? Don't Sit Next to the Photocopier," *Daily Mail*, March 15, 2011, retrieved from http://www.dailymail.co.uk/health /article-1366304/Want-heart-lungs-healthy-Dont-sit-photocopier.html, September 9, 2011.

5. Sabrina Rogers, "What to Eat & Drink Before and After Workouts," AskMen.com, retrieved from http://www.askmen.com/sports/foodcourt_60/94_eating_well.html, August 6, 2011.

6. Mayo Clinic Staff, "Eating and Exercise: 5 Tips to Maximize Your Workouts," MayoClinic. com, December 18, 2010, retrieved from http://www.mayoclinic.com/health/exercise /HQ00594_D/NSECTIONGROUP=2, August 6, 2011; and Mayo Clinic Staff, "Dehydration: Symptoms," MayoClinic.com, January 7, 2011, retrieved from http://www.mayoclinic .com/health/dehydration/DS00561/DSECTION=symptoms, August 6, 2011.

7. Benjamin Wedro, M.D., F.A.C.E.P., F.A.A.E.M., "What Are the Signs And Symptoms of Dehydration?," MedicineNet.com, retrieved from http://www.medicinenet.com/dehydration /page2.htm, August 6, 2011.

8. Mayo Clinic Staff, "Dehydration: Definition," MayoClinic.com, January 7, 2011, retrieved from http://www.mayoclinic.com/health/dehydration/DS00561, August 6, 2011.

9. Dennis DiClaudio, *The Hypochondriac's Pocket Guide to Horrible Diseases You Probably Already Have* (New York: Bloomsbury, 2006), 173.

10. Jane Kay, "Home Water Filters May Leach Lead, Study Finds," *San Francisco Examiner,* June 19, 1998, retrieved from http://www.sfgate.com/cgi-bin/article.cgi?f=/e/a/1998/06/19 /NEWS2231.dtl&type=printable, March 4, 2010.

11. Mayo Clinic Staff, "Lead Poisoning: Symptoms," MayoClinic.com, retrieved from http:// www.mayoclinic.com/health/lead-poisoning/FL00068/DSECTION=symptoms, March 4, 2010; and "Lead Poisoning Symptoms," Online Lawyer Source, retrieved from http://www .onlinelawyersource.com/lead_exposure/lead_symptoms.html, March 4, 2010.

12. Charles P. Gerba, Ph.D., cited in Brownstein and Chitale, "10 Germy Surfaces."

13. Allison Janse with Charles P. Gerba, Ph.D., *The Germ Freak's Guide to Outwitting Colds and Flu* (Deerfield Beach, FL: Health Communications, Inc., 2005), 175.

14. Rebekah George, interviewed on the *Early Show,* CBS News, April 25, 2009; and Brian Dakss, "Germs' Hiding Places," CBSNews.com, April 26, 2009, retrieved from http://www.cbsnews .com/stories/2009/04/25/earlyshow/health/main4968164.shtml, May 2, 2011.

15. "Tenants Banned from Using Welcome Mats over 'Serious Health and Safety Fears,'" *Daily Mail*, February 3, 2010, retrieved from http://www.dailymail.co.uk/news/article-1248174 /Tenants-ordered-remove-potentially-dangerous-welcome-mats-health-safety-fears.html, April 23, 2011.

16. "Health and Safety Killjoys Ban Welcome Mats and Pot Plants—Because They're a Fire Risk," *Daily Mail*, June 25, 2009, retrieved from http://www.dailymail.co.uk/news/article

-1195522/Flat-tenants-forced-throw-away-welcome-mats-pot-plants-health-safety-risk.html, April 18, 2011.

17. "Cute but Contagious—and Coming, Sadly, to a Cave Somewhere Near You," *Economist*, May 21, 2009, retrieved from http://www.economist.com/node/13702854?story_id=13702854, January 22, 2012.

18. "White-nose Syndrome Fungus (*Geomyces destructans*) in Bat, France," *Emerging Infectious Diseases* 16:2 (February 2010), Centers for Disease Control and Prevention, retrieved from http://wwwnc.cdc.gov/eid/article/16/2/09-1391_article.htm, January 22, 2012.

19. Margareta Pagano, "Are Wind Farms a Health Risk? A U.S. Scientist Identifies 'Wind Turbine Syndrome,'" *Independent*, August 2, 2009, retrieved from http://www.independent.co.uk/environment/green-living/are-wind-farms-a-health-risk-us-scientist-identifies-wind-turbine-syndrome-1766254.html, April 7, 2011.

20. Testimony Before the New York State Legislative Energy Committee, March 7, 2006, by Dr. Nina Pierpont, M.D., Ph.D., retrieved from http://www.savewesternny.org/docs/pierpont_testimony.html, April 7, 2011.

21. Jon Boone, Ph.D., www.stopillwind.org; Pagano, "Are Wind Farms."

22. "Aggressive Fungus Strikes Joplin Tornado Victims," Associated Press, June 10, 2011, retrieved from http://www.carthagepress.com/joplin-tornado/x41284196/Aggressive-fungus-strikes-Joplin-tornado-victims, August 2, 2011; and Timothy Williams, "Rare Infection Strikes Victims of a Tornado in Missouri," *New York Times*, June 11, 2011, A12, retrieved from http://www.nytimes.com/2011/06/11/us/11fungus.html?_r=3&ref=health, August 2, 2011.

23. "Mucormycosis (Zygomycosis): Prevention," Centers for Disease Control and Prevention, July 28, 2011, retrieved from http://www.cdc.gov/fungal/mucormycosis/risk-prevention.html, August 1, 2011.

X

1. Greg Michael, "X-ray Computed Tomography," *Physics Education* 36:6 (November 2001), 442–451, retrieved from http://www.physics.utoronto.ca/~key/PHY138/Suppl.Notes/x-ray_computed_tomography.pdf, June 21, 2011; and "Radiation Emitting Products: Computed Tomography (CT)," November 9, 2010, U.S. Food and Drug Administration, retrieved from http://www.fda.gov/Radiation-EmittingProducts/RadiationEmittingProductsandProcedures/MedicalImaging/MedicalX-Rays/ucm115317.htm, June 20, 2011.

2. Walt Bogdanich and Jo Craven McGinty, "Medicare Claims Showing Overuse for CT Scanning," *New York Times*, June 18, 2011, A1, retrieved from http://www.nytimes.com/2011/06/18/health/18radiation.html, June 21, 2011.

3. Roxanne Nelson, "Thousands of New Cancers Predicted Due to Increased Use of CT," *Medscape Medical News*, December 17, 2009, retrieved from http://www.medscape.com/viewarticle/714025, June 20, 2011.

4. Rita F. Redberg, "Cancer Risks and Radiation Exposure from Computed Tomographic Scans: How Can We Be Sure That the Benefits Outweigh the Risks?," *Archives of Internal Medicine* 169:22 (December 14–28, 2009), retrieved from http://archinte.ama-assn.org/cgi/content/full/169/22/2049, June 21, 2011.

Y

1. "CPSC, National Safety Organization Announce Partnership to Stop the Resale of Dangerous Products," U.S. Consumer Product Safety Commission, Office of Information and Public Affairs, April 14, 2004, retrieved from http://www.cpsc.gov/cpscpub/prerel/prhtml04/04120.html, July 26, 2011.

2. "Resale Round-up—April 14, 2004," U.S. Consumer Product Safety Commission, April 14, 2004, retrieved from http://www.cpsc.gov/roundup/resale04.html, July 24, 2011.

3. Walecia Konrad, "Bargains on Used Goods May Prove Costly," *New York Times*, July 26, 2011, D6, retrieved from http://www.nytimes.com/2011/07/26/health/26consumer.html, July 26, 2011.

4. "Supervolcanoes," BBC Science and Nature homepage, February 3, 2000, retrieved from http://www.bbc.co.uk/science/horizon/1999/supervolcanoes.shtml, July 5, 2010.

5. Cecil Adams (aka "The World's Smartest Human"), "Is Yellowstone Park Sitting on a Supervolcano That's About to Blow?," Straight Dope, January 2, 2009, retrieved from http://www.straightdope.com/columns/read/2834/is-yellowstone-park-sitting-on-a-supervolcano-thats-about-to-blow, July 5, 2010.

6. William J. Broad, "All Bent Out of Shape: The Problem with Yoga," *New York Times Magazine*, January 8, 2011, retrieved from http://www.nytimes.com/2012/01/08/magazine/how-yoga-can-wreck-your-body.html?_r=1=magazine, January 22, 2012.

Z

1. "Definition: Botnet (Zombie Army)," SearchSecurity.com, December 2004, retrieved from http://searchsecurity.techtarget.com/definition/botnet, June 27, 2011.
2. Edward J. Kane, Ph.D., "Dangers of Capital Forbearance: The Case of the F.S.L.I.C. and the Zombie S&L's," *Contemporary Economic Policy* 5:1 (January 1987), 77–83, abstract retrieved from http://onlinelibrary.wiley.com/doi/10.1111/j.1465-7287.1987.tb00247.x/abstract, August 8, 2011.
3. William Safire, "Zombie Banks," *New York Times Magazine*, May 17, 2009, MM26, retrieved from http://www.nytimes.com/2009/05/17/magazine/17wwln-safire-t.html, August 8, 2011.
4. Paul Krugman, "Banking on the Brink," *New York Times*, February 22, 2009, retrieved from http://www.nytimes.com/2009/02/23/opinion/23krugman.html, August 8, 2011.
5. Paul Krugman, "All the President's Zombies," *New York Times* blogs, February 25, 2009, retrieved from http://krugman.blogs.nytimes.com/2009/02/25/all-the-presidents-zombies/, August 8, 2011.
6. Philip Munz, Ioan Hudea, Joe Imad, and Robert J. Smith?, "When Zombies Attack!: Mathematical Modelling of an Outbreak of Zombie Infection," in J. M. Tchuenche and C. Chiyaka, Editors, *Infectious Disease Modelling Research Progress* (Hauppage, NY: Nova Science Publishers, 2009), Chapter 4, 133–150, retrieved from http://mysite.science.uottawa.ca/rsmith43/Zombies.pdf, April 29, 2011; and Clive Thompson, "Zombie-Attack Science," *New York Times Magazine*, December 13, 2009, 70.
7. Patrick J. Kiger, "Is This a Good Idea? Preparedness for Zombie Attacks?," Discovery.com, September 14, 2009, retrieved from http://blogs.discovery.com/good_idea/2009/09/is-this-a-good-idea-preparedness-for-zombie-attacks.html, April 29, 2011.
8. Alstry, "Is America Zombulated," *Alstrynomics: Applying Common Sense to Economics*, July 18, 2009, retrieved from http://alstry.blogspot.com/2009/07/is-america-zombulated.html, January 16, 2011.

ACKNOWLEDGMENTS

CATALOGING EVERYTHING THAT MIGHT THREATEN OUR health and well-being—not to mention the future of humanity and the existence of our very planet itself—and warning people about all these hazards in a timely manner can be a depressing and thankless task, as Cassandra, the namesake of our institute, found out when she was ravished by Ajax the Lesser after the fall of Troy, a defeat that would never have occurred had her dire predictions not been dismissed as fearmongering. Our heartfelt thanks go out to every member of the Cassandra Institute research team, without whose unflagging efforts—and truly alarming findings—there would be no *Encylopedia Paranoiaca.*

We are also deeply indebted to three organizations—Armageddon Online, the Lifeboat Foundation, and Maarten Keulemans's darkly humorous, but scientifically impeccable, Exit Mundi—whose pioneering studies of end-of-the-world scenarios have broken the ground, figuratively if not literally, for our project. Thanks, too, to Nick Bostrom, professor of philosophy at the University of Oxford, who, by specifying four distinct categories of extinction risks—bangs, crunches, shrieks, and whimpers—helped us to find an intellectual framework for our own scholarship. (In paying tribute to those who blazed the trail we have followed, we were tempted to point out, as Neoplatonist philosopher Bernard de Chartres did back in the twelfth century, that if we have seen further, it is because we are like "dwarfs standing on the shoulders of giants." However, after taking note of the extreme risk involved in standing on the shoulders of *anybody,* much less a giant, and of the fact that a growing number of little people find the term "dwarf" abusive, we decided not to do so.)

Space limitations prohibit us from properly acknowledging even a small fraction of the experts whose specific research informed our endeavors, or the broad array of international institutions—both public and private—who funded their investigations. But we would be remiss if we failed to single out for special thanks a few whose contributions have proven particularly valuable. Our book would be far less informative and useful were it not for Charles P. Gerba, Ph.D., of the University of Arizona's College of Agriculture and Life Sciences, whose cutting-edge work on the menace of toilet aerosols—not to mention his relentless flushing out of other household microbial threats—has set an environmental biology standard that few, if any, could possibly meet. We're grateful, too, for the regularity—and unexpected good humor—with which Dr. Gerba and his colleague Allison Janse issue biohazard warnings to the public, and for the funding that the Clorox Company has so generously provided to facilitate the professor's work. (Philip M. Tierno, Jr., Ph.D., director of clinical microbiology at NYU Langone Medical Center, and his frequent sponsor, the makers of Brillo soap pads, deserve similar accolades, as do Jennifer Lance, founder of Eco Child's Play, and Susan Nederost, M.D., for alerting us to the hidden perils of using chlorine bleach and soap, respectively.)

We would also like to thank the United Nations Environment Programme (UNEP), the World Meteorological Organization, the Clean Air Task Force, the National Oceanic and Atmospheric Administration, and, of course, the U.S. Environmental Protection Agency, for helping us elucidate the myriad risks posed by global warming, and we are also appreciative of Senator James M. Inhofe of Oklahoma for explaining, with scientific precision, how economically and politically disastrous it would be to attempt to mitigate it. (A salute to the senator, too, for pointing out the similarities between the EPA and the Gestapo.)

Others whose scholarship, writings, and publications have proven particularly valuable include Cecil Adams (of "Straight Dope" column fame), "Alstry" (the blogger who introduced us to the concept of "zombulation"), the Centers for Disease Control and Prevention (and, in particular, the editors of the CDC's surprisingly readable *Morbidity and Mortality Weekly Report*), the Consumer Product Safety Commission, Dennis DiClaudio (author of *The Hypochondriac's Pocket Guide* to Horrible Diseases You Probably Already Have), Michael Ehline (the accident attorney to end all accident attorneys), the Environmental Working Group, Dr. Marc Faber (publisher of the *Gloom, Boom & Doom Report*), Anne Marie Helmenstine, Ph.D. (About.com's chemistry guru), Dr. Ben Kim (of drbenkim.com and *Dr. Ben Kim's Radio Show*), Ray Kurzweil (the peerless inventor and futurist), Internet health sage Kristie Leong, M.D., the Mayo Clinic, Leuren Moret (who is single-handedly responsible for whatever knowledge the Cassandra Institute has been able to glean about aerosol/chemtrails plasma weaponry), Michael Pollan (the award-winning author and food activist), the *New Yorker*'s superlative Michael Specter, SilentMenace .com, Jack Sim (president of the World Toilet Organization), Rick Smith and Bruce Lourie (coauthors of *Slow Death by Rubber Duck: The Secret Danger of Everyday Things*), antinannyism crusader Paul Joseph Watson, Andrew Weil, M.D., (our college friend, and founder of the Arizona Center for Integrative Medicine), WorldPoultry.net ("the gateway to the global poultry industry"), and, alphabetically last but certainly not least, former U.S. Department of Agriculture scientist Gerald Zirnstein (who coined the term "pink slime").

We are profoundly grateful to our colleagues at the Institute of Expertology, most notably Victor S. Navasky, for deepening our understanding of the role that experts—whom Navasky defines as individuals who "by virtue of celebrity, official status, formal title, academic degree, professional license, public office, journalistic beat, quantity of publications and/or use of highly technical jargon, are presumed to know what they are talking about"—have played in raising public consciousness about the "world of hurt" in which we currently find ourselves. And we are also indebted to documentary filmmaker and former science writer Tom Naughton for his unique insights into how the nimble citation of research studies, and the adroit use of statistics, can help convey the seriousness of perils that might otherwise go unnoticed.

We were extremely fortunate that Gwyneth Cravens and Katherine Vaz were willing to share with us the fruits of their extensive research on radioactivity, on the one hand, and polka-related injuries, on the other; our compendium would be far less definitive were it not for their generosity.

Kyoko Watanabe, our book's interior designer, and Victoria Chiaro, the Cassandra Institute's own Director of Symbology, traveled the extra mile to ensure that our messages, however grim, would always be delivered in a graphically arresting format, and we applaud them for their talent and their dedication. We would also like to thank those who, along with Victoria, developed the ingenious pictograms that grace these pages: the International Organization for Standardization; the Noun Project and its visionary leaders Edward Boatman, Sofya Polyakov, and Scott Thomas; neuroscientist and transhumanist philosopher Anders Sandberg, whose "Warning Signs for Tomorrow" adorn the Lifeboat Foundation's website; Public Safety Canada; the U.S. National Park Service; Maylasian graphic artist Khoon Lay Gan; computer-algorithm whiz Ron Kaminsky; the U.S. Federal Geographic Data Committee Homeland Security Working Group; and—perhaps most important of all—the snappily named United Nations Committee of Experts on the Transport of Dangerous Goods and on the Globally Harmonized System of Classification and Labelling of Chemicals.

The *Encyclopedia Paranoiaca* has also benefitted greatly from the skill and thoroughness of our copy editor, Marty Karlow, and from the consistently thoughtful manuscript preparation and logistical assistance we have received from production editor Lisa Healy and assistant editor Michele Bové. Thank you, Marty, Lisa, and Michele!

Finally, we would like to acknowledge our agent and dear friend, Ed Victor, and another treasured colleague, David Rosenthal, who had the foresight to sign our book mere days before, Cassandra-like, he was relieved of his duties as publisher of Simon & Schuster. We are also deeply obliged to Amanda Murray, who courageously assumed responsibility for our project after David's departure, and who treated us to a memorable "welcome lunch" before, sadly, she, too, found herself among the ranks of former S&S staffers. And, above all, we offer our very special thanks to our *current* editor, Jofie Ferrari-Adler, whose warmhearted support, bemused encouragement, and perceptive advice have not only enhanced our enterprise at every turn, but have also not yet—at least as of this writing—cost him his job.

About the Cassandra Institute and Its "Spiritual (and Spiritualist) Father," William Thomas Stead

THE CASSANDRA INSTITUTE IS AN INTERNATIONAL THINK tank and academic research organization founded in New York City on November 20, 1912, one hundred years to the day before the official publication of the *Encyclopedia Paranoiaca*. Our institute's stated mission is "to promote the general welfare by seeking out, vetting, and, when appropriate, calling attention to warnings, caveats, recommendations, advisories, admonitions, and cautionary (if occasionally apocalyptic) prophecies and predictions that, although offered by individuals or organizations with impeccable credentials and/or unimpeachable relevant expertise, have nonetheless gone unnoticed, or at best, have been underappreciated, disbelieved, ignored, or dismissed by the very public whose health, safety, well-being, and fundamental rights they were intended to maintain or protect."

The inspiration behind the founding of the Cassandra Institute—and all its subsequent work—was the noted investigative journalist, civil rights activist, and spiritualist William Thomas Stead, who passed away tragically a mere seven months before our organization officially opened its doors. One of Stead's most notable writings was a lurid short story entitled "How the Mail Steamer went down in Mid Atlantic by a Survivor," published in the *Pall Mall Gazette* on March 22, 1886. In it, he imagined the sinking of a great transatlantic ocean liner, and conjured up in painstaking detail the mayhem that ensued as hordes of frantic passengers and crew members struggled to secure a seat in one of the pitifully inadequate number of lifeboats with which his fictional vessel, like all too many real steamships of the period, was equipped. Stead concluded his eerily accurate account of a possible future maritime calamity with this prescient observation: "This is exactly what might take place and what *will* take place if the liners are sent to sea short of boats."

In a near-perfect display of both the premonitory powers of our Institute's namesake and the curse that ensured that no one would ever believe any of her prognostications, Stead paid no heed to his own uncannily accurate prophecy. Just as Cassandra's fellow Trojans ignored the star-crossed soothsayer's insightful warning about the giant wooden horse offered by "Greeks bearing gifts" and cheerfully wheeled the huge ceremonial nag crammed with heavily armed commandos into the center of their doomed city, Stead blithely boarded the *Titanic* in the port of Southampton on April 10, 1912, clearly aware that the massive vessel had only enough lifeboats for about half of its 2,223 passengers. He was one of the 1,517 voyagers on the ill-omened steamer who drowned when the "unsinkable" ship slipped beneath the frigid waters of the North Atlantic after hitting an iceberg off Newfoundland on April 15, 1912, his decades-old but still all-too-timely admonition having been fated to fall on his own deaf ears.

ABOUT THE AUTHORS

Henry Beard was a cofounder of the *National Lampoon* and served as its editor during the magazine's heyday in the 1970s. He is the author or coauthor of more than forty humorous books—with their attendant risks of brutally slapped thighs, painfully tickled ribs, and severely split sides—on a number of troubling topics, including the hazards of pet ownership (*French for Cats, Zen for Cats, Poetry for Cats, French Cats Don't Get Fat, A Cat's Night Before Christmas,* and *A Dog's Night Before Christmas*); the perils of ill-considered pastimes (the *Sailing, Skiing, Fishing,* and *Golfing Dictionaries, Murphy's Laws of Fishing, Murphy's Laws of Golf, The Official Exceptions to the Rules of Golf, Bad Golf My Way, Leslie Nielsen's Stupid Little Golf Book,* and *Golf: A History of the World's Most Preposterous Sport*); the hidden dangers in everyday life (*The Way Things Really Work*); the routine transgression of animal rights (*Miss Piggy's Guide to Life* and *What's Worrying Gus?*); the lurking menace of an undead language (*Latin for All Occasions* and *X-treme Latin*); the conspicuous failures of our criminal justice system (*O.J.'s Legal Pad*); and the sinister conspiracies that have threatened the very foundations of our great nation (*The Unshredded Files of Bill*

and Hillary Clinton, Where's Saddam?, and *The Dick Cheney Code*). He has also collaborated with fellow *Harvard Lampoon* graduate Christopher Cerf on several critically important projects, a number of which are described below.

Beard is currently pursuing important research on the very urgent question of whether—based on his personal observations of certain puzzling phenomena affecting the movement of small dimpled balls across randomly curved, closely mown grassy surfaces—there is, in fact, reason to hope that if the earth has the misfortune to encounter a black hole, our home planet will obey the laws of golf rather than the principles of physics and experience a "lip out" and pass harmlessly by the lethal celestial object's critical "event horizon" as it approaches its outermost circumference, thereby avoiding being sucked into the infinitely deep gravity well of the supermassive "singularity" at its core, even though our terrestrial globe is moving on a direct line and at a constant speed toward the absolute dead center of the circular rupture in the space-time continuum.

———

Christopher Cerf is, among other things, an author, a composer-lyricist, a television and music producer, and a former contributing editor of the *National Lampoon.* Cerf has written over three hundred songs for *Sesame Street,* and also cocreated the acclaimed PBS literacy education series *Between the Lions*—work that, despite winning multiple Emmy and Grammy awards, has utterly failed to improve the dismal reading scores of America's young children.

Similarly, although his collaborations with Marlo Thomas and the Free to Be Foundation have produced a #1 *New York Times* bestselling book and an Emmy Award–winning ABC special, the United States, as of this writing, still ranks a depressing seventeenth on the World Economic Forum's Gender Equality Index.

Undeterred by these twin disappointments—both of which bode ill for our nation's fiscal future—Cerf has redoubled his commitment to keeping the public informed about the many dispiriting problems that face us. For example, to call attention to the contagion of unrestrained military spending, he teamed up with Henry Beard to create *The Pentagon Catalog: Ordinary Products at Extraordinary Prices,* which offered readers the historic opportunity to obtain a free hex nut—valued at $2,043 by the McDonnell Douglas Corporation—with every copy they purchased. In addition, he and Beard have collaborated on works addressing the crass commercial exploitation of our precious aesthetic heritage (*The Book of Sequels*, with Sarah Durkee and Sean Kelly), and the hideous price exacted by the demands of cultural conformity (*The Official Politically Correct Dictionary & Handbook* and *The Official Sexually Correct Dictionary & Handbook*).

Cerf also conceived and coedited *Not the New York Times*, a newspaper parody whose success led to the unfortunate clear-cutting of several previously unspoiled forested areas, and partnered with Victor S. Navasky to compile *The Experts Speak: The Definitive Compendium of Authoritative Misinformation*, which cautioned readers not to rely on expert advice. Cerf and Beard urge you to do exactly the opposite as you peruse the *Encyclopedia Paranoiaca*. "Your life could depend on it," Cerf warns.

INSECT PROLIFERATION HAZARD

LAHAR HAZARD

MACROECONOMIC HAZARD

MALICIOUS CODE WARNING

NONSTANDARD SPACETIME HAZARD

NUCLEAR PROLIFERATION HAZARD

OBESITY HAZARD

OPPRESSION AND EXPLOITATION HAZARD

RADIATION HAZARD (IONIZING)

RADIATION HAZARD (NON-IONIZING)

RAILROAD ACCIDENT HAZARD

RECTAL AFFLICTION HAZARD

SEXUAL NONPERFORMANCE HAZARD

SHARK ATTACK HAZARD

SHOULDER INJURY HAZARD

SKID HAZARD

STABLE STRANGELETS HAZARD

STARVATION HAZARD

TERRORISM THREAT

TOXIC HAZARD

UNFORSEEABLE EVENT HAZARD

UNREALISTIC EXPECTATIONS HAZARD

UNWANTED PREGNANCY HAZARD

VISION LOSS HAZARD (FEMALE)

MEDICAL CARE HAZARD

MENTAL HEALTH HAZARD

MULTIPLE PAIN AND INJURY RISKS

NANNYISM HAZARD

PERSONAL FINANCE HAZARD

PLANT CRUELTY ALERT

PRATFALL HAZARD

PREMATURE AGING HAZARD

ROOFTOP ACCIDENT HAZARD

SAFETY INFRASTRUCTURE HAZARD

SEISMIC HAZARD

SELF-REPLICATING DEVICE WARNING

SLIP HAZARD

SNORING HAZARD

SOCIETAL COLLAPSE WARNING

SPECIES EXTINCTION WARNING

TRIP HAZARD

TSUNAMI HAZARD

ULTRAVIOLET RADIATION HAZARD

UNEMPLOYMENT HAZARD

VISION LOSS HAZARD (MALE)

VOLCANIC HAZARD

WATER SUPPLY DEPLETION WARNING

ZOMBULATION HAZARD

Hazard Sign Credits

"Hunger" and "Obesity" symbols by James Stone, "Slip Hazard" symbol by Joel Burke, from thenounproject.com collection.

"Active Nanodevices," "Autonomous Device Warning," "Existential Threat," "Nonstandard Spacetime," "Self-Replicating Device Warning," and "Stable Strangelets" pictograms by Anders Sandberg.

"Automotive Pollution," "Fossil Fuel Pollution," "Injury Hazard," "Premature Aging," and "Unemployment" pictograms © Khoon Lay Gan/123RF.com.

"Automotive Accident Hazard," "Insect Proliferation Hazard," "Lahar Hazard," "Railroad Accident Hazard," "Volcanic Hazard," and "Water Supply Depletion Hazard" symbols based on pictograms developed by the U.S. Federal Geographic Data Committee (FGDC) Homeland Security Working Group.

"False Alarm Risk" and "Geomagnetic Disturbance Hazard" symbols based on pictograms developed by Public Safety Canada.

"Malware Warning Symbol" by Ron Kaminsky.

"Medical Care" pictogram from designofsignage.com.

"Vision Hazard" pictogram from the U.S. National Park Service.

"Climate Change," "Sexual Nonperformance," and "Unwanted Pregnancy" pictograms by Victoria Chiaro, from the Cassandra Institute Collection.